New Tunisian Cinema

FILM AND CULTURE
John Belton, Editor

FILM AND CULTURE

A series of Columbia University Press

Edited by John Belton

For the list of titles in this series, see page 381

NEW TUNISIAN CINEMA

ALLEGORIES OF RESISTANCE

ROBERT LANG

Columbia University Press   *New York*

Columbia University Press
Publishers Since 1893
New York   Chichester, West Sussex
cup.columbia.edu
Copyright © 2014 Columbia University Press
All rights reserved

Library of Congress Cataloging-in-Publication Data
Lang, Robert, 1957–
  New Tunisian cinema : allegories of resistance / Robert Lang.
    pages cm. — (Film and culture)
  Includes bibliographical references and index.
  ISBN 978-0-231-16506-8 (cloth) — ISBN 978-0-231-16507-5 (pbk.) — ISBN 978-0-231-53719-3 (ebook)
  1. Motion pictures—Tunisia. 2. Postcolonialism. I. Title.

  PN1993.5.T75L36 2014
  791.4309611—dc23

2013038574

COVER DESIGN: Milenda Nan Ok Lee
COVER IMAGE: Fatma Ben Saïdane in *The TV Is Coming* (2006) (copyright © Manara Productions. All rights reserved)

CREDITS: Portions of this book have appeared in different form in the following publications: *Lorsque Clio s'empare du documentaire* (Paris: L'Harmattan, 2011); *North African Cinema in a Global Context: Through the Lens of Diaspora* (London: Routledge, 2008); *La fiction éclatée: Petits et grands écrans français et francophones* (Paris: L'Harmattan, 2007); *The Journal of North African Studies* 12, no. 3 (September 2007); *IBLA: Revue de l'Institut des Belles-Lettres Arabes* 199/192 (2007/2003); *Masculinity: Bodies, Movies, Culture* (New York: Routledge, 2001). The illustrations throughout the book courtesy of the filmmakers.

To the filmmakers

Contents

Preface ix
Acknowledgments xix

CHAPTER ONE
The Nation, the State, and the Cinema 1

CHAPTER TWO
"The freedom to be different, to choose your own life":
Man of Ashes (Nouri Bouzid, 1986) 40

CHAPTER THREE
Laughter in the Dark:
Sexuality and the Police State in *Halfaouine* (Férid Boughedir, 1990) 67

CHAPTER FOUR
Sexual Allegories of National Identity: *Bezness* (Nouri Bouzid, 1992) 99

CHAPTER FIVE
The Colonizer and the Colonized: *The Silences of the Palace*
(Moufida Tlatli, 1994) 123

CONTENTS

CHAPTER SIX
"It takes two of us to discover truth":
Essaïda (Mohamed Zran, 1996)   157

CHAPTER SEVEN
"It takes a lot of unruly individuals to make a free people":
Bedwin Hacker (Nadia El Fani, 2002)   191

CHAPTER EIGHT
Inventing the Postcolonial Nation/Constructing a Usable Past:
The TV Is Coming (Moncef Dhouib, 2006)   223

CHAPTER NINE
"Destiny answers the people's call for life, darkness will be dispelled, and chains will break"   259

Notes   281

Filmography   341

Glossary   349

Bibliography   353

Index   369

Preface

Tunisian cinema is often described as the most daring of all the Arab cinemas, reflecting the country's widely perceived status as the most "open" and "tolerant" of the twenty-two Arab states, the one in which Western modernity has been consciously but not indiscriminately embraced, and where the secular and liberal ideas of its first president, Habib Bourguiba, have taken root and flourished. The social and economic success of Tunisia since it gained its independence from France in 1956—a few periods of stagnation notwithstanding—and its relatively peaceful relations with its neighbors and with the world generally, are thought to be the very proof and reward of Tunisia's commitment to its national motto, inscribed in the Constitution: "Liberty, Order, Justice."[1] For many, especially in the West and among non-Muslims, Tunisia appears to be a model of equipoise between "East" and "West," and of how to be a small and sovereign nation in a large and globalized world.

And yet, during Zine El Abidine Ben Ali's presidency, from the coup that brought Ben Ali to power in 1987 to his ouster in 2011, Tunisia would supersede Morocco under the rule of King Hassan II (1961–1999) as the most repressive state in the Maghreb.[2] There was no freedom of political expression whatsoever, and the state's record of human rights abuses contrasted starkly with the country's public image as a safe and friendly tourist destination and as the most progressive society in the Arab world. Against these considerable odds, a generation of Tunisia's filmmakers emerged in the mid-1980s to make films that are to a greater or lesser degree allegories of resistance to the increasingly illiberal trends marking their society and which explore what it means, and how, to be Tunisian in the contemporary world. These directors of what I call the New Tunisian Cinema have kept the cinema alive as a form of public pedagogy and as a unique site of cultural politics that tries to influence the debate about national identity, a debate to which I endeavor to contribute here, through an analysis of a handful of their films dating from 1986 to 2006.

During my two extended stays in Tunisia under the auspices of the Fulbright Scholar Program—my arrival in Tunis the first time coinciding with the day on which Yasser Arafat and Yitzhak Rabin shook hands on the White House lawn in Washington (an event I witnessed on Rai Uno, the only European-language channel with tolerable reception on the television in my room at the venerable Hotel Majestic on the Avenue de la Liberté); and my arrival the second time, on 11 September 2001, coinciding with the al-Qaeda attacks on the Twin Towers of the World Trade Center in New York and the headquarters of the U.S. Department of Defense in Virginia (my first knowledge of which I derived from the grainy images that came into view, as my landlord's son, communicating to me by cell phone from the roof of my villa, turned the satellite dish in the direction that would give me the best "bouquet" of channels from the hundreds now available in Tunisia)—the debate about national identity was on everyone's lips, or so it seemed to me in my milieu, which centered on the University of Tunis. As Fredric Jameson wrote in 1986: "Judging from recent conversations among third-world intellectuals, there is now an obsessive return of the national situation itself, the name of the country that returns again and again like a gong, the collective attention to 'us' and what we have to do and how we do it, to what we can't do and what we do better than this or that nationality, our unique characteristics, in short, to the level of the 'people.'"[3]

Obsessive or not, this question of "the national situation" interests me, and interests me now more than ever, not only as it pertains to Tunisia, but as it bears on my own American citizenship. As an immigrant teenager to the United States from war-torn, white Rhodesia, I was already familiar with the rhetoric of national identity—the "what we do better than this or that nationality, our unique characteristics," and so on—and as an opponent of the racist regime in the country of my birth, I had been forced early to learn about the hypocrisies of power. I had yet to read Albert Memmi's *The Colonizer and the Colonized*, but I knew its lessons by heart, especially the one about "the colonizer who refuses."

It was many years before I came to understand that the United States is fully implicated as well in "the colonial relationship" described by Memmi in his book. Carefully disguised for the most part, and operating globally in neocolonial modes that make the identification of villains and victims more difficult, American participation in concrete oppression is nevertheless revealed in all its sordid reality by the massive political and material support we give to the state of Israel, while turning a blind eye toward its morally repugnant ethnic-cleansing policies and occupation of Palestinian territories.[4] In Connecticut, at my university, I am back in Rhodesia; like the majority of Americans, most of my colleagues are publicly silent about IDF atrocities and Israeli war crimes, even when these are being exposed by the mainstream media for all to see and read about; and my most vocal students only want to talk about Palestinian "terrorists" and how "Israel has a right to defend itself."[5]

This is the context in which *New Tunisian Cinema: Allegories of Resistance* was written. The debate about who we are as Americans—especially after the Bush–Cheney administration between 2001 and 2009 managed to subvert or dismantle nearly everything I thought the United States stood for[6]—continues to rage; only now, significant numbers of Americans seem to think we are engaged in a "clash of civilizations" that is threatening our "American way of life." That "other" civilization is vaguely (or not so vaguely) thought by many to be the Muslim world. The example of Tunisia, then, is of great interest to those of us who care about liberty, equality, and fraternity both within and among nations. Tunisian society really is poised between "East" and "West," in a way that has much to teach us about the world we live in, and about the world we should want to live in.

This book is not a comprehensive survey of the New Tunisian Cinema. Nor is it primarily concerned with periodization or identifying this cinema's masterpieces and most representative filmmakers. If I say the films are those of a generation and of an era, it is because most of the filmmakers were born during the ten years before Bourguiba became their country's first president, and they (still) believe in Bourguiba's vision of a modern, liberal, secular society that, while remaining true to its essentially Arab and Muslim roots, might, in Bourguiba's phrase, successfully embrace "the best of the West."[7]

Postcolonial Tunisia only partially realized Bourguiba's early dream of building a modern, liberal, secular state—like France, or more realistically, Turkey—for Bourguiba would become a dictator long before his residence in the presidential palace in Carthage was brought to an end, and he had laid the foundations of the police state that his successor went on to expand and intensify. In retrospect, we can clearly see what the continuities between the two regimes would be, for Bourguiba's ouster occurred only months after the first film of the New Tunisian Cinema burst onto the scene, Nouri Bouzid's *Man of Ashes* (1986). There are wide differences of opinion about how long the New Tunisian Cinema lasted, and which films belong under its rubric, and even some question about why we should call a group of films the "New Tunisian Cinema." For my purposes, it is the cinema of a generation making films during the Ben Ali era, where "era" is understood to refer to the authoritarian regime of Bourguiba's last days and the twenty-three years of Ben Ali's dictatorship that followed.[8]

Although Ben Ali fled the country on 14 January 2011, providing a definitive end to the era that gave rise to the films I discuss in this study, I designate Bouzid's *Making Of, le dernier film* (2006) the last film of the New Tunisian Cinema (for reasons I explain in my final chapter). My concern, as I have said, is not to provide the last word on which films may be included under the rubric and which not (as we hear, for example, in the kind of argument that insists: "The first *film noir* is John Huston's *The Maltese Falcon* [1941], and the last is Orson Welles's *Touch of Evil* [1958]"). Rather, it is to identify and examine some important factors, themes, and key moments in Tunisia's developing narrative about its national identity during a crucial period in the country's history. It is a period when the filmmakers who came of age during Bourguiba's heyday saw and understood that their shared vision of the Tunisia they believed in was embattled. Unlike the films made before *Man of Ashes*—which tended to locate the causes of oppression or injustice somewhere outside the society, or which implied that the stagnation of Tunisian society, such as there might be, was owed to a cycle of foreign domination—the films of the New Tunisian Cinema would be characterized by a certain intimacy and psychological realism of character development and would acknowledge that the sources of oppression, or causes of malaise, were (or are) *within* the society, which is a way of acknowledging that Ben Ali's police state was in a sense a *symptom* of social, historical, and cultural factors that all play parts in defining contemporary Tunisia and Tunisians.

In *Man of Ashes*, Bouzid tells a story in which we see a character resisting the tyranny of the Tunisian neopatriarchal family. "In our society the individual is nothing," the filmmaker has said. "It's the family that counts, the group. Our cinema is trying to destroy the edifice of the family and liberate the individual."[9] The film's principal character, Hachemi, shows a disinclination to marry, which his uncomprehending family takes as an intolerable affront to societal expectations. Bouzid suggests that the pressure on individuals in his society to conform to the values and dictates of Muslim tradition and Arab neopatriarchy (symbolized on the one hand by the tradition of circumcision, and on the other by neopatriarchal society's insistence on heterosexuality and marriage for all its adult members) is nothing less than a form of *rape*, which he believes occurs at every level of socialization and experience.

In Férid Boughedir's first feature-length film, *Halfaouine* (1990), the director offers an allegory of the Tunisian police state's metastasizing reach into nearly every corner of social life, as the spaces of liberty for the film's young hero Noura are threatened, one after the other. While the real police state can be seen penetrating his neighborhood (in the form of the police agent, "Columbo," or the volunteer police informant, Khemaïs), Noura's authoritarian father is the film's chief agent of repression in the private sphere. Along with the neighborhood's self-appointed guardian of morality, the local sheikh, Noura's (hypocritical) father represents a pervasive climate of interdiction that Boughedir fears has become the hallmark of postcolonial Tunisia. As an allegory that privileges a dialectical relationship between the public and private spheres—in which police violence and arbitrary arrest and imprisonment by the state are scarcely distinguishable in character from the father's style of governance at home—*Halfaouine* implies that the Tunisian police state is inscribed in neopatriarchal structures that derive from a patriarchy that has outlived its useful and proper functions and lost its legitimacy. As a boy who in the course of the film grows into adulthood, and who will remember his childhood with a keen sense of nostalgia, Noura would appear to represent a "lost" Tunisia that, in Boughedir's wistful phrase, was once "a Mediterranean society, exuberant and affectionate, where humor and eroticism always have their place, along with tolerance."[10]

Five years after *Man of Ashes*, and following *The Golden Horseshoes* in 1989 (a tragedy about political repression and Bourguiba's betrayal of the dream—at least for its artists and intellectuals—of a modern and bilingual/bicultural Tunisia), Bouzid made *Bezness* (1992), which attempts to comprehend the impact on ordinary Tunisians of the burgeoning international tourist industry in their country. The three films form a kind of trilogy, in which we see that, as Bouzid wrote:

> The [Arab] male is not [as] strong as he is traditionally portrayed. On the contrary, he is lost and confused and is plagued with a set of dilemmas that shake him to the core. . . . The projected image of a constantly victorious and honorable Arab hero has been abandoned. Admitting defeat, the new realism proceeds to expose it and make the awareness of its causes and roots a point of departure.[11]

The dilemmas experienced by Roufa, the protagonist of *Bezness*, are those of the would-be capitalist whose only commodity is his body. The young hustler becomes increasingly angry and despondent, as he tries to maintain his sense of masculine honor and dignity in a rapidly changing economy that is undermining his sense of agency. The film is fully aware of the "causes and roots" of his malaise, such that it becomes impossible not to read his feelings of subalternity and response to his condition as an allegory of postcolonial Tunisia's struggles to resist neocolonial domination in a context of Western-led globalization.

Alia, the protagonist of Moufida Tlatli's *The Silences of the Palace* (1994), is similarly plagued by a sense of malaise. The narrative is organized as a series of flashbacks, giving it, if not a sense of nostalgia for a happier past, then a feeling that Alia, who grew up in the eponymous palace as the illegitimate daughter of one of the servants, is doomed to suffer a perpetual melancholy. (Alia is never told who her father is, but she infers—and the viewer is in no doubt—that it is Sidi Ali, one of the resident princes.) In a boldly melodramatic and allegorical stroke, Tlatli has her heroine leave the beylical palace at the same historical moment that Tunisia frees itself from colonial domination by the French. It is also the moment that Alia truly becomes an orphan, for it coincides with her mother Khedija's death, which is caused by the botched abortion of the pregnancy resulting from her rape by Sidi Ali's brother, Sidi Bechir. Alia's departure from the palace—the only world she has known—is both an expulsion and an attempt at self-liberation, following an act of resistance that displeases her royal masters. She is inspired to perform her act of resistance by Lotfi, a young revolutionary temporarily hiding out in the servants' quarters; and she will live with him when she leaves. But he will not marry her (because she is a singer and is illegitimate), even though she is now pregnant with his child; and Alia's future—like that of Tunisia itself in the allegory—remains uncertain at the end of the film.

In Mohamed Zran's *Essaïda* (1996), the discourse on social class so eloquently articulated by Tlatli in *The Silences of the Palace* is reprised as a persistent postcolonial problem that has been exacerbated by the so-called "economic miracle" that transformed Tunisia's social landscape under Ben Ali. With the departure of the beys and the establishment of a republic in Tunisia, the plight of the poor and politically powerless (as we see them represented by the servants in Tlatli's film) is not alleviated. The social class to which Khedija's rapist belongs in *The Silences of the Palace* has left its palaces in Tunis and Le Bardo and moved to the northern suburbs (Carthage, Sidi Bou Saïd, La Marsa), where Amine, the protagonist of *Essaïda*, lives. Amine (Hichem Rostom, who plays Sidi Bechir in *The Silences of the Palace*), an artist and aristocrat—in a society that cares little about art, or about what Amine's social class has to offer, but cares a great deal about amassing personal wealth—appears to be undergoing some kind of identity crisis. His (unconscious) search for a muse leads him to befriend Nidhal, a boy from Essaïda, one of the poorest neighborhoods of Tunis. In its depiction of their friendship, and of the consequent tensions between Amine and his upwardly mobile, middle-class girlfriend Sonia, and of Nidhal's spiraling descent into increasingly criminal behavior, the film suggests that the gap between rich and poor in Tunisia has become dangerously wide. The poverty of Nidhal's milieu contrasts with Amine's easeful existence and solipsistic character. And when Nidhal is recruited by Hatem (who in the allegorical reading represents Ben Ali's kleptocratic family and corrupt cronies), the film in effect offers an explanation of the dialectical relationship that exists between the desperation of Tunisia's growing poor and the rapine of the newly rich.

The global revolution in communications technologies that occurred in the 1990s would bring about profound changes in the Tunisian public sphere during the two decades of Ben Ali's presidency. The spread in Tunisia of new media such as satellite television and the Internet would dramatically redefine the relationships of Tunisians to authority, each other, and the world—especially after the 9/11 attacks, which Ben Ali, like many other authoritarian leaders and dictators, would use as a pretext to reinforce his suppression of oppositional voices—and it would eventually lead to Ben Ali's ouster. The youngest of the New Tunisian Cinema's filmmakers, Nadia El Fani, offers an allegorical representation of the impact of this new media revolution on Tunisian society in her quite remarkably prescient film, *Bedwin Hacker* (2002), which protests the surveillance-obsessed state that Tunisia became under Ben Ali, while celebrating the media literacy and technological savvy of ordinary Tunisians confronting the dead hand of censorship.

With the filmmakers of the New Tunisian Cinema engaged in both a kind of national-cultural historiography and what documentary filmmaker Hichem Ben Ammar describes as "a revolt against the injustice of society,"[12] it would be only a matter of time before one of them would make a self-reflexive satire about the state's own role in writing the national narrative. The French historian Pierre Nora has observed that "history [now] belongs to everyone and to no one and therefore has a universal vocation"[13]—but in a dictatorship with an image problem, this is not quite true, as we see in Moncef Dhouib's *The TV Is Coming* (2006). The principal characters of the film are members of a village cultural committee engaged in the organization of a pageant representing three thousand years of Tunisian history; and in keeping with Tunisia's status as a country that depends to some considerable extent for its hard currency on attracting international tourists to its shores, the committee seeks to project an image of Tunisian society as one that is stable, tolerant, and open, with a rich history and a long tradition of hospitality. The film takes an amused look at the fraught politics of representation in a state that is not as progressive as it claims to be, offering insights into what is at stake for Tunisians as they attempt to (re)write their history as a streamlined narrative about a people with a "Mediterranean" identity.

In many ways, *The TV Is Coming* summarizes the project of the New Tunisian Cinema, as the filmmaker and his characters on the one hand try to highlight and celebrate the best of Bourguiba's legacy (equal rights for women, a commitment to family planning, an inclusive notion of national identity, religious tolerance, and so on), and on the other hand critique that legacy's betrayal (the descent into authoritarian, single-party rule, corruption at the highest levels of government, the routine abuse of human rights). The film is an example and illustration of the role played by the filmmakers of the New Tunisian Cinema in the writing of national history and shaping of national consciousness. As we see throughout this study, they seek to construct narratives that, in Nora's phrase, will serve the civic as well as intellectual needs of their time; whereas the objectives of the state, despite the similarity of the discourse and rhetoric it uses, are above all to keep the president and his party in power.

What I attempt in the following pages is an analysis of the efforts of the New Tunisian filmmakers to help define Tunisian collective consciousness and reinterpret Tunisia's past and present in symbolic terms.

A Note about Transliteration and Names

In my attempt to address the inherent problems of rendering written and spoken Arabic in the Latin alphabet, I have not used a consistent transliteration system, such as the one provided by the IJMES Transliteration Guide, nor have I taken a purist approach with a phonetic transcription system. My system for romanizing Arabic is idiosyncratic: while not entirely ignoring the ideologically motivated trend to get rid of the colonial transliterations that are in common use (where *Koran* becomes *Qur'an*, for example), I normally go with the most common local usage in Tunisia, however frenchified, that is, the usage most Tunisians would recognize and use themselves, the usage we would most likely find in Tunisian newspapers (for example: *chechia*, rather than *sheshia*; or *Zitouna*, rather than the classical Arabic *Zaytuna*, or *Al-Zaytuna*). This rule of thumb goes for individuals' names as well, especially when the individual's own preference is unknown to me, as in the case of Aboulkacem Chebbi (أبو القاسم الشابي), which is variously rendered as: Abou-Al-kacem El-chebbi; Abou el Kacem Chebbi; Aboul Kacem Chabbi; Abu al-Qasim al-Shabbi; Abul-Qasim Al Shabi; Aboul-Qacem Echebbi; or (as I am told his mother in Tozeur most certainly would have called him) Belgacem (or Belgassem) Chebbi.

Acknowledgments

I have been helped in myriad ways by several Tunisians who wanted me to write this particular book and by many others who were not aware of its political thrust. It is with great pride and pleasure that I thank the following: the entire Aloui family (Noureddine, Bahia, Sami, Emna, and Asma), the late Ahmed Baha Eddine Attia, Hichem Ben Ammar, Hsin Ben Azouna, Kmar Bendana, Amina Ben Ezzeddine, Maher Ben Moussa, Lotfi Ben Rejeb, Fatma Ben Saïdane, Lamia Ben Youssef Zayzafoon, Férid Boughedir, Hatem Bourial, Raja Boussedra, Fathi Dali, Dhia Daly-Bedoui, Moncef Dhouib, Annie Djamal, Nadia El Fani, Kamel Farfar, Monia Hejaiej, Mohamed Kerrou, Hamdi Khalifa, Hédi Khélil, the late Chaker Mansour, Hassouna Mansouri, Mohsen Redissi, Mondher Saïed, Sami Saïed, Mongia Tanfous, Moufida Tlatli, and Mohamed Zran.

In a police state, any resistance to the regime in power runs the risk of reprisal by the state, which is why some individuals who helped me asked not to be named in these acknowledgments. Those whom I did not dare be in touch with after leaving Tunisia, or whom I have not been able to track down since the political upheaval there in early 2011, or who might reasonably fear a counter-revolution, will understand why your names do not appear here. All the same, I remain grateful for your help, your input, and

ACKNOWLEDGMENTS

your encouragement. To those of you who understood the risks you were taking, I salute your courage and ethical integrity.

My gratitude toward everyone who has contributed to this study extends to individuals who may not think they had anything to do with it, such as Maha Darawsha, my first Arabic teacher, in Connecticut, and Najeeb Al-Daghashi, my second Arabic teacher, at the Yemen College of Middle Eastern Studies in Sana'a. In the decade of intermittent research and writing that finally became this book about the New Tunisian Cinema and the society from which it emerged, I have been helped by more people than can be listed here. I wish nevertheless to offer my heartfelt thanks to the following: Hakim Abderrezak, Nemanja Bala, Jack Banks, Noura Bensaad, Jean-Pierre Bertin-Maghit, Steven Blackburn, David Bond, Laurence Breeden, Philip Breeden, Patricia Caillé, Steve Caton, Laryssa Chomiak, Renaud Claudon, Rodney Collins, Lauren Cook, Craig Cornell, Paul Dambowic, Arturo Delgado, Béatrice de Pastre, Gayatri Devi, Brian T. Edwards, Kevin Ellison, Brad Epps, Elle Flanders, Suzanne Gauch, Terri Ginsberg, Josef Gugler, Kaya Hacaloğlu, Julian Halliday, Tom Harrington, the late Ambassador Fereydoun Hoveyda, Dona Kercher, Samir Khalaf, Andrea Khalil, Souad Labbize, Peter Lehman, Mark Lilly, Chris Lippard, Ken Lizzio, Yosefa Loshitzky, Florence Martin, Ambassador John T. McCarthy, Daniela Melfa, the late Jeanne Mrad, Dorit Naaman, Insaf Ouhiba, Kathy Paras, Robert Parks, Natacha Poggio, Claudia Pummer Hangelbroek, David Queen, Najat Rahman, Wil Rollman, Jeffrey Ruoff, Riadh Saadaoui, Charles Silver, John Sinno, Candace Skorupa, Lynn Thibodeau, Sylvie Thouard, Joe Voelker, Vivian Walker, Michael Walsh, and Alex Williams.

This project has been generously supported by the Office of the Dean of the College of Arts and Sciences at the University of Hartford and has received funding on several occasions in the form of a Richard J. Cardin Research Award, administered by the University of Hartford. My biggest debt of gratitude, of course, is to the Fulbright Scholar Program, sponsored by the U.S. Department of State's Bureau of Educational and Cultural Affairs. As an international educational exchange program designed to "increase mutual understanding between the people of the United States and the people of other countries," the Fulbright program is a remarkable American achievement. Large in spirit, intelligently conceived, and superbly administered, it is an example of what Habib Bourguiba would have described as "the best of the West." Its purpose—to provide participants like me with

ACKNOWLEDGMENTS

"the opportunity to study, teach and conduct research, exchange ideas and contribute to finding solutions to shared international concerns"—cannot be commended enough, and I am sincerely grateful to the program for the confidence it placed in me.

Parts of my work were presented at the Université Sorbonne Nouvelle–Paris 3, in the Chaire Roger Odin Séminaires doctoraux (Cinéma et audiovisuel), and I wish to thank that institution for the opportunity to discuss the ideas behind this book.

After the manuscript was completed, Amy Kallander read it from beginning to end and very generously offered comments, made corrections, and suggested some revisions—which I did my best to respond to in the short time left to me before the manuscript went to press. The book is much better for the careful attention she gave it, although responsibility for any errors or excesses that have nevertheless made their way into print of course remains mine. The final revision of the manuscript took place at a *centre de rééducation* in Lamalou-les-Bains in southern France, where I quite unexpectedly found myself confined for a month, after taking a fall during a hike in the Cévennes. To Dr. Brahim Khenifar at the Polyclinique Pasteur in Pézenas: Thank you for my very fine, new, titanium hip; and to the fantastic staff both at the clinic and at La Petite Paix in Lamalou-les-Bains, my warmest gratitude for your around-the-clock attention and kindness.

My family, ever-supportive of my scholarly endeavors, no matter how grumpy the pressure of deadlines sometimes makes me, deserves to be thanked. My parents, June and Vic Lang, and my sister Lesli-Sharon Lang, my *belle-sœur* Alison Holmes, and beautiful niece Helen Lang—none of whom I see often enough—have shown an encouraging interest in this project, and their commonsense questions and comments (including: "When will it be finished?") have always been salutary. My partner Paul Scovill, whose service in the Peace Corps as an architect working in El Kef, was at the origin of my desire to go to Tunisia. His enduring affection for the country and its people, and his unique perspective, deriving from a deep knowledge of Tunisia's history and culture, have made him an invaluable resource: he has been an ideal sounding board, *compagnon de route*, translator, and sometimes even proofreader.

Finally, I must thank Columbia University Press, especially Jennifer Crewe, in whose friendship I delight and whose skills as an editor and

ACKNOWLEDGMENTS

publisher fill me with admiration; Columbia's editorial and design team; and John Belton, editor of the Film and Culture series in which this book appears, whose regard for me as a scholar and writer has been a much-appreciated stimulus during the long years of the book's production.

New Tunisian Cinema

CHAPTER ONE

The Nation, the State, and the Cinema

Nations are made, not born. Or rather, to exist they must be made and remade, figured and refigured, constantly defining and perpetuating themselves. Classic distinctions in political and social theory differentiate nation and state. Nations are cultural, discursive fields. They are imaginary, ideal collective unities that, especially since the nineteenth-century era of nationalism, aspire to define the state. The state is an institutional site constructed as overt repository and manager of legitimated power. Nation is on the side of culture, ideological formations, civil society; state is on the side of political institutions, repressive apparatuses, political society.

PHILIP ROSEN (2001)[1]

On the morning of 7 November 1987, Tunisia's recently appointed prime minister, Zine El Abidine Ben Ali, broadcast a startling message on national radio: "The enormous sacrifices made by the leader Habib Bourguiba, first President of the Republic, with his valiant companions, for the liberation of Tunisia and its development, cannot be numbered. However, faced with his senility and worsening state of health, based on a medical report, national duty obliges us to declare his absolute incapacity to carry out any longer the office of president of the republic. We, therefore, take over with God's help the presidency and the command of the army . . . we are entering a new era."[2]

This news was met with a collective sigh of relief by Bourguiba's countrymen. He had remained in power too long. The Supreme Combatant, as he had come to be known (and officially "President for Life" since 1975), had started to have a paralyzing effect on the country's economy at least a decade earlier.[3] But Bourguiba's forceful, charismatic personality and his ruthless consolidation of political and personal power, beginning even before the abolition of Tunisia's monarchy in 1957, had over the course of thirty years come to have a paralyzing effect on the Tunisian people as well, producing a kind of psychological malaise from which, many felt, only his

FIGURE 1.1 *The Picnic* (Férid Boughedir, 1972), released in 1975 as part of the omnibus film, *Fī Bilād al-Tararanni*, an early attempt to make "the first specifically Tunisian film." (The picnickers' vehicle, a symbol of the East–West hybridity of Tunisia under the French protectorate, breaks down.)

death would liberate them.⁴ In his biography, *Habib Bourguiba of Tunisia: The Tragedy of Longevity*, Derek Hopwood summarizes Bourguiba's rationale for hanging onto power into extreme old age and infirmity by imagining a rhetorical conversation the eighty-six year-old president has with himself. Visibly frail and demonstrably senile, the delusional octogenarian muses: "Tunisia still needs me. I cannot have stayed too long as I was elected president for life. No-one is fit to take over. I have had to dismiss Mohammed Mzali, my prime minister and friend, I have divorced the love of my life, Wasila, for intriguing, I have had to send away my son. Who is there left to trust? Is Tunisia ungrateful to the man who forged its history? I have fought and suffered all my life for my people. When I die what will they do without me?" (1).

If "few Tunisians mourned the end of Bourguiba's sixty years of public life," Ben Ali's bloodless coup was the best possible way to bring an end to a situation that had become intolerable.⁵

For readers unfamiliar with or rusty on the rudimentary facts about Tunisia and how it became a French protectorate—which is where, for better or worse, I must locate a beginning and sketch a "backstory" for this study of contemporary Tunisian cinema—Hopwood's summary will serve our purpose:

> Tunisia is a small country, only 500 kilometers long and some 175 wide. To the north are fertile areas, to the south stretches the desert. The capital, Tunis, center of government, the upper classes and cultural life, is near the northern Mediterranean coast; Monastir [Bourguiba's birthplace] lies in the Sahel (coastal) region, a fertile area of olives, palms and wine growing stretching some 150 kilometers along the eastern side of the country. . . . In 1881 the French had persuaded the then Bey, a prince of little character or "instruction," to sign a treaty allowing them to install a protectorate over his regency, in practice signing away all independence. There is a French resident-general who becomes foreign minister and has the right to promulgate legislation after signature by the Bey. Tunisia becomes a French-run colony. The French take up residence, obtain land, and French becomes the language of the government, higher education, and culture. Churches and cathedrals proclaim the religion of the occupiers without regard for local feeling. Tunisians feel second-class citizens in their own country.[6]

By way of transition to some of the themes I pursue in this book, the last comment in the preceding quotation—"Tunisians feel second-class citizens in their own country"—allows me to flash forward to a remark made in 2002 by Tunisia's preeminent filmmaker, Nouri Bouzid, during an interview he gave in France about his new film, *Poupées d'argile* (*Clay Dolls*): "We don't own the streets where I live."[7] Bouzid had spent over five years in Bourguiba's jails (1973–1979) for his membership in a socialist youth group. But here, in 2002, he is acknowledging that in the area of civil and human rights, things had not improved in Tunisia since the colonial era or the darkest days of Bourguiba's presidency. Most would agree they had grown worse. As Florence Beaugé observed in *Le Monde* in June 2003, in a short article entitled: "In Tunisia, a 'Cycle of Injustice' Is Perpetuated," the objective of "the palace in Carthage" in creating civil and human rights organizations in Tunisia was not to protect civil and human rights in the country, but to improve Tunisia's image abroad.⁸ The new *Amnesty International Report*, she wrote, confirmed that "on grounds of maintaining security and countering the 'terrorist threat,' political and civil liberties in Tunisia remain subject to significant restrictions. As for defenders of human rights, such as the members of the LTDH [Tunisian League for Human Rights] and the ATFD [Tunisian Association of Democratic Women], they are targets of 'systematic campaigns of intimidation': illegal searches, anonymous phone threats, suspensions of telephone service, arbitrary detention, passport confiscations, violent physical attacks, defamation in the media, etc." (29–30). Beaugé wrote that the report goes on to denounce "the systematic interference of executive power in the functioning of the justice system" in Tunisia, where equal rights as defined by international law and guaranteed by Tunisian legislation are "violated at every stage of the legal process." The resort to torture of individuals caught in the justice system is common (30).

If Bourguiba's (undeniable) accomplishment, with his valiant companions, was the liberation of Tunisia from French colonialism and his (also undeniable and altogether remarkable) social development of the newly independent country, then Ben Ali's accomplishment was the liberation of the country from Bourguiba, and (in due course) the country's apparently spectacular economic development, the so-called Tunisian "economic miracle."⁹ But both leaders became dictators whose suppression of all oppositional voices would become so suffocating that the nature and value of the "development" for which each is known and praised would be called into question.

If, as Bouzid put it, "we don't own the streets" (in Ben Ali's Tunisia), then this was certainly also true in Bourguiba's day—although the style of the country's first two presidents could not have been more different. Like Bouzid, the Tunisian novelist Gilbert Naccache came of age in Bourguiba's Tunisia, and on the occasion of the Supreme Combatant's death on 6 April 2000, at the age of ninety-six, he observed that "today's despair has its roots in yesterday's misery."¹⁰ As will be revealed in the films analyzed in the chapters that follow—films that nearly all date from the Ben Ali era—the causes of this "despair" to which Naccache alludes would change little, if at all; only the infrastructure of the dictatorship would evolve. "The difficulty of speaking, of writing, even of breathing—that is not new," Naccache wrote (224). Bourguiba, who was a brilliant orator and compulsive autobiographer—a raging narcissist of phenomenal proportions, who sought to make Tunisia in his own deeply secular and Westernized image and whose presentation of himself as the "father" of the country would have disastrously infantilizing effects upon the population, particularly its male members—was a very different creature from Ben Ali, who was secretive, uncharismatic, "heavy." But in their suppression of free speech and their addiction to political power, the two men came to resemble one another.

The key element that secured the continuity between Bourguiba and Ben Ali and kept Ben Ali in power almost as long as his predecessor was Ben Ali's commitment to secularism and his deft manipulation of Tunisians' fears in that regard, which would be periodically exacerbated by events beyond Tunisia's borders, such as the chaotic aftermath of the victories in local elections of the FIS (Front Islamique du Salut/Islamic Salvation Front) in neighboring Algeria in 1990 and the 9/11 terrorist attacks on the United States in 2001. "In exchange for protection from the 'green threat' of Islamic radicalism," Kenneth Perkins observes, "the majority of secular Tunisians turned a blind eye to excesses committed by the authorities" (194).[11]

Writing in 1995, Eva Bellin notes about the development of civil society in Tunisia (where her references to the "state" can, in my more allegorical reading of the political economy, be taken to refer to Ben Ali):

> While the country has made notable progress in combating some common sources of despotism (nurturing a culture of *civisme* and civility, dispersing the loci of economic power in society, expanding the reach of some democratic institutions), it has still failed to achieve one important goal—the institutionalization of contestation sufficient to impose accountability upon a despotically-tempted state. The responsibility for this failure lies squarely with the state, driven as it is by contradictory impulses to foster the development of civil society on the one hand, but also to contain the latter's development so as not to cede political control.[12]

It is sometimes boasted that Tunisia's short-lived Constitution of 1861 was the first for an Arab country, but as Perkins points out, it was imposed by the French and British consuls and had little indigenous support. And as far as the Ben Ali era is concerned, the "contradictory impulses" Bellin refers to were there at the dawn of independent Tunisia's making. Even at the beginning, Bourguiba's embrace of liberal values did not extend to the tolerance of contrary views.[13] Naccache writes that under Bourguiba:

> Every word, every line you wrote, every step you took in those days was the product of a constant struggle against fear, and against the negative opinion he wanted us to have of ourselves. He pitted his brainless secret agents, the bright lights of his regime, against what he saw as "pseudo-revolutionaries fresh from the Latin Quarter." And like all his confreres, whether nationalist despots or phony socialists of totalitarian states, he mocked everybody's intelligence except his own. He heaped his scorn on us, and called on the people—of whom he was equally contemptuous—to despise us for using our intelligence. (224)

And, the novelist ruefully acknowledges, Bourguiba to some large degree succeeded in making the people devalue the society's intellectuals. Naccache describes how, when he was arrested by the regime and thereby lost his livelihood, he had to move his family out of their house and into a smaller, more affordable one. On seeing the task before them, one of the two movers helping the writer remarked gravely to the other: "It's not surprising that he was arrested, with all these books" (224–225).

"Yes," Naccache tells us, "under Bourguiba, culture was suspect, dangerous. And is this still the case? Indeed it is. But it goes back a long time. You wrote with a copy of the Penal Code under your arm. You had to be careful—a single word or turn of phrase could get you a year in jail, five years, ten. You'd change a phrase because they could interpret it in such a way as to invoke Article 62 or 68" (225). There is no question that Tunisia under Bourguiba had become a police state—the difference is that under Ben Ali one talked not so much about a *man* as about a *system*, of which Ben Ali had been the chief architect since 1987.[14] When Naccache writes in the year 2000 about the Bourguiba of yesteryear, he is explaining how Bourguiba's Tunisia became Ben Ali's Tunisia.[15] The foundations were laid by Bourguiba—both the regime and the man, in that way in which a very strong personality can leave a deep imprint on institutions and the collective psyche for generations to come—but now the house (or prison) was built, and General Ben Ali had the keys.[16]

National Disenchantment

In 1982, when she was thirty-four, the Tunisian writer Hélé Béji published an essay about decolonization and its discontents in her country: *Désenchantement national: Essai sur la décolonisation*.[17] It attempts to explain the trajectory, which began on 20 March 1956, when everything seemed possible—when, in her striking phrase, "Liberty began to cross the street and History to descend the stairway of our small, familiar world"—and which led to the malaise that set in too soon afterwards.[18] Béji imagines her countrymen on that historic day in 1956, released from the yoke of colonialism, caught up in the "unpredictable quickening of national vitality, progress, liberation, and development" (9); and then she contemplates the present disillusionment:

> Why does something still weigh on us in this indistinct and ferocious manner? What is neocolonialism? What is this *other*, ungraspable thing that has appeared since independence? Why this tremendous feeling of impotence in our thinking and in our social conscience in the face of the absence of liberty and democracy? Why was democracy not born with independence? Why have nationalism and anti-colonialism not been a force for liberty? Why has our national political universe become so closed, so crushing? (13–14)

Béji observes that Frantz Fanon's axiom that "the death of colonialism is at once the death of the colonized and the death of the colonizer" is simply not true. Rather, when the colonizer departs, the energies that were expended in resistance to colonialism or that went into anti-colonial dreams of independence do not dissipate but inscribe themselves deeply in a system of representations in which new, detrimental political practices come into being (15). The nationalist discourse that underpinned Tunisia's struggle for independence does not adapt and evolve after Independence, but hardens into what Béji calls postcolonial Tunisia's "national ideology," which, little by little, comes to permeate all of intellectual life, as the state—which was always held up as a synonym for liberty—in effect discourages intellectual curiosity and crushes all critical thinking (29–30). Without the framework of official patriotism, which is expected of all

Tunisia's citizens, Béji's intellectual life, she observes, feels "dissociated, isolated, without reference":

> National feeling has become the central allegory of all of our mental activity, giving it a rhythm to which it cannot help submitting. We never stop holding up a mirror to this discourse, like a gauge, to measure its depth. My complicity with the national discourse prevents me from seeing the web it has woven around me. (30)

Dialectical thinking gives way to a monological discourse that always revolves around three axes: politics, religion, and poverty. "It is like a heavy raincloud that will not burst," Béji laments. The issue of power, the question of tradition, and the problem of underdevelopment—"these three realities haunt us without ever liberating us" (30–31).

Using Bourguiba's speeches, Béji shows how Tunisia's first president successfully conflated himself—his personality, his point of view, his person—with "Tunisia." During a speech, he could make you believe in him as an allegory of the nation-state, which he ingeniously identified with the Tunisian people. "When you hear one of Bourguiba's speeches," she writes, "you are overwhelmed by its vitality, its coherence, its humor. Whether it be a spectacular challenge or a solemn one, the speech impels you by the immediacy of its authority; it is a verbal game that replaces all the frameworks of reference people have with a single and unique landscape—that of the State" (47). (Béji does not put it this way, but we may do so thus: Louis XIV's "*L'État, c'est moi!*" becomes "*L'État, c'est vous!*" ... which "I"—Bourguiba—incarnate as your "Father.") In 1974, for example, Bourguiba gave a speech in which he said: "Don't forget, the Tunisian state is the state of all the people, the state of each and every person in the nation."[19]

But this was hardly the case. The people registered the discrepancy between the nation they had imagined and the emerging state they hoped would define it. Bourguiba, they would discover, embodied the modern *etatist* state, which Hisham Sharabi, in *Neopatriarchy: A Theory of Distorted Change in Arab Society*, with startling directness describes as "essentially nothing but the medieval sultanate in modern form."[20] Sharabi's book describes the way in which the challenges of modernity to patriarchy have resulted in the metamorphosis of patriarchy into *neopatriarchy*. The traditional patriarch's authority and control (primarily over women and children within the family, but evident in the relations of authority, domination, and dependency characterizing the larger society as well) are no longer supreme. With the rise of the nuclear family, in which there is greater economic and democratic freedom for its members than there ever was in the patriarchal family, patriarchy has not disappeared so much as reconfigured itself in the form of neopatriarchy, which attempts to retain patriarchy's power and privileges, without providing its historic benefits or exercising its traditionally concomitant responsibilities.

Tunisia's first president was what Sharabi calls a "modernized" intellectual, that is, one who embodied most apparently the "structural duality and contradictions of society" (24). Despite his rhetoric and apparent commitment to the liberal values of a Western democracy like France, Bourguiba was an etatist patriarch:

> For the distinctive characteristic of etatism, like that of the sultanate, is personalized (legal and extralegal) power, which finds expression in the coercive and suppressive apparatus of the state and derives its legitimacy not from some formal (constitutional or even traditional) source, but from the reality and possession of power. In this kind of polity the ordinary person is a passive entity, a subject not a citizen, with no human or civil rights or power to influence decisions concerning society as a whole. (65–66)

Little wonder that Béji felt disillusioned! Sharabi goes on to explain that in its structure etatism combined the paternalism of colonialism and the bureaucratic apparatus of the modern state:

> As such it took upon itself all the functions of society. For individual citizens it was something external, poised over and against them. Free public association was impossible, even when guaranteed by the constitution, unless initiated and controlled by the state. Isolated, estranged, and suppressed, the individual subject was driven back to the primary social structures—the family, the ethnic community, the tribe, the religious sect—for security and for survival. (66)

National discourse, Béji observes, was the osmosis by which national identity became "a progressive assimilation of reality to a representation that was more pure, more rational, more perfect" (48). Eventually, however, social contradictions and conflicts rooted primarily in the problems of poverty and unequal development would explode this ideal vision of the nation-state, along with the allegory of which Bourguiba was the mainstay, as Bourguiba grew more intolerant of oppositional voices, becoming more dictatorial, erratic, and finally, senile (50–51).

Twenty-five years after publishing *Désenchantement national*, in an attempt to take her analysis a step further, Béji wrote another book, *Nous, décolonisés*, in which she asks many of the same questions she asked in the earlier work: Why, for example, "left to themselves, decolonized peoples sink back into dependency and experience injustices more subtle than those they suffered when they were occupied, and which they themselves have reproduced"?[21] Like her first book, *Nous, décolonisés* is chiefly an eloquent description of her society's malaise, an enumeration of symptoms, a lament—albeit a poetic one—from which an analysis emerges, primarily by way of allegory.

Perhaps to avoid being thrown into jail for criticizing Ben Ali and his regime, Béji employs the form of allegory known as personification, but does so at one remove or more from the "person" who is, surely, best placed to answer for the malaise she describes and decries. Throughout *Nous, décolonisés*, she refers to "us," "the decolonized," or speaks using the first-person plural pronoun, "we," or even the first-person singular pronoun, "I" (the decolonized/postcolonial Tunisian), when she might refer to Zine El Abidine Ben Ali, chairman of the RCD (Democratic Constitutional Rally) and president of the Tunisian Republic.[22]

Béji's refusal to point a finger of blame at Ben Ali for Tunisia's woes or to cast herself and her countrymen as innocent victims in a postcolonial drama of underdevelopment and repression is perhaps more than an allegorical strategy to avoid ending up in prison, however. She blames the Tunisians themselves, who have "confused the *idea of the State* with the *instinct of power*,"[23] insisting that "the despotic nature of our states" (i.e., the states of decolonized peoples) cannot be explained simply by pointing to the evidently despotic tendencies of the leaders themselves. Rather, the despotic state can be seen as the consequence of a popular tendency to create it as a *necessity*, out of a need to feel secure and invincible. "The personification of power is a collective invention, which deifies the one that destiny has chosen," she writes, adding: "Is it really so absurd to think that our general will is oriented toward dependency rather than autonomy?" (70).

If, as Béji goes on to suggest, the greed for power exists as a (normally suppressed) gene in all of us, she nevertheless acknowledges that bad leadership sooner or later begets bad behavior in those being led. When "people choose to be lazy, cowardly, dishonest, [or] hypocritical," she explains, it is because they see that "the collective rules are not being respected" (81). Without ever proposing that Ben Ali or his mafia-like family be held accountable for the widespread and systemic corruption in Tunisia or for the fact that the country under his watch had become a police state—ranked by *The Economist*'s 2008 Democracy Index as being worse than the People's Republic of China, Egypt, Sierra Leone, and Pakistan[24]—Béji observes that: "Everyone justifies his dereliction by a sort of implicit sanction that emanates indirectly from the general authority. Often, incivility is but a reflection of the public attitude of laxity. The weak justify their cynicism by pointing to the impunity of the strong" (81). The reader who remembers that Ben Ali was often popularly described as "a policeman, before he became a president," will be struck by Béji's choice of analogy to illustrate her point: "Drivers would not break the rules of the road so often if they didn't see policemen doing it" (81).

When she wrote *Désenchantement national*, Béji admitted that she wondered what a "portrait of the decolonized" would look like, written in the manner of Albert Memmi's 1957 landmark essay, *Portrait du colonisé, précédé de: Portrait du colonisateur* (*The Colonizer and the Colonized*).[25] As it happens, Memmi did write that portrait in 2004, giving it the title: *Portrait du décolonisé: Arabo-musulman et de quelques autres*.[26] And, possibly in homage to the work by his fellow Tunisian, he begins with a section entitled: "La grande désillusion."[27]

All the films of the New Tunisian Cinema, whether made during Bourguiba's (by then, senile) watch—such as Bouzid's *Man of Ashes* (1986)— or during the Ben Ali era, offer portraits of the decolonized Tunisian, and all are marked by the postcolonial malaise identified by Béji and Memmi, among others.[28] Whether the root of this malaise is an uneasy tension or outright conflict between *tradition* and *modernity*, as Béji at one point suggests (*Nous, décolonisés*, 118), or whether one of the essential problems is poverty and a class divide defined by the rapacious attitude of the middle classes toward the poor, as Memmi believes (*Decolonization and the Decolonized*, 4),[29] Béji and Memmi—like the filmmakers of the New Tunisian Cinema—do not believe that religion or the Islamists have the answer.

"All religions are intolerant, exclusive, restrictive, and sometimes violent," Memmi insists. "The conception of a 'moderate Islam,' which some willingly defend, is misguided: there is no such thing as a moderate religion, even though there are more or less faithful believers, more or less respectful of its dogmas and rites, believers who, for that matter, also arouse the wrath and irony of fundamentalists" (34).[30] Béji, too, is dismissive: "The quest for non-Western values or policies that would benefit the rest of humanity—what has that led to? This 'more' that we were supposed to have brought to modern life has been revealed to be a 'less.'"[31]

The New Tunisian Cinema, as we have said, is a cinema of resistance—but the question, of course, is *what* a given film is resisting. In an uncompromisingly titled book, which appeared in 2002, *La Tunisie de Ben Ali: La société contre le régime*, the editors claim that the date of publication of their volume was not fortuitous:

> While President Ben Ali crudely maneuvers to legitimate a fourth and unconstitutional term for himself in 2004, it seems to us an opportune moment to revisit his 14 years in office by listening to the voices of the Tunisians themselves, both seekers and actors, who are normally deprived of free intellectual debate and of venues of reflection and expression. It also seems to us the right moment, as the French state solemnly renews its support of the Tunisian regime in the context of "the global war on Islamic terrorism," to make available to the French reader some analyses . . . [and] critiques of the current political regime of this country that is so often presented as a haven of peace and serenity.[32]

The volume's contributors seek to "understand how and why the 'democratic promise' of the 'new era' that was officially inaugurated following the 'medical coup d'état' of 7 November 1987 has not withstood the test of the exercise of power" (ibid.).

Likewise, the films of the New Tunisian Cinema are, broadly speaking, allegories of resistance against the authoritarian state—the state that Tunisia became under Bourguiba and that Ben Ali reinforced during his tenure as president. But if I want to make this argument, I must preface it with a consideration of the allegorical mode of filmmaking and reception, for this study proposes that, in a sense, Bourguiba and Ben Ali are themselves allegorical figures who play important roles in the ongoing drama of Tunisia's decolonization. We know they are real, historical figures; but as every serious analysis of Tunisia's postcolonial condition acknowledges, the postcolonial condition is precisely that: a condition. We cannot say it was caused or is maintained by one man. A filmmaker like Nacer Khemir, for example—who is without doubt a member of the cohort identified with the New Tunisian Cinema—makes films that appear to have nothing specifically to do with Tunisia or the two presidents who have shaped its destiny since Independence. More obviously than most, his films are allegories. But what are they allegories of? And there is the related question: How "Tunisian" are they?

I do not include a Nacer Khemir film among those I study in the chapters that follow, because the style and subject matter of Khemir's films are radically different from the mainstream of the New Tunisian Cinema. Nevertheless, I mention him here, because he is useful to us as a test case as we attempt to answer an implicit question contained in the title of this book: Are all the films of the New Tunisian Cinema perforce national allegories? In "The Poetic Vision of Nacer Khemir," Roy Armes quotes Khemir as saying that his overall concern is to show "an open, tolerant and friendly Islamic culture, full of love and wisdom . . . an Islam that is different from the one depicted in the media."[33] For Khemir, fundamentalism "is a distorting mirror of Islam," and his film *Bab'Aziz—The Prince That Contemplated His Soul* (2005), like its predecessors, is "a modest attempt to give Islam its real face back" (81). Khemir argues that *Bab'Aziz* is "a highly political film, and deliberately so. It is a duty nowadays to show to the world another aspect of Islam, otherwise each of us will be stifled by his own ignorance of 'The Other.' It is fear that stifles people, not reality" (81).[34]

The question of allegory, thus, is broached; but Khemir's allegories are clearly not of the kind that signify two-dimensionally, in a process whereby, in Fredric Jameson's phrase, "an elaborate set of figures and personifications [can] be read against some one-to-one table of equivalences."[35] Rather, they are set in motion when we are willing to recognize that "such equivalences are themselves in constant change and transformation at each perpetual present of the text" (73). As Armes puts it, in the conclusion of his assessment of Khemir's work:

> No answers are given to the question of how to change the modern world: problems are hinted at, but no issues are resolved. The title figures of *Les*

Baliseurs du désert [1984], for example, may stand in relation to the dispossessed youth of today's Maghreb, but they are exiled into a timeless desert, not subjected to the capitalist pressures and racial oppression of an exploitative Westernized world. Those who destroy the city in *Le Collier perdu de la colombe* [1991] may be barbarians, but they are given no ideology, fundamentalist or otherwise. Yet Khemir's commitment is always apparent: "No mission seemed as urgent to me as this one: to give a face to hundreds of millions of Muslims who are often, if not always, the first victims of terrorism caused by some fundamentalist." (81–82)[36]

The *désenchantement national* that Béji writes about, then, is not only local—that is, confined within the geographical borders of Tunisia—but global in the dialectical sense, in which we cannot speak about the local without also acknowledging the totality, the big picture.

Allegories of Resistance

When Fredric Jameson famously and somewhat controversially observed in his 1986 essay, "Third-World Literature in the Era of Multinational Capitalism," that all third-world texts are necessarily allegorical, particularly when their forms develop out of predominantly Western machineries of representation, he argued that they are allegorical in a very specific way—they are to be read as *national allegories*. "The story of the private individual destiny," he wrote, "*is always an allegory of the embattled situation of the public third-world culture and society*" (69; emphasis in original). If we infer from this statement that a third-world culture and society is one that can, very broadly, be defined by its "embattled situation" (i.e., in relation to hegemonic forces, or a dominant system), we can see, as Jameson himself acknowledged, that third-world cultures may be found anywhere—in the United States, for example—where the third-world culture in question escapes the categories in which one describes hegemonic culture.[37] The "larger pre-established identity" within which one might identify differences between two cultural situations (i.e., the differences between a first-world situation and a third-world situation) is identified by Jameson as one in which "American bankers hold the levers of the world system," a system, "late capitalism, [which] is the supreme unifying force of contemporary history."[38]

Before commenting on Jameson's article, which has been very productive in helping me make sense of the relationship of cinema to politics in the decolonizing world,[39] I should clarify what I generally mean when I use the term "Third World." Although I shall more often use the attributive adjective "postcolonial" in place of "third-world," I understand, following Ella Shohat and Robert Stam in *Unthinking Eurocentrism*, that the "Third World" refers to "the colonized, neocolonized, or decolonized nations and 'minorities' whose structural disadvantages have been shaped by the colonial process and by the unequal division of international labor."[40] Shohat and Stam are right to observe that "three-worlds theory not only flattens heterogeneities, masks contradictions, and elides differences, it also obscures similarities (for example, the common presence of 'Fourth World' indigenous peoples in both 'Third World' and 'First World' countries)" (26).[41] They also correctly note that third-world nationalist discourse "often assumes an unquestioned national identity," when in fact "most contemporary nation-states are 'mixed' formations" (26)—a problematic that Tunisia's filmmakers (or at least those whose works I examine here) are acutely conscious of and see as crucially relevant to their task of articulating an authentic *tunisianité*.[42] Nevertheless, as Shohat and Stam acknowledge, the term "Third World" does retain heuristic value "as a label for the 'imperialized formations' (including some within the First World)" (27), which, they point out, thereby confers majority status on a group that constitutes three-fourths of the world's population.

When Jameson acknowledges that it would be presumptuous of him to offer some general theory of third-world literature, "given the enormous variety both of national cultures in the third world and of specific historical trajectories in each of those areas" (68), it occurs to me that my general claim about the films of the New Tunisian Cinema being "allegories of resistance" may also be a little presumptuous, given the variety of genres and modes of address that exist in contemporary Tunisian cinema. Not all contemporary Tunisian films are national allegories in the sense Jameson gives the term; but the ones I have chosen belong to a specific class—a canon of films dating from the mid-1980s to the end of the Ben Ali era, which has more or less fallen into place and become legible as such—that is clearly both *political* and preoccupied with *national identity*.[43] We should not be misled by the phrase, "national identity," however, as though it referred somehow to an uncomplicated relation to the nation-state, for as

Jean and John Comaroff have pointed out, "there is no such thing, save at very high levels of abstraction, as '*the* nation-state'":

> The processes by which millennial capitalism is taking shape do not reduce to a simple narrative according to which the nation-state either lives or dies, ebbs or flourishes. Its impact is much more complicated, more polyphonous and dispersed, and most immediately felt in the everyday contexts of work and labor, of domesticity and consumption, of street life and media-gazing.[44]

Nor should we limit our understanding of the term "political" as pertaining only to the state (i.e., to "political institutions, repressive apparatuses, political society")[45]—the films of the New Tunisian Cinema are inevitably political, because it is understood that "in the third-world situation the intellectual is *always* in one way or another a *political* intellectual."[46] As Réda Bensmaïa observes in *Experimental Nations: Or, the Invention of the Maghreb*:

> If it is indeed true that an allegorical dimension persists in most so-called postcolonial texts, allegory is clearly almost never the primary or sole ambition of the authors in question. When it is, however, experience has shown that we often find ourselves faced with texts that could be called didactic, the artistic or literary value of which is slight or nil. This is true for literature proper—as in novels and poetry—but also for films. Legion are the novels and films produced by postcolonial writers and filmmakers that can be read as allegories, though not so much as allegories "of the embattled situation of the public third-world culture and society" as right-thinking and familiar discourses on good and evil, on the pure and the impure, on true and false identity, on the glorious past scorned by colonialism, and so on.[47]

Writing about the vast number of short stories and serialized novels written in the many languages to be found in India and published in Indian-language newspapers and magazines, Thomas Palakeel observes: "The truth is that many canonical works in these languages are often overlooked by those who choose representative fictions for translation into First World languages because 'national allegories' are able to travel beyond regional languages, not as literature, but as ethnographies, as anthropological and political document."[48] His observation should alert us to the way in which a similar process of selection for "translation into First World languages" occurs in the Tunisian cinema, to create the kind of canon I am talking about here.

In the cinema, with the cost of filmmaking and film distribution and exhibition so high, the ability "to travel beyond regional languages," as it were, is nearly always a necessity. A feature-length film is rarely made for a local audience only, because it cannot be produced for the relatively low cost or in the manner of a short story or serialized novel (although, from the consumer's point of view, we can perhaps say that the television drama series functions like short fiction in a newspaper or magazine: it is consumed inexpensively and with regularity).[49] A film must reach a large, paying public for the producers to earn a proper return on their investment. Whether or not investors in Tunisian films include European producers—which invariably they do—it is always hoped that these films will be able to "travel beyond" Tunisia's borders, at least to western Europe, if not as ethnography—as "anthropological and political document"—then as commercial releases in the "foreign film/art cinema" market. The films chosen for inclusion in this study are precisely "representative fictions" in the sense Palakeel gives the term: they "translate" into the first-world language of the art house theater or college film course, because "national allegories" are indeed able to travel beyond the "regional" space, say, of Tunisian film programming on television during the holy month of Ramadan, when the nation's cinematic heritage is reviewed.[50]

But the Tunisian cinema has never been only, or even primarily, about entertaining local audiences, or seeking to "travel beyond" the country's borders in order to generate a greater margin of profit for its producers, or providing product for exhibitors abroad. Its role, as Bensmaïa has also pointed out, has been like that of literature (in the colonized and decolonizing world), as described by Edward Said:

> In the decades-long struggle to achieve decolonization and independence from European control, literature has played a crucial role in the re-establishment of a national cultural heritage, in the reinstatement of native idioms, in the re-imagining and re-figuring of local histories, geographies, communities. As such, then, literature not only mobilized active

resistance to incursions from the outside, but also contributed massively as the shaper, creator, and agent of illumination within the realm of the colonized.[51]

In this sense, one function of Tunisian cinema has indeed been to offer allegories that "speak" the public culture and society. Jameson's article, however, in which he wrote that *all* third-world texts are *necessarily* allegorical, has been attacked by a number of critics over the years for its totalizing aims. In "Who's Afraid of National Allegory? Jameson, Literary Criticism, Globalization," Imre Szeman writes: "The presumption that it is possible to produce a theory that would explain African, Asian, *and* Latin American literary production, the literature of China *and* Senegal, has been (inevitably) read as nothing more than a patronizing, theoretical orientalism, or as yet another example of a troubling appropriation of Otherness with the aim of exploring the West rather than the Other."[52] Like Szeman, however, I think these critics have misread Jameson's essay, whose apparently sweeping generalizations are part and parcel of an argument on behalf of totality, which Szeman, following Jameson, sees as "the possibility of metacommentary . . . as a condition of interpretation per se" (805).[53] Szeman argues that "what national allegory itself names are the conditions of possibility of metacommentary at the present time," and he is interested in "the relationship of allegory (as a mode of interpretation) to the nation (as a specific kind of sociopolitical problematic) and what this relationship entails for a global or transnational literary or cultural criticism" (805).

In "Historical Allegory," Ismail Xavier echoes what Jameson and Szeman mean when they argue on behalf of "totality":

> As historians and political scientists have taught us, the nation . . . is a product of modernity, of market culture and industrialization, a social construct able to create a sense of totalization, a cohesive collective entity that refers to heterogeneous groups belonging to a complex society at a time when any single homogenous community of experience is out of reach.[54]

Allegory, with its dialectics of fragmentation and totalization, brings within reach this "community of experience" that Jameson sees the "cultural logic of late capitalism" as having done so much to erode.[55]

Xavier observes that cinematic allegory underwent significant change throughout the world in the 1980s and 1990s, arguing that "filmmakers from different continents now share a common historical ground that, in spite of all difficulties, challenges them to express encompassing views of the contemporary scene that engenders allegories" (359). He suggests that allegory's contemporary appeal can be explained by the fact that it is "the language of crisis," as the rapid technological and economic change that characterizes our contemporary world forces people to "revise their views of identity and shared values" (359). He emphasizes the (re)appearance of allegory as a symptom of the global zeitgeist, which he sees as marked by a general sense of "fragmentation, discontinuity, and abstraction" (360).

For Jameson, however, the reemergence of allegory as a kind of dialectical criticism is a positive development. He insists that "the allegorical spirit is profoundly discontinuous, a matter of breaks and heterogeneities, of the multiple polysemia of the dream rather than the homogenous representation of the symbol" (73). Or, as Szeman puts it: "Far from reducing the complexity of third world literary production, the concept of national allegory enables us to consider these texts as the extremely complex objects that they are and *not* just as allegories of one kind or another of the Manichean binaries produced out of the encounter of colonizer and colonized (however ambivalently one might want to understand these)" (812–813). Paraphrasing Jameson, I see the films discussed in this book, then, as vital responses to infrastructural realities; they are attempts to resolve more fundamental contradictions.[56] In short, they are a particular kind of cultural strategy—they are engaged in a "cultural revolution," a strategy that not only seeks to "imagine" the nation, but to overcome the phenomenon of "subalternity," namely (in Jameson's summary), the "feelings of mental inferiority and habits of subservience and obedience which necessarily and structurally develop in situations of domination—most dramatically in the experience of colonized peoples" (76).

There is a sense, however, in which we can say that every film ever made is an allegory, because every film presents *a* world, none presents *the* world. And, because there is no reality apart from its representation (in language), every representation is inherently allegorical—or, as Craig Owens observes, turning this fundamental semiotic truth around: "Allegory . . . is revealed as a structural possibility inherent in every work."[57] But one cannot say that all representation is inherently allegorical, and leave it at that, for the term would then lose its usefulness as designating a specific kind of structure demanding a certain kind of reading. The question, perhaps, is how *self-conscious* an allegory is, and whether that hypothetical creature, the "average viewer," discerns a film's allegorical aspects as an "intentional" element among the filmmaker's strategies of communication. Of course, a filmmaker may not be aware that he or she has made an allegory, or that this or that character or situation can be read as "allegorical," and so one must make the further distinction between political allegory (what, in a loose correspondence, Jameson calls "national allegory")—allegory that refers to (a situation in) the public sphere—and ordinary, everyday allegory, a structure that is essentially no different from the psychoanalytic process we call "identification." The moment we stop talking about *intentional* allegories, however—those allegories that presumably even the "average viewer" understands are allegories—we are inevitably returned to the question of the viewer's interpretive competence. Xavier suggests that "alongside intentional allegories there are also 'unconscious' allegories, where the intervention of a 'competent reader' is indispensable. Recognizing an allegorical dimension in a text requires the ability to perceive homologies, and national allegories require the understanding of private lives as representative of public destinies" (335).[58]

There is no doubt that allegory is a notion "that changes definition and value according to cultural context," and so Xavier is right to ask: What kind of demand do most allegories try to answer? (336).[59] For an example of the kind of allegorical reading that functions in the private sphere, we might consider why some people love watching prison films. As the author of a popular film studies guide puts it: for such viewers who feel, for whatever reasons, that they have insufficient authority or control over their own lives, the prison film provides a situation with which they can identify and that is in some way analogous to their own situation. How the main character of these films accommodates to the restrictions of prison life—"yet preserves some kind of individual freedom and dignity, by surrender, sly conformity, defiance, or outright intimidation"—provides viewers with a range of options. If nothing else, prison films "can provide minimal recognition and perhaps compensatory fantasies for people who feel similarly trapped in their own circumstances."[60]

I choose this quite ordinary example of how prison films can function as private sphere/personal allegory, because one of the theses I shall develop about the allegorical imperative in Tunisian cinema is that there is a dialectic at play in several of the films I discuss between themes of incarceration and freedom.[61] (This dialectic is invariably inscribed in a discourse on sexuality. Some of the Tunisian cinema's singularity can be found in its willingness—unusual in contemporary Arab societies—to present the allegory of the embattled situation of the public third-world culture and society in the private, individual terms of sexuality.) These films, as I hope to demonstrate, transcend their stories of the private, individual destiny, to speak not only to Tunisians—to help them account for their contemporary social reality—but also to all viewers who seek to understand society and our position within it.

Jameson makes the point that identity and difference should not be seen as fixed and eternal opposites (the first- and third-world cultural situations as having nothing in common between them), but rather as inscribed in a dialectical—which is to say mobile—relation to each other. Tunisia, as I have suggested, both is and is not a third-world country, which puts its filmmakers in something of a bind as they attempt, on the one hand, to speak to a wide range of audiences, and try, on the other, to avoid the intervention of the government censor. Tunisian society during the Ben Ali era was one in which allegory was seen by the filmmakers as a vitally useful way of participating collectively in a (subversive) dialogue with their fellow citizens; but in fact audiences frequently yearned to go *beyond* national allegory, which, by its very presence in their cinema, attested to the unhappy fact that they still felt themselves as Tunisians to be in an "embattled situation."

Like the cinemas of most postcolonial societies, that of Tunisia is preoccupied with the politics of emancipation and identity; but in their role as active participants in the construction of a national/cultural identity, the filmmakers find themselves confronting dilemmas on several fronts. Whereas the first generation of post-Independence Tunisian films focused on emancipation from colonial or first-generation neocolonial oppression (in which the "villain"—be it France or the predatory features of an American-led, "global" capitalism—is perceived to be essentially external to the society), New Tunisian Cinema considers oppressive/repressive structures within the society itself: the neopatriarchal family, government corruption, the authoritarianism of the state, the mafia-like activities of President Ben Ali's extended family, the growth of political Islam, and so on. The Tunisian public, moreover, by and large craves an imported, commercial cinema, and the allegorical content of the best Tunisian films is often disdained or ignored.[62] The reasons for this are complex and contradictory, but the prestige of a distinctive, recognizably Tunisian national cinema nevertheless provides a valuable repository of representations in the public sphere of what we call *tunisianité*.

"Being Tunisian" in the World

Férid Boughedir, one of the founding directors of the New Tunisian Cinema and perhaps its most visible and peripatetic member on the global stage, identifies Bouzid's *Man of Ashes* as "the miracle" that launched the "golden age" of Tunisian cinema, which he judges to have lasted ten years. For the success of this remarkable coming-of-age of Tunisian cinema, he credits the following: a Tunisian tradition of cinephilia;[63] the successful resistance by filmmakers to any suggestion that they should have a state-run film industry; the boldness of Tunisia's directors in being willing to tackle subject matter that would be deemed taboo in other Arab countries; and the resourcefulness of an energetic group of producers (including Ahmed Attia, Hassan Daldoul, and Selma Baccar in the first generation, and Dora Bouchoucha, Ibrahim Letaïef, and Néjib Belkadhi in the second).[64]

As he is eager to point out, however, "Tunisian cinema had already been a star on the international festival scene" for at least a decade. Films Boughedir mentions include: *The Ambassadors* (Nacer Ktari, 1975); *Hyenas' Sun* (Ridha Behi, 1976); *Aziza* (Abdellatif Ben Ammar, 1980); *The Trace* (Néjia Ben Mabrouk, 1982); *Crossing Over* (Mahmoud Ben Mahmoud, 1982); and *Les baliseurs du désert* (Nacer Khemir, 1984)—before *Man of Ashes* broke the Tunisian cinema out of the "ghetto" of the art house and prestigious foreign film festival.[65]

The "Tunisian" film—and for that matter, the "Moroccan" and "Algerian" film as well—nevertheless often still finds itself grouped by film festivals, scholars, and critics (especially those who live and work outside the Maghreb) under the rubric of "Maghrebi cinema." In "Le cinéma maghrébin vu de l'autre côté de la Méditerranée," Will Higbee suggests that "Maghrebi cinema" is to some extent an invented category, a *lieu imaginaire*, and notes that "the filmmakers of the Maghreb have always preferred to take up 'Maghrebi' realities within a national and local context" and rarely think of their films in a regional context or as examples of "Maghrebi cinema."[66] But Maghrebi cinema, he argues, is always simultaneously local, national, regional, and diasporic, and there is a complex interplay among these real and imaginary spaces. He cites Denise Brahimi's notion of the three *lieux* of Maghrebi cinema that she proposes in her book, *50 ans de cinéma maghrébin*: the first being the Maghrebi country itself, as a geographical, cultural and economic zone; the second being the countries where the films have significant audiences—most importantly, perhaps, France, not only because France shares a colonial history with the Maghreb, but because it is the principal co-producer of the films, and a large number of Maghrebi filmmakers now live and work in France; and the third *lieu* being one that is "more mental and cultural than geographical," an intermediate, virtual space that constitutes a sort of synthesis of all the different meanings we bring to the term when we think or talk about Maghrebi cinema—"not a real space, but a constructed one" (104–105). Citing research done by Patricia Caillé on the reception of Maghrebi films in Europe, Higbee notes that of the twenty-two "Algerian" films that were released in France between 1997 and 2007, twenty-one were co-productions with France, of which thirteen were for the most part French-financed. As for the French co-production of films of other Maghreb countries during the same period, one can count, respectively: seventeen Franco-Moroccan co-productions among the twenty-two Moroccan films released in France and twelve Franco-Tunisian co-productions among the seventeen Tunisian films released in France.[67] The implications of these statistics, reflecting the complex ties that bind France and the Maghreb by virtue primarily of the Maghrebi diaspora in France, are further complicated by the compressions of time and space that characterize contemporary globalization, which exacerbates both global and local categories.

The New Tunisian Cinema, regardless of how individual films might be seen and discussed abroad, remains decidedly *national* and *local* in its concerns. Like Boughedir, who observes that the Tunisian cinema "excels at intimism,"[68] Kmar Bendana, in "Ideologies of the Nation," notes that the singularity of the Tunisian cinema, especially after Bouzid's *Man of Ashes*, can be identified by its focus on the concrete and specific.[69] The postcolonial problems and issues that dominate are located in the quotidian reality of contemporary Tunisian lives. For example, when Bendana remarks on the success of Bouzid's sketch in the omnibus film *The Gulf War . . . What*

Next? (1992),⁷⁰ she identifies one of the most recognizable characteristics of the New Tunisian Cinema and a typical strategy of allegory: while the Gulf War of 1990–1991 was "an event [that was] translated into a spectacular worldwide phenomenon by its televisual hyper-mediatization," she writes, Bouzid's sketch addresses it "through the lens of the everyday life of a Tunisian family" (40). The Tunisian films that have achieved the greatest success both at the Tunisian box office and abroad, she observes, have been those that are "local, particularistic" films that embrace their "specificity" in a way that makes them "globally accessible." She cites as examples Tunisia's three most famous and internationally successful films: *Man of Ashes*, *Halfaouine*, and *The Silences of the Palace* (40).

As members of the first generation to be imbued with Bourguiba's secular, liberal values, the directors of these films are essentially "modern." They are the first—and for the time being, possibly the last—generation with these values to lead the public debate about national identity. Whether or not, following the upheaval in 2011, they or their worldview can remain relevant and influential in this debate, remains to be seen—but for more than twenty years, they were willing and able to speak about the embattled situation of Tunisia's public third-world culture and society in films underpinned by a coherent, progressive ideology.⁷¹ As Boughedir insists, his cohort of filmmakers tried to bring about "a revolution in the way people thought, their habits of thinking: in this, they were directly political."⁷² Their self-conscious modernity and their success in articulating the modernist vision they shared with Bourguiba, I contend, make them Bourguiba's best legacy in the field of artistic representation.

Tunisians are proud of their "modernity." The official rhetoric proclaims that their country by nature is exceptional, a status deriving from the perfect equilibrium it has achieved among three components: Western modernity, a distinctive national identity, and a shared heritage with the Arab and Muslim worlds. This equilibrium, or synthesis, they believe, is signified by their reformist tradition, which they insist dates at least from the mid-nineteenth century and the policies of the great reformer Khayr ed-Din al-Tunsi.⁷³ Reformism and *tunisianité* are understood to be inseparable, and together symbolize Tunisian specificity.

But as Béatrice Hibou argues in *The Force of Obedience: The Political Economy of Repression in Tunisia*, "reformism is a myth, a central myth of Tunisian governmentality, its principal *imaginaire*" (213):

Nineteenth-century reformism is, like the 1789 Revolution for France, simultaneously a founding event and a real myth which is forever being appropriated in contradictory ways. The problem is not the reality of nineteenth-century reformism, the reality of the Fundamental Pact of 1857 and the Constitution of 1861; it is the statement, affirmed by all, that "reformism has been the specific feature of Tunisia since the nineteenth century," the statement—taken as a principle of truth—of a seamless historical continuity without any break or change in meaning, a smoothing-out which defines a fixed and definite cultural identity. (218)[74]

Hibou describes how in Tunisia reformism is a belief, a way of thinking, an ethos; but it is one that has virtually no concrete content. It is "the elaboration of a consensus"; it is presented as that "which makes it possible for Tunisian society to be a unity"; it "provides a sense of national cohesion"; it is "the bearer of positive values that can be shared by all" (216). In short—although Hibou does not use the term—the discourse on reformism functions in Tunisia as a form of *allegory*, in that (to echo Jameson, Szeman, Xavier, and others) it creates a sense of totalization for a heterogeneous society at a time when any single homogeneous community of experience is out of reach.[75] It enables Tunisians to understand their society and their place within it (as a specific kind of sociopolitical problematic)—a way of managing global, modern identity—by offering a mode of interpretation for this endeavor, that is, by naming the conditions of possibility of metacommentary.

Despite feelings of postcolonial disenchantment, national feeling remains strong among Tunisians. The "national idea" appears to have taken root in Tunisian consciousness and to some extent has been shaped in opposition to the "communities" Tunisians have felt do not fully comprehend them: the supranational community that was the Ottoman Empire (of which they were a part for three hundred years),[76] the "Arab world" (which now numbers some twenty-two nations), and the worldwide *umma* of Muslims (which, at more than 1.6 billion, accounts for about 23 percent of the world's population).[77] While constituted by all of these, Tunisia nevertheless feels itself to be uniquely Tunisian, with a specific history that is significantly different even from those of its neighbors in the Maghreb (Algeria, Libya, Morocco), where climate, food, and customs are very similar to its own.

Hibou suggests, however, that *tunisianité* is a "fictive ethnicity," in the sense given to the term by Etienne Balibar in his essay, "The Nation Form: History and Ideology," in which he describes state-fabricated identities like the one the Tunisian authorities have elaborated about the country having a long history of reformism that makes it (and Tunisians) exceptional. "No nation possesses an ethnic base naturally," writes Balibar, "but as social formations are nationalized, the populations included within them, divided up among them or dominated by them are ethnicized—that is, represented in the past or in the future *as if* they formed a natural community, possessing of itself an identity of origins, culture and interests which transcends individuals and social conditions" (96).[78] Among Tunisians, however, the notion of *tunisianité* quickly developed as a vital element in the struggle for independence.

The notion of *tunisianité* has undergone (and, of course, continues to undergo) shifts of emphasis and meaning according to various significant changes in the global political economy, some of the more recent of which have been: the 1967 Arab–Israeli War, in which the Arab nations that went to war with Israel suffered a resounding defeat that was felt by the entire Arab world and led to the general collapse of Arab nationalism; the first Gulf War (August 1990 to February 1991); the rise of the Qatar-based Arab television network, channel, and website, Al Jazeera; the 9/11 attacks of 2001 by al-Qaeda upon the United States; and the Iraq War (also known as the "Second Gulf War"), which began on 20 March 2003 and was followed by the American occupation of Iraq, which lasted well into Barack Obama's presidency. Each of these "events" has provoked a reorientation of the concept of *tunisianité*.

Despite official rhetoric, a widening gap opened up during Ben Ali's presidency between official *tunisianité* and an emergent counter-*tunisianité* (implicit in the title of Lamloum and Ravenel's 2002 book, *La Tunisie de Ben Ali: La société contre le régime*). With every conflict in the Middle East, for example, Tunisia drifted further away from the image of itself in the official portrait, as ordinary Tunisians adjusted to the reality that their government was complicit with the West in the structures of repression that marked their political and social life. Hibou writes that "it is interesting to note that 'the most Western of countries in the Maghreb' is also the one in which the population looks most at Middle-Eastern media—comparatively speaking, much more than at the European media"

(231). The reasons for this—if we take Hibou at her word—no doubt have something to do with Tunisia's uniquely Westernized character and its increasingly ambivalent feelings toward the United States, symbolic leader of the West and chief sponsor of the West's client state in the heart of the Middle East, Israel.

Tunisia's position on the Palestine–Israel conflict and on wars involving other Arab states has not been without its contradictions, ambivalences, and difficulties. True to its special status as a country at the "crossroads of the Islamic and European worlds" (to echo the title of a book about Tunisia by Perkins) and as a country heavily invested in attracting European tourists for a significant portion of its hard currency, Tunisia has sometimes found itself in a delicate situation when there has been a conflict involving an Arab state and Israel or the United States. Politically, the path has been tricky, starting with the fact that at the time of the creation of the state of Israel in 1948, Tunisia had a population of roughly 85,000 Jews. Perkins explains that, although 6,500 Jews departed Tunisia in the year of Tunisia's Independence, "the number of emigrants declined significantly over the next several years, as none of the misfortunes feared at the end of the protectorate befell the community" (144). Bourguiba's view, he records, was that "the Arab states needed to reconcile the justice of the Palestinians' cause with the acceptance of the existence of Israel" (144–145); and when the Palestine Liberation Organization was created in 1964, Bourguiba made a public proposal that the PLO accept the 1947 UN partition of Palestine as a point of departure for negotiations with Israel. The response from Egypt, the political and cultural leader of the Arab world at the time, was immediate:

> Nasser orchestrated a barrage of ridicule and hostility so scathing that Tunisia severed diplomatic relations with Egypt in 1966. But the outbreak of war in the following year between Israel and its Arab neighbors revealed that few Tunisians shared their president's view on the emotionally charged issue of Palestine. Anti-Zionist demonstrations erupted throughout the country, some of them provoking assaults on members of the Jewish community or damage to synagogues and other Jewish-owned property. Despite Bourguiba's denunciation of these incidents, a sustained wave of Jewish emigration following the war rapidly reduced the community to less than half its 1956 size. (145)

Following Israel's 1982 invasion of Lebanon and fifteen years after the fateful 1967 Arab–Israeli War, Tunisia was pressured by the United States to allow the PLO to establish its headquarters in Tunis, which had the unfortunate result, Perkins notes, of identifying Tunisia with the Palestine–Israel conflict, something which Tunisia had successfully avoided in the past. Then, in 1985 Israel bombed a Palestinian compound in Hammam Lif, on the outskirts of Tunis, killing sixty-eight Palestinians and Tunisians and injuring over a hundred. Air raids by the United States on Libyan targets the following year did further damage to the tourist industry, "with consequences that rippled through the economy" (171).

By the time of the Iraq's invasion of Kuwait in August 1990, and the attack of the American-led coalition on Iraq in January 1991, Arab feeling on the street against the United States had begun to harden significantly, as U.S. foreign policy in the Middle East was perceived to be dedicated to preserving existing patterns of political economy, which is to say, as Mark Tessler puts it: to supporting "a handful of privileged Arab states, like the rulers and associated elites within most Arab countries, [who] are believed to be dedicated to the preservation of a political and economic order that provides benefits for the few and is indifferent or even hostile to the well-being of the majority."[79] The U.S.-led coalition scored a decisive victory in Iraq, yet "in many Arab countries, including all three states of the Maghreb, there was substantial popular sympathy for Saddam Hussein and broad opposition to the United States and its coalition of partners" (104). There was an outpouring of public anger, Tessler notes, but this was not produced by a high regard for the Iraqi president or by support for his actions in Kuwait. "Rather, as in a number of other Arab countries, the Gulf crisis served as a proxy for a very different set of grievances and gave citizens of the Maghreb an occasion to express once again the discontent that had produced disturbances during the preceding decade" (105–106).

If the Gulf crisis of 1990–1991 confirmed a deep discontent felt by many ordinary citizens in North Africa, the American invasion of Iraq in 2003 would have the same effect, except that this time the perception among ordinary citizens of the Maghreb that Israel was behind the American invasion of Iraq would intensify anti-Israel bias. The Israeli destruction of large areas of the Jenin refugee camp in the West Bank in April 2002[80]—only the most recent tragedy in a series of brutal actions against Palestinians undertaken by the Israelis with the tacit, if not official, approval of the

United States—seemed to be proof, if any were needed, of the bad faith of American involvement in Middle Eastern affairs. Anger against Israel and the United States would become more entrenched when, with even greater Israeli vindictiveness and similar American acquiescence, Israel bombarded Lebanon in the summer of 2006, and when it invaded Gaza in the winter of 2008–2009.[81]

Tunisian sympathy is strong for the Palestinians in their tragic predicament, but the ongoing conflicts in connection with the Israeli occupation of Palestinian territory (not to mention the political instability that plagues Tunisia's next-door neighbor, Algeria) contributed to a new inflection in the narrative about what makes Tunisia unique, namely: Tunisia's relative stability (until, of course, the uprising of 2010–2011) in a region marked by political and economic malaise. The "miracle" of the Tunisian economy was held up as a kind of proof of the country's superior management of its economic and political affairs, grounded in an approach that we hear articulated in the Tunisian cinema as early as 1972, in a remark made by the nouveau-riche character Abdallah in Boughedir's short film, *The Picnic* (released in 1975 as part of *Fî Bilâd al-Tararanni*), who says: "A good business is more profitable—politics can only lead to prison!" Tunisians became eager in the Ben Ali era (and after the many, long years of economic stagnation under Bourguiba) to make money. Official *tunisianité*, which includes being "the first" in every progressive, new advance—the first Arab country to have a constitution; the first to have a popular independence movement; the first to have a Code of Personal Status granting women equal rights; the first to sign an Association Agreement with the European Union on agriculture and the liberalization of trade; the first to create a Human Rights League (Ligue Tunisienne de défense des droits de l'Homme); the first to develop the Internet; and so on—has added Tunisia's so-called "economic miracle" to its list of "firsts" (the dubious character of this "miracle" notwithstanding): it has been touted as something of an exception in Africa and can legitimately claim exceptional status among the African and/or Arab countries that do not have oil wealth. Of course, we may now add to this list of "firsts" Tunisia's success in ousting its dictator of twenty-three years, in the first truly popular revolution in the postcolonial Arab world. Indeed, as Fouad Ajami, the Lebanese-born, neoconservative American scholar has suggested, it was precisely Egypt's embarrassment at not being the first in the region to oust its own dictator that prompted the Egyptians to launch their uprising to remove President Hosni Mubarak from office: "The sight of Tunisians, hitherto a marginal people in the Arab consciousness, taking to the streets and deposing their tyrant, both shamed and emboldened the Egyptians."[82]

Since the 1990s, however, Hibou observes, Tunisia has felt itself threatened by the very globalization in which it has been so eager to participate and has responded with a defensive nationalism, expressed as "economic patriotism," which contradicts the international laws signed by the Tunisian government. Hibou goes into great detail in her book on this subject, offering a plethora of examples along the lines of: how the Tunisian bureaucracy is designed to prevent foreign investors from getting their money out; evidence of the Tunisian preference for "sleeping partners," and so on. "It is ... becoming easier to understand what nationalism really means," she writes. "[It is] not just an ideology, but the central power's fear of losing its control over the economy and having to manage an unstable situation." Hibou calls this the "disciplinary instrumentalization of nationalism" (which Hélé Béji felicitously calls "nationalitarianism"), which allows domination to operate through the control of economic activities and behavior (233).

Hibou notes that the colonial experience was a crucial factor in creating Tunisia's defensive nationalism (234) and also explains why Tunisia's economic nationalism is so marked. Despite the rhetoric of support for the liberal economic ideology that is believed to be the key to Tunisia's "economic miracle," economic nationalism in fact expresses and cements a general resistance Tunisians have toward *l'ouverture* (openness to the West/transparency), liberalism, and globalization in general, which they perceive as threats to their national independence: "National-liberalism, a strange alliance of liberalism and economic nationalism, is thus not created by a voluntarist project of the state," writes Hibou, "[but rather] expresses the ambiguity of an entanglement of different ways of being, of more or less well-thought-out strategies, tactics of power, and economic and political activities" (234).

The economy—its complexities, contradictions, ambiguities, opacities— like the *tunisianité* that it expresses (a *tunisianité*, in short, that is paradoxically both "open" and "closed"), is sometimes described in terms of *métissage*, or hybridity, which have become key terms in the ongoing articulation of what makes Tunisia unique and justifies its nationalism. It is in the cinema, rather than in the economy, however, that we shall examine this discourse; filmmakers frequently work the theme of cultural hybridity in the mode of *nostalgia* (i.e., with reference to the Tunisia that was "meant to be" or "used to be," before it became a police state under Ben Ali), as precisely Tunisia's lost opportunity. Hybridity and its related tropes, such as "tolerance," emerge as an official discourse at the very moment they are disappearing as realities of Tunisian social life, which is to say, in the same period of filmmaking that produces the New Tunisian Cinema.

Nostalgia, we know, is a term coined in the seventeenth century by the Swiss doctor, Johannes Hofer, from the Greek *nostos* (return home) and *algia* (longing), to describe the medical illness of those suffering from a severe longing for home. In an article entitled "Nostalgia, Nationhood, and the New Immigrant Narrative," Natalie Friedman notes that in our own time, nostalgia has come to mean more than the physical symptoms of homesickness. Quoting Svetlana Boym in *The Future of Nostalgia*, she describes the contemporary nostalgic in a way that offers a perspective on how we might view much of the New Tunisian Cinema:

> Today's nostalgic is, according to Boym, "a displaced person who mediates between the local and the universal." In her characterization of nostalgia as a condition in which a person moves between the poles of local/individual and universal/collective, Boym suggests a polarization between place of residence and place of origin, thereby creating the imagined feeling that the place of residence is not really "home"—home is someplace far away. Nostalgia becomes more than just a longing for the familiarity and comfort of home; it is sense of having lost ties to a nation and a national identity.[83]

Although Friedman is writing about Gary Shteyngart's *The Russian Debutante's Handbook* and the post-Soviet experience, and her references to a "place of residence" and a "place of origin" are to countries and/or cities, we may understand her terms in a way that also explains the sense we have in so many films of the New Tunisian Cinema that the Tunisia of the filmmakers is being mourned as a "home" that is now "someplace far away."

"We went to war, we chose to fight, using our films"

In 1994, Nouri Bouzid gave a lecture in Villepreux (France) in the "Sources of Inspiration" script-development workshop series sponsored by the

European Union, in which he described his approach to filmmaking.[84] His lecture serves as a kind of manifesto for the New Tunisian Cinema. Despite Bouzid's insistence that his "sources of inspiration" are based on his own personality ("not the laws of the market") and are therefore "difficult to trace," he in fact outlines very clearly the sources of inspiration, as it were, for the filmmaking wave we have been calling the New Tunisian Cinema.[85]

Bouzid recognizes that the filmmakers of the New Tunisian Cinema belong to a generation: "I am one of a group of filmmakers all from the same generation, who, without getting together, without coming to any prior agreement, went in almost the same direction and almost all worked in a similar way. What we have in common is that we decided to make films that were like ourselves" (46).[86] He is also correct in identifying his cohort as a group of auteurs, in the sense of the term articulated by Andrew Sarris, as filmmakers each with his or her own distinctive voice, style, and worldview.[87] "Generally," Bouzid observes, "if we take Egyptian or Algerian films of the 70s, it's virtually impossible to guess who directed them. With our films, after seeing five minutes of Nacer Khemir you know it's Nacer Khemir, or five minutes of Mahmoud Ben Mahmoud, you can guess it's him, and the same with Férid [Boughedir], which is a quality to be welcomed. They already had a cinematic mode of discourse, and that's the only way to be a good filmmaker" (46).

The directors we associate with the New Tunisian Cinema are indeed auteurs, each with his or her own "cinematic mode of discourse," which was undoubtedly formed by their education as filmmakers during the 1960s and 1970s—what Bouzid calls "the Golden Age of Cinema" (46).[88] In Khémaïs Khayati's book, *Cinémas arabes*, in which there is a chapter devoted to "the strange battle that rages between two Arab countries [Egypt and Tunisia] on the cinematic field,"[89] the author writes that "all these [Tunisian] filmmakers treat themes that have never been approached before by other Arab filmmakers, at least, not with such frankness, which has become their hallmark. . . . One can say that for a Tunisian auteur, a film is a vision of the world, not [merely] a story told" (143).[90]

As these filmmakers came of age, Tunisia's own ideological/cultural development—as envisioned and promoted by Bourguiba—was on the same track, launching its own promise of a Golden Age. The bilingual/bicultural Tunisia that Bourguiba was trying to build was embodied in Bouzid and his cohort of (future) filmmakers, who were, as we have said, the first generation to be so formed. "*Cinema is the mode of expression associated with the best period of liberalism,*" Bouzid believes: "*This is very important: cinema does not sit well with feudal ideas.... Cinema is the art of an era, of democratic and liberal ideas, and if it's not free, it dies*" (46–47; emphasis added). The core values and essential meaning of the New Tunisian Cinema are contained in this assertion. But we see that, already, the idea of *resistance* appears in Bouzid's statement. The implication is that although the art of the era has come to the country of Bouzid's birth, and the democratic and liberal ideas that sustain it are officially endorsed there, those ideas are in fact under siege in Tunisia. The society that Bouzid's cohort of filmmakers seeks to help build is embattled. "So we went to war," he says. "We chose to fight, using our films" (47).

Bouzid explains that the first thing the filmmakers felt bound to fight was "the old cinema, in particular the Egyptian cinema which dominated the Arab market and shaped our emotions, our tastes, our morals" (47). He characterizes the Egyptian commercial cinema as melodrama, a form to which he and his fellow Tunisian filmmakers are for ideological reasons fundamentally opposed.[91] (One of the very few auteurs working in the Egyptian film industry that Bouzid singles out for favorable mention is Youssef Chahine.) "We declared war on the old emotions. Hitherto the idea had been to make people weep at fate with all the simple, melodramatic tricks. We were fed up with that cinema and wanted to go the other way. So we waged war on the aesthetic and all the models on which that cinema was based" (47).[92] On one of the hallmarks of melodrama for example— the staging of a struggle between good and evil—Bouzid explains why he is emphatically against rendering this kind of conflict as a confrontation between two characters: "[In my scripts] the conflict is no longer between two people but in each other. There is no confrontation between good and evil with the prospect of victory for one or the other. With me good and evil are in one and the same character and the conflict becomes an internal conflict. This is what made the break with the old Egyptian cinema, with melodrama" (53).

There is an entire universe of meaning in these statements.[93] Bouzid is not overstating the (sense of) mission of the Tunisian filmmakers when he says that: "We were bearers of a social, cinematic and political project" (47). Indeed, he and his cohort understood that "making a good film is not a question of telling a story, but of bringing an audience into a discourse that's new, aesthetic, cinematic, stylistic and dramatic in its totality, and in the second place, ideological" (47).[94]

The task of "winning over a badly educated public" (that had been shaped by the Egyptian cinema, signifying dominant Arab-Muslim society) was not easy. But as Bouzid points out, he and his fellow filmmakers "were the only ones making films" in Tunisia and "could not be marginalized," as Chahine and others had been by the Egyptian film industry (47–48). The absence of a film industry in Tunisia actually helped the Tunisian filmmakers, who, to their great surprise, received phenomenal public support for their first films (48). The critical response from the mainstream Tunisian press, however, was not favorable—"Instead of helping us to condition the public and teach it a new way of seeing, they went to war against this cinema. So we had yet another confrontation to deal with" (48).[95]

Bouzid places *character* first in his poetics of cinema and insists that writing a script is like "making a child, not a piece of knitting":

> The character is going to be the source of everything. He is going to impose his own evolution, he is going to claim complete freedom and he is going to impose his own needs, provided he is a character with roots. But, before writing, you live with him, you get inside his skin, you talk to him, you watch him, you dream with him, you shut yourself away with him. If you find him, if you hold him, he does everything because he is real, he is authentic, because he has roots, because he settles into a strong reality. (49–50)[96]

Bouzid's concern, clearly, is not so much that his audience be entertained (in the sense, perhaps, that Hollywood cinema and Egyptian commercial cinema have traditionally put entertainment values above most others) but that it be able to share and understand the point of view of his characters. "I have no need to tell a story," he insists, "but my character or characters must have a goal to aim for." The film "must contain a *stake*. The stake is the character's." In other words—and this is "the most important thing"—the character "absolutely must have a point of view.... Once I have chosen my character's point of view, the structure decides itself, since it's my character that's going to structure the film" (51).

A willingness to trust one's unconscious, Bouzid suggests, will also contribute to a film's successful structure. He is well aware that in artistic production, "there are conscious things and unconscious things." Like Sarris's dictum about the technical competence of a director as a criterion of value (summarized by his remark that "a great director has to be at least a good director"), Bouzid suggests that the good filmmaker must consciously master those elements that are conscious ("Everything that's dramatic is very conscious . . . because drama is a science" [50]), but he or she must "respect" those elements that are unconscious: "If you see [your character] dressed in black, you must dress him in black. If someone asks you why and you don't have an answer, you just say, 'I don't know, I don't care, that's how I see him. I see him bald, I don't know why.' Perhaps if you visit a psychoanalyst you will find explanations, but it's not up to me to provide them" (50).

This kind of cinema Bouzid is describing "regards the viewer as an adult." He believes that the kind that "treats the viewer like a child who has to have everything spoon-fed, explained, settled, is a cinema that despises the viewer and sets itself up as his guardian" (62). His observation is not unrelated to his dislike and suspicion of realism. For him, "reality is unaesthetic," and realist films do not "transform" reality, which is what a filmmaker must do, he believes, to make true cinema (63). His point that the filmmaker's responsibility is to *transform* reality (not mimic it) is Eisensteinian in its ideological thrust:

> You should avoid realist scripts. . . . My duty and my purpose are to put forward a new aesthetic that's not realistic. I have to sublimate . . . reality, transform it, give the impression that it's true, that it's the reality. But it mustn't look like reality, you mustn't say "that's what life is like" when you're writing a script. If you say "that's what life is like," you revert to life and put a stop to cinema. Cinema, as Godard said, is life 24 times a second. (63)

He concedes that, dramatically speaking, the conflicts treated by the narrative have to be settled at the end—"the stakes must be clear at the end of the film"—but the resolution of the conflict "must always raise certain questions that will haunt the viewer." These questions, however, are not to suggest that the film should leave important questions unanswered; what matters is that "the fundamental issues have to be clarified" (63). He firmly does not believe that cinema should be prescriptive ("I'm against cinema that puts forward ready-made solutions"); nor should the filmmaker "have to answer to everything." He knows Tunisian society is one "where we have so much to catch up on" and that there are many Tunisians who invest too much hope in the cinema as an agent of change, but he is very clear about the limits of what cinema can or should do, and what it should not try to do: "Cinema should not be a replacement for politics, or theory, or science" (63).

Since "there is no national cinematic language" on the level of the cinematic signifier—Tunisian films and European films share the same cinematic language—the question of how Tunisian films are different from European films has to be located elsewhere (53).[97] In the eleven scripts Bouzid had written by the time he gave his lecture at Villepreux (eight that he had written for other members of his filmmaking cohort and the three for the feature-length films he had directed to date), there are "six constants" that he is able to identify, which he believes "give our films an identity" (53).

Briefly, these are: (1) "memory as baggage"; (2) "defeat as destiny"; (3) "the filial relationship"; (4) "the image of the body"; (5) "pain as emotion"; and (6) "the face and the veil." As I shall show in the analyses of individual films in the chapters that follow, these themes (as I think we can loosely call them) recur in the New Tunisian Cinema, even in films that Bouzid has not worked on as a scriptwriter or as a collaborator in some other capacity.

By "memory as baggage," Bouzid is referring to memory as "the only thing left to [a character] as a legacy among the loss of values" (53). The overriding preoccupation of characters in Tunisian films, he suggests, is cultural identity. They are searching for an identity, and—standing on the threshold of a very uncertain future—they have only the past to guide them in this search. The question of identity keeps recurring: "Are we Arabs? Are we Tunisians? What does it mean to be Arab? What is being Tunisian? Where do I come from? Why have I always been ruled? Could it be that there was a time when I was not ruled? Are we Berbers? Are we a mixture?" (54). Exacerbating this question, he adds, is the fact that "we [all educated Tunisians] have gained our knowledge through the medium of a language [French] that is not our mother-tongue."

The constant of *memory* in the films is related to the sense of *defeat* felt by characters in Tunisian cinema: "It's like a destiny, a verdict, almost a feeling." The article Bouzid wrote in 1988 entitled, "The New Arab Cinema, or the Cinema of Defeat," (later published as "New Realism in Arab Cinema:

The Defeat-Conscious Cinema") was widely and roundly attacked by Arab critics—which confirmed Bouzid's perception that "it's something which is shared by everyone" in the Arab world (55). Defeat—although, really, the more accurate word, he thinks, is "decadence"—is "a feeling that is rejected, unrecognized, unknown." It leads to tragedy, because people will do anything to "get themselves out of this [sense of] defeat" (55). As an example of what he means by "defeat as destiny," Bouzid offers a remark made by his character, Shahrazad, in the short film he made in 1992 as part of the omnibus film, *The Gulf War . . . What Next?*: "Whether the Iraqis win or the Saudis win, I'm still the loser." The defeat of the Arabs in the Gulf War—of both the Iraqis *and* the Saudis—is an expression of a condition that has gripped the Arabs for centuries: "If I have talked about the Gulf War, it's because these things are clearer to you, but this decadence is five centuries old and it resulted in the Balkanization of the Ottoman Empire, which in turn resulted in colonization" (55). Successive defeats and the demagogy of leaders, Bouzid explains, have led to despondency, disarray, and distress—which are felt in the home and the family and have their correlatives in dysfunctional domestic arrangements.[98]

"The filial relationship" is the most emblematic of the dysfunctional orders of private life, which in turn distort political life and poison the public sphere. By "filial relationship," Bouzid means the status and functioning of the neopatriarchy, the father, machismo—which he says are "very strong where we come from":

> With us the problem of the father is associated not with the Oedipus complex but with the myth of Abraham, who was prepared to sacrifice his own son. The son submits to the father and serves him. In our society the individual is nothing; it's the family that counts, the group. Our cinema is trying to destroy the edifice of the family and liberate the individual. (57)

Alongside the theme of defeat, which is perhaps inseparable from the "problem of the father" that Bouzid sees as characterizing Arab-Muslim society, the "problem" of the *body*, he believes, is the most important:

> The body is really the heart of the matter. For the fundamentalists the image of the body is a double prohibition, the prohibition of the image and the prohibition of the body. The body is prohibited, the image is

prohibited and the image of the body is doubly prohibited. Can you make films without the body? . . . What are you going to show if you don't show the body? (57)

When Khayati writes in *Cinémas arabes* that Tunisian filmmakers "treat themes that have never been approached before by other Arab filmmakers, at least, not with such frankness, which has become their hallmark," he is referring primarily to their willingness to show the body, and to the frequent exploration in their films of public/societal problems in the private terms of sexuality. A frank treatment of sexuality is indeed a hallmark of the New Tunisian Cinema, because nearly all the filmmakers acknowledge, in Bouzid's phrase, that "the body is something fundamental in cinema, as in drama" (58).[99] Bouzid points to the most famous work in all of Arabic literature, *The Thousand and One Nights*, and says: "The body is very much present there. It even inspired eroticism in the West. So why lose this extraordinary area of expression which is the body? This area ought to be reconquered; the body ought to be rehabilitated, rediscovered somehow. For me the body has always been the most important vector of dramatic technique and conflicts, dramas, characters" (58).

When Bouzid describes the fifth "constant" of his cinema, "pain as emotion," he concedes that it is not common to all the filmmakers of his cohort. Férid Boughedir, for example, "works through pleasure," whereas Bouzid will make his own character "suffer in his internal dilemma" (59). It is a question of temperament: "Everyone works with his own emotion," Bouzid acknowledges. For him, pain is "a kind of ethic, because I am unveiling the hidden side of society. . . . I want [my viewers] to understand this side. So I share their pain with them, and, as this pain is mine too, I merge with them." Bouzid believes that to master pain, to overcome or avoid it, to properly understand its causes, you must confront it: "So I almost rape [my viewers] with my images so that they shan't be raped elsewhere. I think this refusal to be pleasing is necessary as soon as you start dealing with serious matters" (60).

Bouzid's final "constant," like the others, is described in the form of an allegory: "The Face and the Veil." It refers to his approach to his material, and recalls Sarris's third criterion of value by which we define an auteur: interior meaning (which Sarris saw as being "extrapolated from the tension between a director's personality and his material"). Bouzid describes his cinema as an "aesthetic based on prohibition," one that "consists in lifting the veil on society.... Anything goes as long as it's done with respect—there's no other prohibition" (60). This is the balancing act that the New Tunisian filmmakers have so successfully performed. As Bouzid says, they are a "rebellious" group and are distinguished by their refusal to censor themselves—which is no mean feat in an authoritarian state (61). "So what are we to do with the cinema?," he exclaims in mock exasperation. "We'll have to make *The Invisible Man*!" (62). He folds the problem of the authoritarian state and all six of the recurring themes of his cinema (which we are saying are also the dominant themes of the New Tunisian cinema) into a problem of Islam, when he declares unequivocally: "The problem with cinema is that it's in complete conflict with Islam, from start to finish. The problem of representation, the problem of the body, the problem of the veil, the problem of interdictions, of showing things" (62). Clearly, "Islam" in Bouzid's lexicon is a broadly allegorical term—a way of referring to the whole, intertwined business of culture and history that has contributed to the making of him and his fellow filmmakers as Tunisians and of the Tunisia in which they live, somewhere at the crossroads between East and West.[100] Which returns us to his stated belief that if the cinema is not free, it dies.

The films analyzed in the following pages are conceived and made in the tradition of this kind of cinema that Bouzid believes in. They are the films of a specific place and era, committed to resisting the "feudal ideas" that are always threatening to overtake Tunisian society, films that believe in "democratic and liberal ideas."

CHAPTER TWO

"The freedom to be different, to choose your own life"

Man of Ashes (Nouri Bouzid, 1986)

In 1995, the Institut du Monde Arabe in Paris celebrated one hundred years of Tunisian cinema with a comprehensive film retrospective that lasted three months.[1] The main essay in the printed program was titled "Un cinéma sans tabou," and it suggested that the Tunisian cinema is unique (among the Arab countries, at any rate) in its willingness to confront the major taboos of contemporary society: sexuality, the status of women, the Jewish question, government power, Islamic fundamentalism, national-cultural identity, and so on.[2]

This characterization of Tunisian cinema is accurate, and the film that made it possible—because the reputation to which the essay refers can perhaps only truly be said to date from 1986—is Nouri Bouzid's *Rih essed* (*Man of Ashes*). The film tells the story of Hachemi (Imad Maâlal), a young wood-carver in the old city of Sfax, and the acute anxiety he experiences on the eve of his marriage. Hachemi's nightmare coincides with the public disclosure, scrawled as a graffito on the city wall, that his best friend Farfat (Khaled Ksouri) is "not a man," and with Farfat's subsequent banishment from the family home by his humiliated and angry father. In the ensuing scandal, Hachemi relives his past, as he attempts to come to terms with his reluctance to marry and to weigh the significance of the time when

THE FREEDOM TO BE DIFFERENT

FIGURE 2.1 Anis (Mourad Bejaoui) erases the graffito on the wall that announces: "Farfat is not a man."

he and Farfat, at age ten, were raped by Ameur (Mustapha Adouani), their supervisor at the wood-carving shop where they were employed as apprentices.[3] Finding comfort in friendship (only Touil the blacksmith, Azaïez the baker, and Farfat remain—their Jewish friend "Jacko" having emigrated),[4] Hachemi struggles to become a man who will remain true to himself, rather than one who will allow himself, in Bouzid's phrase, to be "dragged into something [he hasn't] chosen."[5] Farfat reacts to his humiliation with rebellious defiance, while Hachemi becomes more withdrawn and unhappy about both his approaching marriage and his friend's distress. During a bachelor party in a brothel, in which both young men have their first sexual experiences with women, Farfat is overcome with humiliation and rage when Azaïez reminds him that "everyone knows" what happened between him and Ameur. Farfat runs to Ameur's house, and there, on the street, stabs him mortally in the groin. The next day, in an image that suggests he is free at last, Farfat kills himself.

Tunisia's preeminent film scholar Hédi Khélil observes that in the Arab world it is the filmmakers of the Maghreb who have been the most aesthetically innovative and have done the most to push Arab cinema to reflect seriously on cinema's ethical responsibilities. It is thanks to the audacious efforts of certain filmmakers from the Maghreb, he writes—"their spirit of invention, their tenacity in following through on their ambitions, which they achieved by not following the well-beaten path leading to established models of filmmaking"—that has allowed a new Arab cinema to emerge.[6] Khélil mentions films by Moroccans, Algerians, and Tunisians that have all been milestones in this "shockwave" emanating from the Maghreb, but there is one film, he writes, that is "absolutely essential": *Man of Ashes*.[7] He notes that everything about the film, which won the *Tanit d'Or* at the Carthage Film Festival in October 1986, generated controversy: "The problematic presence of Mr. Lévy, the Jew; the rape of the two boys by their Tunisian boss; the disturbing aspect of sexuality in a hypocritical society; the weight of the past and [particularly] of childhood on the present; the personal and intimate tone of the film; the eroded image the film gives of the city of Sfax, where Bouzid was born; [and] the extreme vulnerability of the main characters, whose masculinity is put in question by those around them" (49–50).

Bouzid himself, in an interview he gave to a Tunisian newspaper at the time of the film's release, insisted that the idea for the film originated in his fascination with the "total rupture" between the world of children and the world of adults. In adulthood, he observed, "you put yourself in someone else's skin, in a completely new decor, and you get rid of the old, you throw away a large part of yourself, perhaps the most intimate part."[8] Circumcision is the most significant formal "rite of passage" in a Muslim male's life, followed by marriage, which often separates a man from his group of friends. With marriage, "you are forced to break with your past and your childhood, to get rid of the child in you, or at least to repress it as much as possible." Certainly, the "long and profound friendship [between Hachemi and Farfat] is threatened by this rupture," he said, adding that he wished to tell a story in which these rites of passage would be seen as traumatic, with lasting consequences.

"I believe our society is built on rape"

There is no doubt that Bouzid succeeds in this effort to suggest that circumcision and marriage are traumatic events in his protagonists' lives. We infer that marriage, however, is only traumatic because of circumcision: the mutilation of the boy's penis is the first trauma from which others follow. As Bouzid stated in his "Sources of Inspiration" lecture (discussed in the previous chapter), Muslim societies are not only profoundly patriarchal, but violently so. The "Sacrifice of Abraham"—the ancient religious parable about how the father was prepared to kill his own son in order to prove his unquestioning obedience to God—which is central to Islam (and, incidentally, also to Judaism, which we know historically preceded Islam), is a lesson in "castration" that every (male) Muslim and Jew learns early in his life.

Bouzid believes that Islam has comprehensively structured his culture and society and that it has had the effect of "defeating" the boy by making him subservient to his father—making him *submit* to the father's authority—whose power to "castrate" the son is symbolically rendered in the circumcision ceremony, which is recalled every year throughout the Muslim world in the sacrifice of the ram during Eid al-Adha. This religious holiday commemorates Abraham's willingness to sacrifice his son Ishmael (in the Jewish and Christian traditions, it is not Ishmael, but his brother Isaac) and is an earthly reminder of the terrifying power and mystique of God Himself, with whom the boy's father is identified. As Hisham Sharabi writes about Islam in *Neopatriarchy*:

> The greatness of Muhammad's political achievement rests not so much on his success in dissolving tribal ties and overcoming tribal factionalism, but in the way he was able to fit existing social and psychological bonds into the structure of the new Islamic community. The Islamic *ummah* (nation) turned out to be nothing more than a supertribe, the projection of the universal tribal ethos. God, as Muhammad portrays Him, is a psychologically familiar figure. Submission, the basic relation of pristine patriarchy, here finds its most powerful ideological expression.[9]

Bouzid's word for the ethos of submission Sharabi is referring to is *defeat*: "The true defeat is in one's education and the type of relations one has with individuals; the relations between the social structure and the individual, whether it is the state, the family or the religious structure. This relationship is one that destroys the individual."[10] Bouzid expressed this view even more forcefully in an interview he gave to the French national daily newspaper *L'Humanité* in 1995, in which he made the remark: "I believe our society is built on rape."¹¹ The figure of rape is the *fil conducteur* of *Man of Ashes*, if not all of Bouzid's cinema, and is associated with the father as patriarchal principle that goes all the way back to the founding father of Islam, Abraham (Ibrahim in Arabic). "This attitude that the father is sacred, and the difficulty of ridding oneself of him, is a constant in *Man of Ashes* and is present in all the films I've made," Bouzid said in his "Sources of Inspiration" lecture. "Hachemi needs a father, but all his fathers cause him problems: his biological father beats him, is violent towards him; his initiation father rapes him; and his spiritual father, Lévy, dies" (56).¹²

Sexuality has always provided gendered metaphors for colonization, observes the American scholar bell hooks in her brief essay, "Reflections on Race and Sex":

> Free countries equated with free men, domination with castration, the loss of manhood, and rape—the terrorist act re-enacting the drama of conquest, as men of the dominating group sexually violate the bodies of women who are among the dominated. The intent of this act was to continually remind dominated men of their loss of power; rape was a gesture of symbolic castration. Dominated men are made powerless (i.e., impotent) over and over again as the women they would have had the right to possess, to control, to assert power over, to dominate, to fuck, are fucked and fucked over by the dominating victorious male group.¹³

Whereas hooks describes the rape of colonized women by the colonizer as a reminder to colonized men of their own domination, Bouzid, we note, is describing his own, *post*colonial society, in which men are raped by other men. Even Khélil, when he refers to "the rape of the two boys by their Tunisian boss," seems to acknowledge the allegorical function of the rape in *Man of Ashes* as pointing to a depressing truth about this contemporary moment in postcolonial Tunisia's history: the colonial hierarchy, in which the majority of men are "fucked and fucked over by the dominating victorious male group" has been reproduced as a purely Tunisian structure. The colonial relationship persists not only in neopatriarchal structures of repression in the private sphere (which is too often ruled by domineering fathers and husbands and is vulnerable to the predations of men like Ameur), but it also structures the public sphere (which has been disfigured and traumatized by the rapine of the homegrown political and economic elites, whose

THE FREEDOM TO BE DIFFERENT

FIGURE 2.2 Farfat (Khaled Ksouri) announces to his supervisor Ameur (Mustapha Adouani) that he is quitting his job.

interests are served by the police state), such that Bouzid can say about his own country, as late as 2003: "The streets do not belong to us."[14]

On the one hand, the rape of the two boys is really only a device (an allegory), an "explanation" offered by the film of the origins of a young man's refusal of the sexual role chosen for him by society (for Hachemi and Farfat are two sides of the same character): Why, Hachemi's uncomprehending mother wants to know, does her son "refuse his happiness"? And why does the graffito on the city wall announce that "Farfat is not a man"?[15] As such, the film is a radical critique of an entire sexual system that puts tremendous pressure on individuals to conform. On the other hand, the rape is exactly that: a terrible and deeply damaging violation of the boys' subjectivity. As both synecdoche and metaphor, it represents the logic of castration on which Bouzid is suggesting contemporary Arab-Muslim societies are built—but it is the logic according to which the father castrates the son, not the logic according to which the son removes the father so that he might take his place in the mother's bed, as in Freud's interpretation of the myth of Oedipus.[16] The rape in the film is not meant to be understood

45

as a singular or aberrant act but as an emblem or allegory of the logic of castration that Bouzid believes permeates the kind of society in which the boys live.[17]

In *Que veulent les arabes?* Fereydoun Hoveyda makes a similar, broadly Orientalist observation about Arab culture as a (neo)patriarchal one in which the repressive father's legacy is damaging to the son, when he writes:

> I no longer recall who first drew attention to the fact that in Arab culture there is no legend comparable to the myth of Oedipus. In traditional Arab societies, the father dominates his children, stifles them, almost. They have to wait for his death, before they can come into their own. When they become fathers in their turn, they find ways to restrict their children.... To what extent this style of parenting has an influence on the social and economic development of a society remains a question to be explored. There is no doubt, however, that all Arabs live under authoritarian and repressive regimes. Traditional leaders or military officers conduct *coups d'état*, monarchs and presidents rule as autocrats. How long their regimes last is always decided, finally, by a resort to violence. Throughout the Arab world, human rights are ignored or systematically violated. Censorship, imprisonment, and torture are the common currency.[18]

According to Tunisian sociologist Abdelwahab Bouhdiba as well (from whose book, *Sexualité en Islam* (*Sexuality in Islam*), it is very probable the francophone Iranian Hoveyda drew for his representation of the authoritarian father of traditional Arab societies), Arab-Muslim society is "essentially authoritarian."[19] It is "castrating not only from the sexual point of view, but also from the point of view of individual autonomy in the political, economic, ethical and cultural spheres" (210). Like Bouzid, Bouhdiba identifies circumcision—both the physical/psychological reality of it and its allegorical meanings as well, which are, in any case, intertwined—as the first and most traumatic rite of passage in the life of the Muslim male. "Nothing can justify [circumcision's] systematic use," he writes. "It involves enormous dangers, on both the physiological and psychical plane. It is hardly surprising that some commentators see it as a barbarous, traumatizing experience" (178). And yet circumcision, he notes, "is regarded preeminently as the mark of inclusion in Muslim society. Indeed this practice is more or less unanimously observed at every social level and at whatever

THE FREEDOM TO BE DIFFERENT

degree of development and acculturation. No one—not even free thinkers, communists, atheists, or even partners of mixed marriages—ignores the rule" (174).

Astonishingly, "circumcision is an act that, according to the *fiqh*, is in no way compulsory" (175),[20] Bouhdiba writes; but it is "deeply rooted in Islamic mores and certainly corresponds to something fundamental" (175). He quotes Marcel Mauss—"For me circumcision is essentially a tattoo. It is a tribal, even national sign"[21]—and agrees that "it is a question of marking membership of the group. The words 'We the circumcised' define a relationship of inclusion within the community" (182).

Man of Ashes opens with an image of symbolic castration that recalls a tradition associated with the Muslim circumcision ceremony: a wounded and bloody cockerel flapping about helplessly in the dust (Farfat's name is a distant allusion to this movement of the dying bird, the same movement made by a fish out of water, gasping for its life).[22]

This shot is immediately followed by images of a wedding feast in preparation. The symbolism of the juxtaposition is undeniable: marriage demands a sacrifice, and for the protagonist, we soon see, marriage looms as a social

FIGURE 2.3 The first shot of the film, of a cockerel being killed as a sacrifice.

obligation that he has no desire to fulfill. As the story will be told from the point of view of a double character—a young man who is about to marry and another who, according to the definitions of conventional masculinity, feels he is "not a man"—the mortally wounded bird is a reference to the circumcision ceremony, the Muslim boy's first official rite of initiation into the community of men. Indeed, Khélil in his analysis of the film observes that the entire credit sequence plays in a register of "pure denotation"; the fiction that is the film is "a transposition into drama of a documentary reality" (52).[23] In the traditionally condensed manner of the opening shots of movies, in which the principal meanings of the film can be found encoded, as in a hieroglyph, the scissors with which the women trim the ragged edge of the circular, wedding *baclawa* refer to circumcision (as does the bleeding cockerel), and the knife used by the women to cut the *baclawa* into squares before baking it makes a link, *avant-coup*, to the knife with which Farfat will stab Ameur. Khélil remarks upon the anxiety provoked in the viewer, not only by the film's opening shots of the agonized convulsions of the sacrificed bird but also by the expert and intimidating skill of the women preparing the *baclawa* for the wedding feast: "What is striking about this establishing sequence is the insistent scratching of the knife against the baking sheet, the clicking sound made by the tethered scissors, as they hunt down the unwanted scraps of pastry" (52). Ameur's death by stabbing is the "culmination" of a long sequence of events in the narrative, going back to his rape of Farfat and Hachemi in childhood (and referring even further back in time to their circumcision and its role in the boys' lives as an originary moment of trauma), for which Bouzid prepares the viewer in these opening shots by using a style of editing, writes Khélil, that is "trenchant, sharp, and rigorous, like the incisions of the knife" (52).[24]

"There is a clear correspondence for the boy between circumcision and marriage," writes Bouhdiba. Circumcision is "a passage to the world of adults and a preparation carried out in blood and pain, and therefore unforgettable, into an age of responsibilities" (182). And "the wedding night is the time when the man experiences and proves his virility" (186). Later in the film, when Hachemi is reminiscing with old Monsieur Lévy (Yacoub Bchiri) about his grandson, Lévy reveals that Jacko is now married and "is even a father." Hachemi smiles to himself, and in a flashback we see the three boys giggling as they show one another their penises, with Jacko saying: "Me too, I'm circumcised!" Though circumcision is more a practice of Muslims than a practice of Islam, as Bouhdiba tells us, it is performed nominally as a rite through which the boy accedes to Islam. But this does not explain the powerful sociological imperatives behind the rite, nor is it, of course, how the boy will remember it:

> As for the mutilated child, he could do nothing but cry out in pain and weep in shock at the violence done to his body. This wound in his flesh, these men and women torturing him, that gleaming razor, the strident oohs and ahs of inquisitive, indiscreet old women, the jugs smashing on the floor, the cry of the cockerel, struggling and losing its blood, the din outside and finally the endless stream of people coming to congratulate the patient on "his happy accession to Islam," that is what circumcision means to a child. (178)

It is clear that for Hachemi the "happiness" his mother refers to (and which all of society insists he seize as his masculine prerogative) is not worth the price he is being asked to pay. Obviously, he had no choice in the matter of his circumcision—that first "rape" in his young life—but he wonders if he dare refuse to marry. As we have said, the film's ostensible explanation for Hachemi's unwillingness to take a bride is that he is suffering from a permanent loss of sexual confidence as a consequence of his having been raped as a child. And yet the film offers another, contradictory discourse that suggests this might not be so. Bouzid has said that when he was writing the script for the film, he asked himself, "What would happen if Hachemi said to society, 'Go to hell, I'll do what I like.' Will he make it? But he can't do it, he's not the type of character who can do that. So I had to create his double, the other side of the coin, because the germ of the double existed in the first one."[25]

Love Between Men

What emerges as the narrative unfolds is a complex and contradictory discourse about what Bouhdiba describes as the Arab man's profound alienation by his own masculinity (239). While the film seems to wish to "explain" both Hachemi's revulsion at the prospect of marriage and Farfat's suicide as the unhappy consequences of their rape, it is also quite clearly an appeal, in Bouzid's own words regarding his film, for "the freedom to be different, to choose your own life."[26] The film shows an individual whose family and society specifically reject his sexuality and will not let him "choose his own life." His society is one in which, we are told, the radical separation of the sexes has a warping effect on sexual development and expression—"To what extremities did the system of sexual division not drive one?" asks Bouhdiba (200)—but if Bouhdiba implies that most homosexuality is caused by the Manichaeism of the sexes, Bouzid's film takes a less heterosexist position on the close bonds among men.[27] *Man of Ashes* makes it plain that Farfat's misery and suicide are caused by homophobia (for men do not become homosexuals because access to women is difficult). No less traumatic for the two young men than their rape by Ameur is the fact that their love for each other, their friendship, will be ruptured by Hachemi's marriage, and if Farfat cannot overcome the stigma of the graffito on the wall that says he is "not a man," he can have no future. As the little boy Anis (Mourad Bejaoui) says to him at the dock, "Farfat, your boat has left without you."

There is a scene in the film that powerfully conveys the love Farfat and Hachemi have for each other. Bouzid shoots it in the manner of silent film, without dialogue, to suggest that the emotional bond between them does not need words—it is *physical*—inasmuch as the look, as one of the five senses (described by Freud as a component of the sexual instinct), is physical. Farfat is in a noisy café, playing cards with several other, apparently older, men. He has been losing, and one of the players offers him the consoling remark that it is not his lucky day. Farfat looks up, and sees Hachemi shyly waiting for him just outside the café. He breaks into a smile and winks at his friend, who bashfully returns a radiant smile. Bouzid lingers on the repeated shots of the two men looking into each other's eyes, while on the sound track we hear the refrain of a song playing on the café radio: "Allahu akbar . . . Allahu akbar," a common phrase in Arab-Muslim culture, meaning "God the Almighty," expressing feelings of awe, admiration, and fascination—a kind of *jouissance*, even—when one is moved by God's power, whether uttered spontaneously in response to a reading from the Qur'an, or during a song by a sensual/spiritual performer like the great Um Kalthum.

In the same interview in which Bouzid spoke, as of a tragedy, of the man who marries having to renounce the intimacy of his male friendships, he spoke of a "corollary problem" that also fascinates him: *virility*. The worst thing that can happen to a boy, in a society described by Bouhdiba as "male-worshipping, in its essence and in its appearances, in its deep structures and in its superficial manifestations" (239), is for the boy to have his sense of masculinity fundamentally compromised.[28] And yet masculinity, the boys in the film discover, is defined by their society in terms of castration. Masculinity is forged, paradoxically, by the very threat of its annihilation. Proper manhood is achieved through an internalization of its meaning as a male trauma that is harnessed for patriarchal purposes, bonding men, with the major moments in this process, as we have said, marked by the rite of circumcision, by marriage, and the abandonment of intimacy in male friendship.[29]

The pressure on young men to organize their affective impulses in exclusively heterosexual terms is of course a phenomenon not unique to Muslim societies. Consider the American critic Molly Haskell's famous remarks in her landmark study, *From Reverence to Rape: The Treatment of Women in the Movies*, on the subject of "love in which men understand and support each other, speak the same language, and risk their lives to gain each other's respect": "But this is also a delusion.... This is the easiest of loves: a love that is adolescent, presexual, tacit, the love of one's *semblable*, one's mirror reflection."[30] Haskell's barely concealed contempt for the male homosocial (but perhaps not homosexual) love she describes comes, no doubt, from knowing how it is frequently implicated in a dialectic of misogyny. But in *Man of Ashes* we are given no evidence that Hachemi and Farfat are misogynistic. If anything, Hachemi's disinclination to marry is a form of resistance to patriarchal structures that we know also subordinate women; his bond with Farfat would appear to be essentially homosexual, not homosocial, and as such does no harm and brings no suffering to the women in their lives.[31]

The precedent for Hachemi's despair at the prospect of losing his friends—of losing the special, intimate quality of his friendships with them, and with Farfat in particular—is the misery he felt when Jacko left Tunisia during a wave of Jewish emigration years before. "I've been around Jews all my life," Bouzid explains. "Hachemi has also lived amongst Jews, and is close to them.... He experiences a double crisis in his childhood: the rape, and the emotional trauma of the 'forced' departure of his friend 'Jacko.'"[32] In effect, Hachemi is forbidden by his society to love Farfat beyond the time frame of childhood, just as he is forbidden by his father to love Jacko (because Jacko is Jewish).

Whether or not this means Hachemi is "homosexual," or—as some of the film's detractors suggested at the time of the film's release—he is a traitor

FIGURE 2.4 Mr. Lévy (Yacoub Bchiri), sings Hachemi a song, and then gives him the lute as a wedding present.

to the Arab people (because he portrays Mr. Lévy sympathetically), should not matter.[33] But it does matter, because, as Bouzid says, in his society "the individual is nothing; it's the family that counts, the group."[34] Hachemi's attempts to defy his family's wish that he marry—seen in conjunction with Farfat's despairing, defiant response to his father's judgment that he is "not a man"—can be seen as courageous. The violent storm that destroys the wedding marquee is nothing less than a cosmic indication of his inner turmoil. The storm is suggested in the film's title (*Rih essed*), which is drawn from the Tunisian proverb "Rih essed yeddi maa y'rude," which refers to a strong wind that sweeps away everything in its path. With this title, and through his main characters' rebellious actions, Bouzid would blow away "the edifice of the family" (and the homophobia that supports it), to "liberate the individual."[35] In resisting the extraordinary pressure on him to marry, Hachemi is showing bravery, not cowardice. He is indeed trying to say, "Go to hell, I'll do what I like."

Hachemi's nightmares suggest that his fears have to do with entrapment, just as Farfat's dreams have to do with flight. But when Hachemi and Farfat are taken to the brothel by their friends in the hope, or on the assumption, that all they need is a positive heterosexual experience to launch them into a lifetime of heterosexual "happiness," Bouzid leaves the question open as to whether he "believes" in this scene, just as the best Hollywood melodramas allow for ironical readings of their "happy endings." (As I discuss below, Bouhdiba believes that for the Arab male confronting his anxieties about marriage, "in the end, everything seems to settle down without too much difficulty and heartache.")[36] The scene is altogether extraordinary, especially when one considers how Bouzid conceives Farfat and Hachemi as two sides of the same subjective experience. For example, at the very moment Hachemi and the prostitute Amina (Sonia Mansour) are rolling about on the bed in a carnal embrace, in a different room Farfat is attacking Azaïez because he believes Azaïez was flirting with him (with the intention of humiliating him), and the two men roll about on the floor in the same manner as the couple having sex upstairs. Just after Hachemi has finished having sex with Amina, we get a shot of Hachemi's mother hysterically slashing the wedding *baclawa* we saw being prepared in the opening shots of the film, signifying, perhaps, that Hachemi will not marry, even after this "proof" that he is capable of having sex with a woman. Though Farfat also finally succeeds with his prostitute, Hasna, their coupling is brief, and he withdraws, saying to Azaïez as he leaves the brothel, "You don't deserve anything else!"

In a curiously revealing choice of words, Haskell sums up the heterosexist point of view of homo(sexuality)—one perhaps shared by the majority of American society, and widely held among Tunisians as well: "The homophile impulse, like most decadent tropisms, like incest, is, or can be, a surrender, a sinking back into one's nature. Just as we have lost faith in narrative forms, we have lost our sexual confidence" (28). These remarks reveal that Haskell, like the society in which Hachemi and Farfat live, believes that there is only one, true narrative—the heterosexual narrative—and any other is proof that "we have lost faith in narrative forms." Indeed, in a voice-over, we shall hear Hachemi's mother say: "On your wedding night, I shan't be able to sleep until I know you have consummated it" (i.e., until she knows that Hachemi has successfully followed the script of the conventional heterosexual trajectory to its proper conclusion).

There are several indications in the film that Hachemi is not sexually interested in women. He is not necessarily afraid of them (his experience with the prostitute, Amina, for example, is apparently not traumatic), and we see that he has a relaxed and easy friendship with his sisters Hend and Amna (whose name, like Amina, means "keeper of secrets" or "trustworthy confidante"). But at the beginning of the film, we see Hachemi flee the aggressively sexual advances of an attractive, married woman who tries to entrap him. As he begins to draw water from the well in the courtyard of the house where the young woman lives, she comes up behind him, puts her arms around him in a way that hampers his movements, and whispers into his ear: "The pleasure lies in going deep ... let me show you how to do it." For the moment, the film will leave open the question of why Hachemi runs in fright—her bawling infant is witness to the event, giving the scene a traumatic aspect, which is compounded by the loud crash of the metal pail falling to the courtyard floor—but in retrospect, we can interpret the scene as an echo of the motif of rape in the film, which is to say, of *coercion*: the "feeling of helplessness faced with something we're being dragged into, something we haven't chosen."[37]

Fathers and Sons

In Bouhdiba's discussion of the trauma that accompanies circumcision and marriage in Muslim society, he seems to think that "if, in the end, everything seems to settle down without too much difficulty and heartache it is certainly because of all the forms of socialization set in train, but also because of the early age of marriage [*sic*], which follows soon after circumcision" (183–184).[38] But for Hachemi and Farfat, everything does *not* settle down without too much difficulty and heartache. Or rather, Hachemi (within the limits of what his half of the composite character represents in the allegory) embodies the Muslim man's ambivalence when confronted with the imperative to marry, and Farfat is a representative example of what happens when a young man categorically refuses to submit to his tribal destiny. Bouhdiba's attempt to explain the link between circumcision and marriage implies a dire theory of desire founded in (symbolic) castration:

> We now understand why sexual mutilation (circumcision and excision) hold such an exceptional place in our Arabo-Muslim societies, whereas there is nothing in the law that would lead one to expect it. It amounts to

an initiation into love, not in its more hedonistic aspects, but in its most negative ones. It is a warning that life is anxiety and danger, but it also teaches how this danger may be overcome and resolved. Circumcision and excision are like a vaccination against the dangers of sexuality. (185)[39]

Bouhdiba's logic only makes sense if one accepts his premise that "life is anxiety and danger," or that sexuality is fraught with "dangers," or if one fails to recognize that the castrating father is the first and chief "danger," which quite naturally would be a cause of "anxiety" for the boy. So which comes first? The anxiety and danger or the vaccination against the anxiety and danger (which, apart from being itself a cause of anxiety, is a warning of even greater, potentially mortal, danger from the one administering the vaccination)? As with the Jews, the answer, it turns out, has less to do with "love"—as Bouhdiba here seems to want to suggest—and more to do with group cohesion:

> In any case the deflowering of the virgin on her wedding night is much more an equivalent of the circumcision of the boy than is the excision. Through festivities, violence, blood, pain and exhibitionism, too, we have in each case different types of traumata wittingly inflicted by the group in order to maintain its own cohesion: the sacrifice of the hymen is a rite having the same nature and the same meaning as that of the foreskin. As we have seen, there is a clear correspondence for the boy between circumcision and marriage. The wedding night is the time when the man experiences and proves his virility and when the girl proves her honesty. (186)

It must be said that Bouhdiba's representation of desire's dialectic as springing from a matrix of oedipal imperatives is essentially no different from Freud's (which also falters when it comes to accounting for entrenched adult homosexuality).[40] The normative account of the boy's evolution toward fully heterosexual desire, culminating in marriage, is the same for the European societies that were Freud's focus (his claims for the universality of the Oedipus complex notwithstanding), as is Bouhdiba's description of Muslim variants (whose book, we remember, is entitled *Sexuality in Islam*).[41] The main difference, perhaps, is Bouhdiba's implication that Muslim societies tend to be more "authoritarian" than the Western societies that are the background against which he presents his findings:

THE FREEDOM TO BE DIFFERENT

> Circumcision is carried out at an age when the boy has long been aware of the importance of the difference between the sexes. Very often a state of anxiety is induced in the boy by his family and friends. He is soon made aware of the exorbitant privileges that go with being male. He has been made well aware of the importance of that "little thing that hangs down," as little Muslim girls invariably refer to it. Hence the fear that it will be cut off if it is not circumcised or, even, that what remains will be cut off after circumcision. Such a fear is part and parcel of the paradox and contradiction of childhood experience. There is a symbolic valorization of the phallus and an obsessional fear of losing it. This situation is likely to last for a long time, especially in an authoritarian society and one in which the terrifying father holds all kinds of goods, pleasures, wealth—and women—in "trust" for him. (183)

At one point in the film, we see Hachemi and Azaïez standing below a balcony on which a beautiful young woman is bending over as she washes a window. She pretends not to notice the two men, although Azaïez is staring longingly up her skirt and is caressing his bare chest in frustrated desire.

FIGURE 2.5 Hachemi (Imad Maâlal) listens while Azaïez (Mohamed Dhrif) loses himself in an erotic reverie.

Hachemi does not so much as glance at the girl. Rather, he is turned toward his friend and standing very close to him. As Azaïez murmurs appreciatively to Hachemi about the girl, it is as if Hachemi were putting himself in her place, shyly accepting his friend's declarations of desire.

The scene is followed by an even more blatant example of how Hachemi's desire is different from that of his friend, who urges him to value heterosexual love above the bonds of male friendship. Hachemi has come to Azaïez for some money for Farfat, who has resolved to leave Sfax and start a new life in Tunis. As he paces about the bakery, Azaïez grumbles that his father has stopped paying his wages since the theft of the motorcycle: "I steal from my father to get drunk. . . . [But] I respect my father. With his mustache, you don't play the kid!" Hachemi responds violently: "Is that what you think it means to be a man! To have a mustache! . . . Have you forgotten what [Farfat] did for you?" (Bouzid reveals here that Azaïez' father is precisely one of those described by Bouhdiba as "terrifying"; he is one of those Muslim fathers who have the power to *withhold* all kinds of goods, pleasures, wealth—and women—from their sons.) Azaïez tries to explain to Hachemi: "I'm in a tight spot. It was because of [Farfat] that we argued. Who would have believed that our friendship would be touched? You know, friendship . . . even when it is reduced to ashes, burns whoever touches it."[42] Azaïez urges Hachemi to stop feeling responsible for Farfat: "Think of yourself a little. Now, finally, you will know life, warmth. . . . Forget our misery, forget bachelorhood and the empty bed, the long nights." Hachemi turns and leaves in disgust, as Azaïez continues, in a reverie: "Love's thirst, cold sheets. . . . You have found warmth! Don't think about others, we're of no account. Forget us, and taste life before it's too late! I've reached my age without knowing tenderness."

The irony here, of course, is that Hachemi (perhaps only unconsciously) wants to know "life, warmth. . . . tenderness"—but with another man, perhaps even Farfat. Nothing in the film suggests that homosexual love would be a poor substitute for the heterosexual love Azaïez dreams of knowing. Indeed, the film makes a claim for Hachemi and Farfat's right to make their own choices about whom, and how, to love, even if these choices will be "different" from those made by the majority of society.

Like his father, Azaïez wears a mustache, the ubiquitous symbol of virility in Arab culture. Hachemi's fair coloring and beardlessness—in a culture that Bouhdiba tells us fetishizes hair and in which "the mere sight of pretty boys is regarded by the *fiqh* as disturbing and terribly tempting" (32)—signal his desirability (to men) as much as they function as signs of his youth. To use an Islamic metaphor, we may see his beardless beauty in terms of *fitna*, or revolt against God. As Bouhdiba puts it, "*fitna* is both seduction and sedition, charm and revolt" (118). He quotes Al-Hassan Ibn Dhakwam, the fifth-century Cordovan judge who cautioned: "Do not sit next to the sons of the rich and noble: they have faces like those of virgins and are even more tempting than women" (32–33). Bouhdiba then comments: "Thus we pass imperceptibly from a world based on the dichotomy of the sexes to a world based on the dichotomy of the ages, since youth is quite simply projected on to the feminine side—and duly repressed!" (33).

Near the beginning of the film, shortly after the flashback in which Hachemi remembers the happy days of his childhood, when he and Farfat and Jacko used to play together at the beach, Hachemi recalls in aural flashback his paternal aunt Aïcha saying: "Hachemi has such white skin, he should have been a girl." (In disgust, he glances at himself in the mirror on the wall.) "My father takes me for a child," he later tells his friend Touil (Habib Belhadi), who comments: "You talk like Farfat. One would say you were twins!" And when a group of Hachemi's friends at a bar decide they should give him a bachelor party ("Enterrons sa vie de garçon," as the French subtitle puts it), one of them says: "Is it a celebration or an interment?"

There is a strong theme in the film of male childhood being understood as a feminine or feminized period and of a properly masculine adulthood being achieved primarily through a conscious rejection of the feminine. Certainly, more than once in *Man of Ashes*, we see Hachemi as a little boy being embraced by his mother, in images that suggest an erotic element in the bond between mother and son, and in a key scene, we see him being bathed by her after he has spent the afternoon playing with Farfat and Jacko on the beach. "My son has grown up," she murmurs, "I must get him married." Hachemi's parents do not allow him to go to the beach without adult supervision, and so when she realizes that his skin is salty, she mildly reprimands him. Overhearing this, Hachemi's father Mustapha (Mahmoud Belhassen) angrily blames the Jewish boy for Hachemi's disobedience ("It's his fault!" he says) and tells Hachemi that he does not want him to see Jacko anymore. In this and earlier scenes, the father is associated with interdiction. He is unambiguously the oedipal father who is jealous of the mother–son bond, and whom the boy fears, with good reason (and no doubt remembering the occasion of his circumcision), as the one with the power to castrate. Love for the mother, in other words, and sensual pleasures (the feeling of the sun and the sea on his skin as he plays with Farfat and Jacko; his mother bathing him when he gets home) are threatened by the father. *Man of Ashes* suggests that the world Hachemi inhabits, which he is obviously reluctant to give up, may very well be far preferable to the "adult" (heterosexual, patriarchal) world so valorized by his society. Hachemi has no desire to become his father, has no wish to take his place, so that, in Hoveyda's phrase, he might, in turn, be in a position to "suffocate" his own children.

Trauma and Fantasy

As Lizbeth Malkmus and Roy Armes note in their book *Arab and African Film Making*, Bouzid's film is marked by "the delicate, tactile, sensual perceptions of the young carpenter hero," and the film is structured as a battle between the senses and the elements, in a way that "is fairly rare in Arab cinema, which is not awash with the sensuality supposed by nineteenth-century Orientalism."[43] *Man of Ashes* in this way is entirely sympathetic with Hachemi's point of view and expresses the filmmaker's desire. The "sensuality" of the mise-en-scène, as an index of Hachemi's psychic reality, in a sense is at odds with the film's claim that he is a victim marked by a childhood trauma. If Bouzid is torn between two fundamentally different points of view (that of the desiring subject and that of the traumatized victim), which imply two different ways of answering the film's central questions— Why is Hachemi reluctant to marry? And why does Farfat believe he is "not a man"?—it is because he wishes to tell the truth about the desire treated in the film, but must disguise that truth in order not to alienate his (potentially homophobic) audience. Bouzid has to find a way to get his cards on the table and to make his audience take responsibility for his characters. In a sense, Bouzid has to trick his audience into acknowledging that homosexual desire is the issue, by pretending that the intertwined story of Hachemi and Farfat can be explained in terms of a childhood trauma—even though the discourse on trauma is not only legitimate, but is the dominant one in the film. It is dangerous to combine these discourses, as Bouzid has done, for the resulting implication is that homosexuality is caused by homosexual rape. Françoise Vergès sheds some light on [Bouzid's] dilemma in her comments about why sodomy, or anal rape, comes to acquire such an overdetermined and intolerable emotional significance in representations of colonization in the work of Frantz Fanon:

> Fanon always privileged trauma over fantasy. "Fantasy" did not belong to his psychological vocabulary. With fantasy one admits that there is a psychic reality; there is a domain which resists total mastery and control, is heterogeneous and speaks in many voices. It is the construction of a narrative in which one's own desire is expressed. This domain cannot be assimilated to reality. With traumatism you are a victim: there is no conscious desire. One can attempt to find the source of the trauma which has wounded one's psyche and then find a cure.[44]

To suggest that Hachemi has a horror of heterosexuality because of a childhood trauma is a way of disowning responsibility for the complexity of sexuality—which is why Bouzid also offers a counter-discourse (he wants to allow for the possibility that Hachemi and Farfat are gay) in telling the story from Hachemi's point of view.[45]

One night, while saying goodbye to all his friends, Farfat becomes thoroughly drunk and afterward makes his way to the atelier where he used to work. As it happens, Hachemi is there, and he tries to calm Farfat, whose maudlin shouts become increasingly despairing as he stumbles about chaotically. The scene is marked by eroticism, as Hachemi, bare-chested, struggles to subdue his violently unhappy friend, who is also shirtless. The key to *Man of Ashes*' latent currents of desire can be found not only in Bouzid's blatantly associative, thematic editing, but in mise-en-scène such as this, in which close-ups of the young men's naked torsos glowing in the dim light of the darkened workshop say what the characters themselves do not acknowledge in the narrative, namely that their friendship contains an element of suppressed physical desire. As Martin Stollery puts it in "Masculinities, Generations, and Cultural Transformation in Contemporary Tunisian Cinema":

> In one unusually framed shot towards the end of a sequence where the two get drunk, the camera is positioned beneath the table in the workshop

where they were abused as children. Within this frame, Hechmi gently lifts Farfat onto a makeshift bed, as if they were lovers. This shot crystallizes two conflicting currents within *Man of Ashes*' exploration of subordinate and hegemonic masculinities and male intergenerational relationships. Affection, tenderness and egalitarianism confront physical and psychological violence. The former qualities are constant in the film's representation of the relationship between Hechmi and Farfat. The latter prove difficult to eradicate.[46]

This scene follows one in which Hachemi, in obvious distress, has recalled his rape by Ameur in this very workshop, where Hachemi is now the supervisor, with young apprentices in his charge; it is followed by an almost surreal scene showing Hachemi coming home to his overwrought family (his mother meets him at the front door—and with the complicity that is wont to enrage Hachemi's father—urgently whispers to him: "My darling! I've missed you! It's as if I'd just given birth to you all over again. But, you smell of wine... your father will kill us! Come inside... he'll see us!") and his then being prevented from leaving the house again by a family member standing in every doorway.

The memory of his molestation, the suppressed eroticism of the two half-naked friends wrestling with each other, followed by this powerful image of familial entrapment, as a cacophony of ringing bells dominates the sound track (Hachemi brings his hands to his ears in an attempt to block out this imaginary din), obliquely reveal that Hachemi's trauma is colored by fantasy.

The mix of fear and desire that characterizes oedipal yearning, and which in sexual contexts gives castration anxiety its uniquely conflicted quality, is in fact condensed in the poster for the film, which is of a drawing, in close-up, of a man's bulging crotch, with the man's hand clutching at his bloodstained groin. The image is extraordinary, because it announces that the film is about a wounded man, desire, and murder; or about a murderous desire; or perhaps about the victim of a (sexually motivated) attack. It also makes unambiguous reference to the film's controlling metaphor of circumcision as a bloody "rape," which every Muslim male suffers, creating that sense of "defeat" described by the filmmaker as a "feeling of helplessness faced with something we're being dragged into, something we haven't chosen." The drawing would seem to be of Hachemi, wearing chinos and a cotton shirt (Farfat wears dungarees, without a shirt, throughout most of the movie), although we must infer, from the events that occur in the narrative, that it is of Ameur. As a wounded man (*"un homme blessé,"* to echo the title of a 1983 French film about a young man's brutal awakening to his gay sexuality),[47] Hachemi feels like a victim, despite his father's conviction that he is merely being perversely ungrateful for not taking up his heteropatriarchal privileges in marriage. "We're like puppets in your hands!" his father shouts, when Hachemi gets home from comforting his distraught friend. "Do you want to turn the wedding feast into a funeral? The marriage is on Tuesday! It was decided, between men!"

Hachemi, at his wits' end, sobs: "You're all against me. Even my brother Samir, the doctor! May God deliver me, and leave you in peace! I don't want this marriage. God didn't want it." Hachemi's father responds by beating him violently, lashing him repeatedly with a leather belt, as he crouches on the floor, and all the women wail in fright. Hachemi's invoking the name of God is a last resort, for even his brother, the doctor (the secular voice of modern science, as it were), has betrayed him, and the frighteningly ugly old woman his family brings in to exorcise his demons also fails. She moans and cries out to various saints to help deliver Hachemi of the "fire" consuming him and to "return him to health." She even calls on the barber of the Prophet to help him. But, as Bouzid wants to make clear, Hachemi is what he is. The proposed marriage is society's way of containing and organizing his sexuality, for patriarchal purposes. And if Hachemi is to remain true to himself, the institution of marriage must be revealed as precisely that: an institution, which is to say, an *ideological* (and therefore malleable) structure, capable of evolution. For the modern, secular Tunisian, Hachemi's example represents a head-on collision with the "feudal ideas" Bouzid has said his cinema is trying to overcome.[48]

"You will always be my apprentices . . . "

In his "Sources of Inspiration" lecture, as we have noted, Bouzid admits that as a filmmaker he has had to put some effort into "winning over a badly educated public" that was used to the ideologically retrograde Egyptian commercial cinema. He sees himself as one of a group of Tunisian filmmakers seeking to challenge Tunisian audiences and trying to "put forward something different and accustom them to seeing new things" (47). His contention that Arab-Muslim society ("the state, the family, the religious structure") in effect "destroys the individual" has been profoundly shocking for Tunisians to hear, and yet the phenomenal success of *Man of Ashes* at the box office, the succès d'estime of his subsequent films, and widespread agreement within Tunisia that Bouzid is their country's preeminent filmmaker, attest to the fact that there is some truth to his diagnosis of an identifiable malaise in Tunisian society. In *Man of Ashes*, how the individual is "destroyed" is obvious (Hachemi's fate remains undecided at the end of the film, but Farfat dies). The ambiguities of the film's ending, however, suggest that there is hope—for all those who might recognize something of themselves in Hachemi and Farfat. Bouzid edits the ending of the film in such a way that we understand that Farfat both dies *and* lives. Farfat is wearing a dark blue shirt and similarly dark pants when he fatally stabs Ameur. As Ameur falls forward—muttering the dying words, "You will always be my apprentices. I nevertheless initiated you."—Touil throws Farfat across his shoulder, and with Hachemi disappears into the nighttime safety of the narrow streets of the medina. The next day, we see Anis, Farfat's young companion, tip Farfat off that two plainclothes police officers are looking for him. A chase ensues, throughout which Farfat is still wearing the dark pants and unbuttoned shirt of the night before. He laughs with abandon as he plays cat and mouse with his pursuers. Finally, having made his way to an open space traversed by a railroad track, he pauses. Anis, standing on the overpass above the track, whistles to Farfat to indicate that his pursuers have located him. At this same moment, Farfat becomes aware that a train is approaching. He stands beside the track, smiling; and in the moment before the train reaches him, Farfat throws himself in front of it. As the train pulls away from the camera, and the two police officers run to the spot where Farfat's body would be, Anis—as if out of nowhere—steps onto the track in front of them. The boy is wearing denim dungarees, without a shirt, as we have seen Farfat wear throughout most of the film. With his hands on his hips, he says to the men: "Let him be." Bouzid then cuts to a medium close-up of Anis, who, turning his head and shoulders to face the departing train, looks back into the camera, and with a smile, winks [at me; at Farfat]. In the shots that follow, we see Farfat running and jumping in slow motion, with his arms outstretched, as if flying across the rooftops of the city. He is again wearing his denim dungarees, without a shirt. In the very last shot of the film, we see Anis erase the graffito that announced to the world that "Farfat is not a man."

The film's message is clear: there will always be Farfats and Hachemis in the world, who courageously reject their society's definition of what it means to be a man. Farfat and Hachemi have seized their destiny. They have, in effect, found the courage to say: "Go to hell, I'll do what I like." They have resisted and transcended the destiny implied by Ameur's dying words—"You will always be my apprentices"—in that their message has been conveyed to the viewer: *Do not submit to the big lie contained in the parable of the "Sacrifice of Abraham." Do not, as Ishmael did with Abraham, be a (willing) victim of your father's murderous wishes.* While it may be true that Ameur "nevertheless initiated" Hachemi and Farfat—just as every Muslim son has been circumcised (by his father/an Ameur)—the viewer might take courage from Hachemi and Farfat's example, to break the castration dialectic in which, as Bouhdiba says, the mutilated man rapes and the raped woman is mutilating (184).[49]

Becoming a Man

In the concluding remarks of their book *Islamic Homosexualities*, Stephen O. Murray and Will Roscoe note that egalitarian (or "gay") male homosexuality is largely, though not entirely, missing from historical Muslim societies and from contemporary ones, with minor exceptions in the capitals of the relatively secular states of Turkey and Pakistan.[50] They acknowledge, however, that in many non-Western urban centers around the world we are beginning to see "men adopting the new terminology and self-conceptions of a gay identity under the influence of Western examples, while continuing to observe traditional distinctions of older/younger, active/passive, and even masculine/non-masculine in their personal relationships" (313).[51] In *Man of Ashes*, the relationship between Hachemi and Farfat is fundamentally egalitarian; Bouzid is not interested in proposing a Western-style model of gay identity for them (with or without the "traditional distinctions" that Murray and Roscoe suggest continue to characterize most homosexual relationships in non-Western Muslim societies), but rather in showing his two young heroes caught precisely between their society's view of them and how they would see themselves—poised, perhaps, on the threshold of an identity that would permit them to love each other without forfeiting their sense of being masculine.

As "two sides of the same coin," Hachemi and Farfat are very similar, and yet different in significant ways; we can even see how—in relation to each other—some of the dichotomies that are said to mark men in traditional Muslim societies as masculine or not-masculine, are inscribed in the differences between their bodies. For Bouzid, as we have noted, "the body is really the heart of the matter. . . . [It is] the most important vector of dramatic technique and conflicts, dramas, characters."[52] Hachemi, for example, "needed to have a feminine beauty whose purpose is to bring out his drama still more," whereas "Farfat, his counterpart, needed to be volatile, androgynous. . . . Farfat needs fragility in his body" (58). The physical beauty of the two young men—which for Bouzid is crucial to the film's meanings, not least because they attract a male gaze—is acknowledged in the way they are photographed. Although Bouzid insists that "the camera has to caress bodies to bring them closer to the viewer" (58), he somewhat confusingly remarks, "I've never used the body for visual pleasure" (59). He admits, however, that "for the fundamentalists there has always been a confusion between sex and the body, but this confusion is in me too. But while the fundamentalists think that the whole body is sex, for me sex is part of the body, everything is body" (58).

FIGURE 2.6 Hachemi with the prostitute Amina (Sonia Mansour) at Sejra's brothel.

As should be obvious by now, *Man of Ashes* is not without its internal contradictions. But the film's critique of repressive neopatriarchal structures is consistent. The film begins with the question of whether or not Hachemi and Farfat will be able to achieve a satisfactory masculinity, and it asserts, finally—although the price each pays is exorbitant—that they do, in the sense that they remain true to themselves. They do not foreclose on their desire. Bouzid's young heroes go beyond the system that offers them only the options to "graduate" to respectable masculinity (confirmed by marriage and fatherhood) or to be relegated to a twilight zone of nonsubjectivity as "not a man." They insist, in the spirit of a Tunisian *cinéma sans tabou*, on the "freedom to be different, to choose your own life."

CHAPTER THREE

Laughter in the Dark

Sexuality and the Police State in *Halfaouine* (Férid Boughedir, 1990)

Férid Boughedir's first feature-length film, *Halfaouine*—the most successful film ever made in Tunisia[1]—tells the story of a twelve-year-old boy, Noura (Selim Boughedir), who lives in Halfaouine, a working-class neighborhood in the old city of Tunis. Ostensibly about the awakening of desire and Noura's transition to heterosexual maturity, it offers an amused and affectionate portrait of Tunisian society, while at the same time lamenting the encroaching police state. The film's phenomenal success at the box office can be attributed in part to its lightness of tone and comedic aspects, which play on Noura's youth and inexperience, as he seeks on the one hand to be taken seriously as a young adult, and tries on the other to hang onto the liberties he still enjoys as a boy, one who can move with relative freedom in both the public sphere dominated by men and the private sphere dominated by women. Critics tend to follow the director's suggestion that *Halfaouine* is a tale "seen through the eyes of a child trying to find his way in an adult universe, within a conservative society where strict separation of the sexes rules."[2] And it is easy to agree with Boughedir when he insists that he wants to show in his film "a Mediterranean society, exuberant and affectionate, where humor and eroticism always have their place, along with tolerance,"[3] adding:

FIGURE 3.1 When Salih (Mohamed Driss) and Noura (Selim Boughedir) find a mural graffito that reads, "One mind for all, the President's," Salih changes it to read: "Our minds, without the President's."

"I believe in the liberatory virtues of laughter and of eroticism—I believe, like the writer Georges Bataille, that 'eroticism is the approbation of life even unto death.'"[4]

But most critics tend also to avoid almost completely any discussion of the film's darkly pessimistic parallel narrative about neopatriarchal oppression and the brutality of the police state. Roy Armes, for example, in his book, *Postcolonial Images,* describes the film as fresh, funny, and inventive, even while he acknowledges that the element providing the film's narrative suspense—Noura's sexual awakening, from his visits to the women's public baths with his mother and other female members of the household, to "the gratification of [his] desire with the body of a beautiful, submissive young girl"—is entirely predictable (143). In the conclusion of his chapter on *Halfaouine,* Armes remarks that "the film shows us at the end a young man freed from the tyranny of his father and the oppression of the family" (147–148). But nowhere does he address what, for a Tunisian audience, is surely the film's central allegory: the *meaning* of the tyranny of the boy's father. Indeed, the film makes it abundantly clear that the father's heavy-handed authoritarianism should not be taken merely as an unlucky element of Noura's biography, but should be seen as emblematic of an authoritarianism that permeates Tunisian society and finds its ultimate embodiment in the president of the Republic himself. In allegorical mode, the film describes the steady erosion and loss in Tunisia of the individual's liberties and freedoms, as the state reaches deeply into the private sphere and causes unhappiness and dysfunction everywhere.

Halfaouine/The Boy of the Rooftops

The full title of the film in Arabic, *'Usfûr Stah: "Halfaouine"* (*The Bird of the* [Rooftop] *Terrace: "Halfaouine"*), or in French, *Halfaouine, l'enfant des terrasses* (*Halfaouine, the Child of the Terraces*), is potentially confusing to the non-Tunisian, for it implies that Halfaouine is the name of the boy (or the bird). This conflation of place and character in the title is interesting, however, for it reveals Boughedir's intention that the eponymous neighborhood be understood broadly in allegorical terms. The movie is as much, or more, about a place—a society—as it is about a character.

In her brief but perceptive analysis of the film in *Cinémas d'Afrique francophone et du Maghreb*, Denise Brahimi describes *Halfaouine* as an example of the realist trend in North African filmmaking that started in the 1980s and sought to understand the individual's sense of malaise in relation to his or her society. This malaise, which she observes is at the heart of the Algerian Merzak Allouache's film, *Omar Gatlato*, for example, is of the same sort that Noura experiences in *Halfaouine*: "the feeling of an incurable emptiness in his overflowing heart."[5] Without stating explicitly that the film's theme of sexual awakening (and the obstacles facing the boy/young man who seeks to "discover sexuality") might be interpreted as anything other than a representation of sexual mores prevalent in Tunisia, Brahimi nevertheless observes that "in locating this disappointment and lack at the heart of an apparent plenitude, Férid Boughedir expresses an essential truth about his character and about his country" (103). Noura must grapple with the "paradox" that he lives in a society in which "sexuality is omnipresent and exhibited . . . [but] held out of reach by a complex and perverse system of interdictions that forces a boy like him to expend prodigious amounts of energy to see first, and act later" (103).[6]

FIGURE 3.2 Noura adores his aunt Latifa (Hélène Catzaras). Here, she asks him to fasten her bra strap.

Brahimi goes on to remark on the way in which "political and social denunciation" is introduced into the film, which is ostensibly "an individual and interpersonal story that takes place within the tiny frame of an old neighborhood in Tunis, Halfaouine, where Noura daily plies the streets":

> The way in which it represents adolescence and its glimpses of the adult world, however, is conditioned by this particular moment in the city's history, which is witnessing a steady loss of its spaces of liberty. These spaces consist of formerly autonomous zones in which the central government only rarely intervened; they were also spaces where individuals were allowed to be themselves, whatever their singularities, and were assured of the (invariably amused and complicit) respect of the other residents of the neighborhood. The film sets up an opposition between this live-and-let-live life, led undisturbed among the shopkeepers' stalls, and the increasingly brutal incursions of external elements. (104–105)

These comments not only refer to the quotidian reality of how people inhabit real spaces but also acknowledge how films signify through mise-en-scène to reveal political realities, that is, how space is organized in the film, and how Boughedir's mise-en-scène uses the architecture of the neighborhood—its streets and squares, the courtyards of the houses, the shops, the rooftops, and so on—to express the society's social organization and reveal the manifold changes that are transforming Tunisian society.

After the film's opening shots of Noura in the women's *hammam*, and the credit sequence under which we see a panoramic view of Tunis, the camera cuts to Noura, the boy-*flâneur*, on Halfaouine Street. As the narrative unfolds, we will recognize these three spaces as the film's privileged sites of nostalgia: they are the three spaces in which Noura is (or was) happiest and are the three spaces that are under threat from (or have been destroyed by) the police state. The nostalgia of the film is for the boy's soon-to-be-lost childhood; and allegorically, it is for the live-and-let-live attitude that Boughedir is suggesting Tunisians had before Tunisia became a police state.[7] As noted above, Boughedir has been explicit and outspoken about what he correctly sees as the main themes of his cinema, which celebrates a real or imagined *méditerranéité* of humor, eroticism, tolerance, and so on; but his reference to Bataille's dictum, that "eroticism is the approbation of life even unto death," hints at darker, more melancholy sources of his motivation as a filmmaker.

Boughedir echoes Bataille's remark in *L'érotisme* that "erotic activity is in the first place an exuberance of life,"[8] but Bataille is more explicitly somber than the filmmaker about eroticism's yearning for a connection with something that has been lost, which he sees as the wellspring of desire:

> We are discontinuous beings, individuals who perish in isolation in the midst of an incomprehensible adventure, but we yearn for our lost continuity. We find the state of affairs that binds us to our random and ephemeral individuality hard to bear. Along with our tormenting desire that this evanescent thing should last, there stands our obsession with a primal continuity linking us with everything that is. This nostalgia . . . is responsible for the three forms of eroticism in man. . . . [the] physical, emotional and religious. My aim is to show that with all of them the concern is to substitute for the individual isolated discontinuity a feeling of profound continuity. (20)

The psychoanalytic theme of desire as springing from the infant's sense of ruptured continuity with the mother's body is a cornerstone of Freudian theory, and is one that is clearly articulated in the film. From its very first shot and in the shots that follow, in which the motif of water is associated with the maternal and the feminine, *Halfaouine* establishes an image—of Noura in the women's *hammam*—that will provide a key to the boy's desire. (And to confirm its thesis about desire, the film will conclude with a flashback to these same shots.)[9] Noura's yearning for the emotional-sensual, private sphere of the women more or less coincides with, or at least is exacerbated by, his banishment from that world. His desire is lodged under the sign of nostalgia—desire for the woman's body.

Whether we think of Noura's "place of origin" as his infant sense of primal continuity with his mother or as the viewer/filmmaker's nostalgic representation of Tunisia before it became a police state, Natalie Friedman's characterization of nostalgia (in Gary Shteyngart's *The Russian Debutante's Handbook*, a novel about the "post-Soviet experience") as a "sense of having lost ties to a nation and a national identity"[10] is clearly not without resonance for Boughedir, who came of age in the 1960s of Bourguiba's (politically and culturally progressive, "Mediterranean," secular and tolerant) Tunisia, and who, we can infer from the film, feels that the Tunisian national identity envisioned by Bourguiba has been betrayed (by Bourguiba himself). The Tunisia of that era is a "lost nation."

The View from the Terrace

Following the film's prologue of Noura in the women's *hammam*, the camera pans from left to right, in a bird's-eye view of Tunis. The cheerful music on the sound track accompanying this shot suggests that the film will be upbeat, perhaps even a comedy. The identifiable setting of the film speaks to Boughedir's intention that his tale be a *national allegory*. As the camera pans right, it slowly comes to rest on a view of Halfaouine, identifiable by the mosque of Youssef Saheb Ettabaâ overlooking the neighborhood's main square. The camera cuts to an extreme long shot of the more iconic, Ottoman-style Sidi Mehrez mosque overlooking Bab Souika in the medina proper and then cuts no fewer than four times to high-angle shots of individual courtyards or rooftop terraces, where we see women at work, hanging laundry up to dry. Finally, before cutting to street level—where we see female shoppers, concealed to a greater or lesser degree by their all-white *safsaris*, interacting with male shopkeepers and others on the street[11]—the camera offers a high-angle shot of the courtyard of the Youssef Saheb Ettabaâ mosque, where we see men kneeling in prayer.

The film thus establishes at the outset the notion of a world divided into separate spheres—public and private, male and female, or mixed (the street)—and a "free zone" (the view from the terrace). As the title of the film suggests, Noura has unique access to this free zone represented by the rooftops—but, as I shall discuss below, by the end of the film, Noura's position high above the street will make him a kind of exile from his own society,[12] and as Brahimi notes, this "space of liberty" also exists in the shared attitude of the residents of Halfaouine (until, that is, the police state comes to destroy it):

> Noura has the ability to "fly" because he has the nimble charm of youth and the conquering energy of adolescence; but one can see from his lofty perch that the space down below is terribly divided up into squares and hemmed in on every side, and that chances of escape would be slim. Among the residents of the neighborhood, however, of which Noura is a worthy representative, there is a strong communal spirit that expresses itself in humor and in language peppered with double entendres and ingenious wordplay. There is a space here that by definition escapes control, and the residents of Halfaouine would appear to be accustomed to having recourse to it, against all forms of interdiction. Political prohibition, sexual prohibition ... these are the key targets of censorship. *Halfaouine* marvelously shows how to play the game and foil the censor, which is what gives the film its uplifting quality, even though the film's subject-matter is neither light nor anodyne. (105–106)

In the reading of the film that identifies Noura as representative of his society—that is, *Halfaouine* as a narrative of nostalgia, and Noura's character inscribed in a story about a society in malaise—it is difficult not to interpret the film's final shots pessimistically. Noura has not been integrated into the world of men (the men's *hammam* is closed for cleaning, and he has nowhere to go, but up to the roof, alone); and he is in flight from his tyrannical father (literally, for his father is in the courtyard below, threatening to beat him when he comes down from the roof; and Noura's spiritual father and role model, Salih, has been unjustly imprisoned). Nicholas Dames's characterization of narratives of nostalgia "as the set of sites and temporal processes that reflect, and manage, *dislocation*—experiences of dissonance, disconnection, separation from past spaces and certainties,"[13] applies to *Halfaouine* and the boy with whom the neighborhood of the film's title is conflated. The film does not fully comprehend Tunisia's postcolonial condition or the myriad factors that have contributed to Noura's state of ontological homelessness, but in its nostalgic register, the film reveals that it feels something precious has been lost in Tunisia's transformation toward modernity and in Noura's progress toward adulthood.

The notion that Noura can be read as a symptom of his society's internal contradictions is asserted by Lucy Stone McNeece in her article "La lettre envolée: L'image écrite dans le cinéma tunisien," in which she locates the origin of Noura's dilemma in an historical "wound":

> The subtitle of the film, *The Child of the Rooftops*, appropriately evokes both the freedom of movement allowed to boys and the privileged access that the hero has to the daily occupations of the women (the preparation of meals, their toilette). It designates ironically both his status and his role in the community: Noura, who enjoys a decidedly ambiguous privilege, is the symptom of an occulted disorder that enflames disturbed identities and mixed-up destinies. Child of the rooftops, Noura has no place of his own—he is always "between"—in a society that can no longer contain its own contradictions, its own pathology. The rejection that Noura will experience on several occasions reveals the incoherence that undermines this society, and that perhaps afflicts all societies that suffer from an historical wound and that seek a strong identity. Noura provokes the *uncanny*, what Freud describes as a projection onto the Other of that which returns in ourselves, but which we cannot recognize as such.[14]

McNeece draws a parallel here between the young protagonist and his quest for an adult identity, and Tunisia itself as a young country poised on the threshold of meaningful independence. She perhaps overstates her argument in having Noura signify some sort of societal "pathology" arising from Tunisia's colonial history—but her point is well taken, if we consider that the Tunisia of the film has been independent for more than thirty years. It should be enough to acknowledge that Noura, like the Tunisia he represents, is in a transitional phase, that is, in a normal stage of development (between childhood and adulthood, just as the country can be defined as moving toward, say, a cultural or economic modern nation-state maturity). But here we see some of the potential pitfalls of allegory: Is it "normal" or is it "pathological" to be still "between" colonialism and independence thirty years after Independence was officially proclaimed?[15] If Tunisia's status as a French protectorate was infantilizing for Tunisians, the colonized country at least knew, for better or worse, where it stood in relation to its "protector." But now, caught somewhere between two worlds or two "phases of development"—the First and Third worlds, say; or Europe and North Africa/the Middle East; or economic "independence" and a neocolonial bind—Tunisia, McNeece would seem to be saying, enjoys the decidedly ambiguous privilege of belonging everywhere and nowhere.

We can, however, like Hakim Abderrezak, choose to be optimistic about the final shots of the film and not see the image of a grinning Noura merely as symbolic of the film's philosophy of "laughter in the dark" (the title of Noura's mentor Salih's new play) but rather as proof that an ordinary Tunisian can be an agent of change. In an article subtitled "L'individu-oiseau face à la communauté," Abderrezak writes that he is interested in how Noura goes from being an unwillingly marginalized figure to one who voluntarily claims a marginal status within the community:

> I call the space in which society confines its marginal figures the "peri-community." [And] by the "para-community," I mean the space created by individuals who voluntarily marginalize themselves, a space *to one side* of the community, *sheltered* by it, and from where one might attempt to revolt *against* it. Only from the para-communal space can a free subject emerge, this Maghrebi subject who, having left the women's sphere and refused to integrate into the men's sphere, negotiates in a fundamentally original manner his transition to adulthood.[16]

Thus, for better or worse, the narrative (in keeping with Tunisian societal norms) codes Noura's childhood as inscribed within the "women's sphere," which is relatively powerless in relation to the masculine sphere of adult men, wherein the (repressive) rules of society are written and enforced. Noura's originality—representing the only hope for a society of "free subjects"—resides in his refusal, upon reaching adulthood, to join the men in their system of oppression.

The *Hammam*/Harem

The scenes that take place in the women's public baths are without doubt the most controversial of the film and remain the first and only such scenes in all of Arab cinema.[17] Their point of view, moreover, is marked as belonging to Noura, whose nascent adult sexuality adds a voyeuristic dimension to the scenes that—if they were not so integral to the plot—might be upsetting to the film's equilibrium.[18] Abderrezak acknowledges that Noura is rather old to be accompanying his mother to the *hammam*, and quotes Moroccan scholar and writer Abdelfattah Kilito in support of this observation: "And then, one day, one had to stop accompanying the mother and resign oneself to accompanying the father to the *hammam*; one had to leave the world of women in order to enter the world of men; around the age of five, one had to submit to a second weaning, a second separation" (85). Abderrezak also quotes Saïd Graiouid, whose interviews with several habitués of *hammams* in Morocco "confirm the precocity of the weaning" ("the moment of expulsion usually occurs at the age of four or five" [85]), and he agrees with Ahmed Bouguarche that the age of seven would appear to be the upper limit: "In Arab-Muslim countries, women take their male children with them to the public baths until the age of six or seven years" (85).

Why, then, does Noura's mother take him with her to the women's *hammam*? When she tries, over the protestations of the matron in charge, to gain him entrance to the baths ("He's young and innocent," she insists. "He's very big for his age!"), the old woman is incredulous: "Your son has grown up! He has a mischievous eye. He even has acne!" Abderrezak observes that: "In *Halfaouine*, and in Tunisian society generally, the boy is not perceived quite as an individual, but rather as a body that is foreign to the community of men—sometimes masculine, sometimes feminine—that must be incorporated as soon as possible into this [adult male] community" (85). He concludes that Noura's mother wants him to accompany her and will resort to subterfuge "out of habit; for practical reasons; and because [she] has a complicit relationship with her son" (85). Abderrezak also suggests that she seeks to infantilize him in order to prolong her prerogative as a mother to keep him at her side.

There is a level on which we may read the film not only as a common (heterosexual, male) adolescent fantasy but also as a kind of Orientalist harem narrative (i.e., Boughedir/Noura seeking to know what is under the veil), thus: beginning with the scene in which Noura observes his friends Moncef (Jamel Sassi) and Mounir (Radhouane Meddeb) flirting with the veiled young women on Halfaouine Street;[19] followed by his largely successful visit to spy on the naked women at the *hammam*; to his triumph in persuading the beautiful servant girl Leïla (Carolyn Chelby) to strip naked and have sex with him. The harem, as Emily Apter observes, "loomed large in Europe's phantasms as an archaic erotic idea—one man to many women, unchecked sexual domination over totally submissive members of the weaker sex, proliferating penis-envy in a world of women libidinally organized around the sultan."[20] Noura's desire is similarly narrativized in these terms. He has been conditioned since infancy to embrace the logic that his (phallic) mastery of the woman will be his only path to adult self-liberation. Boughedir mimics the Orientalist's harem fantasy by privileging the *hammam* in the film as a site of voyeuristic-exhibitionistic erotic reverie and by having his young hero (who, in one of the film's boldest strokes of fantasy, is a boyish twelve-year-old) accede to his culture's definition of adult, heterosexual masculinity by having sex with a beautiful woman who is clearly older (and taller!) than he is. Noura is unaware, or unconcerned, that Leïla decides to have sex with him as a means of getting back at his family for mistreating her; he believes it is the phallic glamour of his masculinity that she responds to.

Apter acknowledges that "one would be hard-pressed to dispense with the phallic paradigm in dealing with the harem," but argues that "the sexual fantasies codified in harem texts may [also] be used to construe an antiphallic, gynarchic model of 'what a woman wants,'" and she examines how "the erotics of claustration shape the representation of the French enclosure and domination of North Africa" (102). My own comments about the *hammam* in *Halfaouine*, while echoing some of Apter's analysis of the harem as a site of an "erotics of claustration," see Boughedir's tale rather as an allegory of resistance in which a claustrophobic neopatriarchy—which for all intents and purposes is synonymous with the police state—is defied (by Noura) in an act of transgression. The *hammam*—like the harem to which, as we have said, it bears some similarity—signifies the restriction of male access to the community of women, which explains why both Noura's illicit penetration of the *hammam* and his transgressive first sexual experience with a woman must be seen as symbolically and dialectically linked to his defiance of his father, Si Azzouz (Mustapha Adouani)/the Father (i.e., the sultan of the harem/the president of Tunisia as head of the police state). Apter reminds us of an important factor in this oedipal drama that is at the heart of Noura's coming-of-age story, specifically, the element of resistance to the (neo)patriarchy and its inscription in a harem structure:

> In *Totem and Taboo* Freud evoked a primal horde dominated by a patriarch who had secured for himself exclusive property rights over all the women in the socius. Though the story proceeds with disgruntled younger men banding together, committing parricide, and sharing the women among themselves, it is interesting to note that what Freud placed at the psychic origin of civilization was nothing other than a harem. The old man and his seraglio, according to Freud's mythic scenario, functioned as a spur to the world-historical enactment of the Oedipal drama. In the beginning, was a harem.... (102)

Possession of the woman carries great symbolic importance in a society in which paternal interdiction is strong. In the Oedipus story as interpreted by Freud, the prohibition on incest is maintained by the paternal threat of (symbolic) castration. In *Halfaouine* this drama is played out on every level of society, and according to the film's logics of displacement, it culminates in the circumcision of Noura's brother and the arrest and imprisonment of Salih (Mohamed Driss), who is guilty of nothing, except his refusal to play the part assigned to him in the (neo)patriarchy, which is a system of repression and which, in the allegory, is structured like a sultan's harem, according to which Ben Ali is the sultan, and all men must either be complicit with him in the system or be turned into eunuchs. As a bachelor who freely admits to enjoying the company of women, but who has no intention of marrying (until, that is, he falls in love with Noura's aunt Latifa), Salih poses a threat to the neopatriarchy (and therefore the state), in which the sexuality of men and women alike must be contained.

All the female characters in *Halfaouine* are reduced to their sexuality. In David Spurr's phrase, echoing Foucault, the feminine body (in the Western discourse of sex since the eighteenth century) is so saturated with sexuality "as to define a set of specifically feminine biological and moral responsibilities: duties of regulated fertility, of devotion to family, etc. Within such a system of representation, the woman is constituted as her body, and her body as its sexual nature.... [It is] a reductive process that also has its integrative function, establishing the feminine role within the mechanisms of knowledge and power."[21] Spurr writes that he wishes to borrow "Foucault's notion of a rhetorically constructed body for that strain of discourse which represents the colonized world as the feminine and which assigns to subject nations those qualities conventionally assigned to the female body" (170). This "eroticization of the colonized," as he calls the set of rhetorical instances "in which the traditions of colonialist and phallocentric discourses coincide," is a representational strategy that we find throughout *Halfaouine*. Tunisia may no longer be a French protectorate, but Tunisia's sons and daughters remain colonized—subordinated to neopatriarchal imperatives and in thrall to the phallus. Noura's maternal aunt Latifa (Hélène Catzaras), for example, is a divorcée, who allows herself to be courted by Salih and eventually becomes his lover. Noura's paternal aunt Salouha (Fatma Ben Saïdane) remains unmarried as she approaches middle age, and is given to alarming fits of real hysteria when her desire for Sheikh Mokhtar (Abdelhamid Gayess) goes unrequited. The shots at the beginning of the film of Moncef and Mounir flirting with the girls on the street show that the girls secretly enjoy the attention and relish rebuffing the two boys. There is a scene in the middle of the film, in which one of Noura's mother's friends, Zakia (Aziza Boulabiar), the wife of a grocer, leads a group of women in a ribald discussion about sex. She then sings a song about her wedding night (in which she refers to her husband's penis in metaphorical terms as a large cucumber), and the women in the group follow each of Zakia's verses with the chorus: "Zakia, Queen of the Orchard / Loves all fruits in great number / But prefers above all the cucumber...."

There is the family servant Leïla, whom we have already mentioned; and there are the young women who accept Si Azzouz's discreet caresses when they enter his shop (where he also keeps his stash of pornographic magazines). And there is the folktale recounted in the film as a leitmotif, about Aïcha, who (metaphorically) loses her virginity to an ogre, while her father is on a pilgrimage to Mecca.[22] Finally, there are the extradiegetic shots at the end of the film of a smiling Noura, back in the *hammam*. Whether we read these shots as pure nostalgia on Noura's part (fondly—and falsely— remembering his visits to the *hammam* as the happiest moments of his life) or as evidence that Noura judges his expulsion from the *hammam* (his "expulsion from Paradise"—as Boughedir himself has referred to it) to have been worth it (because, paradoxically, it has gained him admission to

FIGURE 3.3 Noura is expelled from the women's baths by the deaf-mute *hammam* attendant (Zehira Ben Ammar).

the adult world of male heterosexuality), we cannot fail to remark on their resemblance to the "happy ending" that is so often tagged onto a film in which the ideological contradictions of the subject matter are impossible to resolve. As Jarrod Hayes points out in his fine analysis of the film in *Queer Nations*, Noura seems to forget the price he has paid in order to "become a man"—he forgets that "his heterosexuality was violently imposed."[23] Until these shots of "Noura's postexpulsion fantasies of the *hammam* as a heterosexual utopia" (260), "the loss that heterosexuality requires seems not to be worth the privilege it will later grant" (261).

In the allegorical reading, the deaf-mute *hammam* attendant (Zehira Ben Ammar) who suspects that Noura is at the baths under false pretenses, is an allusion to the pervasiveness of the surveillance-obsessed Tunisian police state. She keeps an eye on him and follows him when he goes to fill his bucket with water. Like the secret police on the streets outside, she takes care to remain "invisible" (her invisibility being not only coded in her deaf-muteness, but represented also in shots of her peering fiercely at Noura from the shadows)—until the moment of arrest, which is rendered as a scene of trauma, when she grabs Noura violently by his hair and begins shrieking unintelligibly and drags him through the entire *hammam*, back to his mortified mother, who angrily tells him that he has brought shame upon her.

Halfaouine Street

The *hammam*, we have said, is one of the spaces defined by the film as a site of nostalgia; it is a space where—*après coup*—Noura was happy, but from which he has been banished, and to which he can never return (except, in a manner of speaking, covertly, in pursuit of various substitute objects). So, too, we have said, is the street such a space. By the end of the film, it is no longer one of Tunisian society's "autonomous zones in which the central government only rarely intervene[s]" (Brahimi 103), but a minefield of hidden dangers and threats to its citizens: we will see Salih dragged from his house and escorted through the street, to prison; the deaf-mute *hammam* attendant, lurking in a doorway, will frighten Noura as he passes by; and if Noura leaves his safe perch on the roof and descends to ground/street level, his father will beat him (as Salih has already been beaten by the police, and will almost certainly be tortured in prison).

Boughedir makes it clear from the start that the child's paradise-world of Halfaouine has already been infiltrated by the spies of the police state. The film's "image" of happiness, which quite properly comes at the beginning of the film, is offered in the scenes of flirtation between Moncef and Mounir and the girls on Halfaouine Street. To echo Brahimi again (who, it should be noted, writes in the past tense), Halfaouine Street represents a space "where individuals were allowed to be themselves, whatever their singularities—assured of the (invariably amused and complicit) respect of the other residents of the neighborhood." It is the loss of "this live-and-let-live life, led undisturbed among the shopkeepers' stalls," that Boughedir will mourn the most. And he is uncompromising in his indictment of the unholy alliance between the repressive and hypocritical neopatriarchy and the self-appointed guardians of official morality: this happy scene of life on the street includes a shot of the forbidding Sheikh Mokhtar, whom we see spying on Noura from a butcher's stall, and who will report to Si Azzouz that the boy (by his association with Moncef and Mounir) has been involved in disreputable behavior. Indeed, the shot of Sheikh Mokhtar, dressed in black and standing behind a severed bull's head, is the very image of the threat of symbolic castration that he will represent throughout the film.

When the sheikh calls out to Noura, the boys flee. They climb up onto the roof of the mosque and make their way to an adjoining warren of rooftop sheds and storerooms, where they search for empty wine bottles, which they can exchange for a few millimes and thus earn some pocket money. When later they hand over the bottles to Ali (Aïssa Harrath), the wine merchant who runs a small concession behind a café, we overhear a conversation between two men playing cards at a table nearby. One of them says to Ali: "The police raided his place last night—took his radio and emptied his refrigerator!" The other cardplayer says: "Wasn't he supposed to come here today?" To which Ali replies, with wry humor: "Must've gone somewhere else for a drink!"

It is disturbing for the viewer to be alerted so early in the film to the (offscreen) presence of the police state in the midst of this society that, as Boughedir himself wants to insist, is "exuberant and affectionate," and "where humor and eroticism always have their place, along with tolerance." When Noura eventually gets home, he will be punished by his father for hanging out with Moncef and Mounir and "pestering girls" on the street; and we see that Sheikh Mokhtar will even aid Si Azzouz in the administration of the punishment, by holding the struggling boy by his ankles, while Azzouz beats him savagely on the soles of his feet. As in other Tunisian films in which we see a father beat his son (Bouzid's *Man of Ashes* and Mohamed Zran's *Essaïda* being just two of the most obvious examples, while Bouzid's *The Golden Horseshoes*, made the year before *Halfaouine*, bypasses allegory altogether, to include a brutal scene of police torture of the film's hero), a woman comes to the boy's rescue. Here, Noura's aunt Salouha intervenes to stop Azzouz from going too far. But if, as the film would have us understand, there is a continuity that exists between paternal/domestic violence and state violence, there is nobody who can rescue the citizen who is arrested by agents of the police state—as the scenes that culminate in Salih's arrest and imprisonment will prove.

"Colombo" (Taoufik Chabchoub), the police agent and head of the Ministry of the Interior's surveillance network in Halfaouine, is a familiar figure in the neighborhood, and the residents of Halfaouine know who his informers are. So, when he enters the barbershop—one of the neighborhood's all-male spaces of liberty—the men who are chatting there amongst themselves suddenly fall silent. Through Noura's eyes (it is his first day at work there, where his father hopes he can be kept out of trouble, and where perhaps he will learn how to appreciate the society of men), we catch a glimpse of a workers' demonstration taking place outside on the street. The men in the barbershop have been discussing the demonstration, and it is clearly the intention of Boughedir (who appears in this scene in a cameo, wearing a *chechia* and reading an American comic book) to show that—before Colombo enters—the men feel free to express their differing opinions. The barber himself, Abdelwahab (Kamel Touati), perhaps to mask his frustration at the workers' impotence in the face of the government's use of force, says: "More trouble again—soon they'll be whining again for forgiveness." One of the men (Taoufik Jebali, who wrote the film's dialogue) expresses sympathy for the demonstrators and informs the others that some of them have already been killed. The man sitting next to him (Raouf Ben Amor) lifts his newspaper and says: "As for me, I only believe what I read in the paper!"[24]

When Colombo says he is looking for one Youssef Soltane (a reference to Hichem Rostom's character in *The Golden Horseshoes*, who is imprisoned for "subversion"), the barber says facetiously: "What's he done to you? Did he try to overthrow your regime?" He is smiling when he says this, as is Colombo; the two men clearly despise each other. "It's my boss who wants him—dead or alive," says Colombo. "He's causing us a lot of trouble. To think we ever considered him one of us!" Still grinning, and facing Colombo squarely, Abdelwahab replies: "Tell your boss that all of us barbers are on his side. If anyone sticks his neck out, we'll be pleased to give him a shave—with scissors or a razor! Believe me."

The scene is reminiscent of Pépé's predicament in Julien Duvivier's classic *Pépé le Moko* (1937) and his pursuit by the Arab-Algerian police inspector in the pay of his French overlords. For Pépé (Jean Gabin), who is wanted by the metropolitan police, the Casbah of colonial Algiers is both a refuge and a prison, because the inhabitants of the Casbah are "on his side" and will protect him, but cannot help him if he steps out of the protective labyrinth of the old city.[25] Writing about "the city of refuge" within the "inhospitable state," Mireille Rosello notes: "Inside the Casbah, Pépé is always already arrested (since completely cornered by a law that has already condemned him) and forever free (since the Casbah symbolizes the margin of latitude within a repressive system, the room for maneuver that even the most totalitarian regimes fail to completely eliminate)."[26]

But if Pépé's situation is at all different from that of Youssef Soltane, or Salih, or Noura, it is that Pépé's Casbah (in its relation to the "European" city, or *nouvelle ville,* and to the power that rules from Paris) describes a colonial situation. For the Europeans, the Casbah is "the incomprehensible labyrinth [that] symbolizes the supposedly impossible presence of the other at the very core of the city of Algiers" (163), which is precisely what guarantees Pépé his safety—even though he sees the city of refuge as a prison. The residents of Halfaouine, however, are caught in a postcolonial situation—their city is not immune from what Brahimi refers to as "the increasingly brutal incursions of external elements." The policemen who are trying to capture Pépé are "rendered powerless by the complex geography of a place that excludes them" (162), but this is not so for the policemen who come looking for Salih in Halfaouine. In the end, only Noura is able to escape the "policeman's" reach; but his predicament, finally, will resemble Pépé's almost exactly: he is a prisoner in his own Casbah (i.e., in the network of rooftop terraces that are his place of refuge).

In the character of Khemaïs (Fethi Haddaoui), Boughedir obliquely offers a partial explanation for this breakdown of trust among Halfaouine's inhabitants by implying that, in a formative and traumatic homosexual experience involving Ali the wine merchant, Khemaïs' own trust was once betrayed. (Khemaïs' first significant act of vengeance for the unnamed hurt he feels is to have Ali's shop boarded up by the police.) The source of Khemaïs' anger is not specified, but his actions—and the objects of his anger (Ali, Moncef, Salih)—imply that he seeks revenge for having been the victim of an abuse of power (which the film codes in sexual terms). Moncef's adolescent horniness and Salih's guilt-free approach to sexuality would appear to exacerbate Khemaïs' sense of loss and grievance; and like the battered child who will in turn become the battering adult, Khemaïs acts out his history of feeling unloved. Halfaouine Street (as a place where humor and eroticism always had their place, along with tolerance) never belonged to him. The lesson he took from his unspecified childhood trauma is that he can trust nobody in his society; and he resolves to put his faith in the hard power of brute force.

Trust, Francis Fukuyama explains, "is the expectation that arises within a community of regular, honest, and cooperative behavior, based on commonly shared norms, on the part of other members of that community. Those norms can be about deep 'value' questions like the nature of God or

FIGURE 3.4 Ali (Aïssa Harrath) mockingly asks the bully Khemaïs (Fethi Haddaoui): "What, sweetie, don't you know who the sweetest flower is?"

justice, but they also encompass secular norms like professional standards and codes of behavior."[27] Writing about the link between "the social virtues and the creation of prosperity," Fukuyama refers to this trust as "social capital," which "can be embodied in the smallest and most basic social group, the family, as well as the largest of all groups, the nation, and in all the other groups in between. Social capital differs from other forms of human capital insofar as it is usually created and transmitted through cultural mechanisms like religion, tradition, or historical habit" (26).

As a social scientist, Fukuyama is interested in the economic consequences of social capital and the proclivity for spontaneous sociability. As an artist, Boughedir is less obviously interested in performing an economic analysis of his society in *Halfaouine* (as, say, his fellow filmmaker Mohamed Zran does in *Essaïda*), than he is preoccupied with the question of Tunisian national identity as it is understood and experienced by ordinary Tunisians in quotidian life. His metaphors are not economic, but he is nevertheless concerned about the price his countrymen are paying for their abandonment of the historical ideal of Tunisia as a "Mediterranean" society. Fukuyama notes that "people who do not trust one another will end up cooperating only under a system of formal rules and regulations, which have to be negotiated, agreed to, litigated, and enforced, sometimes by coercive means. This legal apparatus, serving as a substitute for trust, entails what economists call 'transaction costs.' Widespread distrust in a society, in other words, imposes a kind of tax on all forms of economic activity, a tax that high-trust societies do not have to pay" (27–28). There is a sense in which Boughedir's film is all about this "tax" that Halfaouine's residents have to pay.

Khemaïs is the informer who betrays Salih and arranges to have him arrested. The order of the scenes leading up to his appearance in the film establishes unequivocally the nature of the threat he poses to the live-and-let-live Halfaouine of Noura's childhood (the Halfaouine that will disappear with his accession to adulthood): when Noura's mother Lella Jamila (Rabia Ben Abdallah)[28] learns that, while working at his summer job in the barbershop, her son witnessed the "trouble" on Halfaouine Street, she declares that she does not want him to work there anymore. She proposes that instead he help with the preparations for his brother's circumcision ceremony. The camera offers a cutaway of the bawling child; and then Khemaïs is introduced in the very next scene. Salih, seated in front of his shop, is about to sing a song for Noura and Mounir, when Khemaïs comes down the street, followed by a crowd of men and dragging Moncef by his ear. Upon reaching Salih's shop, Khemaïs delivers a sharp jab to Moncef's chest, which makes the boy fall to the ground at Salih's feet, and announces: "This boy was pestering the girls on our street!"

When Mounir steps forward to defend his friend, saying, "How dare you hit him!," Khemaïs shoves Mounir to the ground as well and orders him to "keep out of this!" The barber Abdelwahab and Sadok (Mounir's father) appear on the scene and try to restrain Khemaïs, who, with real menace, warns them: "Keep your hands off me!"[29] Salih joins in: "I don't believe it! A big man like you, attacking children!" To which Khemaïs replies: "It'll be your turn soon, Uncle Salih!" He slaps the shoemaker aggressively on the shoulder: "One day, your impudent songs will land you in jail!"

"This is a new interest!" Salih retorts. "You're starting to hit notes now, rather than people!" The crowd laughs appreciatively, and Khemaïs is momentarily disconcerted. He grabs Salih roughly by the neck and turns to the crowd: "I swear I'll clout him unless he sings for me!" Salih refuses: "I don't sing for animals." Khemaïs becomes more agitated: "*Tell him to sing!*"

he demands. (We see Noura slip away from the gathering crowd—to get help from Ali.) Sadok implores the shoemaker: "Sing, Salih, so that we'll be rid of him." But Salih refuses. Khemaïs then threatens: "I'll smash up your shop." Hamadi Karama, the cross-eyed street sweeper (whom earlier we have seen receive a shave at the barbershop, in a scene that is meant to reveal how this cohesive and tight-knit community has affection even for members who are lowest on its social scale),[30] offers his reasoning: "Sing— he's getting angry!" But Salih is adamant: "I'd rather die!"

Then Abdelwahab has the idea: "We'll *all* sing for you!" The crowd immediately begins clapping rhythmically and starts to sing: "I've picked you, my sweetest flower / I've chosen you, my sweetest flower . . . " For a fleeting moment, Khemaïs is suspicious of their choice of song, but decides to go along with it. As the crowd claps in unison, Khemaïs makes vulgar, threatening hip movements in Salih's direction; but before they can start a verse that would reveal to the bully that the joke is on him, Ali makes his way through the crowd, toward Khemaïs, and demands to know: "What's going on?"

We see that Ali is a magnificent figure of masculine sexuality—tall, thuggishly handsome, mustachioed, and muscular. Boughedir frames him in a low-angle shot that emphasizes his sexual charisma and the potency of his presence; and with his swaggering gait, a gorgeous orange scarf draped across his shoulders, and a bouquet of jasmine tucked behind his right ear, Ali's arrival on the scene brings the singing to an abrupt stop. Khemaïs quickly kisses Salih on both cheeks and explains to Ali: "I was just having a joke with Salih." But when he tries to kiss Ali in greeting, the older man pushes him away, saying: "What, sweetie, don't you know who the sweetest flower is?" He tweaks one of Khemaïs's nipples, adding: "Or, have you forgotten?"

The crowd laughs knowingly (and we realize that Noura also knew of the relationship between Ali and Khemaïs and that only Ali would be able to bring the young man to heel). Khemaïs' mortification deepens, as Ali continues: "When the cat's away, the mice play, eh? Did you think I'd died?" The camera cuts to a new arrival on the scene, a beautiful woman in a scarlet, satin dress that is partially covered by her loosely-worn *safsari*. She has been attracted by the commotion (it is Noura's aunt Latifa), and she is curious to see what it is about. When the camera returns to Khemaïs, he is asking Ali: "Why are you humiliating me in front of men? I was only having a joke." Ali replies smoothly: "I'm joking, too." Looking Khemaïs up and down, then turning to the crowd, he says mockingly: "See how he's grown up, now! He's become a little man. Ah! He's even growing a beard! Let me feel. Let's have a touch!"

Salih catches Latifa's eye. She has a suitcase in her hand, and gives the impression that she is newly arrived in town. (We do not know whether Salih knows who she is, or whether Noura recognizes his aunt.) With the tables now turned in his favor, Salih smiles winningly at Latifa and, in a clowning gesture, makes as if to punch Khemaïs in the stomach. She bursts out laughing, which distracts all the men in the crowd, who turn to look at her. She throws back her head and continues to laugh, and the confrontation with Khemaïs is dissolved, as the men stare at her in wonder and admiration.

This is a crucially important scene in the film. Boughedir hints that Khemaïs' damaged character was in some way "caused" by his initiation into sexuality by Ali, that is, however it began—whether Khemaïs as a boy was coerced into sex with Ali or whether, despite their age difference (which would have been more dramatic when Khemaïs was still a boy), it was in some sense consensual—their relationship was, and remains, an unhealthy one. Boughedir implies some sort of equivalence between Khemaïs' (bad) homosexuality/(or compromised heterosexuality) and Noura's (good) heterosexuality, with each mode of sexuality carrying with it an array of evil or good associations and outcomes. The drastic power imbalance characterizing the rape of a boy by a man, not to mention the Tunisian society's taboo on homosexuality in general—as in Bouzid's *Man of Ashes*, where it is a prominent motif—is alluded to here as the ultimate horror and defining catastrophe for a boy, with its inevitably negative, long-term consequences.[31] Khemaïs' vengeful and violent personality is never explained by the film, except in this scene, in which it is plausible to infer that it has something to do with the sexual hold Ali has over him. (It should be noted, moreover—because the scene would appear to confirm Boughedir's belief in the liberatory virtues of humor and of heterosexual eroticism—that only a woman's amused laughter can dissolve the tensions among the men.)

Eventually, as we have already mentioned, Khemaïs will lead Colombo to Ali's shop, which Colombo orders his police deputies to board up. "That's one subversive bolt-hole that will give us no more trouble!" Khemaïs pronounces with satisfaction. "He can't hide forever. Sooner or later, Ali will be denounced." At this moment, Salih and Noura arrive on the scene. "Congratulations! Bravo!" says Salih. "First it was children. Now you attack empty shops. How courageous!" Khemaïs replies: "It's not a shop. It's a meeting place for political activists and drunks. And you will be one of the first to be affected by its closure!" In an overtly symbolic image, Boughedir offers a shot of Mounir with Ali's caged bird, followed by shots of the butcher and his assistant (and Moncef) with Ali's ram, suggesting that Ali's sudden expulsion from the community of Halfaouine will be permanent (or that soon he will be led to slaughter).

As an allegory, *Halfaouine* thus creates an opposition between a certain idea of healthy, heterosexual masculinity (embodied by Salih and his young protégé Noura) that is synonymous with a tolerant society; and another idea of masculinity, forged in a matrix of homosexuality and perhaps coercion (embodied by Ali and Khemaïs) that produces or is synonymous with an intolerant society. The film's negative representations of masculinity, which include the ogre, the sexual hypocrite Si Azzouz, and Sheikh Mokhtar, are weighted heavily on one side of the equation, to suggest that the intolerance and authoritarianism that characterize Tunisia's government have their origins in a perverse sociosexual dynamic that is embedded in the neopatriarchal family. As we have noted, *Halfaouine* is set in the Bourguiba era, but was made in the Ben Ali era. So, when Salih is caught editing a mural graffito on Halfaouine Street that reads, "One mind for all, the President's" (he changes it to read: "Our minds, without the President's"), the viewer understands that the presidential authoritarianism being referred to applies as much to Ben Ali as it did to Bourguiba. Halfaouine Street, once an "autonomous zone in which the central government only rarely intervened"—a space "where individuals were allowed to be themselves, whatever their singularities"—now has eyes and ears that watch and listen, day and night, for any signs of subversion, real or imagined.

The Father

When Habib Bourguiba died at the age of 96 on 6 April 2000, having spent the last thirteen years of his life under a form of house arrest in his palace in Monastir, the Tunisian writer and political activist Gilbert Naccache observed that there were many in Tunisia who, for quite some time, had been waiting—if not hoping—for his death, for it seemed to them that only his death would release the Tunisians from an impossibly paralyzing situation.[32] Once knocked from his pedestal, they believed, Bourguiba would belong to history, and his death would have significance only for those near and dear to him or "for those in power who feared or invoked his shadow whenever they did something they believed was risky" (223). After spending more than a decade in prison (1968–1979) for his contributions to the left-wing publication *El Amal Ettounsi (The Tunisian Worker)* of the *Perspectives tunisiennes* movement, Naccache was ambivalent about his feelings in 2000, but he could not help recalling that:

> [Bourguiba] would say to us: "I am your father." At the time, there were still a few of us to tell him: "No, we are not your children, and as such, we don't owe you anything."
>
> He would say to us: "I have sacrificed my life for this people, I have devoted myself to them."
>
> And we would say: "You are lying. You have devoted your life to your passion: to control, to command, to dominate others. And you use brute force, resorting even to murder—did [you] not publicly claim responsibility for Ben Youssef's assassination?—as easily as you use [displays of] emotion, or blackmail. And to legitimate your power and insinuate yourself into Tunisian national identity, you did things." (224)[33]

Naccache goes on to say that those who wish today to give Bourguiba his due and to forgive him, and who are moved by "filial emotion" and sad feelings of nostalgia for the (imagined) "Golden Age" of his presidency, seem to forget—indeed, they do not want to see—how "the despair of today has its roots in the sadness of yesterday": the severe constraints on freedom of speech, the difficulty, even, of "breathing" in contemporary Tunisia "is nothing new" (224).

All this, we have observed, is written into *Halfaouine*, which contains at least three bad fathers, if not more: Noura's father, Si Azzouz; Sheikh Mokhtar (who becomes some sort of legal guardian to Leïla when she is orphaned); and Colombo's "boss" (who answers to someone up the line that leads straight to the Presidential Palace in Carthage). And as we have said, there is Ali, who is a father figure for Khemaïs (until Khemaïs transfers his allegiance to Colombo and the network of power he represents). Only

FIGURE 3.5 After taking a sip of *boukha* from his bottle of "Vicks® Cough Medicine," Salih sings the song he has composed for the occasion of Noura's brother's circumcision. (The song is covertly aimed at Latifa, whom Salih is trying to woo.)

Salih, Noura's adoptive, spiritual father is anything like a positive paternal figure in this neopatriarchal society that only understands the paternal function in terms of interdiction.[34]

Central to the film's meanings as a coming-of-age story is the folktale Noura's mother tells him—a story about Aïcha and how (in the metaphors of the folktale) she loses her virginity. "Aïcha, que faisait donc ton père l'ogre?" ("Aïcha—What, then, was your father the Ogre doing?") is included in Abdelwahab Bouhdiba's analysis of ten Maghrebi folktales for children, *L'imaginaire maghrébin: étude de dix contes pour enfants*. Bouhdiba points out that in all the tales he discusses, almost without exception, the woman gets out of some difficulty by using her intuition and intelligence:

> She repeatedly gains victory over the man. In "The Mighty She-Goat," the male is emasculated. His horns are broken off. He is made ridiculous. In "The Shrill Mother," he is wicked, a cannibal. In "Seven Virgins," he is at the very least fickle, cowardly, and a cuckold. In "Counsel We Received," he is a liar and a hypocrite. He is ineffectual and, in the final analysis, profoundly

evil and capable of the worst sort of snare. In "Half-Cock," except for the case of Half-Cock himself, the male element is jealous, greedy, envious, wicked, and tyrannical. In "Mr. El Baggouri," he is witless, wicked, foolish and simple. In "They Took Flight," he is greedy, tyrannical and wicked. In "Superintendent of the See-Saw," he is witless, fickle, jealous, sadistic and self-tormenting. In "Aïcha—So, What Was Your Father the Ogre Doing?" he is clueless, cruel, slovenly, disgusting.[35]

This is astonishing. What strikes this reader is not the ingenuity and resourcefulness of the woman in these tales, but the comprehensively negative depiction of the male figures. Despite the implication that these folktales in some sense reflect a widespread social reality of wicked and tyrannical men in the Maghreb, one should, as Augustus Richard Norton warns, be reluctant to conclude that the "dearth of political freedom" in the region is "a cultural trait," when rather it is "the result of specific government policies and practices, specifically the tendency to closely monitor, regulate, restrict, and, when necessary, annihilate associational life."[36] Authoritarian rule may be the norm in the Arab world, but as Norton insists, this is "precisely not a cultural artifact, but a modern condition" (32), with its origins in the European colonial era, which established the idea of the modern state and offered a Western political model for government.

The theme of the problem of authoritarianism in Tunisian society and the persistence of an outmoded style of patriarchal rule in the private sphere are central to *Halfaouine*, where the graffito on the wall acknowledges that the president of Tunisia is an autocrat, and Noura's father Si Azzouz is depicted as a neopatriarch. Si Azzouz brings in the money (we see him in his shop; and we see him bring home the basket filled with vegetables, which the women will prepare), while the women of his household are not wage-earners in the public sphere. We see how the patriarchy confines women to the home. It offers them a bargain: the patriarch will pay the "rent," as it were, in exchange for which those who live under his roof "tax free" (i.e., the women and children) will forfeit any right to hold him accountable.

The ogre in the tale that Lella Jamila tells Noura (various aspects of which the boy will visualize at certain moments in the film) refers unequivocally, on one level, to the sexual danger posed to children by men, and on another level, to Si Azzouz as a forbidding figure of interdiction, and by extension, it refers to the police state. Unlike the tale as it is recounted by Bouhdiba in *L'imaginaire maghrébin*, the story Noura's mother tells him puts the emphasis not on Aïcha but on the ogre's predilection for little boys (indeed, in the "original" tale—if one can even speak of such a thing—Aïcha has no "little brother," and no mention is made of the ogre's especial interest in "little boys like [Noura]"):

NOURA. What's the ogre doing with the blood?
LELLA JAMILA. He's tracking the blood, drop by drop, to Aïcha's house. Then he takes hold of her little brother and scrunches him all up.
NOURA. Why does he need a golden needle?
LELLA JAMILA. Because Aïcha's a virgin. The ogre knows it's forbidden. If he touches a virgin, his hands will burn. If he lifts her dress, he'll go blind. The ogre is only interested in children of your age. Little boys like you, he scrunches down to the last bone!

Lella Jamila/(Boughedir) freely adapts a known Tunisian folktale to suit the purpose at hand, just as we shall hear Salouha do later, after the circumcision ceremony, when she tells a tale to a group of small children gathered around her in the courtyard, about an uncle who is really "a robber of hearts":

SALOUHA. The man isn't their uncle. He's a wizard. A robber of hearts. He goes out each night looking for small children. When he finds one, he puts him in his bag, and takes him to a deserted place. There, he looks at the child's palm for the mark. If he finds a ring there, or a white dot on his iris, he kills the child and rips his heart out. Then he burns him to find the treasure hidden in the earth.

There is a sexual theme in the film developed around Salouha's "hidden treasure," which she hopes the sheikh will discover; and we can see how she weaves her own concerns into the tale, much as Lella Jamila will modify the tale about Aïcha in response to her concerns about Noura's budding sexuality (which might attract the interest of men and throw its proper development off course—as we infer happened in the case of Khemaïs).

The economic and psychological dependency that the neopatriarchy imposes on women is wittily illustrated in the scene of Salouha laboriously

LAUGHTER IN THE DARK

FIGURE 3.6 Latifa urges Salouha (Fatma Ben Saïdane) to act on her desire: "Go after him [Sheikh Mokhtar]! Find out where he lives!"

untying the knotted handkerchief in which she keeps the few coins that are the only money she has to her name. She instructs Noura (since she cannot leave the house alone): "Get me some cigarettes—but don't let your father see!—and buy me 200 grams of *halwa*, and a bottle of almond syrup. Hurry! I'm dying for a smoke!" She hands him a coin, which Noura looks at in disbelief: "All that, with 100 millimes?!" She replies: "It's all I have. Keep the change, and buy some chocolates for yourself."

When Leïla is banished from the household, Sheikh Mokhtar comes to pick her up, in order to sell her to another bourgeois household (the theme of poor or orphaned girls who are in this fashion sold into servitude is the theme of Bouzid's 2002 film, *Poupées d'argile/Clay Dolls*). Salouha, who has long had a crush on the sheikh, watches him bargaining with Si Azzouz over the severance pay he is owed, and she urgently mutters under her breath, but out of his earshot: "Take me with you, Sheikh! Take me! Ask me to go with you!" Latifa, standing next to her, whispers: "Go after him! Find out where he lives!" The lovesick spinster explains: "I couldn't! He must make the first step."

By the film's end, however, even Salouha will find the courage to defy the Father and "make the first step" toward her self-liberation from the constraining rules of the neopatriarchal system that keeps her in a position of female subordination to masculine prerogatives. As her sister-in-law Latifa is wont to do, she announces that she is going out for her "injection"—a (slightly vulgar) reference to the male company she seeks. The film's feminist discourse thus rests on the assumption that men are necessary—desirable, even—but that the male-dominated system itself, like the "strongman" leadership of nearly every Arab country in the world, is a fact of life for which no satisfactory alternative can even be envisioned.

Laughter in the Dark

Toward the end of the film, after the circumcision ceremony, Salih and Noura sit in a café on Halfaouine Square. "Stop looking gloomy," Salih tells his young friend. "You'll miss your family, when you leave. Look at me: I'm alone—no children; no family—but I can't fly away. My wings have been clipped." He takes a bottle of Vicks® cough medicine from an inside pocket of his waistcoat, and smiles: "Luckily, I've this friend." He pours some of the *boukha* (fig alcohol) from the bottle into his tea glass and drinks. Then, addressing the bottle, he sings: "You help me laugh, cry, forget, and chatter / I've given you my all, but what have you given me? / You wicked bottle, you dear old bottle."[37]

The darker meaning of the title of his new play, "Laughter in the Dark," is thus revealed.[38] When later in the evening Noura escorts his now very tipsy friend home, and on the way Salih edits the graffito on the wall ("Our minds, without the President's"), the shoemaker-poet, looking up at the graffito, will repeat the phrase, "I've given you my all." The film's indictment of the country's leadership is unequivocal: Bourguiba–Ben Ali betrayed the Tunisian people, who, whether they were coerced or gave their support willingly, now understand that their leader's will to power, in Naccache's words describing Bourguiba, was more selfish than altruistic. The president's passion has been "to control, to command, to dominate others," and he has had no scruples about using "brute force, resorting even to murder." Like Khemaïs, who gave his all to Ali and now perceives his vulnerability was exploited by Ali for his own selfish ends, Ben Ali—the son of Ali, as it were—has done the same to the Tunisian people.³⁹ As a coming-of-age story about Noura's "choices" (i.e., as an allegory about Tunisia's "destiny" following Independence), the film articulates two possibilities: Noura can end up like Salih (exuberant and affectionate, but alone, without children or family, his "wings clipped"); or he can become like Khemaïs (angry and resentful, driven by a sense of grievance, and bent on the ruthless acquisition of personal power).

If *Halfaouine* is depressed about the situation in Tunisia, it insists that all hope is not lost. The film itself might have been called *Laughter in the Dark*, for it seeks to offer humor and eroticism as the best responses to political repression, while attempting also to examine the nature and the causes of the darkness that it sees slowly enveloping Tunisian society. Viewing the film now, more than twenty years after it was made, one is forced to acknowledge that its answer to the police state amounts to no more than a minor form of rebellion—a way of avoiding the father's anger when it is provoked. Laughter and eroticism are merely survival techniques. As a real defense against tyranny, they were truly ineffectual.

The "eroticism" that Boughedir celebrates in *Halfaouine* has a correlative in Tunisia's embrace of consumerism. Many of those who were able to participate in Ben Ali's "economic miracle" embraced consumerism with a vengeance. Indeed, Ben Ali's "political economy of repression" (Hibou) was used by him as a form of blackmail: the majority of Tunisians believed a stable economy was far more important than the protection of their human rights. In May 2002, for example, Ben Ali, who was due to retire in 2004 after fifteen years in office, proposed a constitutional amendment that would allow him to stand for a further two terms. In a referendum that was condemned by human rights groups inside and outside the country as rigged, he won 99.52 percent approval for the constitutional changes. Souhayr Belhassen, Vice-President of the Tunisian Human Rights League, dismissed the referendum as a "masquerade" and "indecent," because "even in the craziest dictatorial regimes one dares not announce such figures."⁴⁰ The online newsletter, *CPJ* (Committee to Protect Journalists) reported in its "Attacks on the Press in 2002" that "through a combination of censorship and intimidation, Tunisian authorities have all but stamped out independent voices in the country's media, with the exception of a few courageous dissident journalists who publish their work underground, on the Internet, or in Western newspapers." Not surprisingly, "those who write critically about political affairs have faced an array of official reprisals: physical attacks, imprisonment, the banning of their publications, the withholding of state advertising, anonymous telephone threats, cut phone and fax lines, the removal of accreditation, and travel restrictions. The result is a press that—although mostly privately owned—is almost completely subservient to the regime."[41]

The future envisioned for Noura is bleak. As we have already observed, his tyrannical father has threatened to "murder" him, if and when he should come down from the roof. The only positive male character in the film, we have noted, is an alcoholic bachelor (i.e., his usefulness as a role model for Noura, Halfaouine's representative citizen, is limited); and by the end of the film, he will be incarcerated by a paranoid police state that will always regard the artist as a threat to its authority.[42] Salih's status in the community of Halfaouine is marginal—or, in the sense Abderrezak gives the term when he refers to the "para-community," Salih is marginal to the idea of Halfaouine as an organic community of families engaged in the business of reproducing itself, as societies have done all over the world since the beginning of time. As a playwright and poet who speaks truth to power, he is a subversive figure; and to the Khemaïses of his society who find him troubling, he is most especially a threat because he is *seductive*. (Like Boughedir, who is the most French of the filmmakers of the New Tunisian Cinema in this regard, Salih understands the superior value and power of charm over the kind of boorishness and force employed by Khemaïs and the police state he serves.)[43] From the antipathy Khemaïs feels toward him, we infer that one of Salih's chief crimes is that he is lovable. He is sensitive to what a woman wants, for example, and knows how to go about getting the love he needs from her. He explains the balance of power between men and women to Noura this way: "Women always know what they want. And as the sage Sidi Ali Douaji says: they never give themselves by halves . . . it is they who decide both the time and the place!" (The film's subtitle in English reads, simply: "A man proposes, but it's the woman who disposes.")

Just as Salih is the only viable male figure of identification for Noura, so is Noura's aunt Latifa the only fully positive female figure in the film. She too is unmarried, although we should note that this fact speaks to the film's progressive, even feminist, discourse, for her divorce has liberated her from an unhappy marriage. But Salih and Latifa's future together must be postponed—and this is the only hope that the film (as an allegory about Tunisia's political present and future) can offer in the end. As he is led off to prison, the ever-optimistic poet calls out to Noura: "Tell your aunt that I've been called away. Ask her to wait!"

CHAPTER FOUR

Sexual Allegories of National Identity
Bezness (Nouri Bouzid, 1992)

The term *bezness* is a generic expression in Tunisia for someone resourceful, or the activities of such a person, who tries to set up a "small business" with no capital at all. The term is associated with the activity of hustling, but is not necessarily pejorative. Bouzid's film, *Bezness*, is an astonishingly daring work that directly confronts the subject of male Tunisians who work as sex hustlers on the streets and beaches of Tunisia's tourist towns and is additionally interesting for the way in which it invites the viewer to see the film as emblematic and allegorical of Tunisia's precarious economic and cultural position in a rapidly globalizing world.

The movie follows the trajectories of three characters in the old city of Sousse—a handsome young hustler, Roufa (Abdellatif Kechiche); his fiancée, Khomsa (Ghalia Lacroix); and a French photographer, Fred (Jacques Penot). Like a professional Orientalist, the Frenchman wanders about the city, avidly taking photographs of its inhabitants. Khomsa becomes his favorite photographic subject, as he finds himself touched by her and drawn toward her ambivalence. She is half-attracted and half-repelled by his increasingly relentless pursuit of her, which is both a seduction and, it comes to seem, a perversion.

SEXUAL ALLEGORIES OF NATIONAL IDENTITY

FIGURE 4.1 Roufa (Abdellatif Kechiche) cruises a female tourist.

Eventually, the Frenchman (who is only once referred to by name in the film) is able to lure Khomsa out of the walled city where she lives, and he drives her to his hotel suite in the *nouvelle ville*. Throughout the film, in snatches of interior monologue and to her friends, Khomsa expresses her doubts about the Frenchman—What are his real intentions? Will he seduce and then abandon her? How similar to or different from a Tunisian man is he?—and at the same time, she is fascinated by him and the unnamed possibilities he seems to be offering her. She finds him beautiful and wonders if she is really tempted by the implication of her friend Ghalia's teasing suggestion: "Do you like him? It will be more than a sin! He's not even circumcised!"

Meanwhile, Roufa cruises the streets, beaches, hotel swimming pools, and nightclubs for female tourists who will pay to sleep with him. In one scene, we see that Roufa knows a police officer whom he hopes will help him get back his passport, which has been seized by the authorities. The officer shows a fatherly concern for Roufa (although of course as a police officer—that is, as a representative of the powerfully repressive state apparatus—he offers Roufa a highly ambivalent figure of identification). As soon as his passport is returned to him, Roufa intends to go to Germany, where, with the help of a former lover, an older German man who lives in Tunisia, he will get a job and save enough money to marry Khomsa. Already, in an irony that is typical of the film, he has bought Khomsa a ring with money he has made from sleeping with European tourists. The officer urges Roufa to stop having sex with men, for the risk of contracting the HIV virus has become too great: "If you had become a tour guide, and given up [male] prostitution, it would have been better for you.... But you only think about leaving! You'll end up on your knees! A blind man falls... And then you'll want only one thing: to come back!"

The officer, becoming increasingly exasperated, shouts at Roufa: "Go on dreaming about leaving! There are those who've died, those who are in hiding, those who are begging. And there are those who've caught AIDS. There are those who've become drug dealers, those who've gone to prison, and those who've been deported. Only one out of every hundred is saved!" Roufa begs the policeman to change the subject: "I don't want to hear about it! I don't care!" he almost sobs. "Don't counsel an orphan about how to take care of his soul!" He reassures the officer that he no longer sleeps with men. Women, he says, are especially attracted to him, making the work relatively easy. Moreover, he uses condoms now. When the officer, despite himself, remarks admiringly on Roufa's success as a hustler, Roufa jokes, in a very telling phrase: "We are the national wealth! Good for export!" Then he again asks the officer when he might get his passport back.[1]

The hustling scenario, which of course is a reality for many young Tunisian men, is in this film both an emblem and allegory of the bigger picture of Tunisia as a third-world country prostituting itself in order to survive in a globalized world, in which the economically weak and culturally disadvantaged find themselves nearly overwhelmed, their native or "traditional" identity compromised or eclipsed. The tourist industry represents the neocolonial grip of free-market capitalism on Tunisia's destiny, a destiny it shares with all third-world countries in that, precisely, the supreme unifying force of contemporary history is now global. Roufa's story is an allegory of the embattled situation of the Tunisian/public third-world culture and society, which reflects the world system, in which there are always those who are oppressed and those who are the agents of oppression. If, as Jameson observed, "American bankers hold the levers of the world system," Tunisia's dictator holds the levers of the Tunisian national system, and in turn, ordinary fathers hold the levers of the repressive system of control that is the neopatriarchal family. In the psychoanalytic metaphor, the Law of the Father is reproduced at every level. But ordinary fathers are powerless to mitigate the destructive impact of economic liberalism on the traditional family, and young men like Roufa find themselves adrift, without a proper place in either the familial order or the economic order. Whether or not we wish to ascribe to "American bankers" (and their clients—corrupt, third-world dictators) the control of "the levers of the world system," we recognize that in the metaphors of Bouzid's film, it is the paying customer—the tourist—who, in the final analysis, confers identity. Roufa would not be a hustler, but for the tourists who make his *bezness* possible.

"Self" and "Other"

Some of the film's principal themes are organized around the signs of gender and sexuality, as they can be identified in the opening shots. Through the activities of the Frenchman, the Sousse medina is represented as a body to be discovered—penetrated, photographed, investigated. Its labyrinthine streets, its courtyards, its shuttered houses also have their correlative in the city's inhabitants, who are veiled, or silent, or who speak a language the Frenchman does not understand, or who perform roles (such as "shopkeeper," or "hustler") that imply there is another—"true," "real," "authentic"—identity underneath or elsewhere, which is inaccessible to the Frenchman, because he is a foreigner here. But these natives are not so different, the film says. There are ways in which they are the same as he is; but they are different.

This is why the film contains the motif of the double, which is repeated in the motif of homosexuality. The Frenchman is not only an allusion to Tunisia's French colonial past, which made Tunisia—or a significant portion of its educated middle classes—a nearly bicultural and bilingual society, he is a representative more generally of the West. Moreover, he can be seen to represent capitalism itself, which is omnivorous and predatory: he photographs men and women, old people, young people, boys and girls, separately and together . . . there is almost nothing of this exotic Orient that the Frenchman's hungry camera does not seek to capture, in order to make a photograph for sale. (We infer that he works for a magazine that is published in Paris.) The Frenchman loves *looking*. His desire is to *see*. He is both a voyeur and a fetishist (as we find out when we see his photograph-filled hotel suite), whose sexuality—if we measure it by a Freudian norm—is no less alienated than that of Roufa, who believes he can sleep with men and women of all ages *and* love Khomsa, the ultimate prize whom he expects to be a virgin when they marry. Khomsa expresses her doubts that Roufa's subjectivity—his sense of who he is—will not be harmed and confused by this commodification of his body and by his insistence that personal identity can be located somewhere completely outside the realm of sexual desire.

From Freud, we know that the love of looking—scopophilia—is a component of the sexual drive that exists independently of the erotogenic zones. In the case of the Frenchman in *Bezness*, the act of looking itself as a source of pleasure is clearly represented as an erotic activity, although, in the allegorical reading, what the Frenchman does—his "taking [of] other people as objects, subjecting them to a curious and controlling gaze"[2]—is marked as an Orientalist enterprise, which in the late twentieth century can only refer to the neocolonialism of a Western-led globalization.

The film has a bifurcated point of view. Quite appropriately, the narrator (by which I mean the film itself or "Bouzid" as a signifier designating the narrating sensibility) has a foot in each of two worlds—France/Europe/the West and Tunisia/the Orient/the Third World. The film appears at first to understand the Frenchman and to understand Roufa and Khomsa as well, giving nearly equal time to the point of view of each, and yet it preserves the final mystery of each—the mystery that each character beholds not only in the other, but in him- or herself. It is perhaps the image of the photograph that expresses most eloquently this mystery of identity—the paradox or conundrum that the *self* can only be discovered and known through the *other*—which the film treats as its central theme.

From Khomsa's point of view, the photograph is an emblem of her alienation, of her self *as* other, as described by Roland Barthes in *Camera Lucida*, when he writes that "the Photograph is the advent of myself as other: a cunning dissociation of consciousness from identity."[3] "No doubt it is metaphorically that I derive my existence from the photographer. But though this dependence is an imaginary one (and from the purest image-repertoire), I experience it with the anguish of an uncertain filiation: an image—my image—will be generated: will I be born from an antipathetic individual or from a 'good sort'?" (11). Barthes goes on to remark: "[It is] odd that no one has thought of the *disturbance* (to civilization) which this new action

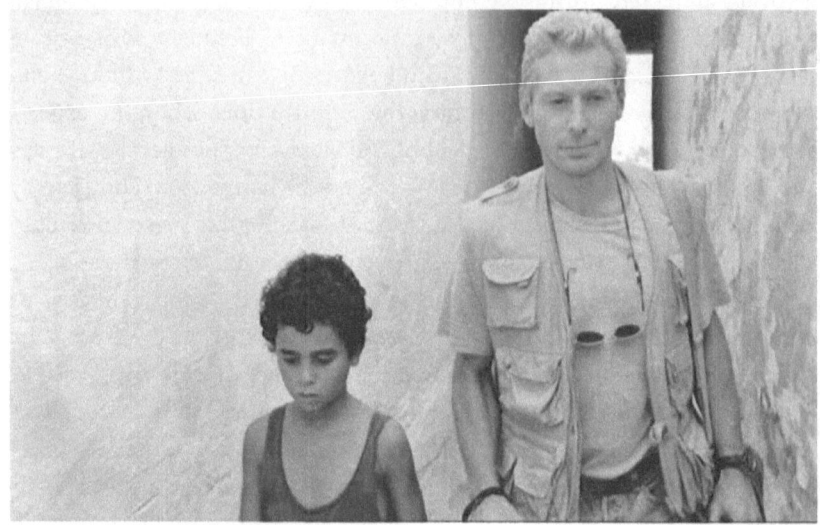

FIGURE 4.2 "Navette" (Ahmed Ragoubi) accompanies Fred (Jacques Penot) on one of his photographic forays into the medina.

[photography] causes.... This disturbance is ultimately one of ownership. Law has expressed it in its way: to whom does the photograph belong?" (12–13).

Roufa and Khomsa's anxieties—which are essentially the same (for these characters are two expressions of the same side of the self/other dialectic that the film explores)—can be summarized as deriving from the relationship of the Tunisian to his or her Western other, articulated here by Bouzid in a story about the twin mainstays of modern identity: sexuality and the image (or sexuality in the field of vision). The Frenchman is not unaware of his role in this new development in the evolution of Khomsa's subjectivity, occasioned by "the Photograph." When he discovers the meaning of her name (Khomsa—which is related to *khamsa*, the Arabic word for the number five—is the name for "The Hand of Fatma," a common protective symbol in the Middle East and North Africa, used to ward off the "evil eye"), he says to himself: "I have stolen your image. I am a thief!"

The film begins from his point of view. As he plunges into the medina, a labyrinth of narrow streets and dead ends, a neighborhood where every door and window he passes is firmly closed—the camera dollying forward, like Alain Resnais' famously probing and insistent camera in *Hiroshima, mon amour* (1959), a film to which *Bezness* bears a remarkable resemblance in its preoccupation with cultural and sexual difference, and with the question of whether, in the final analysis, it is possible to know the other,[4] the Frenchman reflects, in an interior monologue that we hear in intimate close-up: "The deeper I go, the more I ask myself questions. And the longer I stay here, the more I feel the journey is an all-consuming one. Everything is different. The *inside* intrigues me. Everything is veiled. The veil that we wear means nothing ... it's the *invisible* veil that intrigues me ... I just can't pierce it. Behind every look is a mystery ... behind every closed door, a city, a world that eludes me. How do they find their way around?"

In the opening shots of the film, almost the first thing the Frenchman encounters, built into the wall of a house, is a carved relief sculpture representing the "evil eye." To each side of the eye is a fish, and above it, another fish. He pauses for a moment to look at the stone plaque, apparently unaware of its possible meanings. This hieroglyph functions much like the "No Trespassing" sign that begins Orson Welles's *Citizen Kane* (1941). Not only does the eye have a talismanic function—to ward off evil and protect the inhabitants of the medina from intruders who might bring harm to them—it is a warning to the outsider, the blue-eyed Frenchman, to *beware*. Indeed, in some cultures in which light-colored eyes are unusual, people with blue eyes are thought to bestow the curse, whether intentionally or unintentionally. The sign on the wall can be seen to refer reflexively to the Frenchman who, (also) with his camera eye, is marked as a potential threat to the inhabitants of this space.[5]

Following the opening shots of the film, when the Frenchman emerges from the streets of the old city and onto the beach, we see him spying on a young woman wearing a veil (the sign, presumably, that she is local and Muslim). She stops, puts down her bag, and then suddenly and quite matter-of-factly disrobes, removing her blouse, long skirt, and veil. She is wearing a bikini under her clothes, and with an unselfconscious air suggesting that she is a regular visitor to the beach (and which her visible tan line would seem to confirm), she turns and walks toward the water. From his vantage point, hidden behind a beach kiosk, the Frenchman furtively aims his camera and takes several quick shots of the woman, who is unaware that she is being photographed. The Frenchman continues his photographing on a more populous section of the beach, where his attention is caught by the image of two female bathers, just a few feet apart, coming out of the water—one, a topless (evidently European) woman, her shoulders pulled back, striding with a confidence that suggests she is defiantly asserting her right to bare her breasts; and the other, a veiled, Tunisian woman in a dark blouse and ankle-length skirt that clings wetly to her legs, angrily and embarrassedly thrashing her way with difficulty past the European woman, who glances at her, as if in surprise and pity.

In the next couple of shots, Bouzid continues this motif of the European/the Tunisian and his or her double. We see two blond, nearly identical European men in bathing suits. They visually scan the beach, as if looking for something, their heads moving in unison, twin-like. (The framing of this shot suggests that the Frenchman notices them but does not take their photograph—perhaps because he rather resembles them physically and recognizes their voyeurism as similar to his own, and, simply, the Europeans do not excite his desire in the way the Tunisians do.) The Frenchman aims his camera instead at a blonde, European woman in a deck chair, as she is approached by a group of Tunisian hustlers, who greet her in English. Beyond this scene, we see two, good-looking, young Tunisian men coming out of the water. They resemble each other, much as the two blond (I want to say German) men resemble one another, with whom they present a striking contrast.[6] The Tunisian men, walking toward the camera, are lean, brown, and muscular, their genitalia outlined by their bathing suits. The European men (who, perhaps significantly, are seen only from behind), are fair and slightly soft, their bodies lacking in muscular definition. There is no doubt that Bouzid is creating a sexualized mise-en-scène in which the theme of hustling is inscribed in images that acknowledge that sex and commerce, the First and Third worlds, and something like fascination with the other are all dialectically linked in Tunisia's tourist industry.

Tourism, Sex, Money

The scenes described above lay out the film's core obsessions, much as Hédi Khélil does with nearly identical preoccupations in his astonishing and scandalous little book, *Sens/Jouissance: Tourisme, erotisme, argent dans deux fictions coloniales d'André Gide* (1988). Based on his graduate thesis, "Des rapports entre colonisateurs et colonisés: Lecture/écriture de deux fictions gidiennes, *Si le grain ne meurt* et 'Carnets d'égypte,'" which he defended at the University of Tunis in 1980, Khélil's book confronts the same nexus of tourism, sex, and money that, with similar audacity, Bouzid explores in *Bezness*. Khélil takes up his subject with originality and daring and with a portion of explicit autobiographical investment that one would never expect to find in a university thesis, least of all one that was successfully defended in a third-world, Arab country.

Khélil, who grew up in Sousse (this same beach town where, as we have noted, Bouzid sets his film), begins the description of his project thus: "In 1893, André Gide sojourned in two North African colonies dependent on France. *Tourism* and *pederasty*. Twenty-six years later, he decides to set down on paper his memories of his adventures in Tunisia and Algeria.... Today, a 'colonized' reader. His country: Tunisia, former colony of France, *officially independent* and with *a touristic vocation*.... A European author and an Arab reader. Colonizer and colonized. A standard, classic encounter?"[7] Khélil describes how, when he found Gide's "Carnets d'égypte,"[8] he devoured everything written by Gide that had in any way to do with North Africa (*Les nourritures terrestres*; *Amyntas*—"Mopsus"—"Feuilles de route"—"Le renoncement au voyage"), but how none of it really grabbed him, because the question that had begun to interest him—*pederasty*, which he had found scenes of in "Carnets d'égypte"—was so sublimated as to be for all intents and purposes nonexistent.[9]

Khélil remarks that he was put off Gide's *L'immoraliste*, partly because he was unwilling to identify with Michel, the narrator. In that novel, the line between the narrator and the author is blurred, and it is far from clear whether Michel's position represents Gide's own. This left *Si le grain ne meurt*, an autobiographical work which, alongside "Carnets d'égypte," Khélil found to be "preponderantly" concerned with pederasty. Khélil observes that none of the pioneering works of postcolonial studies confronts the sexual element of the colonial situation: "Sexual colonization, no doubt because it takes a more subtle route, has been either simply conjured away by sociologists and historians, or considered as some sort of substitute for economic and political colonization (which is just another way of making it disappear)" (17).[10] And Khélil notes that while biographies of Gide cannot altogether avoid discussion of his homosexuality, and some, like Dr. Jean Delay's *La jeunesse d'André Gide* even provide a wealth of detail about his relations with adolescent Arabs, they do not address the *colonial* dimension of those relations.

SEXUAL ALLEGORIES OF NATIONAL IDENTITY

FIGURE 4.3 Khomsa (Ghalia Lacroix) feels ambivalent about the persistent attentions of the French photographer.

Khélil's book is fascinating precisely because it does examine the "colonial dimension" of Gide's sexual encounters with Arabs in Egypt and North Africa, and also because it is written by an Arab who acknowledges his own desire in that Orientalist dialectic that can be found to persist between European and Arab today. Khélil considers the impact of the colonial legacy on his personal and national identity, which he insists is inseparable from questions about his own desire and sexuality, and which is inscribed in a neocolonial relationship that is very apparent in what he calls Tunisia's "touristic vocation."[11] And Bouzid's film, as I have suggested, does the same thing. The Frenchman in *Bezness* and the Tunisian couple Khomsa and Roufa are—all three—inseparable aspects of the question of the sexual/national identity of the film's viewer/narrator; and the questions Khélil asks about the reader/writer of the Gide text (what he calls *la fiction gidienne*) are in effect the same ones posed by Bouzid in his film. Khélil wonders where one might draw the line between the self and the other:

> Coming back to tourism and the myth [of an "Orient" constructed by the West, of which the tourist postcard is the eminent emblem]—what have

I tried to do, but seek to identify myself with Gide, to recognize myself in him, make the same journey, follow his itinerary, and entreat him sometimes to confer a certain legitimacy on my arguments, at the risk—the serious risk—of occasionally speaking about myself and quite forgetting Gide and his text? How far can one take this specular rapport between "colonized" and colonizer? Can the "colonized" know something about his own desires only by deciphering those of the European? To what limit can I push this inquiry into my own reactions as a reader confronting the Gide text? Wouldn't this [going to/beyond some limit] be committing to a crossing-over that can never be satisfied? Wouldn't this be running the risk of making it a master-game of rules and effects? (128)[12]

Khélil admits that, reading Gide, he finds he is caught up in a play of identifications that makes it impossible for him to recognize himself as either "European" (as he identifies with Gide the author) or in any sense purely "Tunisian" (as he identifies with the colonized subject in Gide's text)—these terms, "European" and "Tunisian," in any case, being constructions that reveal their radical instability as signifiers as soon as one attempts to define them. He is a hybrid creature:

> But the *jouissance* that Gideian pederasty stimulates—is it so complete? Are there not resentments that at times, *après coup*, break my identification with the European's desire? In fact, the perversion of the European's gaze (his voyeurism) and his sexual neurosis (pederasty) never go all the way, never exhaust their pleasure, but oscillate between two attitudes: fascination and repulsion. I feel an intense pleasure in opening myself up to the allure of pederasty. But I tell myself that my own *jouissance*—the *jouissance* of the "colonized"—is nevertheless triggered by a fiction in which sexual colonization is at play, a kind of narrative that ought to revolt me, and not give me pleasure. (130)

Khélil adds: "Now, quite properly, indignation arises at the discovery that I find nothing scandalous in the fact that Mohamed or Mériem serve the sexual requests of the European, since I feel closer to Gide the intellectual than to the colonized. And the pederasty narrative—deep down, I want nothing to contradict it" (130–131).

But toward the end of his book, Khélil will conclude that Gide, unlike Khélil himself (a colonized subject), will return to—assuming he ever really deviated from—his essentially Western character and identity. Khélil reflects that Gide never did understand the problems of the colonized and remained profoundly a European. His frequent stays in North Africa did not shake what he held onto most tenaciously, his "*occidentalité*." Gide's last writings on the Maghreb, Khélil observes, reveal that: "Ultimately, Africa is nothing in Gide's oeuvre. [But] pederasty is always there. That is the *vérité gidienne*, and not Tunisia, Algeria, or Morocco. Africa is *counterfeit*. No more *speculation* is possible. It is *bankrupt*" (147).[13] But the colonized subject remains forever marked by the colonial encounter. Indeed, he is transformed by it; he is forged within a complex matrix of Oriental/Occidental identifications that will constitute his very identity.

In *Bezness*, we see a similar trajectory made by Bouzid's camera across the lives of the film's principal characters. Perhaps nowhere in the film is the question of personal/national identity made more explicit than in scenes involving mirrors, of which there are several.

The Mirror and Identity

When we first see Roufa, he is bare-chested and still wet from his morning shower. He goes over to a cracked fragment of mirror fixed to the wall of a communal space in the house where he lives with members of his extended family and (we discover later) Khomsa's family, and he looks at himself. We will learn that his father is dead, and we see that he appears to have voluntarily filled the position of the head of the household. But there is some ambiguity about how far Roufa's authority extends, or how much it is appreciated, for when he criticizes one of his sisters for "working for other people," his mother tells him not to interfere. It soon becomes clear that his perhaps too heavy-handed exercise of neopatriarchal authority within the household is resented, for upon seeing him, a male member of his family (a brother?) will facetiously ask: "Did his majesty sleep well?" And later, Roufa will get into a nasty argument with his sisters about their general comportment—that one of them smokes cigarettes and another walks the streets as a prostitute and that they do not pay enough attention to whether he always has freshly laundered and pressed clothes to wear. His brother(?) will accuse him on this occasion of "ruining everything" and tells him to "stop playing the cock."[14]

Roufa clearly represents the postcolonial man who, despite his country having gained its independence many years before, knows and feels most keenly that he is caught in a neocolonial bind that puts him at a disadvantage. In *Le Maghreb à l'épreuve de la colonisation*, Daniel Rivet, echoing Jacques Berque, describes how the colonized man will often cling to and emphasize certain values, institutions, and discourses he believes constitute the essence of his identity:

> Colonization has exacerbated the Maghrebi man's masculinity. Deprived of the ability to have his own history, the native compensates by folding himself back into his faith and his sexuality. The woman becomes for him the repository of the values of the conquered nationality. The family offers itself as a refuge where the wounds to his narcissism inflicted by the colonial situation might be tended. If the confining of women is stressed, it is in order to remove them as objects of the conquerors' desire.[15]

Rivet even quotes Berque's remark describing the Maghreb as the "land of the frustrated impulse" and notes that "colonization accentuates the separation of the sexes in town, where contact between the communities is higher" (303). He writes that, according to Eugène Fromentin, for example, "from the moment the Europeans began to stare at the women dallying on the balconies and roof terraces of Algiers, the men forbade the women to disport themselves there"; and among other examples he offers, records that Édouard Michaux-Bellaire noted the same interdiction in Salé (Morocco) during the 1920s, "to thwart the tourists' voyeurism" (303). Rivet also quotes Sliman al-Jadoui, a *destourien* (a first-generation Tunisian nationalist belonging to the Destour party), who summarized the Tunisian woman's symbolic function in the struggle for Independence, thus: "Nationality is a secret protected within the women, who remain the bedrock of our social foundation" (304).[16]

Roufa has a proprietary attitude toward Khomsa, and his wish to marry her is bound up with his anxious desire to consolidate an identity for himself as a Tunisian male. The first time the film shows them together is revelatory of Roufa's perhaps unconscious motives. He meets Khomsa on the stairs as he is about to go out and asks if she will iron his clothes. She reminds him that they are not yet married and adds the warning that she may still change her mind. When he says to her, "I adore you!," she snaps back: "Save that for the tourists!" She strongly disapproves of his hustling activities, which he tries to present to her as a legitimate means of making money—money he is earning in order to marry her and put their future life together on a secure financial footing. A little later in the narrative, in a conversation similar to this one, Khomsa indicates that she is fed up: "This pretence of having 'a plan' doesn't cut it anymore. All you do is dream. It's a sham. You're a hustler, and what's more, you're dragging my brother into it!" Khomsa is very fond of Roufa, and may even love him, but one evening when Roufa brings a Dutch woman back to the house, she becomes nearly hysterical with humiliation and rage, and Roufa is forced to take the woman back to her hotel.

The scene reveals much about the real dynamics not only of the bind in which Khomsa and Roufa find themselves but also—in the allegorical reading—of the bind in which Tunisia itself is caught. As the country tries, from an economically embattled position, to participate in the flows and exchanges of capital that are absolutely vital to its survival in a globalized world, Tunisia quite properly seeks also to maintain its dignity as a society with a culture and national identity befitting a sovereign nation in charge of its own destiny. It is Khomsa's brother Aziz who tips her off that Roufa has brought the Dutch woman back to the house (in a silent and sorrowful gesture, Aziz enters Khomsa's room and closes the window that opens onto the courtyard below, so that his sister will not have to see her fiancé and the woman enter the house together); and after Roufa departs on his motorcycle with the embarrassed woman, we see Aziz, still in Khomsa's room, standing beside the mirror on the wall, his head bowed in shame.

Khomsa angrily tells her brother: "Go ahead, you, too! Follow him, until you become strangers in your own country!" Her phrasing recalls the title of Julia Kristeva's book, *Strangers to Ourselves*, in which Kristeva reflects on the psychological and social trauma that is often experienced by the foreigner. Kristeva, however, believes that in the late twentieth century, tourism, migrant labor, and modern mass communications have made foreigners of us all—it is no longer possible for an individual, a group, or a nation to remain entirely isolated in a cocoon of particularity—and that this, surely, is a good thing. Clearly, though, if one becomes a foreigner in one's *own* country—in the sense Khomsa means it, of losing even one's primary (national) identity—the task of coming to terms with "difference" and the "other," which being a foreigner implies, will be more difficult, because

FIGURE 4.4 Khomsa warns her brother Aziz (Adel Boukadida) that hustling will eventually make him feel like a stranger in his own country.

the sense of self against which the other is formed is radically unstable. How can Khomsa know if Roufa loves her—loves her above all others—if he performs the act of lovemaking (or sex, "performed" to resemble lovemaking) every day with European tourists?

Aziz shakes his head in distress and flees the room, as Khomsa approaches the mirror and looks into it. What follows is a statement of her point of view, offered in an overtly symbolic mise-en-scène: the camera pans across her room, taking in a painted frieze on the wall of a caravan of camels and their drivers crossing a desert, as we hear her interior monologue on the sound track: "Take me far away... to where no one will order me about. Let them do whatever they want with me, but not frighten me with their looks. I want to batter the ramparts of the city! And to know its secrets. All my life, I have been reduced to silence. Not a word, not a gesture. In submission to their rule. 'Khomsa, you are a girl. Have you no shame? Khomsa, lower your eyes! Khomsa, get back inside, and close the door! Khomsa, cover yourself! Put up your hair, Khomsa! You have been promised to a man.' A man (*the panning camera returns to her reflection in the mirror*) ... who confines me within four walls, as women are confined."

When she is finally "taken away" by the Frenchman, to his hotel in the *nouvelle ville* (or *ville française*, as it would also be known by the Tunisians themselves, distinguishing it from the *ville arabe*), we again hear her interior monologue: "What will he think? You have your universe . . . and I have mine. *Everything* separates us." When, very nervously, she enters his room, and sees all the photographs he has taken of her, she remarks to herself: "He's mad about taking my picture!" Then, looking at herself in one of the several mirrors in the room, says aloud to herself (in Arabic): "One day, an important photographer knocked on my door. He wanted to take me to Paris with him. (*At this moment, the Frenchman enters the frame.*) He departed, and left me behind." She turns away from the mirror, to face him, and says: "A foreigner. A transient."

The uncomprehending Frenchman tries to caress her cheek, but she pulls away from him and turns to face the terrace and look out at the sea. "The whole world watches me. Not like you, Roufa . . . Roufa, the hustler. It's better that I should remain an old maid, than find myself in your bed." Her voice rises in defiance: "You will never lock me up! What do they have that is so much better, your tourists? I could beat them all!" The Frenchman gently puts a hand on her shoulder, but her response is ambiguous, reflecting her ambivalence. She reaches, as if to brush his hand away, but instead holds his hand in hers for a moment, as she continues: "If only there weren't this fear—this fear of people, this fear of myself."

There will be more scenes in which Khomsa looks at herself in the mirror. But Bouzid creates a symmetry in which Roufa, too, is shown regarding himself in a mirror and responding to his image in a similarly (or rather more extremely) unhappy fashion. (The Frenchman, of course, is never shown looking at himself in a mirror—although it can be said, echoing Jacques Lacan's dictum that "all sorts of things in the world behave like mirrors,"[17] that his photographs function like mirrors.) On the evening that Khomsa does not return home—because she is with the Frenchman at his hotel—Roufa becomes frantic. He searches all over the city for her (a neighbor has told him that she is "with your photographer friend, the fair-haired boy").[18] He asks his brother, "Navette": "Where does that fag friend of yours live?," but Navette does not know.[19] Finally, at his wits' end and exhausted, he stops at a bar in the new town and goes to the toilet, where he washes his face in the filthy hand basin. This lavatory, from floor to ceiling, is spectacularly dirty; the tiled walls are streaked with brown marks, and the

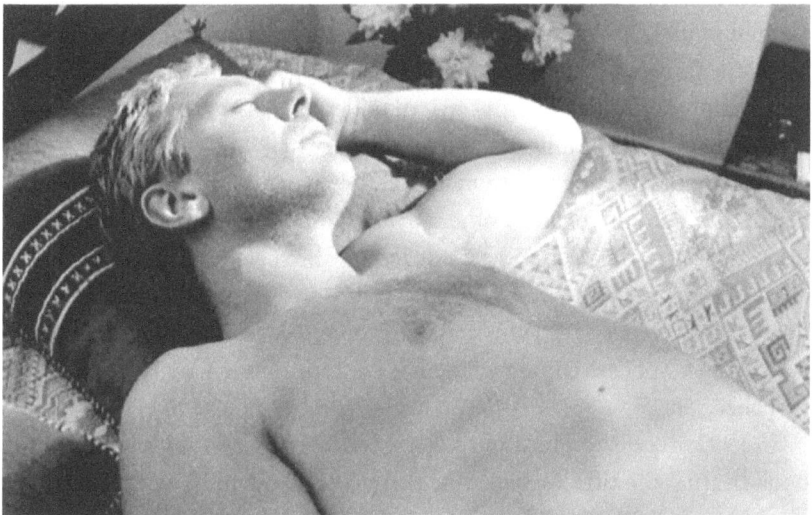

FIGURE 4.5 Khomsa thinks the Frenchman is "beautiful, almost feminine."

door is stained with mildew. When he looks at himself in the mirror, which amplifies the hellish wretchedness of the room, he sees an abject figure staring back at him. And when he tries to leave, the doorknob comes off in his hand! He returns to the mirror, looks at his reflection for another, extended moment, and then smashes the mirror with his fist and howls in despair.

The symbolism of such scenes is obvious and needs no comment, although it is worth noting that Roufa's distress is exacerbated by the Frenchman's pursuit of Khomsa, whose recent behavior strikes at the very core of Roufa's identity as a Tunisian male.

Sexual Allegories of National Identity, and the Dream of Liberation

According to an influential trend in contemporary psychoanalytic theory, the primary way in which it is understood that individual identity is conferred is through the general law of culture that Lacan called the "Name of the Father." It is the agency (not to be confused with the "real" father) that institutes and maintains the law and imposes a sexual identity on the subject. In all dramatic, narrative films—which, because they are representational and are therefore inherently allegorical—this psychoanalytic law of culture is often figured in stories involving "real" fathers. In several of the films of the New Tunisian Cinema, quite remarkably, we see the question of Tunisian national/cultural identity inscribed in allegories about young men and women with complicated, or troubled, sexual identities and in stories about fathers who attempt to maintain the law and impose a sexual identity on their children (or on others over whom they claim authority). As I have suggested, these films, half a dozen of which are notable for being the most daring ever to come out of the Arab world, express some of the difficulties experienced by Tunisia as a postcolonial—and perhaps we should add, Arab—society coping with the Western-dominated imperatives of globalization.

In 1992, five years after Bourguiba was ousted by Ben Ali, a curious little book bearing the title, *Le syndrome Bourguiba*, was published in Tunis. The book is an indictment of Bourguiba and the "social system" that the author, Aziz Krichen, believes Tunisia's first president personified. He writes that it is a system marked by "immaturity" and "underdevelopment" on nearly every level of national life, including, disastrously and most crucially, the way in which fathers and sons relate to each other. Reproduced on the cover—but nowhere referred to in the book itself—is a picture of a sixth-century stele found in Kasserine, in southern Tunisia, representing the "Sacrifice of Abraham." The carved relief sculpture clearly shows Abraham poised to cut his son Isaac's throat.[20] With his left hand tightly grasping the boy's headscarf, and his right hand holding high above his head a large knife, the rather crazed-looking father is ready to do what he believes his God has asked him to do: sacrifice his son as a burnt offering—to prove his faith, which demands blind obedience to God/the (F)ather.[21]

There are many ways to interpret the story of Abraham and Isaac/Ishmael, and many ways to interpret Krichen's intentions in putting this image on the cover of his book. But for the two decades of Ben Ali's rule following Bourguiba's ouster, there was ample evidence (such as that of the Amnesty International reports) to suggest that Tunisia's politics and government continued to be marked by the castrating paternalism Krichen describes in his book; and not surprisingly, we find its allegorical correlative in Tunisia's cinema, where problematic filiation is a frequent theme.

Le syndrome Bourguiba is basically a book of political economy, but it has an unusually psychosociological slant, and begins with analyses of *Man of Ashes* and the film Bouzid made two years later, *The Golden Horseshoes*, which illustrate or reflect the "crisis of filiation" that Krichen identifies as both a cause and a symptom of Tunisia's continued economic and political "underdevelopment." Krichen describes this crisis as the inability to recognize oneself in the father and the resulting incapacity, in turn, to see oneself in the son.[22] He believes not only that Tunisia's colonial experience under the French was infantilizing and humiliating for Tunisians, but that it has had a lasting and damaging effect, and that Bourguiba's regime, following Independence, perpetuated the sense of inferiority and dependence that the people had felt under the protectorate. Krichen's style of writing at times seems melodramatic, but if we hold to the notion that Tunisian films are allegories of national identity, we can confirm that these films suggest there is a crisis in Tunisian society around questions of national/cultural identity, brought about, or exacerbated, by the authoritarianism of the neopatriarchal Father in both the public and the private sphere and by the (dialectically related) pressures of globalization.

In *Bezness*, Roufa's father is dead, but Roufa is not yet himself a father, nor has he been successful in taking his father's place in the family. We have seen how he struggles, on the one hand, to assume the patriarchal responsibilities he believes are expected of him, and how on the other hand, he yearns for some kind of personal liberation. We recall Bouzid's observation that, "our cinema is trying to destroy the edifice of the family and liberate the individual"[23]—and we see that Roufa is caught in a trap that denies him a proper and satisfactory place in society. In one brief, heartbreaking scene, Navette asks Roufa what is troubling him: "I'm worried about you. Who's getting on your case?" Roufa puts his arms around the boy and says: "You can't understand." Navette asks anxiously: "You don't want me to be around you?," to which Roufa replies, by way of explanation: "At your age, I used to go to North Beach, in the center of town. I'd go on foot—that was before all the hotels." Navette is astonished to learn that there was a time, in the not-so-distant past, when there were no big hotels in Sousse. Roufa continues: "We were the only people who lived here—us, and Khomsa's family. Our father was alive." Roufa pauses for a long moment, pondering the meaning of what he has just said. He looks at his young brother, and asks: "Do you want to be like me?" Navette nods vigorously. With gratitude, and smiling sadly, Roufa hugs the boy tightly, and to hide his emotion, buries his face in the boy's shoulder.

Bouzid invokes the father's memory in this scene in order to link it to the present social and sexual disorder of Roufa's family. Krichen is correct in his analysis that French control during the colonial era was infantilizing for Tunisians. But in the neocolonial era, in which countries like France and Germany still control the levers of the world system (as figured in *Bezness* not only by the Frenchman but also by "the German"—who, for the very reason that his role is allegorical, is never named—and by the various northern European tourists in the film), an independent nation like Tunisia discovers that the very meaning of national identity has changed—it no longer means what the nationalists who fought for independence said or thought it would mean.

When he meets a young European woman in a bar one evening, Roufa tries to hustle her, but she says frankly and with good humor: "I like men, but I don't like to be hustled!" She goes on to explain: "A good-looking guy is part of the trip, part of the fantasy. I'm like you—I like having the choice." Intrigued, and perhaps a little disconcerted, Roufa asks: "What do you do in life?," to which she replies: "I'm in sales." When Roufa asks her, "Selling what?," she answers: "A little of everything, and nothing." Roufa is silent for a moment. Then, as the camera moves in to a close-up of his face, his eyes wide with emotion, he says softly: "Like me . . . I sell a bit of fantasy." The camera remains fixed on Roufa, as the young woman asks: "Do you like it?" His voice trembling, he answers: "*I have a family to take care of!*" It is a complex and surely humiliating moment for Roufa: the young woman is not a prostitute, after all, and so her reasons for wanting to have sex (or not) with a good-looking guy like him are not the same as his reasons for approaching her. Her "I'm like you" is unintentionally cruel. There is, finally, a world of difference between her situation and his, an undeniable divide between the First and Third worlds.

This scene, while clearly allegorical, also invites the viewer to reflect on Roufa's sexuality and adds to our understanding of Khomsa's anxieties regarding his subjectivity, the subjectivity of the hustler. The reflexive fantasy of the "dream," surely, is one of freedom. (Both Roufa and the young woman, speaking French, use the word *rêve*, although neither of them is a native speaker of the language.) Roufa needs the dream of sexual and subjective freedom as much as the men and women to whom he "sells" it.[24] Following the scene in which Roufa smashes the mirror in the lavatory at the bar, we see Roufa have a conversation with a musician friend who

FIGURE 4.6 Khomsa discovers that Fred has taken pictures of Roufa.

has just been fired from his job in the orchestra for showing up drunk for work. (The young man suffers from the same malaise as Roufa—the sense of oppression that comes from feeling that one is not in charge of one's own destiny.) Roufa suggests to his friend that he become a hustler, but the young man says it's not for him, adding: "Each to his own desire."

When Roufa runs out of ideas and feels he is losing all hope of extricating himself from his misery (the immediate cause being Khomsa's renewed ambivalence about marrying him, the existential reasons for his unhappiness being unnamed, but turning full circle in the song Navette sings both at the beginning and at the end of the film, about how every hustler eventually grows old), he returns to his former lover, the German. Earlier in the film, we see Roufa introduce a friend of his to the German with the express intention that his friend take his place in the German's affections. But when Roufa arrives at the German's villa and is greeted warily by his friend at the door, Roufa announces that he has changed his mind—he wishes to go to Germany, after all. The friend explains coolly: "Sorry, everyone has his turn. That's the way it is."

The conversation that Roufa and the German will have represents the nadir of Roufa's spirit. The German, for his part, is still kind toward Roufa, even though Roufa has on more than one occasion been irresponsible in his dealings with the older man. But as Khélil observes about Gide (as revealed in Gide's last writings on the Maghreb), the German does not—perhaps cannot—understand the problems of the "colonized." "You are mysterious," he says to Roufa, as the young Tunisian tries to explain his distress. "What are you hiding?" With tears in his eyes, Roufa says that he feels utterly abandoned and that even his "dream" has been stolen from him, a dream that no one has tried harder than he to pursue.

The film in the end offers a dispiriting picture of Tunisia's predicament. Khomsa becomes distraught and seeks to exorcise her demons (is there any other phrase to describe her action of last resort?) by going to a marabout—the tomb of Saint Regaïa—where she joins several other women in need of "healing," dancing convulsively to the loud, cacophonous beat of drums and tambourines, until she collapses in a kind of faint. Roufa discovers her there and at the same time catches sight of the fleeing Frenchman, who had tried to photograph the frenzied spectacle but was forcibly turned away by the woman supervising the therapeutic ritual (or *zār*, as it is known in the Maghreb). In a strange and disturbing scene, Roufa leaves the marabout and follows the Frenchman on his motorcycle. When he catches up with the photographer on the beach, he slowly circles him several times, revving his motorcycle engine in a menacing fashion. The two men stare intently at each other—and the Frenchman understands not only that he is under threat but that he has been the cause of Khomsa's crisis and Roufa's anger. When, having made his point, Roufa eventually rides off, the Frenchman angrily smashes his camera on the side of an upturned boat on the beach and then throws it to the ground. He has gone too far and knows it. He is the evil eye, after all.

Strangers to (Them)selves

There are two scenes in the film that are both funny and painfully revelatory of Tunisia's cultural and economic bind in relation to the West. Early in the film, we see that Roufa has taken it upon himself to teach Khomsa's brother Aziz how to be a hustler. But Aziz shows himself to be ill-suited for prostitution. He finds that when he tries to hustle a female tourist, he starts to have genuine feelings for her; he cannot properly alienate his sexuality for the task. "You are really hopeless!" Roufa tells him disgustedly. "You have to have an eye, and to aim straight!" (Aziz's example suggests, however, that there is hope for Tunisia: in the allegorical reading, not everyone has sold his soul to the devil of Western-led capitalist imperatives.) Roufa—who is widely acknowledged by his friends and admirers to be the supreme hustler, the master of his game—decides there and then to show Aziz how it is done. In the scene that follows, however, we see that he may know (or think he knows) the difference between sex for sale and sex as an expression of his authentic identity as a lover; but he no longer necessarily knows who is, and who is not, a Tunisian—which is another way of suggesting that he perhaps no longer knows who he is. The scene, as an allegory, suggests that Tunisian identity has evolved beyond an Orientalist dialectic in which self and other are clearly distinguished.

Roufa singles out a young woman he sees on the Sousse boardwalk, and follows her. She is wearing a short, red skirt and has long, straight hair. She walks with a confident gait and has a freshness about her that seems to match the sunny weather and the gentle breeze that occasionally blows her hair in front of her eyes. When she stops at an outdoor café, Roufa jumps off his motorcycle and almost runs up to her; and before she can sit down at one of the tables, he takes off his sunglasses and addresses her (in French): "Hey, beautiful! How do you like the country? Would you like me to show you around?" Affronted, she looks him in the eye for a moment and turns to leave. He follows her, persisting in his effort to engage her in conversation: "You know, you really are very beautiful!" he tells her. "I know a quiet corner not far from here." She stops, swings around to face him, and says in Tunisian Arabic: "Who do you take yourself for? Stop being such a jerk!"

Roufa becomes flustered. "Uh . . . I'm sorry. I never realized you were Tunisian," he stutters. "It was a mistake, I'm sorry!" And to compound his humiliation, Aziz at that moment catches up with him and says, laughing: "You're right. You have to have an eye . . . and to aim straight!"

The economic bind in which Tunisia is caught—recalling its infantilizing former status as a French protectorate—which is inseparable from the cultural bind illustrated by the scene described above, is expressed with humor in a brief scene toward the end of the film. Navette and one of his young friends compare how the day went for each of them (we have seen Navette doing the rounds of the beach cafés, trying to sell his plush toy camels): "How much did you make today?" the boy asks. Navette replies:

"I got five dinars from my mother and I bought a couple of camels. I sold one to a tourist, an old woman, for a dinar. She asked if I would like to become her son." Navette's friend is impressed: "Lucky dog!" he says. "And so, you accepted?" Quite matter-of-factly, as though the choice were entirely his own, Navette explains: "No, I don't want to. My brother Roufa would miss me. My mother, too."

There is no doubt that *Bezness* aims in this "story of the private individual destiny" to offer "an allegory of the embattled situation of the public third-world culture and society" of contemporary Tunisia. In the early 1990s—when Tunisia still stood apart from most of the rest of the Arab world as a society that seemed almost unique in the way it deftly straddled the "East" and the "West," and when culturally and economically it seemed to offer contrasting images of itself as a third-world country that at the same time was not a third-world country—Tunisian cinema is of especial interest to the viewer who sees the potential in allegory for resistance to oppression. Tunisia's self-perception, or national narrative, continued to emphasize the country's "modernity," although by then it had become obvious that Ben Ali's regime was using this image to distract both the Tunisians themselves and the tourists upon whom the economy so heavily depends from the baleful realities of the police state and the lack of a vibrant public sphere.

If Roufa and Khomsa, representing a particular postcolonial generation, are in disarray around the question of national identity, there is nevertheless hope for the next generation, represented by Navette, whose French nickname refers to a shuttle, something that plies to and fro. There will perhaps be no need, in the future, to choose between (two) identities, to be torn between (two) cultures, to become an exile, like the German in the film, or to feel ambivalent about one's own identity, as Khélil does when he reads André Gide writing about his encounters with adolescent Arabs in Egypt and North Africa. And perhaps, like Julia Kristeva, Tunisians will come to see the liberating logic of being strangers to themselves.

CHAPTER FIVE

The Colonizer and the Colonized
The Silences of the Palace (Moufida Tlatli, 1994)

> The diffuse and impressionistic character of this oppression, which cannot be described in the same manner as that of the historical occupation, is as elusive as a state of the soul. The oppression is no longer located outside us, and being indirect, seems more troubling and comprehensive. There are no longer two realities that confront each other, the colonial and the national, but two realities that intertwine.
>
> HÉLÉ BÉJI (1982)[1]

The Silences of the Palace, Moufida Tlatli's first film, is set in the melancholy present of the mid-1960s and the highly charged past of a decade earlier, during the last days of the French occupation of Tunisia. In an autobiographical series of flashbacks, it narrates a young woman's memories of growing up among the servants in a beylical palace as an illegitimate daughter of one of the resident princes, who, in a conspiracy of silence with the servants and his own family, will not acknowledge his paternity.[2] The film's many overlapping and intersecting discourses—chief among which are the status of women in contemporary Tunisia, the problems of social class and political power in an ostensibly emerging democracy, Tunisia's complex relationship with its Ottoman heritage and colonial past as a French protectorate, as well as a discourse on the contemporary malaise produced by the country's corrupt and decadent leadership—are grouped around the idea of *samt*, or "not to speak": the "silences" of the film's title.[3] This silence refers, finally, to the repression and self-censorship that characterize Tunisia at the time of the film's making, not so much as legacies of colonialism, but as features of a neopatriarchal society with a long history of authoritarian government that have crippling effects on men and women alike in the private sphere and make any kind of political or artistic

FIGURE 5.1 Lotfi (Sami Bouajila) teaches Alia (Hend Sabri) how to write her name.

expression a dangerous enterprise, rendering genuine public intellectual debate virtually impossible.

Tlatli remarked in an interview published in *Télérama* in 1994 that when she was a child, women were called *"la colonisée du colonisé"* ("the colonized of the colonized"),[4] adding: "It was while thinking about my mother and all that was unsaid and could not be spoken, [a condition] that reigned throughout her life, that I wrote the script."[5] Like the title of this chapter, Tlatli's phrase is an allusion to Memmi's famous book, *The Colonizer and the Colonized* (1957), in which, according to the author himself, he tried to "reproduce, completely and authentically, the portraits of the two protagonists in the colonial drama and the relationship that binds them."[6] Tlatli attempts something similar in *The Silences of the Palace*, as if in answer to the feminist *pied noir* writer Hélène Cixous's exhortation that "women should break out of the snare of silence. They shouldn't be conned into accepting a domain which is the margin or the harem."[7] Tlatli's portrait of the "colonizers"—Sidi Ali (Kamel Fazaâ) and his brother Sidi Bechir (Hichem Rostom); the aristocratic family of these beys and the social class they represent; the French, who are ever-present, but mostly offscreen—is complex, as is her analysis of the drama that binds Sidi Ali and his lover, the servant Khedija (Amel Hedhili), and their daughter Alia (Ghalia Lacroix/ Hend Sabri).[8] With the film's central theme of identity articulated through Alia's efforts to come to terms with her paternity, Tlatli offers a strikingly oedipal analysis of Tunisia's postcolonial condition.

The Woman as Allegory

In an interview with Laura Mulvey in 1995, Tlatli commented on the rich allegorical possibilities of the cinema for the Arab filmmaker:

> I think that poetry and an oral tradition are particularly significant for Arab culture. Poetry was something that existed in the spoken word. At the same time it frequently had to make use of symbols and metaphors to express something that could not otherwise have been spoken. . . . Perhaps cinema is the same. It too has to make use of metaphors and symbols, in keeping with this lack of directness that so characterizes Islamic [sic] society.[9]

Tlatli refers to her culture as a "culture of the indirect. . . . Here everything is a little bit devious, a bit unformulated—the unsaid, and so on. This is why the camera is so amazing. It's in complete harmony with this rather repressed language" (18). Indeed, she believes the cinema is "something right for and specific to this culture" (18). She adds that, furthermore, in the Tunisian cinema there is a striking preoccupation among both male and female directors with "the question of women." She correctly observes that "the theme of women's liberation is the one that [among the cinemas of the Maghreb] has been special to Tunisia" (18), but she often wondered why it was that *male* directors should be so preoccupied with the theme, until she realized that, "for them, woman was the symbol of freedom of expression, and of all kinds of liberation. It was like a litmus test for Arab society: if one could discuss the liberation of women then one could discuss other freedoms" (18).

As an allegorical statement, the opening shot of *The Silences of the Palace*—a close-up of adult Alia's mournful face, as she stares sightlessly at her audience, before beginning her song—reveals everything about the "diffuse and impressionistic character of [the] oppression" felt by postcolonial Tunisians, and by postcolonial Tunisian women most especially, upon realizing that the dreams and hopes they had invested in the revolution have not been fulfilled.[10] It turns out that Alia is feeling unwell. She is pregnant; but her condition would be better described as *psychological depression*. In her role as an allegorical figure, Alia, the illegitimate child growing up in the servants' quarters of the palace, represents Tunisia prior to Independence. As an adult, after she has left the palace and Tunisia has gained its independence, she remains troubled by the question of her paternity (she both is and is not the daughter of a bey, for example), and now—pregnant, but not married to her unborn baby's father, Lotfi (Sami Bouajila)—she hesitates. She wants to keep the baby. "Every abortion is painful," she explains to Lotfi. "I'm losing a part of me." But Lotfi, who wants her to abort, insists: "You're crazy! Every child needs a name, a family, a marriage."

Tlatli explains in her interview with Mulvey that the reasons Lotfi will not marry Alia have to do with social and family pressures that were typical in Tunisia in the 1960s (the fact that Alia is both a singer and illegitimate would compromise the honor of Lotfi's family), but Tlatli also confirms what the viewer quickly understands, namely, that the promise of freedom Lotfi represents when he first meets Alia has not been fulfilled. When Mulvey asks: "Isn't it Lotfi, arriving on the scene almost as the means for Alia to emerge from her silence and literally to 'find a voice' with her singing, who offers the possibility of synthesis, of resolution?" (20), Tlatli replies: "But it's an illusion, as we discover at the end. Though it is indeed present at the beginning, before the first flashback into Alia's childhood. He does seem to offer the possibility of escape. It's only through him that Alia begins to identify with the nationalist struggle" (20). In short, and for whatever reasons, Lotfi "is unable to live out his revolutionary ideals" (20).

The film begins with this impasse, the recognition that in some fundamental way not yet fully understood by the characters, the revolution has failed. The *désenchantement national* described by Béji in her book of that title is legible on Alia's face; and as Tlatli suggests, Alia's return visit to the palace, occasioned by Sidi Ali's death, will offer her an opportunity "to relive everything that had happened before Lotfi arrived" (20). What Alia realizes, Tlatli explains, is that "Lotfi had done nothing to change her life and it's at that moment that she takes control of her own fate" (20).

The centrally important question of the film becomes, then: *Why has Lotfi done nothing—or why has he been unable to do anything—to change Alia's life?* As Gil Hochberg puts it in her analysis of how the film self-consciously uses national allegory, the oedipal narrative about Alia's attempts to gain her father Sidi Ali's recognition and affection is tied ("as if naturally") to the "national story." The shift Alia makes from her father to her lover is associated with a shift from one political position to another: "from the passive collaboration of Sid' Ali with the French government, to the active rebellious spirit of Lotfi, the young fighter in the ranks of the national revolution."[11] But Lotfi—the revolution—has not had a positively transformative impact on Alia's life, because the national agenda Lotfi represents is articulated within a neopatriarchal framework that, for all its apparent commitment to the emancipation of women, does not allow full and free expression (in Hochberg's metaphor) of the "female voice" and is ultimately committed to keeping women in a position of subordination to men.

In her elegant analysis of the film in her book, *Liberating Shahrazad: Feminism, Postcolonialism, and Islam,* Suzanne Gauch notes that in a number of ways Alia's situation improves on her mother's, even as it mirrors Khedija's fundamental disenfranchisement.[12] Alia earns her living as a singer, and with Lotfi enjoys a degree of intellectual independence. But the "decisive silences" highlighted by her tale indicate that "Alia's obsession with her father's name is simply a screen for a more critical lack" (30). This lack, clearly, is produced by the fact that as long as Alia tries to define herself and live by the rules of the patriarchy into which she was born, or to accommodate herself to the neopatriarchal rules of her life with Lotfi, she will *always* find herself lacking—she will always be confined to the margins of a social order that identifies her as illegitimate.

What we see in the film is the breakdown of the patriarchal extended family and its replacement by the neopatriarchal nuclear family.[13] Lotfi and Alia, in their apartment in the city, are not yet a true nuclear family (they are not married and have no children), and Lotfi is a would-be, or failed/pseudo-, (neo)patriarch, in a world in which pristine patriarchy no longer obtains, and in which he is a humble, salaried *fonctionnaire* (i.e., an employee of the state, and therefore potentially subject to government budget cuts, corrupt or incompetent supervisors, the horrors of the bureaucracy, and so on). The patriarchy—as represented in the film by the beylical family in the palace, with its dominion over the servants; and this aristocratic family as reflecting/representing the national political order, that is, Tunisia as a monarchy—will be reconfigured after Independence as neopatriarchy, which is underpinned, Sharabi tells us in *Neopatriarchy*, by the same imperatives as those of the patriarchy that preceded it. He explains that the "inner structure" of neopatriarchy, its "essential core and building block," is the patriarchal family, which is "historically the origin and model of neopatriarchal society."[14] The basic internal relations of the patriarchal family, which are reproduced in the structures of neopatriarchal society, are those of *authority, domination,* and *dependency* (41).

These relations are challenged by the nuclear family structure primarily in three areas. The first challenge, Sharabi explains, is an *economic* one: "In a household where the children have received a degree of education and acquired specific skills, they have by the same token gained independence and mobility. The children [in the nuclear family] are no longer dependent on the father as in a rural or precapitalist setting. The father now finds himself forced into a new relationship within the household and with each of its members" (31). (Here, we consider the revolutionary importance of Alia's learning how to write, which is offered by the film as a symbolic first step toward gaining her independence from her "father"/the patriarchal organization of the beys' household.)

The second implication of the nuclear family structure for patriarchal hegemony has to do with *democratic* relations: "If the essential relation of patriarchy is subordination, that of the nuclear family is equality. Economic independence is the basis of the nuclear family's democracy, the condition for the overthrow of patriarchal tyranny" (31–32). (As we have said, Alia will eventually earn her own living as a singer and as such will be able—as it was never possible for her mother—to say "No" to the beys.)

The third way in which the patriarchal family is threatened by the nuclear family, Sharabi argues, "centers on the *emancipation of women.* In the transition from the patriarchal to the modern family, women are certainly the primary beneficiaries. Familial patriarchy provides the ground for a dual domination—of the father over the family household, and of the male over the female" (32). The structure of the modern family makes the woman's liberation possible, but does not guarantee it, for the precondition of her liberation is that she have access to education and to work, that is, to economic independence. (Alia as an adult, earning her own money, is still not liberated. This contradiction, we have said, becomes the film's hermeneutic thread, for the question as to why, despite escaping the palace and a life of servitude, she has not [to use her word] been "saved" from a continuing sense of oppression, remains opaque to her until the end of the film, when she finally seems to understand the role Lotfi has played in shaping her destiny.)

Sharabi reminds us that "waiting for the revolution to change the status quo is not a revolutionary stance. Truly radical action will undertake the difficult task of addressing feasible possibilities: possibilities to be found in the structures and institutions of the status quo, not in a utopian vision" (151–152). He lists a number of vehicles for social and political action that he believes help make the "conditions of possibility" for radical democratic change—professional associations (academic, medical, legal), trade unions, peasant cooperatives, students' and women's organizations—and argues that, of all the autonomous organizations and groups one can think of, "potentially the most revolutionary" is the women's movement: "Even in the short term, the women's movement is the detonator which will explode neopatriarchal society from within. If allowed to grow and come into its own, it will become the permanent shield against patriarchal regression, the cornerstone of future modernity" (154). We see that, although it cannot really be said that Alia "waits" for the revolution to change the status quo, she only starts to become a feminist when, at the end of the film, she decides to have her child (which may very well cause Lotfi to leave her or prompt her to leave him). In her voice-over at the end of the film, addressed to her dead mother, she says: "I thought Lotfi would save me. I have not been saved. Like you, I've suffered, I've sweated. Like you, I've lived in sin. My life has been a series of abortions. I could never express myself. My songs were stillborn. And even the child inside me, Lotfi wants me to abort. This child . . . I feel it has taken root in me. I feel it bringing me back to you. I hope it will be a girl. I'll call her Khedija."

Her realization is that she had put her destiny entirely in Lotfi's hands, and her hope that he would "save" her was misplaced. Now she must take charge of her own destiny as best she can—even though at no point in the film is any evidence offered to suggest that Alia has become a modern woman. She is caught between patriarchy and modernity, enjoying the benefits of neither and suffering the ills of both. At the end of the movie, she stands poised on the threshold of a new life that she is resolved to build for herself; but the viewer is uncertain about how far she will get.[15] It is not clear whether Alia (and what she represents in the allegory) has the means or the political will to fight the forces that oppress her—for, as Sharabi, quoting Marshall Berman, puts it: "The possibility of genuine rebellion is a product of the new age. Because modern individuals 'know how to think

FIGURE 5.2 The last shot of the film, in which we hear Alia (Ghalia Lacroix) express the hope that her child will be a girl.

of, by, and for themselves, they will demand a clear account of what their bosses and rulers are doing for them—and doing to them—and be ready to resist and rebel where they are getting nothing in return.'"[16]

After leaving the palace, Alia is well and truly cut off from the patronage system of the patriarchal society it represents, where, despite being in a sense the lowliest member of the community, she had been socialized into accepting the supremacy of the established authority of the beys and had been more or less successfully trained in the ways of dealing with it.[17] In the world beyond the palace walls, she will feel very isolated, for the state, in Sharabi's phrase, is "an alien force that oppresses one, as is equally civil society, a jungle where only the rich and powerful are respected and recognized" (35). As a singer-for-hire, Alia is sometimes an object of the unwelcome attentions of men. "Don't worry, they know you're with me," Lotfi tries to reassure her. But this is no reassurance at all, for Lotfi is neither rich nor powerful, and he is in no position to provide real justice or protection to anyone.

As Kenneth Perkins and others note, the Personal Status Code (PSC) introduced in 1957 altered certain practices that are sanctioned by Islamic law but which are regarded by progressives as prejudicial to women:

The code strengthened the nuclear family and fostered a more equitable relationship between the genders. Women won new rights, including those of divorce and the approval of arranged marriages, and expanded existing entitlements in questions of child custody and inheritance. At the same time, the code explicitly placed obligations on women, such as contributing to the maintenance of the household if their means allowed. Other provisions outlawed polygamy, ended the male right of repudiation, and set minimum ages for marriages.[18]

In order to educate women about the PSC and to "encourage them to venture beyond habitual limits, and offer them opportunities to improve their day-to-day lives," a group of women related to Néo-Destour leaders formed the *Union Nationale des Femmes Tunisiennes* (UNFT) in 1956. Perkins notes that the UNFT "concentrated its initial efforts on urging women to exercise their right to vote, granted in 1957, on sponsoring literacy classes for the 96 percent of the female population who could not read or write, and on developing health programs, some of them devoted to family planning" (138). In both areas—women's literacy and family planning—the results in the decade between 1956 and 1965 were dramatic, which helped to put independent Tunisia on a sound footing for the transformation of the social environment envisioned by Bourguiba.

But the situation in which Alia and Lotfi find themselves is disadvantageous to both: Alia's emancipation by the PSC—which Bourguiba hoped would tap into the energies of women, as part of Tunisia's post-Independence commitment to national regeneration—and Lotfi's release by the abolition of the monarchy from a class system characterized by old-fashioned paternalism rather than relative social justice, have been only partially successful. The worm in the apple of the hopes and dreams of young people like Alia and Lotfi is surely the neopatriarchal framework of Bourguiba's vision, as revealed by a speech Bourguiba gave on the occasion of the Woman's March on 1 January 1957:

> The Woman must not exaggerate.... The man remains the head of the family, and he will always remain so. The woman cannot at any moment seek refuge under "Mr. Habib said." She must know that she has responsibilities to assume and that the man will always have the last word.[19]

Echoing Sharabi's argument about the comprehensive and debilitating logic of neopatriarchy, Lamia Ben Youssef Zayzafoon observes in *The Production of the Muslim Woman* that "under the centralized government of Bourguiba in post-Independence Tunisia, there was a shift from family to state patriarchy. In Bourguiba's own words, 'the family is no longer limited to the circle of parents. It extends to the village, the country, and beyond the frontiers, to encompass the Greater Maghreb, the Arab community, the entire continent'" (122).

This somewhat megalomaniacal metaphor in which the family—and by implication, the body of the Tunisian woman as devoted wife and caring mother—is not only associated with or symbolizes the *umma* (the "nation," which Ben Youssef Zayzafoon reminds us is etymologically linked to the word *um*—"mother"—and is closely tied to notions of identity and origin), but is extended to encompass the whole continent of Africa puts an impossible symbolic burden on the Tunisian woman. We understand, then, why Alia feels that her songs are "stillborn," and conversely, perhaps, why Lotfi is reluctant to marry her. Alia may be legally protected by the PSC, but (as an unmarried woman, with no family to protect her socially or confer on her a legitimate identity) she clearly has no place in the society, no identity, except as one of society's marginal or abject figures. When Lotfi picks her up at the hotel where she has performed for the guests at a wedding, his first words to her are: "You're late." He complains that he nearly fell asleep (waiting for her). It is a strange and sad scene, with Alia's evident melancholy compounded by the irony that, like her mother before her, she must present herself as an object for other people's pleasure—other people who see dancers and singers as socially inferior, sometimes on a par even with prostitutes—and here must endure a form of private humiliation, singing at the kind of bourgeois wedding in which she would never be allowed herself to be the bride. Lotfi asks her: "Did they bother you?," and she answers dully: "The usual harassment." They drive off in silence, into a sort of no-man's-land, and are swallowed up by the dark.

When they reach the apartment where they live, Alia lies down on her bed. As he follows her into the bedroom, Lotfi turns on the light. "Switch it off," she pleads. We catch a glimpse on the wall of a reproduction of a painting of a bey (or sultan) on his throne, with his courtiers before him on bended knee, representing a vanished order that for Alia is doubly and irretrievably lost (because she actually grew up in such a family, albeit on its

FIGURE 5.3 Khedija (Amel Hedhili) fears that her daughter will be unable to avoid the same destiny she has had.

margins, and her bey/father is dead; and because Tunisia is now a republic). "I'm scared," she tells her lover. "What of?" he asks. "Of the neighbors," she says. "They stare. They stare at me all the time. All eyes accuse me, as if they could read my thoughts." Lotfi tells her she is "imagining it"; but we know that this kind of fantasy is common among individuals who feel they are in some way frauds, illegitimate. Gauch remarks that the (both real and imagined) looks of the neighbors indicate how Alia is "trapped by a web of internalized as well as societal taboos" (20). Alia's "secret," which causes her so much anxiety and pain, is not only that she is pregnant (out of wedlock), but that in the eyes of the law, she herself in fact is illegitimate. She cannot name her father, in a society that designates the father as the phallic signifier that gives symbolic meaning to the entire social order, and in which a woman's virtue, defined in terms of her role as mother and wife, is held up as the emblem par excellence of the country's religious and cultural heritage.[20]

With the establishment of state feminism at the time of Tunisia's independence, an authentic feminism through which a woman like Alia might forge her emancipation becomes somewhat compromised. The creation of the UNFT in 1956 was a decisive moment in Tunisia's feminist movement, for it would be the death blow to the many feminist organizations that had been established in Tunisia before Independence, including: *L'Union Musulmane des Femmes de Tunisie* (created in 1936); *La Section Féminine de l'Association des Jeunes Musulmanes* (1944); *L'Union des Femmes de Tunisie* (1944); *L'Union des Jeunes Filles de Tunisie* (1945); and *Le Club de la Jeune Fille Tunisienne* (1954). Henceforth, state feminism—feminism that in this case is monopolized by the state and held firmly under its control—would be the order of the day; and as Ben Youssef Zayzafoon correctly observes, following her analysis of what the modern "Muslim woman" meant to Bourguiba and the UNFT, the modern Tunisian woman occupies a decidedly ambiguous position between "authenticity" and "modernity" (124).

"Things are going to change. A new future awaits us"

One of the first requirements of a modern society is that its members be literate; and the momentous scene in which Alia learns to write her name can be seen as pivotal to the film's meanings. It is Lotfi, the tutor of Sidi Bechir's two legitimate children, Selim and Sarra, who teaches Alia how to write. One day, from his ground-floor classroom in the palace, he hears her singing in the garden. When she finishes her song, Alia passes in front of the barred window of the classroom, and he takes the opportunity to compliment her: "You have a beautiful voice," he says. "Pity it's locked up inside." She smiles at him and replies: "You're locked up, too. Why don't you live with your family?" He explains that they live in El Kef; and she asks, "Where is El Kef?" Lotfi's reply—"It's a city far away"—speaks volumes not only about Alia's profound ignorance of the world beyond the palace gates (for El Kef is a well-known hill town west of Tunis, close to the border with Algeria), but also about Lotfi's reflexive condescension as a tutor. In a manner of speaking, Lotfi will always be her tutor; it is his preferred role; he wants Alia to be educated, but not so educated that his role as her teacher will be rendered superfluous. It is perhaps not too much to say that his reply is an unconscious neopatriarchal strategy to keep Alia ignorant—for, as he says the words, a gentle lute melody rises on the sound track, and the two young people look into each other's eyes. He reaches through the window bars, and gently touches her cheek. She pulls back, a gesture that the film treats as an appropriately demure response: it is precisely Alia's innocence and vulnerability that Lotfi finds so attractive; and the viewer understands that if, at any time in the future, after they have become a couple, the balance of their relationship should shift to reduce Alia's dependency on Lotfi, their relationship might very well founder.

Following this scene is one in which we see the female servants in the kitchen engaged in the preparation of a dinner party their masters will host that evening. One of the women, Shemshouma ("Shema," played by Sabah Bouzouita), feels disinclined to work and announces irritably: "We can't remain slaves forever!" Nothing Khalti [Aunt] Hadda (Najia Ouerghi) can do or say will make Shema return to her chores. "I'm sick of this! Sick, sick, sick of this!" the disgruntled servant repeats. "I'm suffocating!"

When the narrative returns to Lotfi and Alia in the next scene, showing Alia learning how to write her name on the blackboard in Lotfi's classroom, the notion of literacy as an important step toward human liberation and self-determination in the modern world is underlined. Following his example, she writes her name (in Arabic). He tries to guide her hand while she does this, but she says: "Let me do it myself!" "You see! It's easy!" he says. Then Lotfi asks: "Can you write your last name?" The smile fades from Alia's lips, and she turns away from him. As the camera pulls back, we see that the blackboard behind Lotfi is filled with writing in French, traces of his earlier lesson with Selim and/or Sarra.

"Are you scared?" he asks. "It's you I'm scared of," she replies. "Then don't be," he says. The film's boldly conceived allegorical strategy, which designates Alia as Tunisia on the eve of Independence, is signaled when he continues: "You're as indecisive as your country! One word thrills you, the next scares you." Lifting her head up by her chin and looking into her eyes, he says: "Things are going to change. A new future awaits us. You will be a great singer! Your voice will enchant everyone!"

Later, as the political situation grows worse and the princely family decides to move to their country house for safety, Khedija urges Alia to join them. Alia tells her mother that she does not want to go with them, and Khedija becomes exasperated: "You're too willful! Is that what your Lotfi taught you?" As we have said, in the allegory Lotfi represents the revolution that will bring about Tunisia's independence from France; but it is significant that he is a teacher. As a poetic text that makes its meanings through metaphor and allegory, *The Silences of the Palace*, we have said, suggests that literacy will be a tool of liberation for Alia. But if the film gives us a (brief) image of Alia learning how to write, it does not give us an image of her learning how to *read*. Sharabi points out that in the Arab world, traditional patriarchal culture never promoted the *reading* of the Qur'an (Sharabi's emphasis): "To this day it is still recited, chanted, and repeated by heart but not, or rarely, *read*.... In this context attention should be drawn to the subversive and liberating function of reading, and the primary concern of all established orthodoxy to protect itself against all *critical* reading or interpretation, that is, understanding" (87).

Arabic—classical or modern standard Arabic (الفصحى /*al-fuṣḥā*)—is not the language Alia already speaks. The everyday colloquial language she speaks is an (unwritten) Arabic dialect that is "structurally related but essentially different" from the language Lotfi will teach her, which, as for all Arabs everywhere who seek to become literate in their official language, she will have to "appropriate ... as *another* language, much as a foreign language" (84–85). Sharabi points out the astonishing fact that "there is no other society in the world today that uses its traditional classical language practically unchanged as its basic means of bureaucratic communication and formal discourse" (84–85).

The implications of this for Alia's destiny (and for the revolution) are enormous. (We have already seen that the film acknowledges the class difference between Alia and her aristocratic cousins by revealing that at least some of Sarra and Selim's lessons are conducted in French.)[21] The teaching of modern standard Arabic—or Lotfi's role in Alia's education as her tutor—becomes a metaphor in the film that explains why Lotfi does not, or cannot, "save" Alia from subalternity. "If language structures thought, classical Arabic structures it in a decisive way," argues Sharabi:

> This is not only because of the essentially ideological character of this language with its rigid religious and patriarchal framework, but also because of its inherent tendency to "think itself," that is to say, to impose its own patterns and structures on all linguistic production. It is a "received language," "a language of others," and it favors, as Halim Barakat puts it, "literary over scientific writing and rhetoric over the written text and speech over writing."[22]

The relevance of these insights to our analysis of *The Silences of the Palace* is striking. When Sharabi suggests that the *monologue* is central in all forms of neopatriarchal discourse and that this mode appears in the very structure of the discourse itself—"not just authority produces the monological discourse, but also the language itself, in that it privileges rhetoric and discourages dialogue" (87)—we have the key to why, as Tlatli remarked, "the possibility of escape" that Lotfi seems to offer Alia turns out to be an "illusion." He is "unable to live out his revolutionary ideals," because he is a neopatriarchal male, which is to say: when it comes to gender equality, and all that it implies, he is the very opposite of a revolutionary:

> The monological discourse may be expressed in different forms and articulated in different voices, depending on its setting. Thus in the household the father's is the dominant discourse, in the classroom the teacher's, in the religious gathering or tribe the sheikh's, in the religious organization the *'alim*'s, in the society at large, the ruler's and so forth. This discourse derives its perceived sense of signification from the structure of language itself rather than from the individual utterance. While the structure reinforces authority, hierarchy, and the relations of dependency, it also produces oppositional forms typical of the neopatriarchal discourse: gossip, backbiting, storytelling, and silence. (88)

When Lotfi predicts for Alia that "things are going to change" and that "a new future awaits us," he fails to take into account that *he* will have to change, if they are not to reproduce a new version of the old order. (At the beginning of the film—in the strand of the narrative that takes place in the post-Independence present—when Alia struggles to explain to Lotfi why she has a headache, she blurts out, almost as a non sequitur: "You always have to win!") In the event, he does not learn to think "outside the box" of traditional discourse, the aim of which, Sharabi tells us, is "to bring about not awareness, understanding, self-consciousness but its opposite—to reinforce an affective, noncritical state rooted in external dependence and inner submission" (96). The challenge for Alia, to echo Mulvey in her 1975 landmark essay, "Visual Pleasure and Narrative Cinema," will be how to fight the unconscious structured like a language (formed critically at the moment of arrival of language) while still caught within the language of the patriarchy.[23] Mulvey argues that the unconscious of patriarchal society has structured film form, making it a voyeuristic, scopophilic language of desire, with woman as image and man as bearer of the look, and observes that the one who controls the look controls language, and the one who controls language controls the world (19).

Mulvey's thesis about the cinema as an advanced representation system in the service of (primarily heterosexual) male interests applies to the languages of neopatriarchy in Arab societies, among which *Arabic itself*, Sharabi tells us, plays a central role. Like Sharabi's argument about Arabic—which, even in its "modernized" form (what he calls, "newspaper" Arabic, a language that is "streamlined to fit the requirements of the times"), is "in structure and tone essentially the same as the classical language of medieval Islam" (97)—the language of neopatriarchy (also "modernized" to fit the requirements of the times) is a language that reflects the antidemocratic social formation it serves:

> The claim that the "newspaper" Arabic of neopatriarchal society constitutes a synthesis between the colloquial and the classical... is an exaggeration, more wishful thinking than reality. This simplified classical Arabic, like the social formation it reflects, is neither fully traditional nor really modern; it is an uneven combination of the two.... This fact has been instrumental in preserving the social and cultural divisions of neopatriarchal society, in maintaining the epistemological compromise of the Arab Awakening, and in blocking the possibility of a genuine break with the patriarchal discourse. Clearly, under these conditions, no breakthrough toward full modernity was possible. (98)

Where Mulvey, writing about the cinema, calls for "a new language of desire" (16), Sharabi, quoting the Maghrebi scholar Mohamed Arkoun, believes that written and spoken Arabic itself needs to be reconceived: "Change must involve the way in which reality is expressed in and by language. Language must be changed, that is, it must be *secularized* and *rationalized*."[24] In the film, the language of patriarchy, as we see it hold sway in the household of the beys, is *monological* (to use Sharabi's word) and not innovative in the least. Among the servants, various tribulations and tragedies are usually explained as being "the Will of God"; and among the aristocrats, the hierarchical order of things is understood to be determined by "tradition," which is perpetuated by patriarchal prerogatives according to which husbands have dominion over wives and children, and the word of the father who is most senior in the hierarchy of the extended family has final authority. When Sarra, for example, excitedly tells Alia that she is engaged to be married, Alia asks her who her fiancé is. Sarra tells her that it is her cousin, Mehdi. "Do you love him?" Alia asks. Nonplussed by the question, Sarra replies: "My father chose him." Of course, the film does not show how Sarra's marriage will turn out, because—allegorically speaking (i.e., because she is a princess)—Sarra is from the beginning a marginal figure. History tells us that hers is a doomed class. (Already, we see that her aunt Lella J'neina [Sonia Meddeb] is infertile; and her mother Lella Memia [Michket Krifa] is a silent, spectral figure.) Sarra does not represent Tunisia/the future, as Alia does, and so, once Alia leaves the palace (on the night of Sarra's engagement party), Sarra for all intents and purposes ceases to exist. The Tunisia that Sarra represents in the allegory—a decadent, feudal society—cannot be saved by another of what Alia will call "these terrible marriages."

According to Catherine Slawy-Sutton, in an article that reads *The Silences of the Palace* as a feminist allegory about a country going through a traumatic period of its history, the focus of the film is on the three servants, Khalti Hadda, Khedija, and Alia, whom she sees as "personifications of historical moments."[25] Khalti Hadda symbolizes the colonial order; Khedija, the end of passive obedience; and Alia, "the birth of a nation that is probing its future" (89). She interprets the developments and illnesses of their bodies as metaphors for stages of Tunisia's recent history—Khalti Hadda's blindness toward the end of her life as a metaphor for the final stages of French colonization; Khedija "is Tunisia in the mid-fifties, pregnant with potential, but agonizing" (95) (Tlatli allegorizes Khedija's beautiful body as a Tunisia that is "forever raped and abused, yet in gestation" [96], writes Slawy-Sutton); and Alia, who is a product of her "double heritage and of a past that is impossible to bury," is also (or rather—unlike her mother, whose pregnancy ends in an abortion—will remain at the end of the film) "a body pregnant with possibilities" (97). (Slawy-Sutton seems to have overlooked the fact that Alia, in the strand of the narrative that takes place in the present, has a headache—or certainly behaves as if the headache she has at the beginning of the film has never left her—which I see as far more important to the film's theme of postcolonial melancholy than her pregnancy is to the film's fragile coda of "hope" for a happier future.)

If marriage and family are neopatriarchy's privileged institution—the one that "speaks" neopatriarchal ideology's contradictions most clearly—we can see in the film's framing narrative that the "marriage" Lotfi and Alia have is in some ways as terrible as any familial arrangement Alia knew when she was living in the palace.

"These terrible marriages..."

The allegorical claims of *The Silences of the Palace*, the temporal structure of the film, and its setting in a beylical palace nearly fifty years in the past, clearly suggest not only that some women in Tunisian society still feel oppressed *as women*, but that there are also men who feel emasculated by the neopatriarchal society and state. To the extent that the character of Sidi Ali, for example, can be seen as a colonizer in relation to Khedija and the other servant women, and given that he is a member of an aristocratic ruling class of Ottoman origin, we observe that he does not seem to be aware that he is an oppressor nor does he feel any guilt about the social arrangement that maintains him in a position of great privilege. Nor do Khedija or Alia seem quite able to bring themselves to inculpate Sidi Ali for his complicity in this system—colonial, patriarchal, and rooted in class privilege—that keeps all women, and female servants most especially, permanently subordinated. He is portrayed as a lonely character (because, it must be said, he is reactionary and devoid of imagination), doomed to play his role to the end, even if it oppresses him.

Historically, the last beys of Tunis found themselves in a rather curious and humiliating position not unlike Sidi Ali's in the film. Although Tunisia was a French protectorate during the period in which *The Silences of the Palace* is set, the Bey of Tunis, a distant Ottoman (thus, also a colonizer),[26] was the country's nominal ruler. But, with little real power from 1881 to 1957, the Husseini monarchs could not disguise the fact that they, too, had become colonial subjects.[27] As Tunisia's feudal political imaginary responded to the pressures of modernity, the legitimacy and authority of the Bey—that is to say, his usefulness to the Tunisian people—would be challenged. From the point of view of the Tunisian people under the colonial "protection" of the French, the Bey could now be seen as "one of us"—but, with no power to change their colonized condition (because colonized himself), he was perceived as having forfeited his right to call himself their king.[28] The historical reality in which Lamine Bey was forced to consent

FIGURE 5.4 Sidi Ali (Kamel Fazaâ) asks Khedija if she will bring his tea later to his room. His wife Lella J'neina (Sonia Meddeb) and his father (Bechir Feni) stare in silence at his effrontery.

to the abolition of the Tunisian monarchy in July 1957 finds its correlative in *The Silences of the Palace*: not only is Sidi Ali's decadence suggested by showing him as unable to produce a legitimate heir, the film also criticizes his "right" to father a child whose paternity he cannot, or will not, assume.

When she hears of Sidi Ali's death and goes to the palace to pay her respects, Alia visits Khalti Hadda in the servants' quarters. The old woman is now blind and sits alone in her room. Alia asks her: "What did Sidi Ali die of?" The former servant replies: "The doctors couldn't do anything. They gave up. I nursed him like a baby. My eyesight was failing . . . and I couldn't go on. So, Mroubia took over." The conversation is entirely allegorical, describing the end of the Husseini dynasty of beys. The "doctors" represent everyone who had ever tried to keep the ruling bey on his throne when he was weak—at least from 1881 onward, if not before—and Khalti Hadda's proud claim that she had "nursed [Sidi Ali] like a baby" suggests that the beys, who had ostensibly ruled in the name of the Ottoman sultan in Istanbul (i.e., they had come from elsewhere, were foreigners), had finally become Tunisians: they were born in Tunisia, and they died there. Khalti Hadda's phrase evokes an image of Sidi Ali as her son and speaks to the notion that the class system that historically maintained a gulf of difference between her and him broke down toward the end, as the (by now largely ceremonial) power that gave the beys their standing eroded and finally dissolved.

Sidi Ali's role as a father, like that of the Bey to the Tunisian people, had been emptied of any real meaning. When Alia remarks that her mother "never wanted to tell me who my father was," Khalti Hadda retorts: "Is a father simply a name? A father is sweat, pain, and joy. An entire life, daily care. Listen, my daughter, some things in life are better left unknown." We recall the earlier scene in which, hearing on the radio that French soldiers have shot at nationalist strikers, Khalti Hadda's son Hussein (Kamel Touati) says: "The Bey can do nothing" (but he adds: "The struggle must continue"). For the first time thinking the unthinkable, Khalti Hadda says fearfully: "If the Bey leaves, the country is lost." A short time later, sitting with his family at the dinner table upstairs, Sidi Bechir acknowledges the truth: "The country is slipping through our fingers. May God protect us."

The question of national identity—what is Tunisia's cultural specificity? What does it mean to be a Tunisian?—is framed by the film, we have said, in familial terms. When Alia learns that Sidi Ali has died, she is reminded of the sources of her malaise. "The old torments resurface," she says in her voice-over narration. She then refers vaguely to "these terrible marriages." It is a curious phrase, suggesting that if contemporary Tunisia has problems—and according to the focus of the film, these would be, like her own, problems of identity—the blame for them might be laid at the door of bad governance, ill-suited partners, and unsatisfactory alliances: in short, the colonial situation. Colonialism has returned as neocolonialism; and patriarchy has reappeared—or reconfigured itself—as neopatriarchy. Sharabi puts it this way: "Cultural development is . . . a relationship between a center of power and domination on the one side and a dependent and subordinate periphery on the other. It can be fairly said that neopatriarchal society was the outcome of modern Europe's colonization of the patriarchal Arab world, of the marriage of imperialism and patriarchy" (21). Or as Mulvey observes: "The silence that has surrounded the politics of colonialism and rising nationalism achieves a certain articulation [in the film]. . . . But the silences that surround [the servant women's] sexual exploitation by the beys never find a voice."[29] When Alia says: "Sidi Ali is dead, gone with another part of my history," we understand that Sidi Ali, as representative of a class that collaborated with the colonial order and was itself once a colonizer in Tunisia's long history of foreign domination, is gone. But Sidi Ali as representative of the patriarchy is not dead.

Alia's own birth, we see, was painful, suggesting that something was "wrong" with the situation. What was wrong, of course, is that she was not born into a normal family; her paternity was never acknowledged. After she is born, the first question we hear, from one of the servant girls, is: "Who is the father?" Khalti Hadda commands the girl to be quiet (it is one of several direct allusions to the film's title). Alia is born into servitude, which reminds us of Memmi's observation that "the idea of privilege is at the heart of the colonial relationship—and that privilege is undoubtedly economic."[30] The source of the wealth of Sidi Ali's family is never explained, and we never see any members of the family engaged in "work," as such. But a clear link is established between the constant activity of the servants and the relative inactivity of their masters. Indeed, the servant women never stop working—washing, sewing, cooking—whereas, like his brother Sidi Bechir, Sidi Ali is always seen at leisure: we see him taking a walk in the palace gardens or taking a nap in a deck chair in the shade. We see him playing cards, smoking cigarettes, and dining with his family in the splendid palace dining room. He hosts a party; and on one occasion we see him playing the lute. In Mark Sinker's phrase, the role Sidi Ali plays in "the story's damaged, doomed society" is "fatuous and impossible," and his palatial home is a "mausoleum to uselessness."[31] Noting that the film is "distinctly allegorical," Sinker correctly observes that, "when the disaster comes it is presented as Alia's combined revolt and personal catastrophe, but it also marks the bankruptcy of an ancient system, in which the powerful exploit, betray and destroy those they profess to protect, all the while pimping for colonial France" (ibid.).

Although Khedija feels tender toward Sidi Ali (which is a kind of love, after all), and young Alia adores him, Tlatli's attitude is properly ambivalent. (The only moment in the film in which Alia herself more or less personally indicts the ruling class to which Sidi Ali belongs occurs during the nationalist song she sings at Sarra's engagement party, which contains the lyric: "You have handed Tunisia over to its enemy.") When Sidi Ali's wife J'neina asks her husband, "What do you see in them [Khedija and Alia]?," he replies: "What do you mean?" His incomprehension seems genuine, although he would surely understand both her jealousy and her class prejudice. She retorts contemptuously: "Don't be a hypocrite, please. You're attached to them. You've sunk so low." Although "class" is clearly understood as a positive value denoting a certain refinement of taste and manners, we observe—especially in the behavior of Sidi Ali's brother, Sidi Bechir—that it is not synonymous with nobility of character. In the scene following J'neina's reproach, the film again comments directly on the sterility and illegitimacy of the class to which J'neina belongs. We see Hussein flirt with one of the younger servant women: "I say, Shemshouma, I saw you this morning in the garden. What class! Just like J'neina." (There is a pun embedded in his compliment, as *j'neina* means "garden" in Arabic.) Shema replies playfully: "Why not? What's she got that I haven't?" And Hussein presses his advantage: "Quite so, you're far more delicious!" (The other women—who appreciate the cruel irony of the barren J'neina being so named—smile with affectionate complicity, as Shema, lifting a plucked chicken from a boiling pot, and with the smile still on her face, gives Hussein a resounding rebuff.)

In a later scene, when Sidi Bechir observes ruefully that "there are no powerful men left in the [Bey's] palace," Sidi Ali explains: "They're on the other side." Sidi Bechir replies disgustedly: "But they have no class! Class cannot be seized. It takes generations to nurture." Sidi Ali's response is the only direct comment Tlatli allows his character to make that suggests he has some sort of insight into his likely fate: "The country's had enough of us. We may end up facing the same sad fate as Farouk of Egypt." When his brother snidely asks, "Do you share these ideas with those . . . who share your nights?," we indeed wonder what Sidi Ali's response will be, for Tlatli is vague about his politics and ambivalent about how seriously we should take him as a character. His angry retort—"It's better than sinking into depression!"—suggests, finally, that Sidi Ali is hardly a three-dimensional character at all. Or that he is merely conventional, which is to say, a banal example of the colonizer who chooses to ignore his role in the catastrophic human oppression all around him, because he loves his comforts and privileges too much.

Strangely, the film seems to ask the viewer to like Sidi Ali—to see him, perhaps, as kind and gentle, in contrast to his brother Sidi Bechir, whose rape of Khedija, which Alia witnesses, will traumatize the girl profoundly and for a long time render her mute. It is necessary to the film's focus on Alia to make Sidi Ali not so much a character as a representative of a whole social class and system of oppression. As Memmi points out:

To tell the truth, the style of a colonization does not depend upon one
or a few generous or clear-thinking individuals. Colonial relations do not
stem from individual good will or actions; they exist before his arrival or
his birth, and whether he accepts or rejects them matters little. It is they,
on the contrary which, like any institution, determine *a priori* his place and
that of the colonized and, in the final analysis, their true relationship. (38)

Sidi Ali is not, as Memmi's chapter headings put it, a "colonizer who
refuses," but a "colonizer who accepts." But, as Memmi observes, "accepting the reality of being a colonizer means agreeing to be a nonlegitimate
privileged person, that is, a usurper," adding: "To be sure, a usurper claims
his place and, if need be, will defend it by every means at his disposal"
(52). The fact that Khedija seems to love Sidi Ali hardly makes him any less
contemptible—but as I have tried to suggest, Sidi Ali must somehow perform the impossible twin functions of being a sympathetic character *and*
serving the allegory as a colonizer, whether that colonizer be the French,
Tunisia's Ottoman aristocracy, or the (neo)patriarchy in general.

There is no question that Tlatli's film seeks to be an allegory of the contemporary Tunisian social reality, in which relations between classes, as too
often in the postcolonial world, are governed by rapine. ("When have the
privileged ever given up their privileges except under the threat of losing
them?" asks Memmi rhetorically.)[32] Taking Tlatli's hint that the allegorical
dimensions of her film are easy to identify, requiring only "a small amount
of imagination" from viewers, which is to say, no special interpretive competence, Gauch writes: "If spectators positioned on the inside of Tunisian
society in the mid-1990s employ only 'a small amount of imagination,' they
can read Tlatli's film as a critique not just of the national government's failure to uphold its revolutionary promises but of their own collusion with
the status quo" (20).[33] And this status quo, there can be no denying it, is
already—only seven years into Ben Ali's dictatorship—as dire as any to be
found in the Third World. As Waïl Hassan puts it in his review of Anouar
Majid's book, *Unveiling Traditions: Postcolonial Islam in a Polycentric World*:

> Much of what used to be called the "Third World" is caught today between
> a sordid present, in which autocratic ruling elites have stifled social, political, and intellectual freedom and wreaked havoc on economies already
> devastated under colonialism, and a bleaker future which promises even

greater economic and cultural devastation in a world increasingly dominated by capitalism.³⁴

Ben Ali did not wreak havoc on an economy already devastated under colonialism, although his policies led to unemployment, inflation, and a high cost of living. He grew and intensified a police state that allowed no press freedoms whatsoever, censored the Internet, monitored phone and email communications, tortured dissidents, and retained only a token opposition in a toothless parliament. As it had with Bourguiba, the state-run media maintained a cult of personality around the president, whose portrait hung everywhere, and promoted an image of him as the reformist leader of a thriving, modern, secular state that owed its good fortune entirely to him and to his chairmanship of the Democratic Constitutional Rally. The nation felt humiliated and insulted by his regime and by the rampant greed and corruption permeating his system of governance (which would be exacerbated after his marriage to Leïla Trabelsi in 1992). He wrought havoc on the intellectual, cultural, and spiritual life of ordinary Tunisians, whose sense of grievance eventually converted to outrage. By the time Ben Ali was forced to flee the country in January 2011, an overwhelming majority of the population had joined to protest his dictatorship and to demand a restoration of their sense of autonomy and personal integrity, much as Alia does on the night of Sarra's engagement party.³⁵

"We were taught one rule in the palace: *Silence*"

Tlatli's great achievement in *The Silences of the Palace*, we have said, is to offer an oedipal analysis of the colonial drama. By showing how both Khedija and Alia love Sidi Ali, their oppressor, she suggests some of the complexity of Tunisia's post-Independence struggles for "identity." And as a film that successfully speaks to its contemporary audience nearly half a century after the events it describes, *The Silences of the Palace* offers a feminist point of view that does not simply blame "the patriarchy" as a system that privileges men and subordinates women—a point of view that old-fashioned melodrama's binary vision tends to favor—but recognizes, in Béji's phrase, that "there are no longer two realities that confront each other, the colonial and the national, but two realities that intertwine."

Alia's lesson, which we are given to understand she has learned by the end of the film, is that Sidi Ali may have been her father—and indeed he seems even to have loved her—but he remained, to his death, a "nonlegitimate privileged person... a usurper," who claimed his place and defended it by every means at his disposal. Sidi Ali could never formally recognize Alia as his daughter—and she will eventually come to terms with this obdurate fact in order to get on with her life. Alia's insight occurs when Sidi Ali dies, and she recognizes that Lotfi, who will not assume his paternal responsibility for their unborn child, is repeating the same cowardly, decadent, (neo) patriarchal pattern. Like the psychoanalytic cure that brings to consciousness what has been repressed, the moment of self-knowledge for Alia will set her free (i.e., her headache will lift, and she will confront Lotfi with an ultimatum). Thirty-eight years after Independence, the film is issuing a challenge to its Tunisian viewers, asking, in effect: "*Are we modern people, or are we not?*" Berman, quoting Marx, puts it this way: "Unlike the common people of all ages, who have been endlessly betrayed and broken by their devotion to their 'natural superiors,' modern people, 'washed in the icy water of egotistical calculation,' are free from deference to masters who destroy them, animated rather than numbed by the cold."[36] Have post-Independence Tunisians, by this definition, become "modern people," as Bourguiba claimed he wanted them to be? Can Alia—who has not only been betrayed by the beys but (without his quite understanding how) has also been betrayed by Lotfi—break free of the tradition of deference that enslaved and destroyed her mother and almost destroyed Alia herself?[37] The image Marx conjures is striking—it even recalls (for this viewer) the scene in which, upon hearing that Sidi Ali is dead and seeking to relieve herself of her headache, Alia takes a bath. We see her fully immerse herself in the water, as in a ritual of rebirth, before setting out for the palace to confront the past that contains the key that will unlock the door to her new future.[38] In the film, the ultimate colonizers (the French) are for the most part offscreen; they are all but invisible. But the effects of their colonization are real, like the repression and self-censorship that haunted the latter years of the Bourguiba era and permeated Ben Ali's police state, or the predatory forces of contemporary global capitalism. As an allegory, *The Silences of the Palace* is very clear about how Alia's drama of identity represents not only the traumatic period of Tunisia's transition to independence, but also how it represents the society's difficult confrontation with its own, evolving character, forged by its long history of foreign rule and patriarchal domination.

As Denise Brahimi suggests in *Cinémas d'Afrique francophone et du Maghreb*, self-censorship is more insidious than direct censorship by the state, and it is quite as crippling to artistic vitality. An anxious, authoritarian government, however kindly its public face might be, rules by force and fear, which results in a colonization of the mind that is as baleful in its effects as the rule of silence that reigns in the palace of the film. Paraphrasing Boughedir, Brahimi suggests "the censorship that African cinemas are forced to submit to is in the end not as constraining as one might fear—perhaps because the governments do not take their cinemas seriously enough to gravely reprimand the filmmakers, or because self-censorship precedes censorship anyway, and as such, does the job by itself. This, however, makes it all the more difficult to assess precisely and accurately the damage that is done."[39]

Tlatli herself, we have noted, thinks that the cinema as a storytelling medium that "has to make use of metaphors and symbols" is well-suited to a society like hers, for it offers ways of saying what cannot otherwise be said. Like Bouzid, she refers to "Islam" in culturalist terms (which may or may not suggest that she believes the religion itself is the template from which the social organization we are calling neopatriarchy originally derives), to make the broad claim that "Islamic society" is one characterized by prohibition and repression.[40]

The acknowledgement by *The Silences of the Palace* of the corrosive power of repression and (self-)censorship is articulated first of all through mise-en-scène, in the conventional manner of melodramatic filmmaking (i.e., as in silent film, wherein it is primarily the image that tells the story). The scene near the beginning of the film, in which a French photographer makes a portrait of the extended family living in the palace, is a good example of Tlatli's style of self-consciously investing mise-en-scène with allegorical possibilities.[41] We see Alia sitting with Sarra in the gazebo in the garden, while Sarra receives her lute lesson. Sarra is called to join the family for the portrait, and Alia goes with her and stands beside her in the front row of the assembled group of princes, their wives, and children. But the photographer says to her (in French): "Move aside, you're in the frame." He evidently recognizes that she does not "belong" in the picture, for all the members of the family are dressed in white, except Alia, who is wearing

FIGURE 5.5 The photographer making a portrait of the beylical family asks Alia to move out of the frame.

a floral dress. Alia's humiliation is shared by the palace servants, who are standing nearby in a group. Khedija lowers her eyes in shame, and perhaps anger, as Alia comes over to stand next to her mother. After the photographer has taken the picture, however, Sidi Ali calls out: "Alia, come here." Under J'neina's sullen and watchful eye, Sidi Ali directs the photographer to take a photograph of him with Sarra and Alia. He puts an arm around each girl and—not smiling, exactly—the three of them face the camera: a father with his daughter and his niece. (Later in the narrative, in a moment of contradictory feeling about her parentage, Alia withdraws the photograph from a box in which she keeps her few, treasured possessions and cuts herself out of the picture with a pair of scissors.)

But Tlatli also develops the way in which *samt*—that which is not, must not, cannot be spoken—*can* speak, by deploying an oral tradition and a tradition of performance in the vernacular, most tellingly through song, dance, and the ribald gossip of the servant women, which allows everything, finally, to be said. After the scene in which the family photograph is taken, Tlatli cuts to the present. Alia has returned to the palace to offer her condolences to Sidi Ali's family, and goes down to the servants' quarters to see Khalti Hadda and to look at Khedija's room. (The extended family as a social unit living under one roof would appear to have become obsolete; there are no servants to be seen anywhere; there are no children in the household representing the next generation.) The door to the room is locked, and Mroubia (Fatma Ben Saïdane) brings the key. "Mroubia, you're still here!" Alia exclaims, to which the servant replies: "Where would you expect me to be?" At this point, Tlatli cuts to a flashback that functions in effect as a flash-forward (although we never see the scene contextualized later). The scene shows the servant women washing the wool from the slaughtered sheep after an Eid al-Adha. With smiles on their faces, they sing a song that would seem to be about a bey's infidelity toward his wife, the lyrics of which are as follows: "Beya, I'm sorry / Please don't worry so / I've fallen awfully low / I've debased myself / For the girl who was once with us / The girl who left in a whirl."[42]

There are several such scenes in the film, some of them narrativized within a framework of realism, some of them not. The culmination of the film's theme of silence—of silence, above all, about the horrors and humiliations of subalternity—rendered as an overdetermined emblem of the melodrama's core meanings, is the scene in which Alia witnesses her mother's rape by Sidi Bechir and in her imagination tries to escape from the palace. Alia has narrowly escaped being raped by Sidi Bechir herself—a scene preceded by one in which, consistent with the film's oedipal understanding of the importance of personal identity and of how human selves are formed within a familial matrix, Alia espies her mother and Sidi Ali together on Khedija's bed. Khedija is wearing a black, lace petticoat, and is smiling, as she gently presses her hand against Sidi Ali's chest. He strokes her hair, and holds her closely to him. The viewer is jolted by the recognition that it is Alia's "primal scene," for the girl suddenly turns and flees into the garden, where she throws her hands up against the aviary and looks distractedly at the small, chirping birds within.[43]

In Freud's formulation of the "primal scene," as one in which sexual intercourse between the parents is observed (or fantasized) by the child, the child usually fantasizes the scene as an occasion on which violence is visited upon the mother by the father. Because it is psychologically necessary for Alia to preserve her image of Sidi Ali as a glamorous figure, a "father" who is both and loving and stern, complicit and remote—it would be intolerable for her to cast him as a repugnant figure—the plot of the film itself will (conveniently) split the father figure into two characters: one that embodies the disgust the child feels about parental sexuality, and the other that can remain idealized, untouched by the sordid implications of the scene and her own place within it. The trauma of Alia's "discovery"/confirmation/fantasy of her origins thus is not only frightening and repulsive, but contains an oedipal element of rivalrous hostility toward Sidi Ali as well, which will be displaced by the narrative onto Sidi Ali's brother—a man who is *like* her father, but who is not her father.

Alia stands at the aviary for a few moments and then runs to the center of the lawn beside the gazebo. She runs frantically in small circles until, dizzy from the effort, she closes her eyes and collapses in a faint. Sidi Bechir, walking through the gardens at this moment, and reading aloud to himself in French, sees Alia lying on the grass and approaches her. The sound track is silent, except for the distant sound of the birds in the aviary. He slowly drops to his knees and leans over her supine body. The scene becomes thick with a menacing atmosphere of sexual transgression, as the camera cuts to a close-up of his (startlingly hairy) hand reaching for the hem of Alia's dress. Very slowly, and scarcely daring to breathe, he lifts her dress halfway up her smooth, brown thigh, decides to pull it back down, and then takes her into his arms and carries her to the servants' quarters of the palace. He makes his way to her room and lays her out on the bed. "What a beauty!" he whispers to himself in wonder.

It is only Khedija's entry into the room at this moment that deflects the prince from what appears to be his rapacious intention. He turns to Khedija instead, who tries to pull away from him. They struggle, and he roughly pushes her against the wall, at which point Alia awakens and sees what is happening. Sidi Bechir forces Khedija onto the bed, and while he rapes her, Alia stares sightlessly up at the ceiling. The sound track falls unnaturally silent, as Alia slowly brings her hands up to her temples and closes her eyes. (As she begins massaging her temples, which we saw her do near the beginning of the film, when she had a headache, we are reminded that this scene is being remembered by Alia ten years after the event; and so, like a recurring nightmare that is triggered by a headache—or a headache that is triggered by the nightmare—Alia's pain is a cycle of suffering from which there would appear to be no escape; both the headache and the nightmare are permanent: they have become a malaise.) The camera then cuts to an extreme long shot of the palace at night, as seen from the street side of the (open) palace gates. In the absolute silence of this nightmare shot, we see Alia running toward the camera, as the gates start to close. It is a zoom shot, which eventually comes into focus in a close-up of Alia's open mouth. The gates firmly close at the moment Alia reaches them, the double movement of her forward trajectory and the false movement of the zoom expressing precisely her sense of entrapment, from which her fantasy/nightmare of escape cannot release her, as she screams silently into the void. All the traumas of Alia's young life—and in the allegory, those of Tunisia's experience not only of colonialism but also of postcolonial dictatorship, which is structurally similar to the experience of female oppression under neopatriarchy—are concentrated in this scene. As Florence Martin describes it, Alia's scream is "inaudible literally and figuratively, for no one could stand to hear such a scream."[44] The silences of the palace—the silence of the palaces—refer to this moment: the absolute and abject suffering of the rape victim, who is helpless, vulnerable, abused, annihilated, deprived of all sovereignty, personhood, humanity.

The palace gates figure several times in the film. They sustain the theme of carceral oppression, not only in the lives of the servant women, but in the allegory also, to suggest that all of Tunisia has become a prison. After Khedija's rape by Sidi Bechir, Alia falls into a deep psychological depression that nearly resembles a catatonic state. She remains confined to her bed, and her condition inevitably affects the mood of the servant women, who keenly identify with the girl's despair. One day, while polishing the beys' silver cutlery, Mroubia becomes unbearably sad: "I've been waiting so long," she says to Falfoula ("Fella," played by Hélène Catzaras), who is folding table napkins at her side. "I'm getting old. After all, I have family, too!" A painful memory rises up in her: "My cousin came to see me, and they slammed the palace gate in his face." She begins to sob. "He kept calling for me, until dawn. But no one answered." As the tears stream down Mroubia's anguished face, Fella reaches out and puts a comforting arm on her shoulder: "He'll come back," she says softly, "and next time, they'll let him in." They both know, however, that Fella's reassurance is empty. Mroubia turns toward Fella, and as the camera pans slowly to follow her gaze, we see Fella frown in distress, and look away. They both know that "they" will not let Mroubia's cousin in "next time"; indeed, there will never be a "next time."

After Khedija falls pregnant, and it becomes clear to the other women in the kitchen that she is resolved to induce an abortion, the servant women

FIGURE 5.6 The nationalist song that Alia sings at Sarra's engagement party results in her expulsion from the palace.

again cannot avoid reflecting on their own condition as prisoners in the palace. The atmosphere in the kitchen is tense, for Khedija's misery coincides with reports that the political situation between the Tunisian nationalists and the French—with the Bey caught in the middle of the conflict—is rapidly deteriorating. One afternoon, on the radio, they hear an announcement that "the French government, in agreement with the Bey, and in view of the dangerous situation, has declared a state of emergency from 9:00 P.M. until 6:00 A.M." One of the servants remarks: "Our lives are like curfews." Shema, lost in her own feelings of abjection, says: "We have nothing to be afraid of. I don't belong to myself . . . I want to go out in the street, to run unhindered, naked and barefoot . . . and scream, and shout out loud. Only their bullets can silence me . . . as they run through me, turning my body into a sieve." She breaks down into uncontrollable sobs.

One of the challenges facing Tlatli, making a film about a private individual destiny that inevitably or by choice is an allegory of the embattled situation of the public third-world culture and society, is how to articulate that identity in such a way that it can speak to a broad audience, so the allegory will function successfully and ring true. When, for example, one of the servants in the film observes that their lives "are like curfews," and Shema says: "I don't belong to myself," the viewer understands these women are speaking for and to a wide range of viewers, and they are saying something about women in general or women in Tunisia (in the 1950s and 1960s, and still, in the 1990s), and about class prejudice, neopatriarchal structures, Ben Ali's authoritarian regime, and so on. The palace where these women live and work is all of contemporary Tunisia; the beys' regime is the (neo) patriarchy that now structures the whole society; the *silences* of the palace are the silence of the *palaces*. Allegory is everywhere. And so, when Tlatli herself says that, as a child, she remembers women were called "*la colonisée du colonisé*," she is deploying an allegorical image. She is not unaware that there are difficulties involved in using terms like these, however, and that she bears a crucial responsibility as a filmmaker (especially in a country that produces only one or two films a year) to articulate the embattled situation of her public third-world culture and society—for her society, as we have said, both is and is not a third-world society, and like her fellow filmmakers of the New Tunisian Cinema, she is committed to the cinema as a form of public pedagogy and as a means of influencing the debate about national identity. Carthage (the wealthy suburb of Tunis, where the Presidential Palace is located) and Sidi Bouzid (the impoverished city in the center of the country, where Mohamed Bouazizi set himself on fire, starting the social and political conflagration that became the uprising that ousted Ben Ali) are not the same kind of town, but they are both in Tunisia, and the one is no more or less "authentically Tunisian" than the other. And so, how do you make a film that "speaks the national" and articulates a notion of *tunisianité* that is not reductive or shared by too few? The issues are complex and refer not only to problems of native self-marketing and image production in a global (and neocolonial) context—wherein type can become stereotype, and stereotype can veer into caricature—but to problems that come with appropriating third-world discourse for first-world universalizing ends. A feminist like Moufida Tlatli is not, of course, automatically exempt, by virtue of her birth in the Third World, from the kind of charge made by Emily Apter, who writes in *Continental Drift*:

> Western feminists from Simone de Beauvoir and Hélène Cixous, to Gayle Rubin, Judith Williamson, and Sandra Lee Bartky have drawn on the language of apartheid, racism, and colonization to dramatize the

world-historical situation of women. Economically and socially "enslaved," sexually conquered as "Other," placed under the dominion of a despotic superphallus identified with the Orientalist sultan, their bodies "trafficked," their voices quelled by the "silence of the harem," feminist critics have qualified their subordination to a phallic regime through the language of colonialism.[45]

But Tlatli is the very opposite of a self-Orientalist, as Apter's remarks might imply (if applied to *The Silences of the Palace*). Tlatli is quite properly outraged by the suggestion that she has ever done anything in her films specifically "to please the West." As she told Hédi Khélil in an interview published in 2002: "You cannot imagine the impact that such an insult has on me. This is a political insult. Is it possible to want to please those who have colonized us and made bad critics of us, bad filmmakers, eternal beginners ... ?"[46] By setting her film in a kind of contemporary harem, Tlatli draws on a complex repertoire of images. She acknowledges the Western stereotype in which "the word [harem] functions as a synecdoche of what the West most desires and fears in the Other—polygamy and domesticated prostitution" (*Continental Drift*, 106), but she also suggests, as Fatima Mernissi writes in *Le harem et l'Occident*, that the harem is "a word synonymous with prison," a place that was for Mernissi's grandmother, "a cruel institution that mutilated women, that deprived them of their rights, starting with their right to the freedom of movement."[47] Tlatli's film offers a counter-image to the Western representation of the harem "as a place of sexual satisfaction, pleasure, eroticism, and sensual plenitude," writes Dina Sherzer in her article about the film, "Remembrance of Things Past." The filmmaker represents it "as a place where a strange ballet of desire, power, domination, attraction, and rejection is enacted, thus harming the women and making the men unhappy. Unspoken rivalries between brothers, between wives and servants, between mother and daughter, and between servants fill the silences of the palace, as do tension, jealousy, sadness, and frustration."[48]

The Silences of the Palace is what Ella Shohat calls a "post-Third-Worldist" film—by which Shohat means that it offers a perspective that "assumes the fundamental validity of the anticolonial movement, but also interrogates the divisions that rend the Third-World nation." As a feminist film, moreover, it "functions as a simultaneous critique both of Third-Worldist anticolonial nationalism and of First-World Eurocentric feminism." Shohat argues that "while still resisting the ongoing (neo)colonized situation of their 'nation' and/or 'race,' post-Third-Worldist feminist cultural practices also break away from the narrative of the 'nation' as a unified entity so as to articulate a contextualized history in specific geographies of identity."[49]

This is why, when Gauch makes the observation that Alia's obsession with her father's name is simply a screen for a more critical lack, it is the same thing as saying that Tlatli's story about Alia—the story of a private individual destiny—is an allegory of the (still) embattled situation of the ongoing (neo)colonized situation of her "nation" and/or "race" (i.e., it is a contextualized history articulated in a specific geography of identity).

When, during her final meeting with Khalti Hadda, Alia remarks that her mother would never tell her who her father was, the old servant says to her: "Listen, my daughter, there are things in life one is better off not knowing. What your mother went through could drive you mad, too. It is the will of God. We were taught one rule in the palace: *Silence*." Alia turns away, heartbroken, as the camera moves in to a close-up of Khalti Hadda's face in profile. In the dim light, the blind, immobile woman looks like a statue carved in stone. It is as if she were already dead, for Khalti Hadda is as silent as the grave—the secret that she will never reveal, her adamant refusal to utter the name of Alia's father, becomes a metaphor of the "silence" that speaks both woman's repression and her complicity in patriarchal structures.[50]

In the tradition of melodrama, the film ends on a note that means to be hopeful but leaves the viewer looking toward a future that is not at all certain. As we know, the class and gender divide in Tunisia separating a woman like Alia from the (neo)patriarch in the palace who controls her destiny (i.e., until he ceases to control her destiny), did not close or become more narrow, but in some ways grew wider during Ben Ali's so-called "economic miracle," as the rich got richer, and the poor got poorer. The singular success of individual women, like Ben Ali's second wife, Leïla Trabelsi, a hairdresser more than twenty years his junior, only highlighted the fact that generally a woman's social and economic power still depended on her place in an extended family. There would be a painful irony in the spectacle of Leïla Trabelsi Ben Ali styling herself a champion of women's rights and of Ben Ali's state feminism using her as its chief spokesperson, for Ben Ali's regime would become a kleptocracy, led by none other than Madame Ben Ali herself.[51]

CHAPTER SIX

"It takes two of us to discover truth"

Essaïda (Mohamed Zran, 1996)

Mohamed Zran's first feature-length film, *Essaïda*, confronts the question of Tunisia's national identity through the prism of social class. In the spirit of its epigraph, a quotation from Khalil Gibran's *Sand and Foam* (1926)—"Should you really open your eyes and see, you would behold your image in all images; and should you open your ears and listen, you would hear your own voice in all voices"[1]—the film insists that the widening gap between Tunisia's rich and poor is a social calamity that cannot endure indefinitely. As an allegory, the film addresses its message to Tunisia's educated elite, represented in the film by Amine (Hichem Rostom), a wealthy, middle-aged artist suffering a crisis of creativity, who befriends Nidhal (Chedli Bouzaiane), a boy from Essaïda, a poor neighborhood on the outskirts of Tunis. The film makes a statement about the social responsibility of the artist/intellectual in society and echoes Marx's argument in *The Eighteenth Brumaire of Louis Bonaparte*, in which he wrote that the French peasantry (in 1851–1852) lacked cohesion as a class and as a consequence fell into the trap of Bonapartism. "[The peasantry] do not form a class," Marx wrote, and because "they cannot represent themselves, they need to be represented." Where Louis Bonaparte's coup, in the phrase of one writer, "showed the drive for total domination by the modern bourgeois state,"

FIGURE 6.1 "In Nidhal's eyes . . . you see the life of the whole neighborhood of Essaïda." (Chedli Bouzaiane)

with its baleful consequences for both the proletariat and the bourgeois democrats themselves,[2] Zran's film similarly describes the link between the contemporary policy in President Ben Ali's Tunisia of economic growth at any cost and the growing dysfunction and despair of the urban poor.

Essaïda is not self-consciously analytical about the causes of the poverty that characterizes its eponymous neighborhood—it cannot really tell us whom or what to blame for the fact that Nidhal's father is unemployed and often resorts to violence when he becomes drunk; nor can it explain (except as an allegory of the rapine characterizing Ben Ali's regime) why Hatem, the petit-bourgeois son of the capital's wealthy *banlieue Nord*, who will recruit Nidhal into his gang, has become a professional thief who steals from the houses of the rich and, by his own admission, even from his own family. But it knows what everybody knows—that, as Albert Memmi (himself a native and once also a poor boy of the Tunis medina) forthrightly puts it in *Decolonization and the Decolonized*: "Poverty engenders instability and instability violence. The inability to create an adequate number of stable jobs leads to long-term unemployment and endemic uncertainty."³ From the evidence, moreover: "Poverty leads to and helps prolong ignorance and superstition, stagnant forms of social behavior, the absence of democracy, poor hygiene, sickness, and death" (5).

Essaïda is reluctant to point a finger squarely at Amine, to indict his social class as the direct or indirect cause of the social conditions and train of events that lead to Nidhal's death. But again, in Memmi's words, it knows that:

> The Tunisian exception, even when held back by the incomprehensible police pressure found there, proves that anything is possible. Illiteracy has nearly disappeared, the condition of women has improved substantially. But here too aren't we ignoring the real reasons for poverty, which are internal and, therefore, susceptible to change? Namely, that the wealthy and the rulers want to distract the attention of the people, convince them that their poverty is inevitable, the result of fate or some foreign plot, hoping to disarm resentment and prevent revolt. (23–24)

The short answer to the question that haunts *Decolonization and the Decolonized*—How do you explain "the extreme poverty of the third world"?—would seem to be that third-world countries are characterized by poor leadership and moral bankruptcy. "Are the wealthy citizens and leaders of those countries convinced of the need for change?" Memmi asks rhetorically. "Can we not assume rather that they prefer stasis? That the current situation, in the end, is convenient for them?" (23).

In *Abécédaire du cinéma tunisien*, Hédi Khélil writes that we would be wrong to think of *Essaïda* as picking up "the theme of social engagement so dear to the generation of Tunisian filmmakers of the 1970s, as certain people claimed at the time of the film's triumphant release in 1996."⁴ Although the film's "Manichean clichés depicting Tunisian society as one riven by glaring inequalities between poor areas and privileged enclaves perfectly suit those who are nostalgic for a Marxist discourse of uncompromising class struggle," Zran's success with the public is due, rather, to a populist vein that he mines so sympathetically (133). Khélil observes that the film would appear to be an indictment of social conditions in Tunisia, but in fact does no more than offer a series of impotent gestures toward the idea of political engagement (133):⁵

Essaïda is not an example of art that glorifies political engagement and the commitment of the intellectual to the struggles of the underprivileged, but a fiction that shows the impasses, and confirms the decay, of such an illusion. It is hardly a question, then, of being a call for a collective protest against exclusion and marginalization, but simply [a film about] two individuals whose paths cross in a particular place, who come together, draw apart, come together again, and separate. (133–134)

But as I shall argue, the film does deliver an indictment, however embedded or imperfectly understood by the filmmaker himself, of the following: Amine's social class, which is ineffectual and has entirely given up the struggle for social justice (if indeed it was ever engaged in that struggle); the dysfunctional neopatriarchal structure of the Tunisian family (at least as it persists in the social class to which Nidhal belongs); and Tunisia's political economy of repression (which produces a character like Hatem, who should not be seen merely as one of his society's bad apples—an aberration, a melodramatic character representing "Vice"—but as a representative of the mafia-like regime that rules from the Presidential Palace in Carthage and controls every aspect of economic, social, and cultural life in Tunisia). Zran's method, precisely, is contained in the last line of the epigraph he chooses for his film: "*It takes two of us to discover truth: one to utter it and one to understand it.*"

"A Child Is Being Beaten"

Just as there is an epigraph that concludes the film, there is one that begins it: "*Look at ourselves as we are, that we might become better than we are.*"[6] The viewer may wonder: Who are "we" in this exhortation? To whom is this epigraph addressed? As I indicate above, the film would appear to address its message to Tunisia's educated elite; but, of course, the message is to any viewer who feels that he or she is interpellated by these epigraphs (which, as such, make an intellectual rather than an emotional appeal). A viewer may identify emotionally with Nidhal, the poor and ignorant boy of Essaïda; but it is to any and all of us possessed of self-consciousness and an ethical sense of citizenship that the film makes its appeal to bring about socioeconomic change.

The opening shots of the film show Nidhal and his friends hanging out on the streets of Tunis and begging for money. They give each other tips on which begging strategies work best: one suggests that pretending to be blind is most effective, while another, to amuse the other boys, gives an exaggerated demonstration of how to perform economic desperation. An old man wearing the traditional *djebba*, scarf, and *chechia* says to the boy, as he passes: "Why don't you get a job!" Not far from the boy, in the background, we see a man selling oranges from his cart (an example, perhaps, of the sort of work the old man has in mind). Superficially, this would appear to be a "modern" society: other pedestrians include young women in modern dress—some in miniskirts, others in tight jeans—and still others are wearing the traditional *safsari*. The younger men on the street are dressed in contemporary, Western garb (long pants and short-sleeved shirts).

Following the opening credits, the narrative proper begins—with a scene of Nidhal being beaten by his father. The first shot is an extreme close-up of a woman's hands kneading dough in a shallow basin, an action that is performed with violent gestures that pull and press and tear at the dough, while we hear a man's voice on the sound track, shouting: "You've come back empty-handed!" The boy (Nidhal) is pleading with his father to stop beating him. Finally, as the camera pulls back, we see that there are tears streaming down the woman's cheeks. It is Nidhal's mother, Zeineb (Fawzia Badr). She stops what she is doing and turns to her husband: "Omar, he's your son! I beg you to stop!" Omar (Abdallah Mimoun) continues to beat the boy savagely with his belt and calls him a "son of a bitch!" When Nidhal's mother demands that he "take that word back—he's your son!" Omar turns and strikes her across the head, and she falls to the ground. He continues to beat the boy; but when she declares, "I shall implore God—He will take his revenge on you!" Omar is momentarily distracted. He strikes his wife a second time; and Nidhal seizes this opportunity to make his escape. Breathing heavily and resembling a punch-drunk boxer or an exhausted bull facing his torero, Omar turns to his wife and says: "You always take his side! You're all against me!"

It is a scene that is familiar in Tunisian cinema, yet remarkable. Zran's camera in the film's prologue has prepared the viewer to identify with Nidhal. But here, not only do we see the beating of the boy from the mother's point of view, we are given some insight into the father's subjectivity as well. In his case study, "A Child Is Being Beaten" (1919), in which Freud

FIGURE 6.2 Nidhal and his father Omar (Abdallah Mimoun) dine separately from Nidhal's mother Zeineb (Fawzia Badr) and sister Donia (Mabrouka Chtiri).

explores the childhood beating fantasy ("its transformational stages, its changing cast of protagonists, and the differences between girls and boys in the sequences and meanings of the fantasy"[7]), he concludes that the unconscious fantasy of boys, like that of the girls, is: "I am being beaten by my father."

I invoke Freud's essay not because I think this scene of Nidhal being beaten ought to be interpreted in terms of fantasy, but because I wish to draw the viewer's attention to the complexity and interplay of the point-of-view structures deployed by Zran for the light they shed on the general question of the moral responsibility of the artist (Zran the filmmaker or Amine within the film) and the implications of this question for the viewer. Just as Freud—to borrow Ethel Spector Person's summary of his conclusions—uses the "child-is-being-beaten" fantasy "to explore the genesis and structure of fantasy, its developmental sequencing, and the interplay between unconscious and conscious fantasy" (x), we may ask: Who is the film's implied viewer? What is the film's mode of address, and hence, its ideology? What, or whom, does the child represent in the film as an allegory?

Like the tyrannical fathers of other Tunisian films (*Man of Ashes* and *Halfaouine* come most readily to mind), Omar clings to his paternal and patriarchal prerogatives, even as—or precisely because—those "prerogatives," if we may call them that, have been undermined by seismic changes in Tunisian society brought on by a host of political, social, and economic challenges that, as Benjamin Stora correctly observes, derive from "both the flow and ruptures of North African history over the *longue durée* and the ever-accelerating processes spurred by modernity and globalization."[8] Like so many other New Tunisian Cinema films, *Essaïda* inscribes its themes in terms of sexuality. We see a psychoanalytic understanding of the issues at stake; a story of the private individual destiny (to echo Jameson, once again) is articulated as an allegory of the embattled situation of the public third-world culture and society.

"Where is my father?"

Like Noura in the earlier *Halfaouine* by Boughedir, Nidhal forms an emotional bond with an older man who is more attentive to him than his own father. Where it is easy to see why Nidhal would respond to the attention that Amine focuses on him, the precise nature of Amine's investment in his relationship with the boy will remain ambiguous. When Amine first comes across Nidhal on the street, the boy fixes him with a well-rehearsed, doleful look that is intended to persuade Amine to give him a dinar. But Amine returns Nidhal's look with a stare of such intensity, that the unnerved boy demands to know: "Why are you looking at me? Give me a dinar, or get lost!"

From this first exchange and throughout the film, the question of what Amine wants from the boy is shot through with undercurrents of feeling that are never named. Amine gives Nidhal a dinar, and the boy flees. The older man follows him all the way to Essaïda, which is some distance away by train. When he catches up with him, Amine tells the boy he wishes to paint pictures of him. "I am not a flower or a bird!" Nidhal retorts—but clearly he is intrigued. (It occurs to the viewer that if Nidhal had really wished to evade Amine, it would have been easy for him to do so at any time during the twenty-minute train ride to Essaïda or in the warren of Essaïda's dusty streets.) "I am known. Don't be afraid," Amine tells him.

But Nidhal will not be infantilized by this stranger nor cowed into deference by the class difference between them. "I'm in my own neighborhood, here! I'm not afraid! I don't know you," he replies defiantly—in response to which, Amine says: "I gave you a dinar. Have you forgotten?" Nidhal gives him a contemptuous look: "A dinar! Here's your dinar!" He throws the coin to the ground at Amine's feet and walks away. It is a sort of game, which allows Nidhal to assert his status and dignity as a "known" member of the Essaïda community (Amine is the one who is out of his element here) and serves to bring the point of view back to Nidhal and put the two of them on an equal footing. As Nidhal walks away, a man who has witnessed the entire exchange approaches Amine: "Is everything okay? What's going on with the kid?"

The man's question can be interpreted in a variety of ways. Does he come forward in effect to offer protection to this middle-class man who is clearly not from the neighborhood, and who may have been robbed (or whatever) by this local boy? Or is the man trying to find out if Nidhal—as one of Essaïda's own—needs protection against this outsider? Is there class solidarity in Essaïda? To echo Marx's phrase describing the French peasantry in 1851–1852, do the inhabitants of Essaïda "form a class"? Or is the man merely bored and nosey?[9] In any event, his intrusion is a reminder of the extent to which Tunisia has become a police state under Ben Ali, and how surveillance of the citizenry occurs at every level of society. Writing in 2006, Béatrice Hibou observes in *La force de l'obéissance* (subsequently rendered in English as *The Force of Obedience*) that daily life in Tunisia "is characterized by the conjunction of an apparent normality and a constant and intrusive police presence" (81).[10]

Amine continues to follow Nidhal, and when he catches up with the boy, offers him a cigarette (which Nidhal accepts!). "Don't be afraid," Amine tells him, "I'm not a cop." Again, and still playing the game, Nidhal replies: "I'm not afraid. You press too hard." Amine comes out with it: "I want to paint pictures of you. I'll pay you." Nidhal is not a hustler (i.e., a prostitute), although, for a long time in the movie, this question—of what it is that Amine wants from him and that it might be sex—will hover in the air as a vague possibility. The question of what it is that artists "do" is confronted at the outset (Nidhal's notions about painting as an aesthetic/decorative endeavor—his assumption that artists seek to make representations of things that are "beautiful" or "pretty"—are expressed in his retort that he is "not a flower, or a bird"), although it is never really answered by the film. The commodity exchanged between hustler and john (i.e., sex for money) is different from that between model and artist, but there are similarities between them. The hustling scenario, as Bouzid's *Bezness* reveals, contains many ambiguities; or rather, it is a structure—a piece of theater, a performance, a *fantasy*—that allows a number of possibilities for the subjectivity of those involved. It perhaps goes without saying that what Nidhal might want from the relationship he will forge with Amine is bound to be different from what Amine wants.

After he accepts the cigarette from Amine, Nidhal leads Amine to his family's house, where they find Nidhal's mother cleaning bulgur wheat with her daughter and holding an infant in her lap. "Where is my father?" he asks her peremptorily and without greeting. She asks if there is a problem; and he replies simply: "A man wants to speak to him. Where can I find him?" Her facetious reply is a clear signal that all is not well in this family: "Call his secretary! How should I know? I'm not a bell tied around his neck!" But she knows where he probably is and indicates: "He'll be bumming around over there." As Nidhal and Amine set off again in search of Omar, Amine asks: "What does your father do?," to which Nidhal replies flatly: "Nothing." Not wishing to seem complicit with Nidhal's sarcasm, or perhaps only to clarify his understanding, Amine confirms Nidhal's answer by echoing his first question: "He doesn't work?"

The problem of unemployment is a central concern of *Essaïda*. As Memmi's observation quoted above makes clear, long-term unemployment leads to endemic uncertainty and engenders instability and violence. But to understand *why* the denizens of Essaïda struggle to make a living, when Amine—one of Tunisia's "wealthy citizens" who live in that *other* neighborhood, Carthage—does not have to work for a living, requires an analysis that goes beyond the film; for Amine and his girlfriend Sonia (Myriam Amarouchène) are the film's only representatives of their social class (Hatem, whom I shall discuss below, is not a member of their class, but a criminal member of the nouveau-riche petty bourgeoisie) to which, quite obviously, Nidhal's social class is bound in a dialectical relation.

Essaïda may be a suburb of Tunis, but for all its sprawling chaos, its socioeconomic structure is not that of an urban mass society but resembles that of a village, where ostensibly tribe, clan, and extended family rule.[11] Nidhal's family, as the film's window into the world of Essaïda, reveals that the old kinship system of village and tribe has broken down, and the patriarchal family is in retreat, along with the economic system that supported it. We have seen Omar violently beat his son and demand to know why he has not brought home his "earnings" from his activities on the street. And now, as Nidhal seeks his father's permission to accept Amine's offer of employment, we recognize that, for all its vaunted "modernity," Tunisia retains a large social class that is caught between the values and dictates of the patriarchal family of the precapitalist or rural setting and the imperatives of modern capitalism's nuclear (democratic) family that is both an outcome and motivating force of economic transformation. The myth of the *zaîm* (the leader, or boss) persists in Arab societies, and as Mohamed Kerrou's remarks suggest in his contribution to the edited anthology, *L'individu au Maghreb*, it is both symptom and cause of the kind of dysfunction that marks Nidhal's family: "In the Arab world, the emergence of the *zaîms* is inseparable from the existence of the myth of the undifferentiated and subordinate mass, and not of the society of free and autonomous individuals. By imposing himself as a unique individual, the *Zaîm* rejoins the old symbolic order centered on the figure of the father ('patriarchy'). Now, this order is these days unable to resolve the tensions of modernity."[12]

The development in the Arab world and in the Third World generally of a *dependent* capitalism, in the wake of European capitalism and in a Western-dominated world market, was not foreseen by either Marx or Weber, both of whom, Sharabi reminds us in *Neopatriarchy*, present (autonomous) capitalism as a necessary phase of the transformation of society. Amine's proposal to pay Nidhal (or rather, to pay Nidhal's father) for two hours a day of the boy's time, in order that he might paint pictures of him, offers a sort of allegory of this situation. If modern Europe's colonization of the patriarchal Arab world—"the marriage of imperialism and patriarchy"—created "a relationship between a center of power and domination on the one side and a dependent and subordinate periphery on the other,"[13] Amine's contract with Omar can be seen to reproduce this structure. Carthage and Essaïda might as well be two different countries; and separated as they are by the Lake of Tunis, as France and Tunisia are separated by the Mediterranean Sea (to which analogy Amine and Sonia's occasional resort to French in conversation with each other only adds resonance), we are reminded of the historical conditions of the cultural development that requires Nidhal to seek his father's permission to accept Amine's job offer.

To use Sharabi's term, Omar is not a traditional patriarch, but a *neopatriarch*—he is neither *modern* nor *traditional*:

> A central psychosocial feature of [neopatriarchal] society, whether it is conservative or progressive, is the dominance of the Father (patriarch), the center around which the national as well as the natural family are organized. Thus between ruler and ruled, between father and child, there exist only vertical relations: in both settings the paternal will is the absolute will, mediated in both the society and the family by a forced consensus based on ritual and coercion. (6–7)

For the moment, Omar still commands the obedience of his wife and children (through "a forced consensus based on ritual and coercion"); however, as we shall see, patriarchy and capitalism are on a collision course. The two questions—"Is modernization possible without capitalist development?" and "Is capitalist development possible without modernization?"—are explored by the film primarily through the interactions among its main characters, who put into play an allegory that draws the link between the natural family and the national family. The allegory functions like the fantasy ("A Child Is Being Beaten"), in which the viewer must take his or her place and ask: "Who and/or where am I in this scenario?"—which ought to lead to the question the film in effect asks: "What is my/the viewer-citizen's responsibility [in the struggle to bring an end to poverty]?"

There will be another scene in the film in which Omar beats Nidhal. This time, Omar binds his son's ankles and hangs the boy upside-down from a window bar. As he beats him mercilessly on the soles of his feet, Omar shouts: "You have to work, bring home money! If you're going to be afraid, it's me you should be afraid of! Me, and me alone! Do you understand?" As in the earlier scene, Nidhal's mother at first does not intervene, but struggles with the traditional wife's role of submission to the neopatriarch's will, until she can stand it no longer, and rushes over to her son: "Let go of the boy!" she screams at Omar, "You're going to kill him!" She unties the rope, and Nidhal's body crumples to the floor. Omar is breathing heavily, and he has a wild, desperate look in his eyes. "You're a brute!" she wails. "You ruin our lives. You're making a spectacle for the neighbors. Leave the boy alone!" Then, turning to Nidhal, she says: "I should have told you to obey him!"

"I am an artist"

When Amine first explains to Omar that he wishes to paint pictures of Nidhal, Omar is mystified. Indeed, the first meeting between the two men is comical. Nidhal and Amine find Omar on the street, playing a board game with his friends; and without ceremony, Nidhal says to his father: "This gentleman wants to talk you." One of Omar's friends is heard to whisper, "Who is he? He's not from here." They are polite, and one of them calls for a chair to be brought (the men are all seated on the ground). "No, please! I prefer to sit on the ground," Amine tells them. They offer him some mint tea, which he accepts. After the first sip, Amine declares appreciatively: "It's delicious! It has been a long time since I've tasted a glass of tea so good!" (This is one of the first indications of what Amine feels his life is "missing"—one of the first clues to the nature of his nostalgia.)

Omar gets to the point: "What do you want to speak to me about?" When Amine tells him that it concerns his son, they all turn to look at Nidhal, who is sitting awkwardly at some distance from the group. "This devil?" Omar asks incredulously. One of the old men in the group corrects Omar: "He's an angel!" With fearful concern, Omar leans forward and asks in a hoarse whisper: "What has he done?" After Amine reassures the father that his son has done nothing wrong, he goes on: "There is something in him ... He is intelligent, charming, lively. ... "

"Concretely, what do you want?" Omar interrupts him, nervously. When Amine says, "I wish to do portraits of him," Omar appears not to understand. "What do you mean?" he asks. Amine replies: "Paintings. I am an artist." He puts his hand lightly across his heart, in the traditional gesture of humility, and introduces himself: "My name is Amine. I am a painter."

Zran's framing of the scene—in a series of deep-focus shots, with Nidhal centered in the background, and Omar, Amine, and at least one of the other men in the group visible in the foreground—recalls the famous scene in *Citizen Kane*, in which Mary Kane and Thatcher in the foreground of the shot decide young Charlie's future, while the boy's agitated father paces about the room, and the boy, at the center of the shot, can be seen

IT TAKES TWO OF US TO DISCOVER TRUTH

FIGURE 6.3 Amine (Hichem Rostom) meets Nidhal's father Omar and his friends.

through the window playing outside in the snow. That Nidhal is framed here in this fashion suggests that his destiny is a community affair, and a male one. He belongs to the neighborhood as much as he does to his father. Or to put it another way: his "destiny" is inseparable from his origins in this neighborhood and from his status as Omar's son. But his destiny will also be inflected by Amine, the artist, the one who will "represent" him in a series of portraits. Omar and his friends are puzzled and slightly amused by Amine's desire to paint pictures of Nidhal, a boy whom they think of as entirely unexceptional. The question, then, is what Amine sees in Nidhal, and what purpose the paintings will serve.

When Amine returns to his studio in Carthage, he makes a pot of mint tea. The camera lingers on the shot of him pouring it, in the traditional style, from a great height, into two glasses—one for Sonia and one for himself. We recall his enthusiasm for the tea offered him by Omar's group of friends and predict that his crisis (because this glass, surely, will not equal that other one in deliciousness) is about to be triggered. "What are you thinking about?" Sonia asks. "About the show," he replies. "I no longer feel like doing it. I'm calling it quits."

The camera cuts to a shot of Nidhal and his friend Sami (Abdelkader Boughanmi) sauntering down the street, with Nidhal contriving to bump into various attractive women who walk past him. The camera returns to Amine's studio: "You know, Sonia, this kid, Nidhal . . . I followed him all over the place. I got on the train with him, and went all the way to Essaïda, where he lives. If only you could see Essaïda . . . It's another world. I could never have imagined it! I became crazy! In the streets, people followed me with their gaze. From their rooftops, their windows, as if I'd come from another world. And yet I didn't feel out of place. I felt great!"

It is a bizarre little speech that, apart from anything else, reveals Amine's vanity. He is intoxicated by the experience of slumming; he is stimulated by the Essaïdans' recognition that he is from "another world," and he perhaps imagines that they are impressed, or even envious. Sonia looks at him apprehensively. He walks around the studio, turning his paintings to the wall: "I was finding what I've been looking for. I found it there, among them. In Nidhal's eyes . . . you see the life of the whole neighborhood of Essaïda." Then follows a slightly attenuated pause, such that the viewer, like Sonia, begins to wonder about the hidden dimensions of this emotion that has clearly taken hold of Amine. "It's not the wretchedness, or the poverty . . . or the hatred . . . or the fear. It's something else. It's beyond belief." Music begins to swell on the sound track. "I'm going to bring him to my studio. He will be my model."

The music suggests that (unconsciously) Amine feels relieved at having made a confession of some sort. "I have to go to Essaïda. To live there." The camera remains fixed on Sonia, as he continues: "What I've been doing until now, that's all finished. I have to do something else." She is smoking a cigarette and looking at him suspiciously. The scene plays like the conclusion of a classic lovers' quarrel, in which the woman discovers that her man—before he quite recognizes it himself—has fallen in love with someone else. The "twist" here is the revelation that the "someone else" is an adolescent boy, and this boy, moreover, is from one of the poorest neighborhoods in all of Tunis.

To the extent that the film has an implicit notion of what a "normal" family is, Amine and Sonia do not fit that norm. We see Amine experience a mid-life crisis (Rostom was forty-eight when he made the film); and yet he is not married; he has a young and beautiful girlfriend; and he appears to have no obligations or commitments of any kind to family members, leaving him free—when he is not working at his easel—to hang out in Essaïda's cafés and get drunk with (new) friends, such as Souleymane (Tayeb Oueslati), the blind man whom he will meet through Nidhal. More interesting than the psychology of Amine's character, however, are the possible meanings of his role in the allegory.

Immediately following his announcement to Sonia of the discovery of his new muse, we see him feverishly at work on his first portrait of Nidhal.[14] When, unable to contain his curiosity any longer, Nidhal eventually gets up off his stool to take a look at the canvas, he asks in disbelief: "Is that me?" Amine tells him to "go back to your place—I'll show it to you when I'm done." The boy soon becomes bored and restless, and Amine must repeatedly command him to stop fidgeting: "Don't move! Look at me! . . . Look at me!" Nidhal tries to make a bargain with Amine: "Give me a cigarette, and I'll stop moving." The changes of Nidhal's shirt suggest that this routine keeps up for a few days, while Nidhal slowly learns the discipline of being an artist's model. After seeing his portrait, however, Nidhal becomes dejected. He had hoped that, unlike his father, Amine would really "see" him. But all the portraits Amine does of Nidhal are unrecognizable to him.

Their arrangement can be loosely interpreted as an allegory of the socioeconomic contract between rich and poor in Tunisia. Amine is getting what he wants ("Look at me! . . . Look at me!"); but Nidhal is not (the five dinars a day that Amine pays Omar notwithstanding). Eventually, Omar will decide to bring an end to his agreement with the painter, complaining that, "to be honest, I didn't think it would be like this. It's just messing about, it's not serious. . . . I'm hoping [Nidhal] will find a real job." Amine asks if it is a question of money; does Omar feel that he is not being paid enough? "It's not that!" Omar insists. "It's not the money. It's my son. I want him to find a real job, so that I can stop being responsible for him! The work he does for you . . . I don't understand it . . . it's shit. It's no good."

But Amine and Nidhal continue to see each other. Some of the rewards, difficulties, and ambiguities of their relationship are expressed one day during a conversation they have while sitting under a tree, as Amine does a drawing of Nidhal on a small sketchpad:

AMINE. What do I see there, in his eyes?
NIDHAL. What? His eyes?
AMINE. They seem sad. Why are they sulking?
NIDHAL. I have a lighter. What it needs is a cigarette. (*Amine throws Nidhal a cigarette; but Amine has trouble lighting his own.*) Do you need a light? (*They giggle.*)

The erotic undercurrents of this scene are perhaps only fully resonant for speakers of Arabic (Amine refers to Nidhal's eyes as plums, for example). The sexual metaphor contained in their exchange regarding the cigarette and the lighter retains its ambiguity (as much for Nidhal, perhaps, as for the viewer—what does Amine want, *really*?); and the deferred question is: What is the future of this relationship? Nidhal's moment of sadness is his premonition that—as Omar has already understood—their relationship is not one that a poor boy from Essaïda can really afford; it makes no real sense; it probably will not lead to anything that will help set up Nidhal for a viable future.

As if to give voice to these anxieties, a passing group of boys, seeing Amine and Nidhal together, make loud comments among themselves, as they speculate on the nature of the relationship between the man and the boy. One of the boys (although Amine appears, or pretends, not to hear him) comes out with it: "They must be fucking each other!" Nidhal tries to ignore the hecklers, but finally says to Amine: "Let's get out of here!" They return to Amine's studio:

AMINE. What's wrong, Nidhal?
NIDHAL. People . . . they talk about us. Bad things.
AMINE. What are they saying?
NIDHAL. Things that are not good . . . I'm ashamed. I can't tell you. . . . These pictures, what are you going to do with them?
AMINE. A show.
NIDHAL. A show? Who for?
AMINE. So that people can see them.
NIDHAL. People? All my friends will tease me. Is that what you want? (*Amine ponders this question for a moment, then gets up and walks over to*

Nidhal. He takes Nidhal's hand in his, and puts his other hand on the boy's shoulder.)
AMINE. Do you trust me?
NIDHAL. I do, but people don't.
AMINE: People . . . you shouldn't care about them! Let them talk. (*Amine takes Nidhal's head in his hands, and looks him in the eyes.*) We don't care about other people. Does it make you happy to work with me?
NIDHAL. (. . .)
AMINE. Take off your shirt!
NIDHAL. No.
AMINE. Take it off, so that we can work!
NIDHAL. No way! You want to paint me without my shirt on? (*Amine grabs Nidhal's shoulders, as if to remove the boy's shirt himself.*) Let go of me!
AMINE. What's up with you, Nidhal? (*They struggle for a moment, as Amine tries to get the boy to take off his shirt.*)
NIDHAL. Stop messing with me. People have their suspicions. I've lost my dignity. If it's about the five dinars, you can keep them. I don't need them, okay? (*Nidhal leaves the studio, as the camera remains fixed on Amine.*)

It is a shocking scene that can only be read metaphorically as an attempted "rape" of Nidhal by Amine. Whatever it is that Amine wants from Nidhal, it is clearly not of much concern to him whether his desires complement or coincide with those of the boy. The question Nidhal puts to Amine—Who are these paintings for?—and Amine's response, lay bare, finally, Amine's predatory egotism; and Nidhal is quite properly incredulous ("People? All my friends will tease me"). As Abdul R. Janmohamed reminds us: "If every desire is at base a desire to impose oneself on another and to be recognized by the Other, then the colonial situation provides an ideal context for the fulfillment of that fundamental drive."[15] In the allegorical reading, Amine is like the colonialist who uses his military superiority to ensure "a complete projection of his self on the Other." With his money, and his superior cultural and political capital, Amine seeks to "compel the Other's recognition of him and, in the process, allow his own identity to become deeply dependent on his position as a master" (20). He is like the colonialist who would destroy "without any significant qualms the effectiveness of indigenous economic, social, political, legal, and moral systems and [impose] his own versions of these structures on the Other" (20).

The destruction of Tunisia's rural/precapitalist/patriarchal society has already occurred, however—it is not Amine's social class (the historical bourgeoisie) that is in economic and political control in Tunisia, but rather the petty bourgeoisie in its neopatriachal formation (Ben Ali's regime, and his representative in the movie, Hatem). In this respect, to a degree, Tunisia has followed the pattern of most of the postcolonial Arab world. As Sharabi explains:

> The petty bourgeoisie's rise to dominance resulted from two main developments: the population explosion of the 1940s and 1950s, which accelerated the movement to the cities and augmented the ranks of the urban petty bourgeoisie; and the seizure of power by petty bourgeois officers and political party leaders during the post–World War II era in the four core countries of the Arab world: Egypt, Syria, Iraq, and Algeria. It soon became clear that the new class, embodied in its leadership, was an ineffective social force, lacking internal unity and coherence and utterly incapable of carrying out the tasks either of the bourgeoisie (i.e., capitalist economic development) or the proletariat (i.e., revolutionary social transformation). (8–9)

Tunisia differs slightly from this trend described by Sharabi in its relative good fortune to have had Bourguiba as its first post-Independence president, and in the qualified success under Ben Ali of the petty bourgeoisie's sponsorship of state-capitalist consumerism. There were real economic gains for the burgeoning middle class after Ben Ali's 1987 coup but dialectically linked to this economic growth was an increase in corruption and cronyism and the proportionate growth of the police state. The traditional bourgeoisie was politically disenfranchised and uprooted, and as in the four core countries of the Arab world, "the petty bourgeoisie has patronized and controlled the urban proletariat and absorbed it into its culture" (9).

Sharabi's broad-strokes description of the rise of the neopatriarchal petty bourgeoisie in much of the Arab world is worth quoting at length, for it neatly summarizes Tunisia's predicament as a "progressive" state and sheds useful light on the apparent contradictions and occasional incoherence of *Essaïda*'s discourse on social class and on the absence of anything but the most oblique acknowledgment of how the economy is structured:

Under the hegemony of the petty bourgeoisie not only did the revolution and Arab unity suffer defeat, but political life in the Arab world disintegrated into domestic authoritarianism and rivalry between antagonistic regimes. The movement of social change and development faltered, leading by the 1970s to a kind of state-capitalist consumer society in the "progressive" states and a distorted free-market capitalism in the conservative ones. Petty bourgeois rule in the former (and its cultural dominance in the latter) contributed to the spread of a peculiar kind of anomie, giving rise to a clear class split between the new petty bourgeois power elite in the "progressive" regimes (in the conservative regimes, the new rich) and the underprivileged and increasingly alienated petty bourgeois-proletarian masses. (9)

Amine is a decadent bourgeois (because politically disenfranchised and culturally besieged), and our measure of his narcissism and selfishness will be confirmed by Sonia. From her very first visit to Essaïda, made at his behest, she expresses her doubts about his plan to rent a space there. As they drive into the heart of the neighborhood in her red sports car, she observes: "There's so much poverty here!" He disagrees: "It only looks that way. You'll see how kind the people are." His response, of course, misses her point entirely. They may be "kind," but they are still poor, and the majority does indeed live in "poverty." Amine and Sonia get out of the car and start to walk. She is wearing skintight jeans and very high heels. Not surprisingly, people stare at them.

"Why are they looking at me like that?" she asks; to which Amine replies: "It's so you don't feel you're passing unnoticed! This way, they'll recognize you when you come to see me here." She is surprised and demands to know what he means. When he tells her that he intends to live in Essaïda, she says: "Here? You're joking!" As they continue, in a mixture of Arabic and French, he explains: "No, I need to be here, among the people. I need that."[16] Sonia is not convinced: "There's something else," she says ambiguously. He is quick to reassure her: "But no, I really mean it. I feel good here. I need to look into their eyes, see their dreams, and be in harmony with them."

They reach some high ground offering a panoramic view of Essaïda. "Look!" he enthuses. "This is what I love." He directs Sonia's gaze toward a building: "My studio, it'll be there, the one with the three windows. Will you be okay with that?" She can scarcely contain her anger (and perhaps fright). "I don't know!" she says gruffly, as she turns away from him and heads briskly back down the hill, to the car.

The viewer is struck by Amine's iteration of his "needs," most especially his stated desire "to look into their eyes" (the French is: *"de saisir le regard des gens,"* which in this context seems to contain a hint of violence, in that Amine, the nostalgic, Westernized bourgeois, wants to seize or steal something from the "authentic," un-Westernized, proletarian Essaïdans that he believes he has lost). His declaration that he particularly loves the panoramic view of Essaïda is extraordinary in its blatant reification of the "Other." Here and elsewhere he claims that he wants, in effect, to lose himself among the residents of Essaïda—to become one among them—and at the same time, he cherishes his status as an exceptional figure that stands above and apart from them. It is the Orientalist maneuver, par excellence. For Amine, the resident of Carthage (that leafy, green suburb of large villas and palaces overlooking the sea), Essaïda represents an internal "Other" of Tunisian society, one that—whether he quite understands it in these terms or not—will allow him to know himself better or confirm his identity (as a member of Tunisia's intellectual elite; a "known" artist).

What he and Sonia can see from their vantage point at the northern edge of Essaïda, standing on the high ground just behind the Faculté des Sciences Humaines et Sociales of the University of Tunis, on the Boulevard du 9 avril 1938, is a sprawl of half-built houses (the upper floors left unfinished, as hopeful plans for the expansion of single-story dwellings must be abandoned, for lack of funds), with the salt lake, Sebkhet el Sijoumi, visible along the eastern edge of the neighborhood, and the Sahel at the southern horizon, beyond. For all intents and purposes, Essaïda is Amine's "Orient," in the sense that Edward Said uses the term in his seminal work, *Orientalism*—"a place of romance, exotic beings, haunting memories and landscapes, remarkable experiences."[17] The Orient, Said writes, "was almost a European invention," and

> Orientalism [has been] a way of coming to terms with the Orient that is based on the Orient's special place in European Western experience. The Orient is not only adjacent to Europe; it is also the place of Europe's greatest and richest and oldest colonies, the source of its civilizations and languages, its cultural contestant, and one of its deepest and most recurring images of the Other. (1)

IT TAKES TWO OF US TO DISCOVER TRUTH

FIGURE 6.4 Essaïda, with the salt lake in the background.

The cultural project of modernity in Tunisia, launched by Bourguiba following Independence, was European in inspiration. But the economic revolution over which Ben Ali presided was not fueled by autonomous capitalism; nor was it in sync with the (faltering) cultural project of modernity, which has been not only hampered by the neopatriarchal structure of contemporary Tunisian society but also undermined by an intermittently promoted and poorly conceived program of *arabisation*. The cultural and economic gap between the Amines and the Nidhals of the society has always been wide; but the rise of the petty bourgeoisie, as the numbers of the urban poor multiply, has had the effect of exacerbating the sense of class injustice (the petty bourgeoisie having little or no sense of stewardship; and the bourgeoisie having lost its function in the rule of the country).[18] The paintings Amine will do of Nidhal and his neighborhood are for a public that visits art galleries in the wealthy and Westernized northern suburbs (Salammbô, Carthage, Sidi Bou Saïd, La Marsa . . .); they are not for anyone Nidhal would know. Considering the taboo in Islam about representational image-making—albeit a taboo that is now very attenuated, except in very conservative countries, like Saudi Arabia—it is not surprising that Zran should make Amine a painter. He is an apt symbol of Tunisia's formerly dominant, but now largely irrelevant, Westernized cultural elite, and it is perhaps inevitable that we should see his activities as a painter in Orientalist terms:

> Orientalism is premised upon exteriority, that is, on the fact that the Orientalist, poet or scholar, makes the Orient speak, describes the Orient, renders its mysteries plain for and to the West. He is never concerned with the Orient except as the first cause of what he says. What he says and writes, by virtue of the fact that it is said or written, is meant to indicate that the Orientalist is outside the Orient, both as an existential and as a moral fact. (20–21)

Sonia experiences her introductions to Nidhal's mother and sister Donia (Mabrouka Chtiri), and later to Nidhal and his friends, as extremely awkward (Nidhal rather too familiarly addresses her as "my sweet" and "my beauty"); and suddenly, she decides she has had enough. She demands that Amine give her the car keys and walks off. Amine hastens after her, and on their way back to Carthage, complains:

AMINE. What a pity! I would have liked to introduce you to other people, another world. Why are you so uninterested in people that I like? Damn!
SONIA. Do you think I *want* to come here? Have you asked yourself, Amine? This is really annoying! I've had enough! Humanitarian relief work is not my thing! (*She says this in French.*) Did you ask what I did today? Did it occur to you to ask how my exam went? Did you ask how I feel today? No!
AMINE. Sonia, listen . . .
SONIA. Shut up! You don't give a damn about the people who care for you! I've had enough. Who do you think you are, giving me lessons in moral responsibility? Who do you think you are? (*She stops the car on the highway, and leans across Amine to fling open the passenger door.*) Leave me the hell alone! Get out!

One day, after a long separation following this argument, Sonia visits Amine again in Essaïda. He is (or claims to be) very happy to see her and

IT TAKES TWO OF US TO DISCOVER TRUTH

FIGURE 6.5 Sonia (Myriam Amarouchène) feels out of place in Essaïda.

tries to persuade her to move in with him there. It is an irrational request, for it is already apparent (to the viewer, at least) that he is in flight from Sonia and what she represents; his "identity" is adrift in a no-man's-land between an imaginary and ostensibly "authentic" Orient and a semi-, perhaps even pseudo-, West. Several scenes have already amply demonstrated that Sonia would never be happy in Essaïda (the residents of the neighborhood stare at her as she passes them on the street; they make vulgar and insulting comments, loud enough for her to hear, or they address her directly, pretending to believe that she is a prostitute). She is puzzled by Amine's contradictory attitude toward her, and on this return visit to Essaïda, dressed, as always, in a chic and tight-fitting outfit that heightens the incongruity of her being there, she confronts him:

SONIA. I'm sick of coming here, Amine. You could come and work at my place, in Carthage.

AMINE. (*He laughs.*) In Carthage? What the hell can I do in Carthage.
SONIA. So, that's it. Carthage, isn't for you!
AMINE, *trying to mollify her, he speaks softly*. Why are you talking to me this way, Sonia?
SONIA. You've really changed, Amine. (*She rises from her seat, and snaps impatiently.*) You're only interested in your own existential experiments. You don't want to make any effort . . .
AMINE. What are you talking about? (*He grabs her arm, as she reaches the door to leave.*)
SONIA. (*She looks him in the eye.*) We can't go on like this.

This is one of the film's allegorical discussions about the place and role of Amine's social class in Ben Ali's Tunisia. Sonia is more correct than she realizes: they cannot "go on like this," in limbo—neither members of Ben Ali's nouveau-riche social class (the reference to Carthage, i.e., the Presidential Palace) nor members of the urban poor (i.e., Essaïda, where Amine is attempting to make himself at home).[19] As Hibou observes, there has been a rupture between Bourguiba's Carthage (which was Amine's Carthage) and Ben Ali's Carthage (represented in the film by Hatem, as I shall discuss below). She notes that the monopoly over resources and the rise of corruption are not specific to Ben Ali's regime, but their significance is:

> Previously, Bourguiba's intimates surely sought to establish personal capital and new wealth. But this quest took place in the context of a war for succession, the rotation of the political elite, positioning in the public sphere, through economic exchanges, and relations of power. Power struggles took place on the public scene of politics, and these economic practices were mostly "collateral damage." Under President Ben Ali, these practices have become constitutive of the system of control, and even of repression, in Tunisia today. All political stakes are stillborn; those who benefit from these monopolies and exactions are close to the President. They are private actors and not political pretenders; their only objective is to accumulate wealth. In other words, the meaning of the personalized management of power has been transformed, and it is in this sense that we can speak of a rupture.[20]

Amine's objectives, as Sonia acknowledges, are "existential"—they are not, in Hibou's phrase, merely "to accumulate wealth," as they were for the petty bourgeoisie in control of Tunisia's political, economic, and cultural life under Ben Ali. "Through the politics of repression," writes Hibou in 2006, "the political field and the public sphere are monopolized by the President; the economic and financial fields are now the only sites of conflict, the only objects in which stakes can be placed . . . . Even if the agents of inveiglement or corruption are private, or even mere hoodlums, politics is always present, being the only thing that tolerates them, uses them, and confers another meaning on their activities" (198).

Amine came of age in Bourguiba's Tunisia, when, for better or worse, his social class still had a role. "Art" (the film's chosen metaphor) had a stake in the political field and the public sphere. Amine's class had a voice; art could make a difference; the educated elite, in some manner, were the ruling class; they participated in the management of the state, although, of course, this management of the state "was largely restricted to political interests and political aims, in a political game that remained, in spite of it all, open to those of the inner circle" (198). With Ben Ali's rise to power, however, "monopolization of resources, corruption, and diverse economic accumulation" became new modes of governing. In short, "the frontiers between the economic and the political [became] increasingly blurred" (198)—that is, Ben Ali's regime "increasingly [based] its power on hybrid means (semi-public, semi-private) through intermediaries recognized as such by the Presidency or, more directly, by a personal allegiance to the President and his discourse" (199).

Hatem (or, "What did he do to get all this?")

Just as Sonia and Amine cannot go on living together as a couple, while she lives in Carthage and he lives in Essaïda, Nidhal cannot continue indefinitely as Amine's model. As Omar correctly points out, there is no future in it. Nor is there any future for Nidhal in Essaïda—there is a sense in which Omar's lack of a job already makes that clear. Omar, however, stubbornly insists that Nidhal find work, even going so far as to deny his son a place at the family dinner table as long as the boy remains unemployed or fails to bring money home to his father.

It is only a matter of time before Nidhal's impossible situation will explode like an intifada, resulting in violence and death. Amine's impotence, not to say blindness, in the face of Nidhal's predicament is harshly judged by the film, although, not surprisingly, the film can do no more than lament the comprehensive system of repression that is Tunisian society. Zran does not identify a villain in the manner of popular melodrama; he does not allow his viewers—in Eric Bentley's famous description of the melodrama audience that does not want to feel guilt or take responsibility—to "identify with angels, and blame everything that goes wrong on devils."[21] He knows, as Hibou demonstrates in her remarkable sociological analysis of power in Tunisia, that "political control and strategies of repression are not held by President Ben Ali and his entourage, nor by the institutions and networks that are somehow supposedly independent of economic and social mechanisms. Instead, economic and social mechanisms otherwise independent of [the] system of political control simultaneously end up serving [a] logic of domination or even repression" (202). Hibou quotes Michel Foucault's analysis of power to describe how this dynamic works:

> Power ... works like a machine. And if it is true that its pyramidal organization gives it a "chief," it is the entire apparatus that produces "power" and distributes individuals in this permanent and continuous field. This is such that disciplinary power is both absolutely indiscreet, since it is everywhere and always attentive, leaving no shaded space and constantly controlling the very people who are supposed to control; and absolutely "discreet" since it is constantly at work and mostly silent. (202)

In such a system, Amine cannot help Nidhal. He cannot, as Omar might wish, find him "a real job." One day, Amine comes across Nidhal sitting by himself on the site of an abandoned factory[22]:

AMINE. Do you come here often?
NIDHAL. It depends. ... The first time I came here, I was ten years old. I was sent home from school. I looked at the power lines. I dreamed of building a machine that would take me far away, so that I could know many other countries and friends.
AMINE. And now, what do you think about?
NIDHAL. About leaving!
AMINE. You don't like anything here?
NIDHAL. I can't have any of the things that I want.

AMINE. Can I help you?
NIDHAL. I want to go to America. In Italy and France, there are too many Arabs.
AMINE. How are you going to do that, without any qualifications or skills?
NIDHAL. I'll get out of the shit, somehow!

This conversation challenges the "truth" of the advice Nidhal's mother gives her daughter Donia after they meet Sonia. Zeineb is gracious and charming towards Amine's fiancée, who, in contrast, is ill at ease, to the point of being rude. But after Amine and Sonia leave, the little girl says: "Mama, she's very beautiful, Amine's wife," to which Zeineb answers: "Yes, but you are even more beautiful." Donia persists: "Will I have clothes like hers?" "Yes," her mother replies, "you will have even nicer clothes. You only have to do well in school." (This, of course, is an open question: Is it a just society? In Ben Ali's Tunisia, can Donia's aspirations be realized by fair and ethical means?)

As for the conversation between Amine and Nidhal, in which the boy reveals his dreams of flight and friendship, it must be acknowledged that

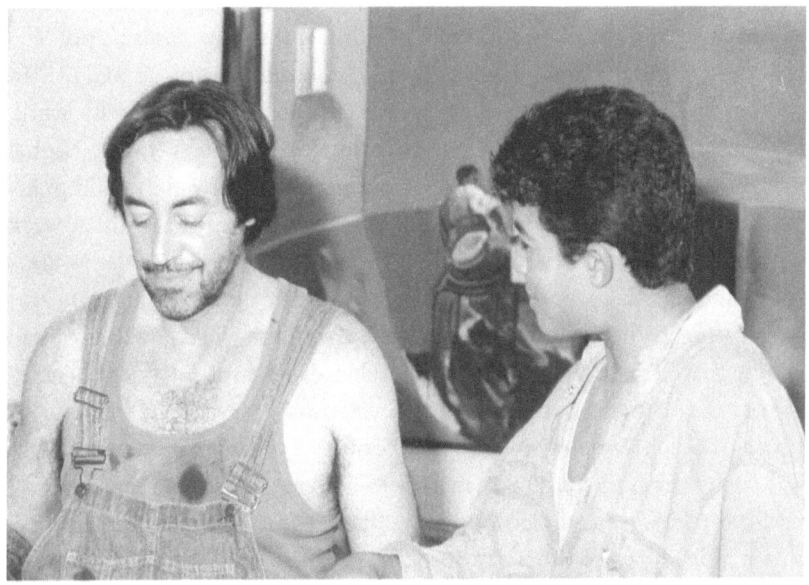

FIGURE 6.6　Amine with Nidhal in his Essaïda studio.

they are both correct: if Nidhal were to emigrate to France or Italy, he might very well encounter some of the racism he fears (but probably more because he is also "without any qualifications or skills," than solely because he is an Arab). The answer, in any case, is not to "go abroad" (as one of the options discussed by Memmi in his analysis of the contemporary predicament of "the decolonized"—even though, at home, "there is no foreseeable hope of change, just an endless stream of lost illusions").[23] An individual may "go abroad," and even find some measure of success and happiness there, but as an allegory, *Essaïda* must pursue the logic of Nidhal's destiny to its proper end, to remind us, as Memmi observes, that the rulers of third-world countries like Tunisia "are immobile by nature and by desire. They have no sincere project to offer since they are incapable of offering one, and moreover do not wish to" (67). Nidhal, as an ordinary boy (the extraordinary qualities Amine projects onto him notwithstanding), must share the fate of all other boys like him, who constitute the large social class of the urban poor.

When Nidhal is picked up in an expensive car on the La Marsa highway by a young man called Hatem (Khaled Ksouri), his destiny is sealed.[24] (The highway connects Tunis and Carthage and here symbolically suggests that the sole—or quickest—path out of poverty for someone like Nidhal is through crime; or as Hibou explains it in the terms of Tunisia's political economy, through membership in Ben Ali's political party, the RCD.)[25] In response to Hatem's questioning, Nidhal tells him he is looking for work. Hatem pretends to be surprised ("Already, at your age?"), but Nidhal explains that he needs to earn money because he is the oldest child in his family, and his father does not work. Hatem proposes that Nidhal work with him as a professional thief, robbing the villas of the rich in the *banlieue Nord*, adding: "If I were in your place, I wouldn't do a job I thought was humiliating." What he says next is as close as the film will come to acknowledging that Ben Ali's regime is a comprehensively corrupt system benefiting first his kleptocratic clan and their social class: "My father is well-off, but I scam the rich. Even my own family. I don't make an exception for them." Hibou describes the RCD as "a machine for giving and controlling, keeping under surveillance and distributing, on the individual and not on a collective level."[26] It is also the party of social revenge—a means of getting back at the traditional elite:

Social revenge thus appears as a significant dimension of the functions filled by the RCD and incarnated by the head of the party—the President himself—in person. And even more, his entourage. This is doubtless one of the explanations—but not the only one—for the widespread corruption and predatory behavior in the presidential circle, also filtering down to the party structure. Or, to be more exact, one of the interpretations of this phenomenon by the national bourgeoisie, the traditional elite and an important fringe of the middle classes: coming from a modest background, Ben Ali and his entourage thus seem to be assuaging a thirst to join the bourgeoisie and a huge need for social recognition. (92)

Nidhal agrees to work with Hatem and to bring his friends Nawfel (Lotfi Akremi) and Sami onto the "team." Hatem will wait outside the villa in his SUV, while the boys grab the items that Hatem has already picked out for theft ("a golden horse, a silver teapot, a bronze statuette . . . then, in the bedroom, a jewelry box"). They will have fifteen minutes.

When the boys enter the villa (of Hatem's next-door neighbor in Gammarth), Nidhal exclaims: "It's Ali Baba's cave! Where did he get all this? How did he do it? And why don't I have the same? I feel so small, like a mosquito! What did he *do* to get all this? Come and see! Look at this photo of these two little cocksuckers!" Nawfel tells him: "Shut up! You're the one who's a cocksucker! They could have all of Essaïda, with you as their slave!" But Nidhal says: "Let me dream." He then muses: "Oh, man, this one's got a judge for a neighbor, and me, all I've got are drunkards! It's too much. I don't know where to begin!"

Nidhal's remarks (and Nawfel's response) summarize what Hibou calls Tunisia's "political economy of repression." Nidhal's reference to the judge who lives next door is an allusion to the fact that there is no rule of law in Tunisia, except the law of the strongman president and the system of which he is the supreme embodiment. Judges in Tunisia, if they do not necessarily or literally serve at the pleasure of the president, are nonetheless fully implicated in the system of corruption.[27] This system is a function of the "totalitarian conception of power," which has the security of the state (or as the regime puts it, "the protection of society") as its first priority. But since Ben Ali's political party *is* the state (Hibou refers to *"le parti-état"*— "a party that operates like an administration" [110]), and since "there is no means of constraining the state" (118), the judicial apparatus, thus, "in concrete terms, and contrary to the Constitution ... is in the hands of the executive power" (117).[28] The independence of the justice system in Tunisia, Hibou observes, is "a pure illusion" (119).[29]

When Nidhal asks, "Where did he get all this? How did he do it? And why don't I have the same?," we note that the film's answer is very indirect (as if to say—as Nidhal does—"I don't know where to begin!"): the villain in this drama is not Amine, but a whole system, of which Hatem is but a symptom and synecdoche. In the familial terms of melodrama, Nidhal seeks a Father to put in place of his own dysfunctional father; but Hatem, like Amine, is more of a brother figure than a father. The Father/the Law is absent from the film as a figurable entity; as already noted, Zran will not furnish a straw-man villain (Ben Ali, for example) because he knows it is more complicated than this. The (corrupt and dysfunctional) Law of the Father/the rule of law (the judge) is everywhere and nowhere—for, to cite Foucault again—while it may be true "that its pyramidal organization gives it a 'chief,' it is the entire apparatus that produces 'power.'"[30] As Hibou puts it:

> The judicial system contributes, by intimidation, fear and social control, to stigmatizing and punishing whoever wishes to set himself apart; it thus appears as a central mechanism of the power of normalization. This control is not exercised on a group of people, a social or professional category or a class, but affects everyone, individually. It operates less as a system of justice and more as a system of individual control; it operates less as a judicial mode and more as a mode of social protection. As is suggested by the systematic way in which, in cases of litigation, judicial decisions favor enterprises, Tunisian justice is a functional justice, and its function is essentially to "protect society"—or rather to protect a certain order of society—and to ensure the proper functioning of measures of security and the realization of the pact of security.[31]

The film offers an allegory of this systemic use of intimidation and fear in the scene in which Hatem orders one of his henchmen to rape Nidhal. After their successful heist, Hatem shows a reluctance to pay the three boys for their part in the robbery, but Nidhal is adamant that they should be paid properly and in a timely fashion. They arrange to meet in a sort of no-man's-land near the Sebkhet el Sijoumi. Hatem's sidekick accuses Nidhal of getting too big for his boots and of being insolent toward his "masters." Just as Nidhal picks up a rock to throw at him, two policemen on horseback appear on the scene. The boys flee, but Hatem is obliged to stay with his car, and the scene ends on an image of the policemen ordering Hatem to put his hands behind his head and to get down onto his knees.

Several evenings later, Hatem and his associates catch up with Nidhal and Sami in a dark alley, where they proceed to beat up the two tearful and frightened boys. We see one of Hatem's gang order Sami to sit on his lap. The man reaches inside his (own) pants and withdraws a wad of money from his crotch: "You see these bills—they're counterfeit. Exchange them for real money, and you get half. If you don't do it, you'll pay with your skin." Hatem, in the meantime—as he shoves Nidhal toward an older man—orders the boy to pull down his pants. The older man repeats the order: "Pull down your pants! Which do you prefer—by force, or gently?" Sobbing, Nidhal reminds him: "Have you forgotten me? You came to the barbershop when you got out of prison . . . it was a morning . . . I gave you a free haircut, without telling my boss!" The man lifts Nidhal's face toward the light: "Yes . . . it's coming back to me. I recognize you." And with a vulgar thrust of his hips, throws Nidhal off his lap and tells him to "get lost."

When Nouri Bouzid says of Tunisia, "I believe our society is built on rape,"[32] he is referring not only to the violence that underpins authoritarian regimes, but also to his perception that in Arab-Muslim societies "the filial relationship"—which is "associated not with the Oedipus complex but with the myth of Abraham, who was prepared to sacrifice his own son"[33]—is grounded in violence also. Indeed, the "social structure" of contemporary Arab-Muslim societies produces what Bouzid calls a "destiny of defeat," "a feeling of helplessness faced with something we're being dragged into, something we haven't chosen" (52–53). Using his films *Man of Ashes* and *The Golden Horseshoes* to illustrate his point, Bouzid observes that the family (the "patriarchy, the father, and machismo"), religion (which commands that the son submit to the father, no matter how tyrannical this father may be), and the state are mutually reinforcing in their destruction of the individual: "The first film speaks of the destruction and rape of a child; the second speaks of another form of destruction and rape of an adult. The true defeat is in one's education and the type of relations one has with individuals; the relations between the social structure and the individual, whether the state, the family or the religious structure. This relationship is one that destroys the individual" (56).

"I've had enough!"

Khélil notes that while Nidhal's name in Arabic means "militancy," Nidhal is not the leader of the outcasts or reprobates, nor is he their spokesman. His final protest, before his fatal fall, is that of an individual who does not identify with the community; indeed, he repudiates it, by repeating the phrase: *"I've had enough!"*[34] The crowd that gathers at the foot of the electricity pylon from which he is threatening to jump begs Nidhal to come down; but he is insensible to their entreaties: "I don't want to live like you! I want to live my life. I want a worthwhile job. I want to be a man. I am going to die in front of you. My father will stop worrying about me, and so will you. I will no longer live the life of a dog, as you do! I'm sick of all of you. Do you hear me?"

Nidhal is speaking to his fellow residents of Essaïda, but the film's protest against the real forces that have brought him to this point of despair—the moral apathy of Amine's class; the brutality of what Bouzid calls "the filial relationship" in Arab-Muslim societies like the one in which Nidhal lives; Tunisia's political economy of repression (in which the only choices for Nidhal are a lifetime of poverty or a life of crime)—is very nearly obscured by his speech. Amine (whose name, Khélil tells us ironically, means "of good faith") joins the crowd, adds a brief entreaty to theirs, then turns away and leaves the scene, without so much as a backward glance. Khélil remarks that on no occasion during their relationship did Amine make any attempt to offer Nidhal moral guidance or set him on the right track: "He didn't come to Essaïda to reform a young boy and educate him, but to take from him the one thing he had that was most instinctive and passionate: his look" (134). (Khélil is referring to the intensity of Nidhal's look—which captivates Amine on the day of their first meeting—in which the older man believes he sees the key to his own identity as a Tunisian, a citizen of a country and member of a society that includes both "Carthage" *and* "Essaïda.")

As if to confirm Sharabi's thesis about the coercive nature of neopatriarchal societies (where the Father is "the center around which the national as well as the natural family are organized" [6–7]), the policeman who has been pursuing Nidhal and threatening him with dire punishment now calls up to the boy: "Come down! You are like a son to me! Don't be afraid, I won't do anything to you!" Moments later, Omar arrives on the scene and positions himself next to Nidhal's anxious mother and sister at the front of the crowd: "Come down, my son! Please! I won't beat you anymore. Come down, I beg of you! I won't do anything to you!"

Omar's entreaty is the only one that moves Nidhal, who very tentatively starts to climb down. But when his mother starts ululating, he loses his footing and falls to his death.

Khélil's complaint is that, in the final analysis, Zran's film is not an example of politically engaged art. *Essaïda* functions, rather, on the level of "anecdote" (135). In one scene, for example, where we see Nidhal and Amine sitting in an outdoor café in the (formerly European) Lafayette district of Tunis, a young man dressed as a soldier "appears like an extraterrestrial, uttering the words: 'Where is my pen? Give me back my pen. I want my pen'" (135). Mohamed Zran is "addicted to the anecdote," Khélil remarks: "Military servicemen have replaced the intellectuals: it's a seductive idea. But the apparition of this character, stuck in a litany [of such anecdotes/characters] going nowhere, is purely illustrative" (135–136).

Khélil is correct in only one sense: the film on one level is unexpectedly apolitical—or rather, despite what Khélil calls its "Manichean clichés" showing a Tunisian society riven by deep inequalities—it would appear to be strangely depoliticized. And it is true that as a call to arms it is less than direct about who or what the real enemies are. But the film is a perfect example of what I have been calling an allegory of resistance; its politics are occulted, but they are clearly articulated for those who are able and willing to read them. The film cannot come out and say: "We want to overthrow our entire system of repression—that is, we want to reform the family structure; we reject the part of Islam that demands submission to the tyrannical Father (as illustrated by Islam's story about Abraham and Ishmael); and we want to modernize the political economy of the state." This is why even the ending of the film, which is where films often summarize their point of view—Nidhal's funeral procession through the streets of Essaïda, and the shots of Amine completing his mural of the neighborhood—must be coded in allegorical terms.[35]

Nidhal's coffin is covered in a green cloth, and the young men holding it high above the crowd, chanting in unison, beg God to forgive them. The funeral procession is clearly an act of protest; the mourners are united in their feeling of solidarity with the dead boy—but Zran, as we have said, draws back from turning his film into a melodrama by pointing a finger of blame at a single cause of Nidhal's death. The general cause is the poverty of Nidhal's milieu. This kind of poverty, Memmi reminds us, "leads to and helps prolong ignorance and superstition, stagnant forms of social behavior, the absence of democracy, poor hygiene, sickness, and death" (5). Nidhal's suicide speech—"I don't want to live like you! I want to live my life. I want a worthwhile job. I want to be a man . . ."—clearly identifies the nature of his distress, from which the viewer infers the causes.[36]

The final shots of the film, of Amine completing a large mural on the site of the abandoned factory, are remarkable: Amine's painting of Essaïda resembles not at all the scene in front of him. The screen image is divided in two: the upper half shows the dilapidated buildings of the factory and its inert chimney stacks; the lower half shows the prettified, panoramic view of the neighborhood as Amine "sees" it. If, as the epigraph that concludes the film suggests, Amine has made an attempt to open his eyes and "see" Essaïda and has failed, we have to consider that the epigraph is and always was for us, the viewers of the film: "*It takes two of us to discover truth: one to utter it and one to understand it.*" It is *we* who must "*look at ourselves as we are, that we might become better than we are.*"[37]

CHAPTER SEVEN

"It takes a lot of unruly individuals to make a free people"

Bedwin Hacker (Nadia El Fani, 2002)

From an apartment jammed full of equipment, Kalt spends her days hijacking the frequencies of foreign television channels and using them to broadcast messages in Arabic, signed by a moving cartoon character, a camel named Bedwin Hacker. When Julia, alias Agent Marianne, from the Paris counter-hacking department recognizes the signature as that of Kalt, her old rival, she uses her friend, the reporter Chams, to collect more information. Chams begins working on the case unaware that he is the catalyst for a game of cat-and-mouse between the two women. Energetic and warm hearted, *Bedwin Hacker* gives a modern portrayal of North African women and culture.[1]

Most descriptions of *Bedwin Hacker* do not identify the film or its protagonist specifically as Tunisian; nor do they give any hint of the terrible frustration and anger so often felt by the Arab world in relation to the West and by Arab and many third-world populations in relation to their own governments—which in fact forms the very matrix of *Bedwin Hacker* as a national allegory.

As the director Nadia El Fani herself has acknowledged, it required cunning on her part to get her political message across—a message that the Tunisian government, certainly, would never have supported in the form of a subsidy, had it understood what she wished to say—and so she approached her theme through humor and used the conventions of genre to accomplish what amounts to a radical indictment of the Tunisian police state. "With this cyber-spy movie," she remarked in an interview, "I am supposedly addressing the West, when in fact I am directly talking about contemporary Tunisian society."[2]

IT TAKES A LOT OF UNRULY INDIVIDUALS

FIGURE 7.1 The Bedwin Hacker intercepts the frequency of a foreign television channel.

Published reviews of the film take the movie's plot premise at face value, that the hacker of the title is a cyber-activist engaged in a kind of awareness campaign aimed at (the complacency, racism, and capitalist greed of) the West. But Tunisian viewers undoubtedly recognize that the film is as much a complaint about how countries like theirs can become victims of a first-world neocolonialism that prevents them from becoming as free and prosperous as a country like France, as it is a critique of the Tunisian state's own paranoid insecurities, especially as these are reflected in the regime's efforts to monitor all electronic exchanges of information among Tunisians and its attempt to have total control over how they use the Internet. The film's theme of espionage is hardly the stuff of fiction: the lived reality of ordinary Tunisians—the way in which the surveillance-obsessed Tunisian state impinges on the lives of its citizens—is the film's real subject, not its plot machinations involving the French DST (La Direction de la Surveillance du Territoire), except inasmuch as the DST may be read as a stand-in for the Tunisian government itself. The film's global theme signals the paradox that produces the humiliation and frustration felt by nearly all Tunisians during the Ben Ali era who had access to the Internet and satellite television and who had some idea about how the rest of the world lives: they are connected to the "global" world, but Ben Ali's regime allows them only limited, closely surveilled participation via the Internet in that world beyond Tunisia's geographical borders. The film's spy theme and its trajectories of pursuit and evasion contain a warning: they are a reminder of the way in which many third-world peoples are caught in a circuit of oppression and resentment. Feelings of resentment among the citizens of third-world dictatorships toward their own repressive governments are exacerbated by Western support of those regimes. These feelings redound to the (growing) resentment felt toward the West, which appears to be in a position to alleviate their plight (one characterized invariably by economic hardship and/or an absence of human rights), but which does—or appears to do—little or nothing to change this order of things.

In the postcolonial era, which coincides with the contemporary era of globalization—wherein globalization, in John Tomlinson's representation of the phenomenon, refers to "the rapidly developing and ever-densening network of interconnections and interdependences that characterize modern social life"[3]—the stakes remain the same as they ever were, only now they are higher, or so it would seem. As Zygmunt Bauman puts it: "The so-called 'globalizing' processes rebound in the redistribution of privileges and deprivations, of wealth and poverty, of resources and impotence, of power and powerlessness, of freedom and constraint. . . . What is a free choice for some descends as cruel fate upon others."[4]

Bauman argues that "the freedom of mobility" is at the center of the processes of globalization, which "puts a new gloss on the time-honored distinctions between rich and poor, the nomads and the settled, the 'normal' and the abnormal or those in breach of the law" (3). We see this in *Bedwin Hacker*, which examines the "new gloss" on the old distinction between colonizer and colonized; and while it is true that Kalt (Sonia Hamza), throughout the movie, until the end, outwits the attempts of Julia (Muriel Solvay) to arrest her,[5] the film not only draws attention to the enduring inequalities and areas of mistrust that characterize the postcolonial relationship (between France and Tunisia), it also registers a keen disappointment in the failure both of decolonization and the transformation of culture brought about by globalization to change the rules of repression and oppression. Embedded in the film's cat-and-mouse game between the French woman and the Tunisian woman is a discourse about *why*—to use the French woman's terminology and point of view—the Tunisian woman would appear to be teaching her ten-year-old niece, Kmar (Lilia Falkat), "how to become a terrorist."[6] (Kalt's response to Julia's accusation is that she is *"teaching* [Kmar] *how to be free!"*) During the decade between the 9/11 attacks upon the United States and the Arab Spring of 2011, the West tended to be suspicious of all expressions of Arab or Muslim discontent in Western countries and was quick to label any act of resistance (to injustice or oppression) by an Arab or Muslim as "Islamic" in character or inspiration. For some Arab leaders, Ben Ali among them, George W. Bush's absurdly named War on Terrorism (sometimes also described as a War on Terror) provided an opportunity to crack down harder, and often with shocking brutality, on the political opposition—in whatever form it was perceived by the regime to be taking—in the name of "national security." As Tunisia's most important Islamic thinker Rached Ghannouchi put it (before he came to power in 2011), Ben Ali's regime succeeded in suppressing all opposition in Tunisia:

> Democracy [has been] the loser. . . . Civil society, as a consequence [has been] weakened because it no longer has any means of protection. The government fabricated a plot and portrayed [the Islamist opposition] as enemies of democracy and human rights. The idea found resonance in the ears of its listeners; but this did not result in more freedom. Instead, it resulted in widespread oppression and an ever-tightening security grip. The Tunisian League for Human Rights [LTDH] is being increasingly weakened. There are no longer any liberties, only the hegemony of the police and the Mafia.[7]

Although El Fani does not invoke or endorse the Islamist "answer" to the "widespread oppression" and "ever-tightening security grip" in Tunisia—and all her characters are thoroughly secular (indeed, they would be viewed with strong disapproval by most Islamists)—the Bedwin Hacker of the film's title is a fighter for liberty in much the same way that Ghannouchi's Islamists claim to be.[8] Its enemies are also "the police and the Mafia," and in Ghannouchi's phrase describing the program of the Islamist opposition political party in Tunisia, Ennahdha, it is committed to making a coordinated effort "on issues such as the question of liberties, defense of civil society, the press, the lower social classes, the formation of a strong

FIGURE 7.2 Kalt (Sonia Hamza) teaches Kmar (Lilia Falkat) how to be a hacker.

national economy, the openness of Tunisia towards its own environment: the Maghreb, and Europe."[9] *Bedwin Hacker* in effect echoes with the similar conviction that, as Ghannouchi has said:

> To achieve democracy, we should never rely on the support of the state. All the experiences which ignored the people's aspirations, their dignity, their fundamental liberties and their identity, all the efforts of persuasion which were concentrated on the state as a means for the achievement of development, modernity and democracy, were but a failure. It is the people who should build the state, their own state, govern it and use it as a means to achieve their goals and objectives. . . . [This approach] is a democratic [one], since it gives priority to society, to culture, to the freedom of man and his dignity.[10]

This is exactly what Kalt means when she says she is teaching Kmar how to be free, and it is a sad comment on the state of Tunisian political culture at the time the film was made: the first lesson Kmar must learn in effect is never to "rely on the support of the state"—which is another way of saying that the state is not to be trusted.[11] Kalt herself, of course, is the best role model for the girl, who will learn from her the Bedwin Hacker's lessons about self-empowerment and resistance to oppression.

"Other periods, places and lives exist"

One of the inspirations for the characterization of the film's protagonist as a fighter for liberty is the nonconformist French journalist, polemicist, and novelist Georges Bernanos, who spent his last days in Tunisia, before he died in 1948. In the film, the writer is quoted by Kalt's Uncle Salah (played by El Fani's own father, Bechir El Fani), who reads to Chams from Bernanos's *Les enfants humiliés: Journal 1939–1940* and asks him: "What do you think of this: 'It takes a lot of crazy youth to make a free people'?" The principal message of *Bedwin Hacker* is perhaps more clearly revealed in the original passage in Bernanos's book:

> Il faut beaucoup de prodigues pour faire un peuple généreux, beaucoup d'indisciplinés pour faire un peuple libre, et beaucoup de jeunes fous pour faire un peuple héroïque. [It takes a lot of spendthrifts to make a generous people, a lot of unruly individuals to make a free people, and a lot of crazy youth to make an heroic people.] [12]

Kalt is not crazy (nor even reckless—if that is the better translation here of *fou*), but she is generous, disobedient, and heroic. At the beginning of the film, we see her save her Algerian friend Frida (Nadia Saïji) from indictment by the French authorities for living in France without a valid visa; and we see that she shares with Frida's estranged husband Mehdi (Ahmed Hafiane) the responsibility of looking after Frida and Mehdi's young daughter, Kmar.[13] Above all, she is the Bedwin Hacker, who hacks into satellite transmissions of television programs to transmit the message, written in Arabic (and sometimes also in French and other languages): "*In the third millennium, other periods, places and lives exist. We are not mirages.*"[14]

Bedwin Hacker is a protest against what Ella Shohat and Robert Stam call "unthinking Eurocentrism":

> Eurocentrism first emerged as a discursive rationale for colonialism, the process by which the European powers reached positions of hegemony

in much of the world.... As an ideological substratum common to colonialist, imperialist, and racist discourse, Eurocentrism is a form of vestigial thinking which permeates and structures *contemporary* practices and representations even after the formal end of colonialism.[15]

To the extent that *Bedwin Hacker* really is about what it says it is about (i.e., a reminder to Western viewers that "other periods, places and lives exist [and that] we [the formerly colonized peoples of the world, among others] are not mirages")—as opposed to being a critique of the Tunisian police state—we can see that the film, as an act of resistance, makes the distinction between colonialist discourse and Eurocentric discourse. Shohat and Stam explain the difference between the two:

> Although colonialist discourse and Eurocentric discourse are intimately intertwined, the terms have a distinct emphasis. While the former explicitly justifies colonialist practices, the latter embeds, takes for granted, and "normalizes" the hierarchical power relations generated by colonialism and imperialism, without necessarily even thematizing those issues directly. Although generated by the colonizing process, Eurocentrism's links to that process are obscured in a kind of buried epistemology. (2)

As a self-described "work of adversary scholarship," Shohat and Stam's book "critiques the universalization of Eurocentric norms, the idea that any race, in Aimé Césaire's words, 'holds a monopoly on beauty, intelligence, and strength'" (3). In effect, El Fani does the same thing with her film and does so in the bold form of an allegory, in which Kalt represents one of Europe's internal and external "others," and Julia represents Europe's historically oppressive relation to this "other."[16] Kalt is represented as more appealing than Julia—but this is to be expected in a work that is a national allegory. For, as Fredric Jameson would remind us, in third-world texts, the story of the private individual destiny "is always an allegory of the embattled situation of the public third-world culture and society."[17] The film must have a "hero," and that hero is Kalt.

In *Cinéma en Méditerranée*, Mohamed Bensalah comments on how "a certain American conception of globalization" has extended Eurocentrism's discursive rationale for (neo)colonialism:

The new information and communication society being established is today nothing less than the triumphant hegemony of a couple of transnational mega-corporations. Practicing a dubious neoliberalism, they impose a global culture of substitution that increasingly marginalizes national cultures. The way in which the Europeans cling to the concept of cultural exception is evidence of the importance of these stakes. Confronting a certain American conception of globalization, the revolt [against this neoliberal-capitalist form of globalization] quickly took on an aspect of resistance, which was accompanied by natural assertions of identity and cultural pluralism in general. With borders blurring, and images proliferating, the logic of the monopolies becomes clearer. They not only give birth to tastes and forge opinions and values, they also choose what they want to know about the world, and make televisual taxonomies of the world's inhabitants.[18]

Although, in Bauman's phrase, Kalt is one of "those who can afford a cosmopolitan identity" (Bauman also calls such individuals "globals"—people who belong to the "relatively narrow category of extraterritorials and globetrotters" [101]), her function in the film, precisely, is to draw attention to the "locals and forcefully localized" (99). El Fani not only celebrates Kalt's worldliness and the ease with which she crosses borders and can operate in a variety of cultural milieux, she also draws attention to the plight of those who are not so fortunate as Kalt—the *sans-papiers* (without papers) we see near the beginning of the film, the Tunisians perpetually under the surveillance of the police state, all those who do not and cannot occupy what one writer calls "the global, culturally hybrid, elite sphere . . . occupied by individuals who share a very different kind of experience of the world [from that experienced by the lower reaches of social reality], connected to international politics, academia, the media and the arts."[19] Even Frida—perhaps because she is an Algerian national[20]—does not have the kind of freedom to travel that one might expect an international singing star to enjoy.

Kalt is engaged in the formation of a deterritorialized, transnational/postnational public sphere, in which "other periods, places and lives" become *visible*—to themselves and to others. Although the Bedwin Hacker writes primarily in Arabic and is figured as a cartoon camel hipster, its message is universal. It (or she), to borrow a phrase from the anarchist philosopher Hakim Bey, is one of "the original freedom-loving hackers &

guerilla informationists, the true pioneers of cyberspace,"[21] and its message is for whoever can recognize and identify with it. The camel is inscribed in a public sphere that transcends national frontiers and cuts across lines of gender, race, class, age, sexual orientation, and any number of other signifiers of identity. In her article about the film, "Transvergence and Cultural Detours," Florence Martin asks:

> What better image to illustrate transvergence [a fluid type of discourse that allows for the possibility of adhering to one statement, then dissenting from it] than the silhouette of a virtual dromedary on European screens? The icon signals neither an invader (it has no colonizing goal) nor a "terrorist" (it is not out to destroy), but an occasional, nonchalant presence; it alludes to the sharing qualities inherent to nomadic life: the desert and the airwaves are anyone's space to be traversed for they belong to no particular entity.[22]

Martin goes on to remark that for Tunisian viewers the cartoon camel may also evoke the fourteenth-century, Tunis-born historian and protosociologist Ibn Khaldun's description of camel herders as nomads seeking food for their animals and, occasionally, refuge from sedentary justice. "Nomads, as wandering rebels against established seats of power," she writes, "resemble Kalt and her tribe in the desert and her dromedary grazing on virtual grounds" (123). The cartoon figure "simply occupies TV's space as a camel would the desert, without asking for a visa or pass" (124).

Kalt and her camel are like those hackers and "defacers" described by Will Taggart in his article, "The Digital Revolt: Resistance and Agency on the Net," who belong to groups who "see themselves as confronting the hegemonic discourses of everyday life and their (oppressed) positions" (3). Kalt, "like all hackers," writes Rosalia Bivona in her article about El Fani's film, "seeks to use her repertoire of skills to bring about real and concrete changes, knowing full well that sometimes, indeed very often, the dice are loaded, so that her mission, while it is subversive, can be perhaps a moral, philosophical one."[23] The Bedwin Hacker is an activist—a fighter for the freedoms of expression and association that are denied not only to most Tunisian citizens (at the time of the film's making) but to nearly every citizen in the Arab world.

In *Bedwin Hacker*, the "imagined" translocal communities (Anderson 1983) or postnational formations (Appadurai 1996) that the cartoon camel interpellates and for which it is a mascot, are implied first of all by the variety and number of television channels Kalt intercepts, and are suggested by the far-flung poles of Kalt's movements (she is everywhere! like her namesake, Um Kalthum, whose voice can be heard wherever Arabic is spoken—and beyond): from Midès, a tiny village in southern Tunisia; to Paris (the 18th arrondissement); to Tunis (in and around the city—the medina, Carthage); and to El Jem, the great Roman coliseum in the Tunisian Sahel. *Bedwin Hacker* is a road movie, as much for the numerous geographical displacements of the various characters and the time they spend on the road, as for their virtual travels also; and as in most road movies, these characters are driven by a quest for freedom.

But there's nothing virtual about Kalt; she is not, to use the Bedwin Hacker's word, a *mirage*. Indeed, she represents a certain reality that exists in Tunisia: the strong, independent, educated, modern woman. Her mastery of the communications technologies represented in the film—so often thought to be an exclusively male domain—and her sexual charisma, which transgresses the gay/straight divide, pose a challenge to what Taggart refers to as "the hegemonic discourses of everyday life" that so many populations in the Third World and elsewhere find oppressive. From the very first shot we see of Kalt, with her short-cropped hair and decisive gait, and wearing a military combat cap, she not only confounds the stereotype of conservative Arab femininity so often depicted in terms of veiled modesty, but she also offers a contrast to the images of "liberated," sometimes sexually provocative women that can be seen on advertising billboards throughout Tunisia. In a striking image that symbolically suggests her phallic power, Kalt checks the retractable antenna she has had Mehdi install for her in a secret location in Midès. "C'est déjà branché!" he tells her, in his Algerian-accented French, as the antenna electronically rises from its hiding place in a wooden barrel. And in the tradition established by Bourguiba, who believed that education was his country's best investment in the future, Kalt reminds Kmar of the girl's promise always to put her schoolwork first.

The "Information Society"

Tunisia has been socially the most progressive of the Maghreb countries since it won its independence from France in March 1956. Certainly, with

FIGURE 7.3 Chams (Tomer Sisley) and Mourad (Néjib Belkadhi) run into Kalt and Frida (Nadia Saïji) in the Tunis medina, while Ben Ali's portrait on the shopkeeper's wall watches and listens.

respect to women, it has the most egalitarian laws in the Arab world. But Tunisia under Ben Ali experienced a dismaying reversal of the progressive trajectory initiated by its first president, to become the most repressive state in the Maghreb. Ben Ali, we know, dramatically expanded Tunisia's internal security apparatus, and after the Internet began to be widely available to the Tunisian public in the late 1990s, he arrested, imprisoned, and tortured many Internet users—some of them only teenagers—who were caught in cybercafés surfing websites deemed by the authorities to be seditious or otherwise a threat to the regime.[24]

It is against this background or in this context that *Bedwin Hacker* must be understood. While the authorities encouraged the use of the Internet— and indeed with 6.4% of the total population using it, putting Tunisia well above the North African average of 2.8%—the authorities also sought to control how Tunisians used the medium, and blocked access to dozens of human rights websites, information websites, and, of course, political opposition websites.[25] Ben Ali's efforts to propel Tunisia toward membership in the "Information Society"—to the extent of hosting the UN World Summit on the Information Society in Tunis in November 2005—were contradictory, to say the least. He had been able to control the Internet within his own country (all Internet service providers were connected to the world network via ATI, the Tunisian Internet Agency, which was therefore in a position to monitor all data exchanged through the ISPs);[26] but at the same time, over half of all households in Tunisia were equipped with satellite dishes and had access to an extremely broad selection of channels from Arab, European, and African regions, providing information that Ben Ali appeared to be less concerned about or able to control. Among the new technologies, it is the Internet—more than satellite television—that has for the Tunisians themselves thrown into sharpest relief the extent to which they have been systematically denied freedoms of expression and association.[27]

Early in the film, when we first meet Kalt's Uncle Salah, we see the old man being approached by a young man on the street as he comes home. Salah is polite in his responses to the man's insinuating questions about why Salah is not keeping his car in his garage (it is because Kalt has turned the garage into her workroom/bedroom), and about how his daughter Malika (Najoua Zouheir) is doing (she is doing fine, and will soon accompany Frida in a concert at El Jem, he tells the young man). Once inside, Salah tells Malika: "The neighborhood informer, the hairdresser, wants a ticket to the concert—he'll be delighted, and it'll keep him quiet for a while." He warns his daughter and her friends that the young man was asking about Kalt.

Clearly, in Ben Ali's Tunisia, the state lived by the dictum that "information is power"—not to promote greater productivity and prosperity for an informed and educated population, as implied by Ben Ali's hosting of the World Summit on the Information Society, but to *control* information. Ben Ali's regime pointlessly expended considerable resources on around-the-clock surveillance of the population (or tried to give the impression that it was doing so) on the grounds that it was safeguarding the Tunisian people and looking after the security of the state, when in fact its first priority was to maintain specifically Ben Ali and his RCD Party in power. Uncle Salah knows this, without having to think about it, which is why, like everybody else, he knows who the neighborhood police informer is, and he is careful not to give away any information that would put him or his family in danger from the state.

When Uncle Salah tells them that a certain journalist called Chams (Tomer Sisley) is in Tunis to interview him and is looking for a place to stay, Malika tells him it is all arranged: Chams will be staying with Salma

(Rinda Dabbegh) and Raja (Habiba Trabelsi). Frida giggles in an aside: "I could have put him in Kalt's garage!" Malika is shocked that Frida would say such a thing within her father's earshot (as it happens, Salah does not hear the remark), but Frida complains: "We may be in a world of satellite technology, but we're still in the Middle Ages here!" This is really a comment by the film on the third-worldness of Tunisia's system of governance, not a complaint about the old-fashioned sexual morality of this modern, middle-class Tunisian family.

Later, when Malika's boyfriend Mourad (Néjib Belkadhi) accompanies Chams into the medina, he tells the visitor: "You know . . . nobody believes your story about an article. Uncle Salah has been writing for thirty years! We say nothing—and you think we don't know what's going on!" A moment later, the two men run into Kalt and Frida. As the four friends greet each other, the viewer notices that President Ben Ali, in a portrait hanging in the small shop behind the group, seems to be observing the scene. As Kalt exclaims, "Tunis is so small! We can't avoid running into one another!," the camera cuts fleetingly to a close-up of Ben Ali's portrait staring down at them, before Mourad enters the shop (in search of a talisman or aphrodisiac for Chams, to "spice up [his] love life"). "It's magic!" Chams says to Kalt, either in reference to the aphrodisiac or the "coincidence" of their running into each other. "Hmm . . . ," grunts Kalt in wry response. The scene exists purely to illustrate the notion that everywhere you go in Ben Ali's police state, you are watched.

Later, at the club where Salma works, we see Mourad reading to Salma and Raja from a newspaper: "They're still talking about the hacker!" he tells them. "They think it's the fundamentalists. They've called in a sociologist, a futurologist, an Islamic expert, a computer expert. . . . " Salma turns to Raja: "He's taking the piss—we haven't received *Le Figaro* for the past few days!" This is another scene intended to illustrate the paranoid attempts by Ben Ali's regime to repress or control access to every sort of information it fears could spread sedition. (The irony is that it is precisely this type and degree of social control that tends to foment—not dissolve or eliminate—sedition.) Mourad laughs derisively: "Hah! *Le Figaro* has become a subversive newspaper!"

A centrally important theme of the film is the education of ten-year-old Kmar, who lives with her father Mehdi on the Tunisian side of the Algerian border, in Midès. In the opening shots of the film, we see the girl with a

IT TAKES A LOT OF UNRULY INDIVIDUALS

FIGURE 7.4 Mourad pretends to read from *Le Figaro* about the investigation into who or what the Bedwin Hacker is. Raja (Habiba Trabelsi) and Salma (Rinda Dabbegh) are amused, because they know that the sale of the French newspaper has been temporarily suspended in Tunisia.

group of other children leading a donkey through an arid landscape. There is absolutely no hint of what will shortly be revealed—that she is not, as the image (slyly, playfully) implies, a poor and ignorant child of a backward society that has remained virtually unchanged for two thousand years, but rather is an intelligent, multilingual apprentice hacker of computers and satellite transmissions who is on her way home from school. Kmar greets her father and Kalt, who are standing beside the antenna, and says admiringly: "I knew you would get it to work! You're really great, auntie!" Kalt corrects her: "Not 'auntie,' if you please! And you stick to your promise: school comes first!" Kalt is teaching Kmar how to be cyber-adept, and the girl clearly has an affinity for the new communications technologies in which Kalt is expert.

It is toward the end of the movie, when Julia finally catches up with Kalt in Midès and confronts her about being "Bedwin Hacker," and accuses her former friend and lover of teaching Kmar how to become a terrorist, that Kalt replies angrily: *"I'm teaching her how to be free!"* adding sarcastically: "It's more honorable, wouldn't you say? Perhaps you'd prefer that I teach her how to get a visa? How to become a Permanent Resident? How to acquire [French] citizenship? Truly, I never thought of it!"

Undocumented Aliens

In *Postcolonial Hospitality: The Immigrant as Guest*, Mireille Rosello notes that national borders do not correspond to linguistic borders:

> The language obstacle is less daunting for some than for others: when immigrants move to what used to be the colonial *metropole* in Europe, they will not experience the language barrier in the same manner as people who have traveled from neighboring states because of wars, for example. The fact remains that cultural competence is indistinguishable from language and may even be defined as a type of language.[28]

Bedwin Hacker puts Kalt's cultural competence—her linguistic abilities and her mastery of the language of the new communications technologies—at the front and center of its discourse about the postcolonial predicament for many Tunisians and others of Maghrebi descent, whether they live in the Maghreb (with virtual access to the rest of the world) or live in what used to be the colonial *metropole*. When the Paris police disrupt the meeting of the undocumented aliens and Frida is arrested, the French officer at the police precinct charged with booking Frida becomes irritated when Kalt and her friend talk to each other in Tunisian Arabic. "There is no need to jabber [*baragouiner*]," he tells them. "We have translators." He himself appears to be of Maghrebi descent, but evidently does not recognize their dialect. Little does he realize that Kalt is one step ahead of him: not only is she adept in whatever "language" it is that enables her to pass Frida off as a niece of the king of Morocco, but adept also in the language of computers, which will allow her to hack covertly and quickly into the officer's desktop and change the data in the "immigration control" file on Frida.

That *Bedwin Hacker*'s narrative should begin with the Paris police raid suggests that El Fani is preoccupied to a certain extent with what Rosello describes as an emerging, "widespread, diverse, and multicultural debate about hospitality" (2). Rosello traces the beginning of this debate (in France) to the "closing of borders" that can be said to have taken place in

1974, when work immigration was officially stopped by President Valéry Giscard d'Estaing (180n8). Those who lived and worked in France but were denied the legal documentation allowing them to stay were put in an untenable legal and social position, and became known as the *sans-papiers*. The most obvious manifestation of the French government's increasingly anti-immigration attitude were the so-called Pasqua laws that led to the 1993 reform of the *Code de la nationalité française*—laws that reflected a "repressive and restrictive philosophy, turning the *clandestin* into an enemy of the state, the most easily identifiable national scapegoat" (1).[29]

The government's anti-immigration policies were eventually challenged, most spectacularly in the summer of 1996, "when French people, perhaps for the first time, had the opportunity to hear the voice of the demonized *clandestins*," in what the media dubbed *"l'affaire des sans-papiers de Saint-Bernard"* (the affair of the undocumented immigrants of the Church of Saint Bernard):

> Approximately 300 African men and women occupied several public spaces in Paris until they arrived at the Church of Saint Bernard in Montmartre. There, they defied the government for months, ten of the *sans-papiers* starting a long hunger strike under the scrutiny of national television cameras. Their goal was to propose an alternative interpretation of their presence in France and to inform the public about the perverse consequences of the Pasqua laws: according to their critics, the new texts were less effective in preventing new immigrants from entering the country illegally than in turning long-term immigrants into undocumented aliens whose administrative status was an inextricable knot of contradictions. (2)

The scene in *Bedwin Hacker* in which the police raid the *sans-papiers* meeting is reminiscent of the brutal evacuation of the Church of Saint Bernard by the riot police ordered by the government on 23 August 1996. But if the film cannot untie the inextricable knot of contradictions in which the *sans-papiers* of France find themselves (albeit that French nationality for Chams—and Julia's attempt to blackmail him, with nationality as his reward—is an important strand of the film's plot), it nevertheless seeks to shed light on the quandaries of national identity in our postcolonial/global era, where we now are all, perhaps, in Julia Kristeva's phrase, "strangers to ourselves."[30]

In *Lettre ouverte à Harlem Désir*,[31] which is included among the essays translated and published in English as *Nations Without Nationalism*, Kristeva outlines a proposal about personal/national identity in our postcolonial/global era, in the context of a discussion about citizenship. Her proposal mirrors the thesis of *Bedwin Hacker*, a film which we could say acknowledges the continued vitality and usefulness of the (idea of the) nation, but advocates "nations without nationalism."[32] Kristeva's starting point is Montesquieu (book XIX, chapter 4, in *The Spirit of the Laws*), who writes: "Human beings are ruled by several things: climate, religion, laws, principles of government, examples of things past, customs, manners; as a result, an *esprit général* is constituted."[33] Following the French philosopher's argument for a relative notion of *citizenship*—which is evolutive and political, rather than the more deterministic one of *nationality*—Kristeva believes that "the nation as *esprit général* (with the heterogeneous, dynamic, and 'confederate' meaning that Montesquieu gives to a political group) is one of the most prestigious creations of French political thought" (57). It involves "the integration, without a leveling process, of the different layers of social reality into the political and/or national unity" (57).

Thus, writes Kristeva, we may define the *national* as being:

1. A *historical identity* with relative *steadiness* (the tradition) and an always prevailing *instability* in a given topicality (subject to evolution).
2. Endowed with a *logical multiplicity* whose diversity is to be maintained without the possibility of having one social (logical) stratum dominate the others. Thus, laws determine the citizens' actions but non-laws determine morals (inner behavior) and manners (outer behavior). (56)

Kristeva is right, however, to ask what we mean, today, when we say that French national identity is *historical*. The question requires "a serious assessment of *traditional national memory*: the 'customs of France' (Montesquieu), its *entire* religious history (Catholic, Protestant, Jewish, Muslim) and transcending that history during the Enlightenment when, precisely, one could think of the 'nation' as having an *esprit général*" (58). At the same time, Kristeva writes, "a bold assessment is called for" of the twofold shock to the "customs of France" of the contemporary tide of immigration inside of France's territorial boundaries and to the confrontation with other

European nations in a broadened concept of Europe (59–60). It comes down to this: "How shall we manage to have citizens of that historically mobile group known as France today be something else than selfish people withdrawn into their own common denominators, more or less integration-minded or even death-bearing, and become 'confederates' in the *esprit général*?" (61). The challenge is to work out how to strike a balance between the *esprit général* and the domain of the *private*:

> The vast domain of the *private*, the land of welcome of individual, concrete freedoms, is thus immediately included in the *esprit général* that must guarantee through law and economy the private practice of religious, sexual, moral, and educational differences relating to the mindset and customs of the confederate citizens. Simultaneously, while the *private* is thus guaranteed, one is committed to respect the *esprit général* in the bosom of which there is a place for its own expansion, without for that matter hindering the "privacy" of the other communities that are included in the same *esprit général*. (61–62)

Implicit in the question of why Frida should be present at a protest meeting of the *sans-papiers*, or why Julia might assume that Kalt is teaching Kmar how to acquire French nationality, or why Chams is seeking the legal documentation that will allow him to stay in France is an acknowledgment by the film that France indeed does offer a national model whose *esprit général* is a desirable alternative to the varieties of nationalism that characterize the nations of North Africa.

El Fani's film, however, asks another question put by Kristeva: "It is time to ask immigrant people what motivated them (beyond economic opportunities and approximate knowledge of the language propagated by colonialism) to choose the French community with its historical memory and traditions as the welcoming lands" (60). Although Kalt herself appears to be a cosmopolitan, and is contemptuous of Julia's assumption that French citizenship is always a better thing to have than Tunisian citizenship, *Bedwin Hacker* nevertheless clearly endorses the values of the French Enlightenment. (The slogans of the *sans-papiers*—"PAPERS FOR EVERYONE," "NO TO EXCLUSION," "STOP THE EXPULSIONS"—suggest as much.) "What does each immigrant community contribute to the lay concept of *national spirit as esprit général* reached by the French Enlightenment?"

Kristeva asks. "Do those communities recognize that *esprit général* or not? What do they expect from that *national spirit*, which is to the credit of the country they are calling on to resolve their *contradictions and concrete needs*, and how do they wish to enrich it without denying it?" (60–61).

While the film celebrates the fact that every nation has its own climate, religions, past, laws, customs, manners, and so forth—which, as "a *layering* of very concrete and diverse causalities," form a part of the *national whole* (55)—there exists (in Kristeva's summary of Montesquieu's argument) "a possibility of *going beyond* the political groups thus conceived as sharing an *esprit général* and into higher entities set forth by a spirit of concord and economic development" (55). *Bedwin Hacker*'s protagonist is emotionally and culturally attached to (indeed, was formed by and in) Tunisia, but the film is harshly critical of the Tunisian police state. Likewise, she and the film are emotionally and culturally bound to France, but critical of the French state (which too often still allows people to regress to the logic of "hunting for the scapegoat outside their group" [51]). Tunisian national identity and French national identity are implicated, one in the other. As we see in Kalt herself, and in Chams and Frida and Julia—indeed it can be said of *all* the characters in the film—personal and national identity are tied in an inextricable knot, but clearly, the time has come to stop seeing this knot as one of impossible contradictions.[34]

Queer Nation/Global Nation

In his literary study, *Queer Nations: Marginal Sexualities in the Maghreb*, Jarrod Hayes elaborates and expands the notion of "combat literature"—which has often been limited to works about independence struggles—to include "sexual allegories of the political," in which Maghrebian writers bring two types of skeleton out of the closet: the sexual and the political.[35] "When writers include marginal sexualities or the transgression of sexual taboos in their novels," he observes, "they reveal what is considered shameful in official discourse and destroy the officially propagated image of the Maghrebian nation as a nation of 'good Muslims' who abide by the strictest interpretation of Islamic family values" (16–17). Hayes notes that these novels do not reject the project of consolidating national identity but seek rather to "articulate a national identity that is heterogeneous in relation

FIGURE 7.5 Kalt knows that Julia has directed Chams to spy on her even at El Jem, where Frida is rehearsing for a concert.

to languages, ethnicities, sexualities, and religions, and that questions any totalizing binary opposition to the former colonizer" (16).

We recognize at once El Fani's progressive agenda in figuring Kalt as bisexual (the fact that Julia, the French DST agent, is also bisexual is less significant in this regard, although it is interesting nonetheless, because Julia is revealed to be a sexual blackmailer—both in relation to Kalt, when they first knew each other as students at the école Polytechnique in Paris; and in relation to Chams, whom she has no qualms about using to entrap Kalt—which thereby throws into question the "authenticity" of her sexual proclivities). Hayes makes the astonishing observation—and I have no basis for refuting or disbelieving him—that "rare indeed is the Maghrebian writer who does not deal with male homoeroticism or same-sex sexual behavior in at least one novel" (18); but he goes on to remark that in Maghrebian literature female homoeroticism is harder to see than its male counterpart. All the more extraordinary, then, that the heroine of *Bedwin Hacker* should be bisexual—she is the first such heroine in Arab cinema—and that the scenes in which we see her in bed with Julia, and many years later, with Julia's boyfriend Chams, are treated with such frankness and complete lack of self-consciousness or awkwardness. There are several scenes in the film as well involving an openly lesbian couple, Salma and Raja, whose relationship is accepted without fuss by all their friends, both male and female. Salma is a professional bartender—again, this is one of the film's acknowledgments of the extent of the Westernization of Tunisia, where a significant number of women can be found in occupations that, while perhaps considered unexceptional for women in the West and not out of the question for women in Tunisia, are unheard of for women in other Arab countries—and the association of Salma's emancipated embrace of her sexuality with her profession as a bartender, like all the scenes of sociability and community in the film in which characters drink wine or beer, is as much a celebration of one of Tunisia's contemporary realities as it is a conscious act of resistance by the filmmaker to the disapproval of the consumption of alcohol by traditionalists and fanatics throughout the Muslim world.

Not surprisingly, the film does not show either Kalt or her cousin Malika as having a mother (we infer that Malika's father, Salah, is a widower). This leaves the narrative freer to have them embody the kind of feminism celebrated by the film. (In other words, the narrative does not become distracted by the mother–daughter relationship, which would be a subject worthy of a film of its own. Kalt is a hero, and heroes, according to the laws of the family romance, are orphans.[36]) Uncle Salah is what we could call a "cool dad"—a progressive, older man who gets along well with his daughter and her friends—although El Fani makes it clear that he represents an earlier generation of activism. He has been a writer for more than thirty years and has built a minor reputation as a poet. But he is not one of Hakim Bey's original freedom-loving hackers or guerilla informationists—which El Fani signals by showing him looking about distractedly for his mislaid pen and asking Chams: "Do you see a pen over there?" He understands his niece, however, and gently offers Chams a piece of advice: "You're going to have to be more flexible, if you want to continue to please Kalthum."

The film invites the viewer to make a comparison between Salah and Chams's father, when we see Salah prepare dinner for "the tribe" in Tunis and see Chams's parents at their dinner table in Paris. Chams's family is more "traditional"; it would appear that his mother does the cooking in her household, and his father is reflexively patriarchal, believing it not worth explaining to his wife what Bedwin Hacker's message means. When Chams's family sees one of Bedwin Hacker's messages on their television screen, Chams's mother asks her husband what it signifies. "It's nothing," he replies dismissively. But his daughter corrects him: "No, it's not 'nothing'! It's you, you don't know how to read!" (At the same moment, Julia's boss—who also, apparently, does not know "how to read"—is explaining to Julia what "Bedwin" means. He breaks the word into two parts: "bed," in English, is a translation of *lit*, he tells her with didactic self-satisfaction; and "win" is the English for *gagner*. The hacker is "a Brit who thinks he's good in bed." Julia corrects him: No, "bedwin" is the corrupted spelling of *bédouine*, a female Bedouin—hackers being generally careless about spelling.)

The homosexual/bisexual motif in the film has a purpose. It has implications for the globalization theme, for example, which is also about the transgression of borders. If queer sexuality confounds the straight/gay divide, so does globalization subvert the notion of the nation as a territorial and sovereign entity with borders. Bauman writes that for some people the advent of high-speed technologies such as the Internet "augurs an unprecedented freedom from physical obstacles and unheard-of ability to move and act from a distance. For others, it portends the impossibility of appropriating and domesticating the locality from which they have little chance of cutting themselves free in order to move elsewhere" (18). In *Bedwin Hacker*, of course, Kalt enjoys this unprecedented freedom Bauman refers to (she is even freer than Julia, who must kowtow to her none-too-bright boss), whereas Chams travels the old-fashioned way and must submit his papers for inspection at the frontier. We see that Chams has not fully mastered the languages that would enable him to travel fast and light (he is duped by his more cyber-adept girlfriend into spying for her and is easily caught when he tries to hack into Kalt's computer; he struggles to learn Tunisian Arabic, and thus remains as much of an outsider in Tunisia as he does in France). To use Uncle Salah's word, he is not as flexible (*souple*) as Kalt is; and this has its correlative in the film's portrayal of him as an ordinary heterosexual (who wants citizenship in an old and established nation with borders).

Bauman writes that "for some people—for the mobile elite, the elite of mobility—[the way in which information now floats independently from its carriers] means, literally, the 'dephysicalization,' the new weightlessness of power. Elites travel in space, and travel faster than ever before—but the spread and density of the power web they weave is not dependent on that travel. Thanks to the new 'bodylessness' of power in its mainly financial form, the power-holders become truly extraterritorial even if, bodily, they happen to stay 'in place'" (19). Although Kalt does not represent an agent of this power in its financial form, she is an example of its extraterritoriality. Even when she is in Midès or visiting El Jem, she is connected to this web—but it is a web that gives her freedom; whereas for Chams it is a web in which he will always feel caught (it "will always be stronger than you are," he tries to convince Kalt).

If, as Bauman remarks, "in cyberspace, bodies do not matter" (19), El Fani reminds us that in the real spaces of real life bodies *do* matter. What Chams is missing in France, we infer, he will find in Tunisia: Kalt as a physical, bodily reality (the scene in which, preparing for bed, she strips down to her G-string in front of him, while kicking him out of her room because he has attempted to hack into her computer, drives home the point: he will never again get from her what he really wants); the sensuality of physical experiences and group activities like those we see Kalt's "tribe" enjoy, such as breaking spontaneously into song after dinner, or dancing in Uncle Salah's living room and at the bar where Salma works, or eating *lablabi* at a hole-in-the-wall restaurant in the middle of the night, or swimming in a natural pool at an oasis in the desert, or sitting around a campfire.

Bauman quotes Georg Henrik von Wright on the erosion of the nation-state in the contemporary phenomenon of globalization:

> The molding forces of transnational character are largely anonymous and therefore difficult to identify. They do not form a unified system or order. They are an agglomeration of systems manipulated by largely "invisible" actors . . . [there is no] unity or purposeful co-ordination of the forces in question . . . [The] "market" is not a bargaining interaction of competing forces so much as the pull and push of manipulated demands, artificially created needs, and desire for quick profit.[37]

The ongoing process of the "withering away" of nation-states, Bauman observes, is surrounded by "an aura of a natural catastrophe," because its causes are not fully understood. It produces a "feeling of unease," because it is a "situation without obvious levers of control" (57). (What third-world peoples know, however, or believe they know—which is central to *Bedwin Hacker*'s meanings as an allegory of resistance—is that, in Jameson's phrase, "American bankers hold the levers of the world system" [late capitalism], which is "the supreme unifying force of contemporary history.") Bauman is writing essentially from a first-world perspective when he observes that "throughout the modern era we have grown used to the idea that order is tantamount to 'being in control,'" and that "this assumption—whether well-founded or merely illusionary—of 'being in control' [is what] we miss most" (57).

Not "being in control" is clearly what Julia as a French citizen and the film's representative of the former colonial power fears most, when she tries to explain to Chams the threat posed by Kalt (a Tunisian, and representative of the former colonized power): "There are laws, and they have to be kept! If not, it's chaos!" Much has been written about the erotics of the colonial relationship,[38] and on one level, we can read Julia's grim determination to track down and arrest Kalt as her unconscious effort to repress her homosexual desire. Kalt produces a chaos of feeling in her that can only be brought under control by eliminating Kalt from the field of play and securing Chams's fidelity as a lover, which she hopes will confer on her the stable heterosexual identity she seeks. When Bauman (echoing the title of a book by Kenneth Jowitt) refers to "the new world disorder," he is alluding to the end of the Cold War, which for nearly half a century imposed some kind of order on the world by organizing it into two power camps, thus keeping it in a precarious equilibrium. Following the collapse of the Communist bloc, however, Bauman writes, one has the impression that *"no one seems now to be in control"* (58; emphasis in original). But we must reiterate that for characters like Kalt in *Bedwin Hacker*, while there may be an agglomeration of systems manipulated by largely "invisible" actors bringing pressure to bear on ordinary citizens, it is perfectly clear who the beneficiaries and who the losers are in this new world (dis)order. If, in Bauman's phrase, there is an "uncomfortable perception [that] 'things are getting out of hand,'" this perception, it must be said, is shared more by the Julias of this world than by the Kalts.

Bauman believes that "the deepest meaning conveyed by the idea of globalization is that of the indeterminate, unruly and self-propelled character of world affairs, the absence of a center, of a controlling desk, of a board of directors, of a managerial office . . . "—which perhaps explains why the world's erstwhile rulers are so anxious. And we know they are anxious: Julia and the agency for which she works think of the Bedwin Hacker as a terrorist; and the degree of repressive state control in Ben Ali's Tunisia is of an order that can surely be described as *hysterical*. The more "unruly" the world seems to be—and we remember Bernanos's dictum that it takes a lot of unruly individuals to make a free people—the more determined are Julia and her team to lock up Kalt for twenty years. The more it is perceived that "no one seems now to be in control"—and we recall that the national motto, inscribed in the Tunisian Constitution, includes the word *order*[39]—the more determined Ben Ali's regime is to demonstrate that things are *not* getting out of hand (at least, in Tunisia) and that—let there be no doubt about it—there *is* "a controlling desk."

The state, as Max Weber defined it, is the agency claiming monopoly over the means of coercion and over their use inside its sovereign territory. The Tunisian state is nothing if not such an agency, and there are many allusions in *Bedwin Hacker* to the state's baleful exercise of its powers of coercion. As we have said, under cover of being "a game of cat-and-mouse" between Julia and "her old rival" Kalt, the film is a fierce indictment of the Tunisian police state. Echoing the subtitle of Bauman's book, it may be read as a critique of the "human consequences of globalization" for countries like Tunisia, where the "levers of the world system" of late capitalism are held by countries like France and the United States. But, overwhelmingly, the viewer is meant to see Julia/"Agent Marianne" not so much as an agent of the French DST (which of course she is, in the plot, with her code name a symbol of the French Republic), but allegorically as an agent of the Tunisian repressive state apparatus. The functions of the French Ministry of the Interior are hardly any different from those of its Tunisian counterpart, and so when we read on the website of the French Ministry of the Interior that the DST "describes itself today as an internal security agency whose primary function is to gather security intelligence and investigate the diverse and uncertain forms of threat," we have no difficulty reading the film, say, as an allegory not only of French attempts at neocolonial domination of Tunisia, or of contemporary French fears about the erosion of "traditional French" national identity, but also, on the other side of this coin, of the Tunisian regime's obsession with surveillance and desire to recreate Jeremy Bentham's Panopticon in cyberspace.[40]

But the allegory is an attempt to make a complex and unwieldy state of affairs comprehensible. The film knows that in the globalized world it evokes there are indeed largely "invisible" actors manipulating an agglomeration of systems we call late capitalism, but that these actors function in the service of capitalism's biggest and most successful players, who are still identified with specific nation-states and their ostensible rulers. These rulers—it is unfortunate but true—work to preserve existing patterns of political economy that benefit them, and they are indifferent, or even hostile, to the well-being of the majority.

Bauman quotes from an article (signed "Sous-Commandant Marcos," in Chiapas, Mexico) which appeared in *Le Monde diplomatique* in August 1997, in which the writer states that he believes nation-states *pretend* they are in control, but in fact are controlled by "the new masters of the world," which are trans- and supranational: "In the cabaret of globalization, the state goes through a striptease and by the end of the performance it is left with the bare necessities only: its powers of repression. With its material basis destroyed, its sovereignty and independence annulled, its political class effaced, the nation-state becomes a simple security service for the mega-companies . . . " (68). National governments are not sovereign in the old sense, but answer to the amoral and often ruthless demands of capitalism. "The new masters of the world have no need to govern directly. National governments are charged with the task of administering affairs on their behalf" (68).

Bedwin Hacker's intentions are not to offer, in fictional form, an analysis of the amoral and often ruthless demands of capitalism, however. The film offers no images of the proliferating sites of consumerism in Tunisia—the gleaming glass-and-chrome shopping malls, for example, such as the Palmarium in downtown Tunis (which could be anywhere in the world), or Géant, the "hypermarché" just north of the capital, with its seventy shops and 3,600 parking spaces—that could proudly signal the Tunisians' membership in the global community of successful consumer-capitalist societies.[41] Indeed, the film does the opposite: when Kalt returns to Tunis with Frida, after rescuing her from detention and deportation by the French justice system in Paris, the two friends go into the medina (not the *nouvelle ville*), where, as mentioned earlier, they run into Mourad and Chams. We understand that one of the things the Bedwin Hacker is resisting is the *commodification* of culture (as we see it alluded to in the television transmissions [she] intercepts). It is as if the film were saying: "We are proud that we have our own, specific history and culture. Yes, we have our own temples of consumption, like any other modern society, but what we will show you—and which you will never find, for example, in Dubai, that Arab 'dream' of pseudo-modernity—are (in Tomlinson's phrase), 'the many aspects of people's cultural experience and practices—their personal relationships, their religious or political affiliations, their sexual orientation, their sense of national or ethnic identity, their attachments to "local" practices and contexts, and so on—which have not been colonized by a commodifying logic'" (88).

Tomlinson notes that "the installation of global modernity does not necessarily represent a continuing cultural domination of 'the West'—as a set of real nation-states rather than an abstract cultural principle—over the rest. Western nation-states clearly do for the present enjoy considerable political-economic dominance in the world—though, as we have observed, there is no reason to consider that this is indefinitely guaranteed" (96). While *Bedwin Hacker* concedes, and even celebrates, that there is something we might call global "cosmopolitan" culture, it is clearly in thrall to the idea of *national culture*. If global culture is inevitable, it does not—it need not—necessarily destroy and replace local culture.[42] As Anthony Smith describes it, global culture is "composed of a number of analytically discrete elements," namely:

> Effectively advertised mass commodities, a patchwork of folk or ethnic styles and motifs stripped of their context, some general ideological discourses concerned with "human rights and values" and a standardized quantitative "scientific" language of communication and appraisal, all underpinned by the new information and telecommunications systems and their computerized technologies.[43]

Where global culture, Tomlinson writes, is "a 'constructed' culture [that] is ahistorical, timeless and 'memoryless'" (101), national cultures remain obstinately "particular, timebound and expressive" and are constructed on the sense of a collective identity shared by people situated in a particular location and involve "feelings and values in respect of a sense of continuity, shared memories and a sense of common destiny."[44] At the heart of *Bedwin Hacker*'s raison d'être, even as it breathes the ether of global culture and depicts a world "underpinned by the new information and telecommunications systems and their computerized technologies," is an acknowledgment of the value and necessity of the *national* idea, which Smith calls "the community's ethno-history," the subjective core upon which modern national identities are elaborated.

This "national idea" is not to be confused with what Tomlinson describes as the "(romantic) ideal of small face-to-face communities," defended on grounds of their immediacy ("the directness and authenticity of the social relations they promote"). Those who defend this ideal, he argues, are "laboring under a 'metaphysical illusion' of the possibility of 'immediate presence of subjects to one another.'"[45] *Bedwin Hacker* in its intimate scenes of Kalt in bed with Chams and (in flashback) with Julia rather "prove" that the "immediate presence of subjects to one another" is no guarantee of an "authentic" and transparent communication between them, for Julia, we discover, is plotting her betrayal of Kalt even as she climbs into bed with her; and Chams's physical relationship with Kalt brings him no closer to understanding her; indeed, at Julia's behest, he will shortly afterward start spying on her.

"What's his password? 'Love,' 'secret,' 'sex,' or 'God'?"

In a sense, the film stages a struggle for Chams's soul. Will he join the global resistance movement represented by Kalt's Bedwin Hacker, or will he continue down the path of assimilation toward French citizenship and, perhaps, adoption of the hegemonic values of the dominant society? Indeed, a hint of the architecture of this allegory is offered in the way his name—which means "sun" in Arabic—illuminates a dialectical relation between the cluster of meanings he represents with that of the film's other highly symbolically named character, Kmar (which means "moon" in Arabic). When Kalt hacks into Chams's computer in his Paris apartment—merely to gain access to the Web, not because she suspects he is a spy (like Julia) or a double agent—she asks Frida rhetorically: "What's his password? 'Love,' 'secret,' 'sex,' or 'God'?" Kalt already knows the answer, because two seconds later, she is online and muttering bemusedly to herself: "It's always the same!"[46]

Although the film is strongly feminist in its depiction of emancipated female characters and shows the men to be generally hapless, ineffectual, or buffoonish, it is nevertheless affectionate in its portrayal of most of the male characters (the exception is Julia's overbearing boss, a blustering know-it-all) and shows some understanding, for example, of the kind of predicament in which Chams finds himself. As we have said, he must choose between Julia, who will ensure that he gains his longed-for French nationality, and Kalt, who represents the morally superior cause of defending an authentic (national) identity and fighting for what is politically right (the liberation

FIGURE 7.6 Julia/Agent Marianne (Muriel Solvay) tries to decode the meaning of the Bedwin Hacker's message, while her boss (Alberto Canova) gives unhelpful advice.

of third-world peoples from the twin oppressions of Western domination and corrupt local regimes).

Following the Paris police raid on the meeting of the *sans-papiers* and their supporters, Chams the journalist starts writing a story about Frida: "The Journey of an Undocumented Woman." Very soon, however, another story will capture his attention: the Bedwin Hacker's messages, which are interrupting television broadcasts throughout France (and beyond?), and the DST's efforts to explain them away. In the meantime, Julia's colleague Zbor (Xavier Desplas) at DST headquarters has told her what happened following Frida's arrest by the Paris police: "Someone altered an ID down at the Eighteenth. Just as the officer logged on, someone tapped in and changed the ID data. Nobody noticed anything!" ("Typical cop!" he adds derisively.)

Chams visits his parents for dinner, where he learns of the Bedwin Hacker's latest message, broadcast in French and Arabic: "I am not a technical error. This is my path. I march to the beat of my own drum. You, who hate the sound of boots, wear your *babouches* tomorrow. Bedwin. It's not over." Unaware of exactly how Kalt had sprung Frida from the police station in the 18th arrondissement, and unaware of the links among the four events—the security failure at the police station; Bedwin Hacker's message ("Other periods, places and lives exist"); the DST's disinformation message; and Bedwin Hacker's follow-up message ("I am not a technical error")—Chams writes another story, the conclusion of which he reads to Julia: "In this wonderful 'world order,' we still have great troublemakers! They broadcast messages of peace ... in Arabic. Is that enough to justify calling them 'technical errors'?" He sympathizes with the Bedwin Hacker's point of view, although it is not until Julia reveals just how different her own ideological position is from his, that he is able to identify his true feelings on the subject: "Frankly, I think [the DST's] disinformation is disgusting!" he tells her. When he glances out the window of his apartment and observes that many of the pedestrians passing by on the street below are wearing their *babouches* in solidarity with Bedwin Hacker's message of the day before, he comments admiringly: "So, the little camel on TV worked!"

Julia is furious at being outmaneuvered by Kalt, and she tells Chams she believes the hacker is a certain "Pirate Mirage," someone she knows personally from the Chaos Computer Club.[47] This hacker was so nicknamed, she explains, "because she covers her tracks like nobody else." When, however, Julia adds ominously: "These hackers are like everybody else," the viewer recognizes that the DST agent has slipped into the "all-terrorists-are-the-same" discourse made popular by George W. Bush's War on Terrorism (or rather: the discourse that identifies an overly broad range of critics of the state as "terrorists"). Chams is neither convinced nor impressed: "Oh yeah? And you think there's a link between 'Pirate Mirage' and Kalt? What's your problem? You want to turn her in? She's gone!"

Kalt's question, "What's his password? 'Love,' 'secret,' 'sex,' or 'God'?," is a way of asking what his politics are. We learn that he is like most left-leaning Frenchmen; his politics are admirable, by the standards of the film, but he is not a committed dissident, like Kalt. Chams's efforts to acquire French nationality are a bid to secure more personal liberty; he is generally not one to fight for a cause much larger than himself—for, as he repeats to Kalt: "They [the forces of oppression, government authorities] will always be stronger than you are!" Notwithstanding his final act of heroism, in which he is nearly killed when he tries to intervene to prevent Julia from turning Kalt in to the French authorities, Chams would appear not to be one of Bernanos's spendthrifts, unruly individuals, or crazy young men who help make a generous, free, and heroic people. But he and the Bedwin Hacker are on the same side (which, if it needed confirmation, is alluded to in Kalt's remark about them both having slept with Julia: "We have the same taste"). He is, as Bivona so perceptively observes, a "young man whose affective life, citizenship status, job, and personal judgment are all at risk. He is incapable of understanding the real reasons why he goes to Tunisia, or of explaining them to Julia and Kalt, for [these reasons are unconscious, and] the object of his journey always was, and remains, none other than Bedwin Hacker, this visionary of an era that is being born in the gurgle of televised images."[48]

"The courage to resist"

In the end, it is the women in the film who come out best. Even Frida, the international singing star whose very lifestyle is asserted (both by her and by the film) as the choice of an emancipated woman, is a fighter for personal liberty in a way that perhaps Chams, in the final analysis, is not. Nevertheless, *Bedwin Hacker* acknowledges that not everybody can be an activist on the order of a Kalt (or the future Kmar). Chams may finally choose Julia and French nationality, but we cannot call him a coward; not everybody can be a popular hero committed to throwing off the yoke of oppression. In *Bedwin Hacker*, it is the women who lead the fight, and the principal weapon of the film's protagonist is a new technology that, as suggested by the film's prologue of old footage showing President Truman in 1945 at the Tennessee River dedicating the Tennessee Valley Authority's (TVA) Kentucky Dam, rivals nuclear power in the magnitude of its potential either to help make the world a better place or contribute to human oppression and misery. In Truman's speech, he said: "We've just discovered the source of the sun's power: atomic energy.... We had to turn it loose in the beginning for a destruction ... but that tremendous source of energy can create for us the greatest age in the history of the world."[49] This in part is *Bedwin Hacker*'s message as well. That "tremendous source of energy" is not only the Internet and the whole matrix of communication technologies underpinning the Information Society, but more importantly it is the *woman*—the kind of power embodied by the female characters in the film.

El Fani dedicates her film to her grandmother "Bibi," who inspires her with the "courage to resist."[50] There is no doubt that Kalt and her creator El Fani have this courage. From the very beginning of the film, over the images of Truman at the TVA dam, we hear Kalt's voice sounding the activist's alarm: as if to herself and at the speed of typing (which we hear under her voice-over), she is saying: "An enemy on the right ... an enemy on the left ... Be careful! There's one behind...." The film thus announces its allegorical strategy. The "enemies" Kalt refers to could be any number of things, but the film will discourage a literal-minded interpretation.[51] More interesting perhaps than Kalt's warning is El Fani's decision to put this footage of President Truman's speech about nuclear power at the beginning of her film.

The official government website for the TVA includes an article about David Lilienthal, the TVA's board chairman from 1941 to 1946. The article is entitled "The Father of Public Power" and describes Lilienthal as "boyish in appearance but hardheaded and knowledgeable." He "built the TVA power system according to one guiding principle: affordable power for everyone in the Tennessee Valley." During his tenure as board chairman, he "oversaw the construction of 12 dams in five years, as TVA power helped win World War II."[52] It is striking that *Bedwin Hacker* should resonate with similarly fervent rhetoric in its presentation of Kalt as an agent of progress in the name of the people (as opposed to special-interest groups). Just as Lilienthal was committed to creating "affordable power for everyone in the Tennessee Valley" and understood that he was participating in an effort to win a war ("he took pride in TVA's role in the war effort and in its rock-solid dedication to public power"), Kalt is working to put power in the hands of the people and is engaged in a war against their oppression. Lilienthal "didn't trust the private power companies; he felt that public power should be distributed publicly, through a network of local municipal power boards and rural co-ops." So, too, does Kalt distrust "private power companies"— this is why the Internet is her medium. She is, to paraphrase Bernanos, one of Tunisia's unruly individuals, committed to teaching "Tunisians" everywhere how to become [a] free people.

The last shot of the film is a low-angled, diegetically isolated one of Kalt in medium close-up, against a clear, deep-blue sky. She is looking out-of-frame, toward the horizon (in the direction, possibly, of the departing couple, Chams and Julia). She puts on her combat cap, turns to look into the camera—*at me, at you*—and smiles.

CHAPTER EIGHT

Inventing the Postcolonial Nation/ Constructing a Usable Past

The TV Is Coming (Moncef Dhouib, 2006)

The premise of Moncef Dhouib's fiction film *The TV Is Coming* is self-reflexive, much like that of a Hollywood backstage musical. When the municipal cultural committee of El Malga in southern Tunisia hears that a German television company is planning to make a documentary film in their dusty, rural village, they busy themselves with the preparation of an itinerary of events, including a pageant representing three thousand years of Tunisian history.[1] They also make a short film of their own, to impress their European visitors and, as one of the characters says, to give them "an idea of what we have accomplished in the very short time since Independence."[2] *The TV Is Coming* is therefore a work of meta-historiography, a movie about how national-cultural history is written, or as I suggest in my title, borrowing phrases from Van Wyck Brooks and Eric Hobsbawm, it is about how a "usable past" can be constructed as a narrative for the purpose of "inventing" the postcolonial nation.[3] The various interests and sometimes conflicting objectives of the different members of El Malga's cultural committee produce a debate about what constitutes the "real" or "authentic" Tunisia and also in effect raise questions for the viewer about how (the real) Tunisia is confronting certain political, economic, and cultural challenges in the global era.

INVENTING THE POSTCOLONIAL NATION/CONSTRUCTING A USABLE PAST

FIGURE 8.1 Hadhria (Fatma Ben Saïdane) angrily confronts the German television company when she discovers it has not come to film "our culture, our history, and our values."

The film functions quite explicitly as an allegory—the village of El Malga, for example, is fictitious (the real El Malga is a tourist theme park in Djerba)—permitting an examination of certain features of Tunisian society not normally acknowledged in public discourse, such as the problem of the extreme authoritarianism of Ben Ali's regime and the complete absence in Tunisia of freedom of political expression. The allegorical form, which plays here in registers of ambiguity, ambivalence, and contradiction, allows *The TV Is Coming* both to uphold the myth of Tunisia as a historically progressive state and to undercut this narrative at the same time.

In an article entitled "Images of Openness, Spaces of Control," Waleed Hazbun describes state-managed forms of cultural production similar to El Malga (the tourist theme park in Djerba) as representing "a dovetailing of tourism development and image making with national identity formation and myth making."[4] The El Malga of the film, not unlike its namesake in Djerba ("a space exposed to the gaze of international tourists and sustained by the flows of hard currency they bring" [28]), offers a performance of (itself as) an authentic Tunisian village, untouched by tourism, with the film satirizing the way in which this space, "like the pseudo-public space of a theme park or shopping mall . . . is a space of control, one that is politically managed rather than defined by the actions and interests of autonomous agents within a system of democratic participation" (28). The film's satire, in part, is directed at the way in which, as Hazbun summarizes it, "media representations of Tunisia's external openness belie the domestic regime of control" (28). Tourism is used "as a means of promoting global economic integration through the construction of enclaves where state authorities maintain the ability to manage the transnational flows of people, capital, and images" (28). What *The TV Is Coming* suggests, most subversively, is that this effort of comprehensive state control is not confined to theme parks like El Malga on the island of Djerba but extends to Tunisian society as a whole.

With a "historical" pageant at its core, and the expectation of the residents of El Malga that the German television company will document their efforts at self-representation, *The TV Is Coming* highlights its allegorical intentions; and like the inventory within the film made by the accountant Lamine of the props used during the tree-planting ceremony and during the opening of the village's new community center, it offers an inventory of what Pierre Nora describes as *lieux de mémoire*.[5] The filmmaker Dhouib and his characters perform a kind of historiography by attempting to construct a usable past, in order to forge for themselves and for the much-anticipated German television company—and of course for us, the viewers of the film—a representation of Tunisia that, to echo Nora, will be suited to the civic as well as intellectual needs of their time. As a satire, *The TV Is Coming* dwells as much on the present as on the past; and as an allegory, speaking frequently to its viewers in code (in order to avoid the heavy hand of government censorship or reprisal), the film functions, of course, as a form of political resistance.

The Community Center, and History's Universal Vocation

Nora notes that (in France, at least), "the institutions that once transmitted values from generation to generation—churches, schools, families, governments—have ceased to function as they once did" (2).

("Globalization, democratization, and the advent of mass culture and the media," he suggests, "have turned the world upside down" [1].) There used to be "three main sources of archives: the great families, the church, and the state" (9), but the relationship between memory and history has changed: the great families, the church, and the state no longer have a monopoly on how history is written. Now, suggests Nora, "history belongs to everyone and to no one and therefore has a universal vocation" (3).

> Memory is life, always embodied in living societies and as such in permanent evolution, subject to the dialectic of remembering and forgetting, unconscious of the distortions to which it is subject, vulnerable in various ways to appropriation and manipulation, and capable of lying dormant for long periods only to be suddenly reawakened. History, on the other hand, is the reconstruction, always problematic and incomplete, of what is no longer. (3)

History, he summarizes, "is how modern societies organize a past they are condemned to forget because they are driven by change" (2).

In this age of the "acceleration of history" to which Nora alludes, in which "societies [that are] based on memory are no more" (2), the community center (by which I mean the actual building or room, which may be no more than an occasionally used *salle polyvalente*, of which there is one in nearly every town and village in Tunisia) plays an important, sometimes even prominent, role in the organization of the past. As a "new" nation—one of those which Nora would include in his description of "societies only recently roused from their ethnological slumbers by the rape of colonization" and "swept into history" by Independence (1)—Tunisia is under particular pressure, *accelerated pressure*, to define its collective consciousness, reinterpret its history in symbolic terms, and identify the *lieux* that embody its collective memory. "The less collective the experience of memory is," Nora observes, "the greater the need for individuals to bear the burden" (11). But where individuals cannot bear this burden and are condemned to forget, because they are driven by change, responsibility for remembering is increasingly delegated to the archive. The community center, like the one we see in *The TV Is Coming*, functions like an archive.

The film begins with a scene in which the six members of El Malga's cultural committee are assembled in their community center. They are seated around a table that has been placed on the stage in their theater (the

FIGURE 8.2 Mr. Fitouri (Ammar Bouthelja) and his deputy, Salem (Ali Abdelwahab) await the arrival of the "prominent official" who will plant a symbolic tree in El Malga and also ceremoniously open the El Malgans' new cultural center.

film thereby declaring its allegorical intentions at the outset and suggesting that democracy in Tunisia, as represented by the committee, is a charade). They are discussing what should be included in the program of activities to accompany their next planned event, Arbor Day (*La fête de l'arbre*). While their *chaouch* Ayed (Tawfik El Bahri) incongruously prepares a pot of mint tea over a smoking terra-cotta brazier on the stage beside the committee, the voice of the chairman can be heard bringing the meeting to order.[6] The camera focused on Ayed pans right and comes to rest on the group. Its one female member is speaking:

HADHRIA. Thank you, Mr. Fitouri. And since Arbor Day is approaching, I propose we start planning the program of festivities.
FITOURI. The festivities are always the same, and so is the program. Do you want to change them?
HADHRIA. This time, a prominent official will be visiting us.
SALEM. Ah! In that case, we have to make an effort. How about a footrace?

FITOURI. Foot racing is a healthy activity.
SALEM. We've grown tired of foot racing.
HADHRIA. Actually, we've had more than enough of it.
BRAHIM. Furthermore, the racers start in the field and finish at home.
FITOURI. Hey, how about *fantasia*?[7]
SALEM. Ah! *Fantasia* is something else! Between us, I like *fantasia*!
HADHRIA. *Fantasia* is old news.
SALEM. Indeed, it is old news and old school. *Fantasia* doesn't exist anymore.
BRAHIM. *Fantasia* is stuck in the mud.
HADHRIA. We are creative people. Let's find something else! (*The camera pans slowly to the right, then pauses on Sghaïer, who is wearing a red beret and a Tunisian scarf, which, to the uninitiated eye, resembles a Palestinian keffiyeh.*)
SGHAÏER, *standing up, and in a state of high excitement, speaking very rapidly.* Comrades! I think the right attitude would be to open up to our young talents—in order to put an end to the plot being sown against our Arab and Muslim culture by America and Zionism.
FITOURI, *turning to Hadhria in exasperation.* Shut this disaster up! He's talking like the opposition.
HADHRIA. Let him talk. So what if he's from the opposition!
SALEM. If he is, we should denounce him.
HADHRIA. The opposition is legal now.
SALEM. In that case, there's no point in denouncing him.
FITOURI. Since when is the opposition legal? Why am I the last to know?

I quote the dialogue of this little scene at length, because it effectively conveys the meeting's tone, which will be maintained in the interactions among these characters throughout the film and reveals the dynamic of their democratic method. Hadhria (Fatma Ben Saïdane), in keeping with Tunisia's reputation as the country with the most "liberated" women in the Arab world, is the feistiest and apparently most progressive member of the group. Salem (Ali Abdelwahab), as Fitouri's deputy and yes-man, will always blow with the winds of consensus. Sghaïer (Chawki Bouglaïa), the youngest member of the committee, representing Tunisia's "youth," is allowed to hold the most left-wing views, as long as those views do not actually excite the imagination of the group and result in a threat to the status quo.[8] Brahim

INVENTING THE POSTCOLONIAL NATION/CONSTRUCTING A USABLE PAST

(Aïssa Harrath) speaks little in this first exchange among the film's main characters, but the viewer, reflecting also on the fact that his character is blind, will soon recognize him as the voice of Tunisia's de-politicized Islam. Lamine (Jamel Sassi), the treasurer, normally preoccupied with whether El Malga can afford the committee's planned activities and projects, is for the moment silent. Mr. Fitouri (Ammar Bouthelja), chairman and local *zaîm* (leader or boss, with links to Ben Ali's hegemonic RCD Party in Tunis)—buffoon though he may appear to be—dominates the proceedings, and as he is sometimes pleased to remind his fellow members, is the final authority in all matters even remotely relating to the business of the committee. Mabrouka, the secretary, silently records the minutes of the meeting.

Fitouri's authoritarian impulses represent the bedrock issue to which, in the final analysis, all of the film's satire redounds, just as Tunisia's democracy deficit is the puzzle at the contradictory heart of its bid for recognition as a "modern" society. When Hadhria informs Fitouri that (political) opposition is now legal, his response ("Why am I the last to know?") is a reproach by the film to Tunisia's leadership. It is a way of saying to Ben Ali: "Have you not heard? Why are you the last to know? Dictatorships are out of style! For modern, civilized countries, authoritarian governments are a thing of the past!" Salem's response, when he realizes that Sghaïer can be defined as being "from the opposition," in effect is to remind his fellow committee members of their duty as members of the RCD ("If he is [from the opposition], we should denounce him!"); but when he is told that "the opposition is legal now," his conclusion—"In that case, there's no point in denouncing him"—is both absurd and funny. It reveals the complete absence, even in a democratic setting, of the right to challenge Tunisia's ruling party, and it exposes Ben Ali's multiparty democracy as a thoroughgoing sham.[9] (Salem says this without any hint of irony, for his response is the reflex of someone who has lived his entire life without freedom of political expression.)

Later in the film, after they have been (mis)informed that a German television company will soon arrive to make a film about El Malga, we see Stoufa (Elaïd Bououni), a performer in the pageant who has been assigned the role of the Tunisian poet Aboulkacem Chebbi (1909–1934), walking around declaiming Chebbi's poetry. "Destiny answers the people's call for life, darkness will be dispelled, and chains will break," he recites again and again, with as much feeling as he can muster.[10] Hichem (Hichem Rostom), the Egyptian theatrical director whom the El Malgans have taken on to design their pageant, makes his way through the crowd of costumed villagers and confronts the young man:

HICHEM. Who are you?
STOUFA. Aboulkacem Chebbi.
HICHEM. Who authorized you to speak?
STOUFA. Why? Do I have to pay to speak?
HICHEM. It's a silent role, without dialogue.
STOUFA. A poet cannot have a silent role.
HICHEM. Keep quiet!
STOUFA. Ah, so, you are telling me to keep quiet? I refuse to keep quiet! Colonization didn't make Aboulkacem Chebbi chicken out, and you are not the one who is going to reduce him to silence! (*He walks off, recommencing his recitation of the same two lines of poetry*: "Destiny answers the people's call for life, darkness will be dispelled, and chains will break....")

In this brief exchange, not only does the film plead for the special role of the artist in the struggle against oppression, it critiques the hypocrisy of the managers of Tunisia's image (the guardians of patriotism—the whole apparatus, both official and unofficial, dedicated to forging a "positive" image of Tunisia, without much concern for historical truth or realities on the ground) and registers the disappointment felt by those who believe the promise of decolonization has been betrayed by Tunisia's post-Independence leaders.[11] Stoufa is correct: a poet who has been rendered silent, who is nothing but an image on a postage stamp or a thirty-dinar bill, or a costumed figure in a parade, is no longer a poet, but a commodity, a symbol whose meaning can be hijacked for ideological purposes or used to sanction behavior that contradicts what the poet himself believed in and stood for.[12] In the present context, of course, the poets who refuse to be silenced are the filmmakers themselves—Moncef Dhouib, the actors, everyone involved in the making of *The TV Is Coming*.

Showing "our culture, our history, and our values"

When Fitouri receives the phone call informing him of the television company's imminent arrival, he announces to his fellow committee members: "If I'm being telephoned from on high, it's because there's a political message underneath, which only I can decode." His first instinct is to seize the opportunity for personal gain. As a politician in a one-party state, Fitouri knows that the promotion of a positive image of the nation is—and must be seen to be—inseparable from an endorsement of the ruling party. As in most societies, patriotism is an effective tool of social control; and whether or not the citizens of El Malga understand that they are being manipulated by their government, we see that they are willing and able to subordinate their differences to the higher, patriotic purpose of burnishing a positive image of their country.

Fitouri decides that El Malga should have a statue in the village square, as they have them in Europe. He commissions Brahim's son, Kafza (H'mida Laâbidi), to make the statue. Kafza, who is an artitst and has actually visited Europe, understands that a public monument of the kind Fitouri wants should be allegorical. Accordingly, he seeks the input of the cultural committee, whose discussion about what the statue should represent—they want it to represent everything positive the nation stands for (allegorized as "the Tunisian Woman")—itself nearly becomes an allegory of what a majority of Tunisians were convinced would be the result if they had real, multiparty democracy: the popular belief, encouraged by Ben Ali's regime, was that Tunisia would become like its neighbor Algeria, a dysfunctional democracy with crippling parliamentary conflicts and protracted violence among several of the society's constituent groups. Out of fear, most Tunisians supported their "strongman" form of government and rarely complained about the absence of a real opposition party, preferring instead the oxymoronic fiction that their leader was democratically elected—usually winning, according to the published figures, around 99.5% of the vote—and that he was maintained in office by the free will of the overwhelming majority of the people.

Without Fitouri's "leadership" guiding them for better or worse toward agreement about how they should represent themselves (he is absent during the discussion about the statue), the committee's democratic process of arriving at a decision does not, in fact, fall apart.[13] On the contrary, it proceeds admirably. The outcome, although imperfect, will not resemble the contemporary Algerian body politic. The significant, if ambivalent, point of the scene is that the committee *is* able to arrive at a decision that is acceptable to the majority. The realized sculpture, of a giant, bare-breasted woman with an amphora under her arm, will resemble the centerpiece of a grand and implausible, eighteenth-century, European fountain; but despite everything, the village is ready for the German television company when it arrives—ready even with a stream of water gushing from the plaster maiden's amphora—all of which, if not effectively symbolizing the authenticity and modernity of "the Tunisian Woman," nevertheless stands as proof of a project conceived, developed, and accomplished in a timely manner.

As an example of democratic teamwork, the committee's achievements are impressive. Examples of Fitouri's authoritarianism, however, also abound in the film. The actor Bouthelja's charm and his expert comic timing perhaps allow the viewer to forget sometimes that Fitouri represents the violence of the police state. "Unlike 'police states' in the region," Hazbun notes, "the Tunisian regime continued to articulate a discourse of pluralism, democracy, and openness to buttress its cosmopolitan tourist image throughout its period of political deliberalization" (29). State control over society was expanded under Ben Ali, whom it is said quadrupled the number of police (including secret police) in his first ten years in office. *The TV Is Coming* makes reference to this practice of police states and to what Hibou describes as the "totalitarian conception of social relations and relations of power" in Tunisia (118). Throughout the film, we see Fitouri's spy Bahoussi (Abdelkhader Dkhil) at work. Although not quite the village idiot, Bahoussi is depicted as a childlike fool, who takes it upon himself to keep Fitouri informed with gossip and the goings-on in the village that he thinks "Uncle" Fitouri will find useful.[14] He also spies on Fitouri himself, which is how he knows that Fitouri will probably be upset to discover that "the Egyptian" has chosen Fitouri's mistress Selma (Leïla Chebbi) for the role of Zezia in the pageant.

When Fitouri threatens, on trumped-up charges, to shut down the Café de la Jeunesse, some unsavory truths embedded in his "Uncle Fitouri" character are revealed for what they are: he is an authoritarian with a state-funded repressive apparatus at his disposal, to use as he wishes—"in the name of the law"—without being accountable to anyone. He marches into the café, where he finds the proprietor (Nouri Bouzid) carefully weighing out portions of tobacco for use in the café's *chicha* pipes ("My waiters are bankrupting me!" Bouzid's character explains).[15]

FITOURI. Listen, I've received a telegram from on high, informing me that a foreign television is coming to film here.[16]
CAFÉ OWNER. What does it have to do with us?
FITOURI. We must make a positive impression.

CAFÉ OWNER. What do you mean, "positive"?
FITOURI. Your café is full of unemployed people, and it gives a bad image of Arabs.
CAFÉ OWNER. Because you like Arabs so much? If you ask me, they get on my nerves.
FITOURI. You insult your race? Fine. (*He walks out in high dudgeon.*)

Fitouri returns the next day, accompanied by a municipal agent charged with closing down the café. When the proprietor protests, Fitouri explains that it need not come to that:

FITOURI. We wish only to present a clean café, with nicely dressed customers holding a newspaper or a book. To read and improve oneself, where's the harm in that?
CAFÉ OWNER. What's in it for me, if you fill my café with intellectuals?
FITOURI. But the reading will only last an hour, it's not for always.
CAFÉ OWNER. Ah! If it's temporary, then the café is at your disposal.

For the Tunisian viewer watching this scene, there is a layer of allegorical meaning contained in the fact that, as noted above, the café owner is played by Nouri Bouzid, himself a veritable Tunisian *lieu de mémoire*. Not only is Bouzid the founding director of the New Tunisian Cinema, as we know, but he was also, throughout the Ben Ali era, the cinema's most fearless critic of Tunisian society and of the Tunisian police state, making films (and contributing to the films of others, primarily as a screenwriter) about government torture, traditions of domestic servitude akin to slavery, the sexual abuse of children, the causes of Islamic fundamentalist violence, and various other evils. Bouzid's iconic value in this scene is inestimable—he is the Tunisian film director most famous precisely for categorically refusing to offer a picture-postcard view of his country, which is why it is so funny to see (his) café cleaned up and resembling a movie set on the day of the German television company's visit. The café's clientele, smartly dressed for the occasion, sit at evenly spaced tables, reading nonfiction books, French-language newspapers, medical journals, and serious film magazines (we even catch a glimpse of Orson Welles in *Citizen Kane* on the cover of one magazine!).[17]

Eventually, after a couple of false alarms and a seemingly endless wait, the now-weary radio reporter, who was earlier present for the tree-planting and ribbon-cutting ceremonies in the village, begins to wonder if the German television company will ever show up. "We are still awaiting the arrival of the TV," he says into his microphone. "And we will continue to wait. But our waiting will not last forever. Because ... as a matter of fact ... we don't need to make our image better in the eyes of the West. We have no need to name all our qualities. And we are warning you not to export your so-called democracy to this noble land."[18] It is one of the film's few direct references to "democracy," and it alludes to the perception, described by Béji in *Nous, décolonisés*, that the West uses the "democracy deficit" in countries like Tunisia as a club with which to beat them: "The Europeans continue to reserve a right to look down on our democratic shortcomings. Democracy serves now as a legitimate means of spreading civilization, and it demands of these very subjects, who yesterday were judged to be unfit for democracy, something that it did not know how to give them."[19] Indeed, the modern conscience measures a society's moral value by the yardstick of democratic virtue, and countries like Tunisia are found wanting. The radio reporter's remarks reveal an awareness (perhaps widespread in third-world societies) that democracy, while no doubt admirable and desirable, is often promoted by Western countries as a way of exercising neocolonial domination.

This same complaint will be articulated by Hadhria, albeit rather differently, toward the end of the film, when the El Malgans discover that the German television company is not in fact there to film them but to observe a species of deadly scorpion unique to North Africa. Just as Béji remarks that, ever since democracy "became a quasi-*religious* moral charge in the world, we [the decolonized] have felt guilty about not knowing how to exercise it properly [and] we tie ourselves in knots trying at least to give the appearance of knowing how" (45), Hadhria stands before the German television crew and blasts them with a fierce reproach:

> Are you entertained? Are you mocking us? For a month we've been preparing! Men and women have rallied to show you our culture, our history, and our values. And you, you just don't give a damn! We look up to you, and you look down on us. We treat you as human beings, and you see us as animals. You are all excited about scorpions and beetles!

The scene is all at once poignant, painful, and funny, for Hadhria then turns to face her fellow El Malgans: "And I say this in front of all of you:

there will be no more drum majorettes—they're finished! I'm going to put a match to their uniforms! Yes, a match!"

The era of the colonized subjects' mimicry of their European colonizers—symbolized by the incongruous spectacle of Hadhria's smartly dressed little group of drum majorettes in their European marching-band outfits, complete with tall, white shakos (or of Hadhria struggling in her high-heeled shoes better suited to Paris streets than the rocky, desert terrain around El Malga)—is over. The film announces, as Driss Abbassi observes in *Quand la Tunisie s'invente*, that in effect the word "homeland" (*patrie*) has replaced the word "nation" in Tunisia's political vocabulary: "It speaks a new conception of the national space, conceived as an inheritance; which is to say, a patrimony transmitted by ancestors. In this way, national identity is circumscribed by a territory (Tunisia), where the memory of earlier inhabitants is properly honored" (9n7). Henceforth, in François Hartog's phrase (echoing Pierre Nora): "the homeland is the *alter ego* of memory" [*"le patrimoine est l'alter ego de la mémoire"*].[20]

This is exactly what the film does in the pageant organized by the residents of El Malga—it seeks to honor the memory of Tunisia's earlier inhabitants—at the same time that it attempts to identify some of the main themes of contemporary Tunisian identity through the six members of El Malga's cultural committee.

"Comrades!"

Of the six members of the committee, Sghaïer in effect represents the most overtly political reminder to the viewer that Tunisia is an Arab nation, which is to say, one of the twenty-two members of the League of Arab States (indeed, Tunis was the headquarters of the Arab League from 1979 to 1990, before the league returned to Cairo).[21] For all its close ties to Europe, and its French connection as a Maghreb country, Tunisia has never not belonged to what is broadly called "the Arab world."[22]

When Sghaïer refers in the film's opening scene to "the plot being sown against our Arab and Muslim culture by America and Zionism," he is voicing a perception that is widespread in the Arab world—which would be overwhelmingly confirmed by the American invasion of Iraq in 2003—that Arab countries, especially those that are vocal in their sympathy for the

FIGURE 8.3 Sghaïer (Chawki Bouglaïa) recites a few lines of Aboulkacem Chebbi's poetry, to demonstrate to Stoufa (Elaïd Bououni) why he deserves to play the role of the famous poet in the pageant.

plight of the Palestinians, are viewed with suspicion and sometimes hostility by Israel's chief protector, the United States. The only country in the world, for example, that pretends not to understand why the United States invaded Iraq is the United States itself.[23] This, briefly, is the context in which Sghaïer's character in *The TV Is Coming* would have been written—an anti-Israel and anti-American context that would be exacerbated by the phenomenally destructive Israeli invasion of Lebanon in the summer of 2006, shortly before *The TV Is Coming* was released, in which over a thousand Lebanese civilians were killed and approximately a million Lebanese were displaced.

Sghaïer repeatedly voices his support for the underdog, and despite Fitouri's attempts to shut him up, reminds his fellow committee members at every opportunity that "Palestine is Arab!" and that they should be vigilant against the predations of "the imperialist plot." (His beret and Che Guevara T-shirt announce clearly where Sghaïer's sympathies lie.) When Fitouri tells his assembled committee that he has received a telephone call informing him of the imminent arrival of a television crew from Germany, Lamine is the first to respond: "I have a suggestion," he says helpfully. "Let's start by picking up all the beggars on the streets. The crazies and the bums. We'll hide them, and then after the foreign TV has departed, we'll release them." Sghaïer's reaction is immediate: "I'm opposed to that!" He repeats his earlier exhortation to "support our young people" and to mount a cultural project "capable of defeating Zionism and the reactionary forces that plot against Arab and Muslim culture." These forces, he explains, "want Western culture to rule over the entire world."

"Our beautiful religion"

If Sghaïer's reminder to his fellow committee members that "Palestine is Arab" is a way of reminding them that Tunisia, too, is Arab, then Brahim's role on the committee, as he sees it, is to remind them that they are Muslims. When Fitouri tells them about the German television company, Brahim's reaction is contradictory. "Don't trust them," he warns, "they don't have our best interests at heart." But he also sees the visit of the television company as an opportunity: "We should show them our traditions, our customs, our values, and our beautiful religion. Who knows! They might otherwise leave out [any mention of] the faith." For him, Islam is not a political vehicle, but the repository of Muslim values. He has always disapproved of his son's marriage to Ingrid (Bernadette Machillot), for example, because it was not arranged in the traditional manner by the respective families of the bride and groom. When Ingrid puts her arm around Kafza and explains, simply: "He is my husband, and I love him," Brahim replies: "Listen, Westerner, you may have overtaken us in technology, but we surpass you in morality! Do I go around saying that I love my wife? Or that she loves me? If and when you embrace Islam, *then* you may marry my son!"

If in Tunisia obedience to the authority of ordinary Muslim fathers (like Brahim) is erratic, the rule of submission to state authority is not. Paternal authority (as illustrated by the parable of the "Sacrifice of Abraham") seems to have been reproduced, first by Bourguiba, then by Ben Ali, in the relationship between the state and the Tunisian people. It has been a coercive relationship, Kenneth Perkins drily notes, which has rendered "compliance all but inescapable":

The most disruptive, unsettling, and far-reaching, but also certainly the most consequential, social debates in modern Tunisian history have centered on the value of traditional beliefs and practices. The enactment of legislation banning or restricting long-established customs and institutions, often in conjunction with other, subtler, forms of governmental pressure, has rendered compliance all but inescapable. From the precolonial era to the present, much of what successive governments have targeted as outmoded, and thus attempted to eliminate or radically alter, has been linked to Islam.[24]

There is a very amusing scene in the film alluding to this social debate, in which Fitouri and Hadhria come upon a group of devotees of the *marabout* Sidi Ben Issa engaged in a ritualistic dance. The two cultural committee members have no idea what they are looking at and are nonplussed; but when they realize that they are witnessing the manifestation of a syncretic religious tradition containing pre-Islamic elements, they express their categorical disapproval:

FITOURI. Tell me, what's with this guy who's eating scorpions?
IMAM. He's an ostrich, and he's in no danger.
HADHRIA. And the other one, who's rubbing himself against a cactus?
IMAM. Him, he's the camel.
FITOURI. This is no longer a fraternity, it's the African savannah!
IMAM. It's a spiritual exercise following the path of Sidi Ben Issa. When a man goes into a trance, he tames the animal inside him. His soul is thereby elevated, and the human is freed.
FITOURI. This is underdevelopment!
HADHRIA. It's underdevelopment that gives a false image of Islam in Europe. We are going to receive a foreign TV, and we want to present a good face. We're proposing a light program for them. For example, a little music, a little bit of folklore, some dance. They enjoy themselves, and then they go home.
FITOURI. And get rid of these scorpions and cactus plants.
IMAM. And what right do you have to alter a Sufi ritual?
FITOURI. (*Drawing himself up.*) I represent the authority here!
HADHRIA. Right. From now on, your Sufi ritual comes under the authority of Culture. It will be listed in the program as the Festival of the Cacti.
FITOURI. That's it. (*They both turn and leave.*)

A religious practice, thus, is made into a folkloric spectacle for the purpose, in effect, of selling the brand "Tunisia." Hadhria's pronouncement, "From now on, your Sufi ritual comes under the authority of Culture," and Fitouri's casting of it into law ("That's it"), recall the radical sweep of Atatürk's secularization of Turkey in the 1920s and 1930s, which Bourguiba, we know, observed with very close interest and sought largely to imitate.[25] Post-Independence Tunisia's orientation was to be decidedly Western. As Perkins writes: "Following independence, the nation's new leaders, virtually all of them products of French educations through which they had assimilated the philosophical underpinnings of Western culture, initiated sweeping social reforms allegedly designed to liberate Tunisians from beliefs and practices they saw as obsolete in the modern world and as deterrents to development" (7).

Brahim's role in the film is handled cautiously. The fact that he is blind and must often rely on Fitouri's stooge Bahoussi to guide him is a comment on the constrictions placed by the regime on the interpretations and practice of Islam in Tunisia.[26] El Malga's imam (the film's official representative of Islam) will grumble about the statue of the bare-breasted maiden placed in front of the mosque, but he does not have the power to have it removed; and when Brahim learns from Bahoussi that his daughter-in-law Ingrid is voluntarily picking up garbage that has been left on the streets of the village—which is the act that prompts Fitouri to announce the "Cleanliness Week" in El Malga ("Let's make our country a paradise on earth!" he enthuses)—the blind patriarch is incredulous. "You came from Germany in order to pick up garbage? Go back to the house!" he orders her. But Ingrid ignores him. Fitouri, however, is filled with admiration: "Look at that! German education!" he marvels. Hadhria agrees: "I've brought up this problem [of garbage on the streets of El Malga] at every meeting; I've written a stack of reports about it. And look, we still have garbage on the side of the road!"

Brahim (whose name refers to the "Father of the Religion," Ibrahim/Abraham) scolds his son Kafza for publicly showing affection for Ingrid. "Aren't you ashamed? You embrace a woman who eats pork and drinks wine!" "But she's my wife!" protests Kafza. The old man nevertheless is adamant in his disapproval: "It's an illicit relationship. This woman is impure, steeped in sin!" Kafza tries to reason with him: "Father, listen, if it's about the wine, it's not forbidden in their religion, you know. Jesus himself drank wine!"

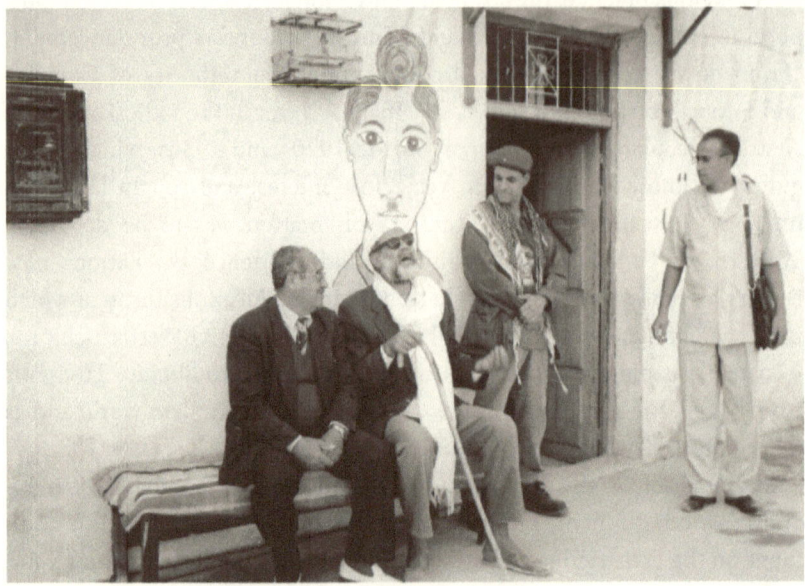

FIGURE 8.4 Salem, Sghaïer, and Lamine (Jamel Sassi), assembled in front of the barbershop, listen to the objections of Brahim (Aïssa Harrath) to one of Kafza's proposals about what their allegorical statue should look like.

The general Tunisian attitude toward Islam is usually described as "moderate," but Dhouib and his fellow filmmakers of the New Tunisian Cinema remain anxious about the dangers of bringing religion into the public sphere of national politics.[27] Brahim will be unhappy to discover that the symbolic representatives of his religion are going to bring up the rear in the pageant being organized, but his indignation goes unheeded: "Islamic civilization is our pride!" he declares. "It ought to be put up front!" Hichem reminds Brahim that the pageant is meant to be historical. Fitouri, too, has priorities that are ahistorical: he wants to put the Romans before the Phoenicians (because the Romans have the more beautiful costumes), just as Brahim wants to put the Muslim Arabs at the head of the parade (to show the proper "respect" for Islam). Hichem can only repeat: "We must respect the course of history!" Brahim shakes his head ruefully and mutters to himself: "History is being turned upside-down. Instead of putting the Muslims in front. . . . Come [*placing his hand on Bahoussi's shoulder*], take me back to the house."

INVENTING THE POSTCOLONIAL NATION/CONSTRUCTING A USABLE PAST

The question of religious tolerance in Tunisia, related to the status of Islam as the official religion of the state and in particular to the status of the Jews (both historically and in the present), is evoked in an exchange between two pageant performers and Fitouri:

"PRIEST". Why have I been put with the non-believers?
FITOURI. Who has put you with the non-believers?
"PRIEST". The Egyptian! All the others get to keep their religion, except me. He's made me a priest.
"RABBI". He made me a rabbi, and I didn't complain.
"PRIEST". Is that so? And is it because a rabbi is worse than a priest?
FITOURI. What! There's a rabbi in the story? (*He finds Hichem.*) What's all this commotion? Why are you introducing Christians into my parade? And you've added Jews. (*He lowers his voice, as the camera cuts to a close-up of his face.*) Are you aware that we are at war with Israel?
HICHEM. (*Shrugs elegantly.*) I am aware of the war, but this is about history.

The possible meanings of this little scene are too numerous to discuss in any detail here, except to remark that Fitouri's question ("What! There's a rabbi in the story?") is an index of how difficult it is for some Tunisians to reconcile their national ideology of tolerance with the terrible injustice wrought by the Zionist cause upon their fellow Arabs, the Palestinians. Fitouri has simply repressed any memory of the Jewish presence in Tunisia's history, just as Hichem (representing Egypt, which signed a peace treaty with Israel in 1979) is on the side of history, and therefore cannot speak to the "war with Israel." The film in effect registers a degree of resentment felt by many Tunisians that Egypt continues to claim for itself the role of leader of the Arab world, despite having caved in to U.S. pressure and accepted the American bribe to sign a peace treaty with Israel.

The film's final comment on the role of Islam and the status of religious tolerance in contemporary Tunisia is perhaps illustrated in the scene in which a sudden storm—a veritable *rih essed*[28]—results in mayhem and sends the pageant's costumed performers running for shelter. The majority makes its way to the mosque, where the imam at the door, to all appearances, looks like Noah deciding which creatures, and how many of each, should be allowed into the ark. Seeing a man dressed as a Catholic monk, he tries to bar the "monk's" entrance: "Where are you going, with that cross around your neck? This is a mosque here!" But the pressure of the crowd is too strong for the imam, who quickly gives up and says, "Okay, fine, come in." The tide of history on which Tunisia is being carried, the scene suggests, is toward pluralism and tolerance, and the world that was once riven (we could even say, defined) by religious rivalries—notwithstanding the dire predictions of those who believe in a "clash of civilizations"—is now committed to a modernity underpinned by Enlightenment values.[29]

"You talk about women's emancipation. Where are they, these women?"

There is no doubt that Tunisia's postcolonial success as a modern, prosperous society is grounded not only in Bourguiba's having made universal education a high priority, but also in his commitment to the emancipation of women. A delightful scene in the film pays tribute to this era of Tunisia's development: on the day of the arrival in the village of Hichem, recommended to El Malga's cultural committee as "Egypt's greatest director," we observe Hadhria leading a family-planning class in El Malga. "Birth control is one of the great priorities of the government," she is saying. "The methods of contraception are numerous and varied. Today, I'm going to talk to you about the condom. [*She goes over to her desk.*] Here's a specimen. [*She holds it up for all to see.*] Known by the name of 'condom' [*as she is saying this, we see Hichem alight from his taxi and approach the open window of Hadhria's classroom*], or 'contraceptive,' or 'rubber.' Its use is simple. You have to fit it delicately in the appropriate place. That is to say, slide it gently there, where it needs to be. [*She slips the condom onto two of her fingers, and holds her hand up high. The camera cuts to a shot of her audience; most of the women are in traditional garb. With considerable aplomb—she is a natural performer—Hadhria continues.*] Then, at the end of the operation, that is to say, when one has properly finished, and had a good time...." A woman interrupts her: "Listen, I tried your 'rubber,' and it's not effective." (We notice that Fitouri's wife is seated behind this woman.) Without skipping a beat, Hadhria replies: "Perhaps you don't know how to use it." The woman insists: "No, my dear, I do. Every evening, I slip it onto my husband's finger before we go to bed. And we have nine kids!" Hadhria suggests to the woman that she try using "the pill," to which the woman replies: "With the husband I've got, neither the pill nor a condom is going to work—the only thing perhaps would be for the government to erect a wall between us!" Hadhria laughs heartily at this, as do the other women in the room... until she notices Hichem standing at the window. Mortified, she hides her condom-clad fingers behind her back, and passes on the message to the visitor that Mr. Fitouri is waiting for him at the café. He graciously thanks her, and turns to leave, as she struggles frantically with the condom, which is refusing to slip off her fingers.

The scene, apart from being one of the funniest in the movie, echoes with a hint of irony, in that Hadhria had been awestruck when she first met the suave and elegant Egyptian. "Mr. Hichem, are you *really* an Egyptian?" she asked (it is the same question Fitouri's mistress, the widow Selma, will ask him), as if his national origin were a wondrous thing, conferring cultural superiority—and yet, in the matter of family planning, where Tunisia has succeeded admirably, Egypt has failed miserably and suffers the consequences of severe overpopulation and widespread poverty.

Hadhria's role in the film is central. She represents the advanced status of women in Tunisia and much that is socially progressive about her society, but she is also an allegorical figure representing the way in which Ben Ali's RCD Party, following Bourguiba's Néo-Destour Party, co-opted the UNFT. She is properly introduced to the viewer at the beginning of the film, when she addresses her fellow committee members in a lively spirit of patriotic complicity: "Listen, my brothers: In the name of the Tunisian woman—take this down, Mabrouka [*she turns to the secretary, who is recording the minutes of the meeting*]—in the name of Tunisian women, and of the women's organization that I represent—you're getting this down?—I propose that we do not miss this opportunity to inform the West about the important achievements of the giant steps made by women on the road toward liberty and emancipation, not counting the gigantic achievements that have accumulated and which redound to the credit of woman. [*She turns to Mabrouka again.*] You got that?"

Her portrait is filmed with affection and with the same pride that Hadhria herself has in "what [Tunisians] have accomplished in the very short time since Independence." The film pretends to be ironic about some of its material, such as the radio reporter's announcement on the day of the pageant to his "dear listeners [that] we have been here since early this morning awaiting the arrival of our TV friends, who are going to acquaint themselves with the depth of our civilization, the authenticity of our culture, the rootedness of our traditions." But in fact the film is completely sincere; and Fatma Ben Saïdane's superbly understated, comic performance as Hadhria helps to ground it in this sincerity of purpose, so that when the reporter adds: "As a sign of friendship and fraternity, we are welcoming them today with flowers." his expression of goodwill is nevertheless believable—despite what we have already seen of the recycled bunch of dusty, artificial flowers presented to the government official on Arbor Day (and again, a few minutes later, when he opens the new community center).

In one of the earliest scenes of the film, during the festivities to celebrate the opening of the new cultural center, we see Hadhria in the front row of the audience attending the dancer Hnia's performance. Watching the dancer triggers a desire in Hadhria to dance as well, and she rushes off to one of the deserted rooms in the community center, ties a scarf around her hips, and dances for a few, frenzied minutes, then returns to her seat, smiling to herself. The scene, we could say, is an ironic comment on the energies of women that have been liberated in Tunisia by the Personal Status Code of 1956: Hadhria is not exactly the liberated woman she wishes she were; nor does she fully embody the image of the woman Tunisia extols as one of its most progressive accomplishments in an Arab world more typically marked by female subordination to neopatriarchal rule. State feminism cannot be expected to make true feminists of all Tunisian women; but this is not the real point of Hadhria's character, whom it must be remembered is an RCD Party member. She is an unwitting stooge for a party that pretends to be progressive, but is not. Her character draws attention to the hypocrisy of Ben Ali's regime, which never shied away from taking credit for the advances and accomplishments of women in Tunisia, especially if the occasion could be used to advance the regime's political agenda and reinforce its stranglehold on the Tunisian political system.

Ben Ali's shameless attempts to imply that Tunisian women had the reformist fervor of his regime to thank for their "gains" and that their emancipation only became real in the years after his ouster of Bourguiba in 1987, make the viewer wonder about the value of women's rights in a country in which their human rights are dispensed with at the slightest perceived threat to the regime.[30] As the film's chief representative of "Benalism,"[31] Fitouri gives the viewer some idea of what may have lain behind Ben Ali's claim to support what the 2008 United Nations Human Development Report on

INVENTING THE POSTCOLONIAL NATION/CONSTRUCTING A USABLE PAST

Tunisia calls: "building the capabilities of women." When Fitouri protests to Hichem about his casting of Selma in the role of Zezia, Hichem shrugs: "Propose some women. You talk about women's emancipation. Where are they, these women?" Fitouri replies: "We'll do it without women."

Hadhria's response, predictably, is immediate: "What do you mean, 'without women'? [*She turns to Hichem.*] I'll provide the women. What do you need?" Hichem says: "We need three women—Elissa, the founder of Carthage; Zezia, the Hilalian [*Fitouri is nodding and grunting his approval at the mention of each name*]; and Kahina, the Berber." Hadhria makes a note of the names.

FITOURI. Kahina! Where does that one come from?
HADHRIA. What!? You don't know the Kahina? She was the Berber queen who fought against the Arab invasion. She defeated Hassan, the Muslim general.
FITOURI. What! A woman defeated a Muslim general? She has to be removed!
HICHEM. (*Amused, stops fanning himself.*) What do you mean, "removed"?
FITOURI. We eliminate her.
HICHEM. Ah, Mr. Fitouri. I will not allow you to interfere with my artistic choices.
FITOURI. Your artistic choices, we leave those to you. But political choices, that's our business—we who are in charge.
HADHRIA. Mr. Fitouri (*she speaks slowly, looking him in the eye*), this is about history. You want us to falsify history?
FITOURI. (*Pointing his finger at her and jutting out his jaw, Mussolini-style.*) I must report this to the authorities!

Fitouri's objection to the inclusion of Kahina is perhaps based on more than his misogyny. Writing about the place of Kahina (or "the Kahina") in the Tunisian political imaginary in the early 1960s—as it can be inferred from an examination of the history textbooks in use in Tunisian schools at the time—Driss Abbassi notes:

> If the primary-school textbooks in Arabic pass in silence over the episode of Berber resistance to Islam, the secondary-school textbooks in French on the contrary underline its importance. The disinterest of the textbooks

in Arabic toward this historical episode can certainly be explained by the fact that the Jewish origin of the Berber heroine (Kahina) does not square with the thesis expounded in these manuals about the Arab and Islamic origins of the Maghreb. We should remember that Kahina symbolizes the antiquity of the Jewish communities in the Maghreb, the vestiges of Christianity, and a Berber identity opposed to arabization.[32]

Abbassi's interpretation of the reason these textbooks pass in silence over the episode of Berber resistance to Islam is debatable, however. In his fascinating book, *Colonial Histories, Post-Colonial Memories: The Legend of the Kahina, A North African Heroine*, Abdelmajid Hannoum observes that "no legend has been adopted, transformed, or used by as many social groups as the legend of the Kahina. No character, real or imaginary, has been metamorphosed as has been the character of the Kahina. And consequently, no legend has articulated or promoted as many myths, nor served as many ideologies as this one."[33] Starting more than a century and a half after the historical events themselves, the legend of this war leader of the Berber tribes in the 680s was initially used to bolster the claims of Berbers in al-Andalus against Arab claims of ethnic supremacy and later reflected most of the modern ideologies in the Mediterranean: colonial ideology, European anticolonialism, Arab nationalism, North African nationalism, Berber nationalism, Zionism, and feminism. "The character herself has been transformed accordingly," Hannoum writes. "She has been changed constantly from a Berber to a Jew, to a Christian, to a Byzantine, to an Arab" (xv). The legend is crucial in Islamic and North African history, he explains, because it is the story of an origin: it tells how North Africa—once Berber, Roman, Byzantine, and Christian—became what it is now, that is, Arab and Muslim (xvi). He observes that one cannot tell when the legend was first appropriated by historiography:

> The legend was part of the memory of social groups (Berbers and Arabs), as well as the memory of historians. The two kinds of memory are not really opposed; they only function differently. . . . When historiography borrows a theme from oral tradition, the theme is no longer likely to be forgotten, but is henceforth part of the memory of history. It is very possible that other themes, other versions of the legend that were not taken up by historiography, were lost forever once they lost their function. (22)

Hannoum suggests that, from the Muslim point of view, the Kahina is an antihero owing to her status as a non-Muslim. In the century following the death of the Prophet, during which the Muslim community elaborated the essentials of its mythology, the story of Islam was represented thus: "The expeditions, the conquests of other people's lands, were not aggression, nor were they motivated by material interests, but they were rather a fulfillment of God's will. Islam, a religion of peace (versus the anarchy of others, in this case the Kahina) and surrender to God (versus surrender to a human being, in this case, the Kahina) must be carried out" (4). With the passage of time, he writes, the legend of the Kahina became firmly entrenched in the Maghrebi Muslim imaginary, and the factors behind its emergence and development were still at work in North African societies in the nineteenth century. During the colonial period, however, "a serious attempt" was made by the French to "rework it" (23). The French considered themselves to be the heirs of the Romans, and thus felt not only that French occupation of North Africa was justified, but that any seizure of Arab lands by the settlers was also justified:

> In short, the French [believed they] had the right, if not the duty, to colonize. They were taking what had belonged to them since the dawn of time. The Kahina represents European origin, just as she represents the change that occurred. She is Berber, and therefore a European in the final analysis. Her legend articulates, for the first time, two myths: the Berber myth and the Roman North African myth. (37)

Fitouri's stated objection to the inclusion of Kahina in El Malga's pageant—"What! A woman defeated a Muslim general? She has to be removed!"—would seem, finally, to be a critique by the film not only of the occasional persistence of an archaic variety of male sexism in Tunisian society, and of the heavy strain of neopatriarchal authoritarianism still to be found in the Tunisian public sphere, but of the rise—especially after the 9/11 terrorist attacks on the United States—of a reflexive chauvinism that insists on Tunisia's Muslim identity.

As for Elissa—or Dido, as she is more commonly known in the West—Hadhria will later explain to Hichem, while they're choosing costumes for the pageant performers, why this queen of ancient history is her favorite: "I admire Elissa. She was in love, and she kept her love secret. And when they tried to force her into a marriage, she set herself on fire." Hichem is appalled by this story: "That's terrible! What a tragic end."[34] But Hadhria tells him: "You men, you have no idea what a woman in love is. When a woman loves, she becomes fire and flames." We know Dhouib is having fun in this scene, not only because we have picked up on hints throughout the film that Hadhria has a crush on the smooth-talking and sartorially splendid (but oblivious) Egyptian, but also because we remember Salouha, Ben Saïdane's character in Boughedir's *Halfaouine*, whose unrequited love for Sheikh Mokhtar results in hysterical fits of passion that leave everyone in her household quite unnerved.[35] (In Boughedir's *A Summer in La Goulette*, Ben Saïdane's character again is unrequitedly in love with a man of religion, the pious hypocrite nicknamed the "Double Hadj.") The scene is additionally amusing, and allegorically charged, because Hichem is dressed at this moment as "The King of Spain" (Charles I, the first King of Spain, who was the grandson of the "Catholic Monarchs," Ferdinand and Isabella, who are credited with driving the Moors out of Spain in 1492); and Hadhria is wearing the Ottoman Sultan Suleiman the Magnificent's outsized turban, which makes her tiny frame seem even tinier. (In a setback for Charles I, Suleiman's naval commander, Khair ad-Din[36]—also known as Barbarossa—defeated the Spanish Fleet at the Battle of Preveza in 1538, securing vast territories in North Africa for the Ottoman Empire, including Tunisia). The allegory is elaborate, but the point about not underestimating the power of women (and Muslims in a Christian-dominated world) is clear.

Zezia the Hilalian is perhaps the most symbolically complex of the three female figures chosen by Hichem to represent the contributions of women to the three thousand years of Tunisia's history. Zezia's pedigree (she is also known in many accounts as Jâzya) dates from the middle of the eleventh century, when the Hilalian tribes, as they are called, spread into the Maghreb from Egypt (they are estimated to have numbered between 200,000 and 500,000).[37] Abbassi describes the way in which this single most important event in medieval North Africa is treated in Tunisian textbooks of the early 1960s. It "is not treated as a fact about religion (i.e., the advent of Islam as a new religion), but as an event of political, social, economic, and cultural importance" (35).

> The influx of a large number of Arab nomads would have provoked a rupture in the socioeconomic equilibrium achieved by both the nomadic and

sedentary Berbers. A series of consequences have been attributed to the Hilalian invasion: the crossbreeding of the Berber population; the arabization of the Berber dialects and spread of the Arabic language; the halt of trade and the economic ruin of Ifriqiya and its political dismemberment (35–36).

Zezia, who was the Hilalian sultan's sister (which allowed her to play an important role within the tribe), is described by the ethnologist Micheline Galley as:

A woman whose personality is exceptionally versatile and powerful. . . . At the time when the tribe has to take decisions of high moment (for instance, before migrating westwards), the Elders ask, and follow, her advice. In all cases she is pictured as the counselor *par excellence*, in the sense that she knows how to disentangle intricate situations (*dabbar*) and find out the most appropriate concrete solution. For the sake of her people in periods of drought, she serves as the barter between the Hilalian tribe and a prince from the city: the latter gives grain, pasture and water, and marries Jâzya (a temporary marriage, in fact, until the Hilalians decide to take their sister back). In all circumstances she appears as the protector of the tribe and the guardian of its ancestral values.[38]

Galley also records that "it may happen that she reminds her peers of the manly qualities required of a Hilalian" (434), and among the examples she gives, includes the "virtue" concerning "the art of speaking and, in particular, the subtle use of 'allusion'" (434). This last, rather curious virtue extolled by Zezia is perhaps alluded to by Dhouib in the scene in which Selma meets Hichem during the audition call for the pageant. Selma, fluttering her eyelashes and playing coquettishly with her veil, says to Hichem, "I've never seen an Egyptian in the flesh, only in the movies. Are you really an Egyptian?" When he assures her that he is the real thing, she lowers her veil a little, to reveal her neck, and says: "You promise?" Hichem, taking off his sunglasses and leaning forward seductively, asks her what her name is. When she tells him, he remarks on how pretty it is. She giggles, and raises her veil again, to cover her mouth, all the while shooting little glances at him out of the corner of her eye. "You know," he says to her, "you could be an actress!"[39] Then, in what could be an allusion to Rostom's role as the rapacious bey in *The Silences of the Palace*, she says, as if quoting from somewhere or trying to reproduce movie dialogue: "Me! I don't have an actress's talent, my handsome bey!" Hichem chortles at this—no doubt because popular wisdom has it that, within their narrow range, prostitutes are often the best actresses—and now says: "You should become a star! [*Turning to Hadhria, he makes the casting decision.*] That's our 'Zezia the Hilalian'!"

Selma, thus, has alluded to the fact that (possibly, like Fella in *The Silences of the Palace*) she is available for sex, if Hichem should desire it; Hichem appears to allude to her allusiveness (and to the historical Hilalian's willingness to serves as the barter between her tribe and a prince from the city) when he casts her in the role of Zezia; Dhouib possibly has Selma allude to Rostom's role in *The Silences of the Palace*.[40] The film does not focus on what Galley calls the legendary Zezia's "exceptional qualities of intelligence and wisdom" (434), but depicts her, rather, in the way an Internet blogger in 2007 described her: as "the fabulous Zezia," one of those women who are able to "motivate the exploits of men, who are thereby transformed into demigods and become larger-than-life in the eyes of these same women."[41] The viewer understands why, contrary to Fitouri's objection, the widow Selma is ideally cast in the role of Zezia!

All three women—Elissa, Kahina, and Zezia—are inscribed in the film within a general context of Arab machismo. Dhouib makes fun of one macho character who auditions for a role in the pageant and is told by Hichem: "You'll shave off your mustache and be a Roman soldier." The man protests that he will be a Roman *with* a mustache. "You heard!" Hichem snaps back. "Shave off the mustache." The man explains that he cannot shave off his mustache, because he is a married man. "My friend," Hichem tells him, "the Romans didn't have mustaches." To which the man replies: "It's not my fault the Romans weren't manly!" Hadhria tells him firmly that there will be no further discussion on the subject and calls on the next person in line to step forward. Later, the man will ask his barber: "Tell me—Mribeh's son, the one who is playing Ibn Khaldun, is he more manly than I am?" The barber says to him: "If you had a beard, they'd have given you Harun al-Rashid."[42] The man expostulates: "A beard! For the one [character] you need a beard to get the job; and for the other, you have to shave off your mustache! Fine [*he gets up from the barber's chair*], I refuse to work!"[43]

As for Fitouri, the film's chief representative of masculine bluster, there is a scene that parodies the ancient dynamic between men and women that

Zezia in the film represents. Cutting a ridiculous figure in his pajamas, as he sits on his bed beside his wife, Fitouri says: "Listen, dear spouse. Highly placed officials have charged me with a very important mission. If I succeed, I shall be promoted, and I'll become an important person." His wife's response—"And as they say: 'Behind every great man is a great woman, but well hidden'"—is all the funnier, because Fitouri, accustomed to hearing only what he wants to hear, pays no attention to it. (The viewer of course might also think of the woman behind Tunisia's president: Ben Ali's second wife, Leïla Trabelsi Ben Ali, who was rather the opposite of hidden.) He tells her not to wait up for him during the coming days, for his time will be taken up with important meetings and lengthy, roundtable discussions that will extend late into the evening. But what the viewer knows (the scene immediately prior to this suggests it) is that he intends to use the preparations for the television company's visit as an opportunity to spend more time with his mistress, Selma.

The Pageant of History

"We have to show them that we have a rich history," Fitouri says. "Our region is ancient. It has at least—*at least!*—three thousand years of history." On this, everyone agrees. Hadhria goes through the list: "Phoenicians, Punics, Romans, Byzantines, Arabs, Turks, Spanish, French—they've all passed through us."[44] Fitouri suggests they show how "our country is a meeting ground." Upon hearing this, Bahoussi turns to Brahim: "Uncle Brahim, what does 'meeting ground' mean?"; and Brahim explains: "It means that civilizations that wanted to meet each other, and had no place to meet, would come to our country."

Of course, the truth is slightly different. In *Tunisia since Independence*, Clement Henry Moore writes:

> During its three thousand years of history, Tunisia was ruled most of the time by foreigners—Carthaginians, Romans, Vandals, and Byzantines, then various Muslim dynasties that usually originated in other Muslim lands. The Hafsids were themselves at the outset only agents of the Moroccan Almohads. Similarly the Turkish Husainid dynasty of the eighteenth and nineteenth centuries ruled in the name of the Ottoman Empire.[45]

FIGURE 8.5 Hichem (Hichem Rostom) and Fitouri discuss what should be in the pageant.

Moore's representation of Tunisian history in this paragraph is potentially misleading, however, for it can give the impression that there has always been a Tunisian people—an unchanging ethnic/religious/linguistic group—that for three thousand years has been colonized by one foreign power after another. The reality, of course, is that, like most peoples, Tunisians are (and have been throughout their history) the sum of their differences. The notion that there was a "pure" Tunisian who was "ruled" by the foreign Queen Elissa, and was later ruled by the Romans, and thirteen centuries later was ruled by the "Ottoman" Lamine Bey, and so on, is false.

Most of the committee members are fully conscious of their historiographic responsibility, although for understandable reasons, they choose not to focus on the narrative describing Tunisia as having been "ruled most of the time by foreigners" (i.e., a history of colonialism). The other narrative—that the residents of Ancient Carthage were "Tunisians" in the same way that the residents of Carthage today are Tunisians (which is perhaps like saying Queen Cleopatra was an Egyptian in the same way that

INVENTING THE POSTCOLONIAL NATION/CONSTRUCTING A USABLE PAST

President Hosni Mubarak was)—is as inaccurate as the notion that there is such a thing as a transhistorical, "authentic" Tunisian.[46]

These differences of emphasis in the construction of national identity are raised in an amusing exchange between the pageant's accountant, Lamine, and its director, Hichem. When Lamine arranges for a manufacturer of tomato-based products to sponsor the "Egyptian" section of the pageant, Hichem becomes upset: "He wants to put [placards advertising] the tomatoes with Ramses! It's indecent!" Lamine asks: "And what does your Ramses have to do with anything? Is he in our history?" Hichem replies: "You, in Tunisia, you have three thousand years of history; while we in Egypt have five thousand! Listen, we are Arabs, brothers—same people, same history—we help each other. We need to do this thing together, okay?"

There is a sense in which Hichem is correct, not because he says contemporary Tunisians and Egyptians are both Arab peoples (which is true), with the same history (which is not true), but because Tunisians and Egyptians are both hybrid peoples. "Proof" of this is given in the delightful scenes showing the auditions (or rather, the selection process) for the pageant. Hichem and Hadhria are seated at a table in the middle of the courtyard of the community center, as the aspiring performers approach the table, one by one. "Demonstrate that you are well organized!" Hadhria orders them. "When you've taken a number, present yourself to the director!"

The line moves fast: "You as well, Roman," Hichem tells the man standing before him. "Spaniard," he tells the next. "You, you will be Punic," he tells another. Protestations about the designation method are useless. "Punic! And why Punic?" one man wants to know. Hadhria waves him on impatiently: "Punic! Punic!" And the "audition" continues: "You, you'll be Spanish... French... You, you'd make a good Hannibal... You, you will be Ibn Khaldun..." and so on, to the very last resident (it seems) of the village.[47] Not surprisingly, the residents of El Malga look like their various ancestors.

Television Has Arrived

When the television company finally arrives, the half-dozen or so Germans turn out to be not a television crew at all, but, as has been noted, a group of scientists and documentary filmmakers engaged in research to find an antidote for the sting of a species of poisonous scorpion. They enter El Malga by the back road, where they are apprehended and held at Brahim's oil mill, until Fitouri can be brought to the scene to decide on their fate. One of the hostages asks for a telephone, so that he might call the German Embassy in Tunis. When Fitouri learns the truth about their identity, he orders them freed at once, but turns to Ingrid, his interpreter for the occasion and asks: "You're saying they're from Germany?" (The camera tracks from one hostage to the next, corresponding to his gaze: the group includes a black man, a blonde woman, a man with Asian features) Fitouri is puzzled. How can they all be Germans? "They're the real thing,"[48] Ingrid confirms.

Fitouri asks Ingrid if, since her "cousins" have finally arrived and have their cameras with them, she might persuade them to film "some souvenirs" of El Malga (he gestures toward the expectant pageant performers). When the Germans discover that they are out of film, Fitouri says: "Just pretend to film—nobody will know the difference."

The fact that the film's credit sequence at the end contains a scene nearly identical to the one that begins the film—of the committee discussing what they should do in their next program of "cultural" events—is a wry comment not only on the gap between the official narrative regarding Tunisian national identity and the realities that complicate and contradict it, but on Tunisia's stagnant political culture as well. The never-ending struggle in the debate about national identity is framed as one between tradition and modernity (in which modernity, as Marx understood it, means constant change). When Salem, for example, argues for couscous as "the best thing in our cultural program," Hadhria proposes a change of menu. "Let's vary it," she says. Fitouri suggests they have a "couscous with tripe," and Hadhria agrees, adding that she thinks the committee should also give its support to some kind of "artistic creation." Fitouri's predictable reply is that they tried that once before, and it produced no tangible return on the investment. All the committee members start talking at once. We see Fitouri, his voice louder than the others', pointing at Sghaïer and telling Mabrouka: "Get all of that down, except the suggestion of the opposing voice."

When the entire cast of the pageant is assembled in front of Brahim's oil mill, however, Sghaïer manages to make himself "heard," after all. Dressed as a Roman soldier, he pushes his way to the front, and at the moment he believes the cameras have started rolling, he unfurls a prepared banner that reads: "Palestine is Arab."

The principal vehicle of our time for the process of inventing the postcolonial nation and constructing a usable past is television. To paraphrase Nora's observation about the writing of history, constructing the Tunisian nation has become a collective enterprise, a task that belongs to everyone and to no one and therefore has a universal vocation. As we have observed, however, the inclusive reach of the media did not prevent the Tunisian government from trying, sometimes heavy-handedly, to control the national narrative, a fact that is illustrated in the film by the scene in which Fitouri attempts to drive the (highly symbolic) municipal minivan.[49]

When Fitouri comes upon Ayed and members of the cultural committee watching a film reel containing all the steamy scenes that have been censored from the foreign movies in the committee's film program, he exercises his authority as "the official censor" by ordering them to stop watching it immediately. (Reflexively hypocritical, like the regime he represents, Fitouri intends to keep the reel of censored scenes for his own viewing pleasure.) When Ayed does not respond quickly enough to his command, Fitouri threatens to fire him. "But Mr. Fitouri," Lamine points out, "if you fire Ayed, who is going to drive the car?" Fitouri replies that he will hire a driver. "And who will pay him?" Lamine asks, adding: "This vehicle is a propaganda car, a projection booth, and a library-on-wheels. If it stops running, all cultural activity will come to a stop." Fitouri answers that he will drive the vehicle himself! Lamine tries to reason with him: "Mr. Fitouri, the car is capricious. It has no gearbox. It goes in reverse instead of going forward." But the chairman of El Malga's cultural committee is already climbing into the driver's seat of the minivan. He looks behind him as he puts his foot down on the gas pedal . . . and the vehicle starts to move forward. He tries frantically to steer it toward the open gate of the community center, but the vehicle follows a haphazard—we could say, "independent"—trajectory, until, with a scrape and a bump, it comes to rest against a wall. (This vehicle implies that, in the final analysis, Tunisian filmmakers are able to resist the control of the state.)

The TV Is Coming acknowledges how important film and television have been in the twentieth century in the stimulation of a renewed national consciousness in Tunisia. The emergence of an authentic national cinema and its role in the formation of something we might call modern Tunisian national identity have imitated the way in which print technology and capitalist imperatives combined in sixteenth-century western Europe to help

INVENTING THE POSTCOLONIAL NATION/CONSTRUCTING A USABLE PAST

FIGURE 8.6 Ayed (Tawfik El Bahri) in the municipal minivan, which is "a propaganda car, a projection booth, and a library-on-wheels." Lamine will explain to Mr. Fitouri: "If it stops running, all cultural activity will come to a stop."

forge what Benedict Anderson calls the "nationally imagined community."[50] He argues that, in its basic morphology, this early notion of the nation set the stage for the modern nation (46). Anderson describes how in Renaissance Europe the dethronement of Latin as an instrument of administrative centralization and as the language of the church (which had made possible "the sacred imagined community" of Christendom) occurred when administrative vernaculars—French in Paris, for example, and Early English in London—began to spread: "In every instance, the 'choice' of language appears as a gradual, unselfconscious, pragmatic, not to say haphazard development" (42). He explains that what made the new, national communities imaginable was "a half-fortuitous, but explosive, interaction between a system of production and productive relations (capitalism), a technology of communications (print), and the fatality of human linguistic diversity" (42–43). He points out that "the determinative fact about Latin—aside from its sacrality—was that it was a language of bilinguals. Relatively few were born to speak it and even fewer, one imagines, dreamed in it" (38).

Then, as now, the majority of mankind was monoglot, but thanks to capitalism and the development of print technology, he notes, "monoglot mass reading publics" were created, which are the bases for national consciousness. The mechanically reproduced print-languages "created unified fields of exchange and communication below Latin and above the spoken vernaculars," and in the process, readers "gradually became aware of the hundreds of thousands, even millions, of people in their particular language-field, and at the same time that *only those* hundreds of thousands, or millions, so belonged." Print-capitalism, as it has come to be called, "gave a new fixity to language, which in the long run helped to build that image of antiquity so central to the subjective idea of the nation" (44). Moreover, it "created languages-of-power of a kind different from the older administrative vernaculars" (45).

The relationship between the emergence of a Tunisian national cinema in the spoken vernacular and the creation of an imagined, uniquely Tunisian identity is illustrated by *The TV Is Coming* on both an allegorical level and quite literally. The presence in the film of Hichem the Egyptian and the El Malgans' choice of a pageant that is staged in order to be televised—and all of it a film, directed by Moncef Dhouib—attests to the existence of those mass "publics" identified by Anderson as the bases for national consciousness, publics that in Tunisia's case were created not so much by the printed word as by the image and the spoken word in the vernacular. The Tunisian dialect—a largely spoken, thus substandard, Arabic—initially lost caste in the struggles to articulate a native Tunisian national identity, for the language of Tunisia's colonial overlords during the protectorate, we know, was French (as, at one time, under the Ottomans, it had been Ottoman Turkish, a composite of Turkish, Persian, and Arabic), which became an instrument of administrative centralization. Under Bourguiba, both French and modern standard Arabic dominated the print media and Egyptian Arabic dominated the largely imported cinema.

The "monoglot mass reading publics" described by Anderson as having been created in western Europe in the sixteenth century were never created in Tunisia. But mass film- and television-viewing publics were created, and these publics—the bases for a uniquely modern national consciousness—have done much to shape the ongoing narrative about who the Tunisians are and what they would like to be. (This modern national consciousness, articulated in the "languages-of-power" made possible by the new communications technologies, would eventually erupt in the pro-democracy uprising in the winter of 2010–2011.) We know that in the early decades of modern Tunisia's self-invention, Egyptian films (or films dubbed into Egyptian Arabic), whether seen in theaters or on television screens in Tunisia, served to remind Tunisian viewers not only of their Tunisian specificity (i.e., that Egyptians are "different" from them), but also that they belong to the *umma*, or Arab world that stretches far beyond Tunisia's national borders. In the character of Hichem, *The TV Is Coming* maintains a running discourse on Tunisia's historical relationship with Egypt in the domains of politics and culture; but the message by film's end is that the era of an Egyptian-led narrative about who the Tunisians are is pretty much over, and despite the fact that there is a sense in which we can still say that the majority of mankind is monoglot, the evolution of global media-capitalism and the emergence of an identifiably national cinema have allowed Tunisia to assert a more confident national identity that is *polyglot*.

This argument, of course, is not only and literally about languages (Arabic, French, English, and so on), but about Tunisia's evolving economic, political and social fluency, that is, its degree of cosmopolitan "globalization." The film shows and is itself evidence of Tunisia's fluency in the contemporary languages of our globalized world. Thanks to an education system that does in fact give Tunisians access to and potential mastery of several European languages, and through satellite television, the Internet, and other communications technologies, Tunisians have been able to construct a usable past and to identify and elaborate a specifically Tunisian/local culture, while becoming thoroughly familiar with, and lively participants in, global culture.[51]

CHAPTER NINE

"Destiny answers the people's call for life,
darkness will be dispelled,
and chains will break"

On 14 January 2011, President Ben Ali and his immediate family fled the country of which he had been the dictator for twenty-three years. His abrupt departure followed protests that began in mid-December 2010 in Sidi Bouzid, a small town in the interior of the country, after Mohamed Bouazizi, a twenty-six-year-old street peddler of fruit and vegetables, set himself on fire in protest against the repeated demands of the local police for bribes and against the humiliation and abuse he had endured at their hands. Bouazizi's plight, which quickly became known throughout the country (he lay in a hospital for more than two weeks, before dying from his burns on 4 January), was recognizable to the hundreds of thousands of Tunisians who were similarly oppressed by poverty and neglect, who were unemployed, or who found their prospects thwarted by corruption and nepotism.[1] Carried swiftly by the new communications technologies, such as cell phones with built-in cameras, and the new social media, especially Facebook, the

---

The title of this chapter comes from two lines in the Tunisian national anthem, "Humat Al-Hima"/"Defenders of the Homeland" (revised in 1987), written by Mustafa Sadiq Al-Rafi'i, incorporating lyrics by the celebrated poet, Aboulkacem Chebbi.

FIGURE 9.1 Bahta (Lotfi Abdelli), in Nouri Bouzid's *Making Of* (2006), leads an impromptu protest march.

young man's tragedy triggered a wave of protest that spread to other towns and cities, including the capital. Ben Ali's police state was overwhelmed by the rapidity and scope of the reaction, and—according to one explanation of events—when the state security forces refused to continue shooting at unarmed civilians (dozens had died in clashes with the police the previous week), Ben Ali and his widely hated wife, after being denied entry into France, boarded a private jet and flew to Saudi Arabia.

Just before Bouazizi's self-immolation on 17 December 2010, the release of U.S. Embassy cables by WikiLeaks describing Tunisia as troubled by nepotism, corruption, and the "sclerotic" regime of aging president Ben Ali had the effect, eventually, of helping to focus and fuel the anger and sense of injustice felt by many Tunisians who would subsequently join the groundswell that led to national revolt.[2] The most damning report of the American ambassador, in a cable dated June 2008 and given the subject heading "Corruption in Tunisia: What's yours is mine," detailed the breathtaking cupidity of Ben Ali's wife's large, mafia-like family; and another, dated July 2009, included the following assessment of the situation in the country:

He [Ben Ali] and his regime have lost touch with the Tunisian people. They tolerate no advice or criticism, whether domestic or international. Increasingly, they rely on the police for control and focus on preserving power. And, corruption in the inner circle is growing. Even average Tunisians are now keenly aware of it, and the chorus of complaints is rising. Tunisians intensely dislike, even hate, First Lady Leïla Trabelsi and her family. In private, regime opponents mock her; even those close to the government express dismay at her reported behavior. Meanwhile, anger is growing at Tunisia's high unemployment and regional inequities. As a consequence, the risks to the regime's long-term stability are increasing.[3]

Satellite television (notably the Al Jazeera network), which is widely accessible in Tunisia, also undeniably played a role in sustaining the wave of anger that led to Ben Ali's overthrow.[4] As the title of Dhouib's film *The TV Is Coming* announces, television—and all the other contemporary technologies of global communication it implies—had indeed arrived in Tunisia. "Television" has played a significant role in the invention and construction of postcolonial Tunisian identity; and it can be said that a certain kind of "history" now is written almost at the same time as the events that form its basis are themselves unfolding. With a speed and immediacy that are unprecedented, the national narrative is sustained and elaborated in photo, audio, video, and text postings via media such as Facebook, Twitter, YouTube, and Dailymotion, while an Internet information site like Wikipedia, "the free encyclopedia that anyone can edit," is continuously being updated and fact-checked for accuracy, becoming in the process a kind of historiographic repository of facts, which—contested, competing, and jostling for position—become the basis for a narrative we call history.[5]

Looking at Oneself in the Mirror

It is, however, the Tunisian national cinema as an institution speaking to both local and global audiences that has most consistently and effectively articulated for the Tunisian people an image of themselves—an image of who they are and aspire to be—giving them a coherent sense not only of what they were protesting *against* in the early months of 2011, but of what kind of Tunisia they feel they deserve and are willing to fight *for*. It seemed everybody could agree that Ben Ali's departure, when it occurred, was a good thing. But it was not a foregone conclusion that after he was gone the institution of some kind of democratic government would result in the triumph of the secular modernism championed by the filmmakers of the New Tunisian Cinema.

In an interview he gave to Hédi Khélil in 2002, Férid Boughedir remarked that "an adult society is one that is capable of looking at itself in the mirror," adding that modern Tunisia seems to have lost its way and regressed when it comes to the question of self-identity. He suggested that although Tunisians have historically had a genius for cultural "*métissage*" (Boughedir more often uses the word, "*synthèse*"), going back to the days of Carthage, their colonial encounter with France would appear to have made "cultural bastards" of them. "One part of the population," he observed, "has its eyes fixed on Cairo and reads everything that is written about the Middle East," while another part "reads Le Nouvel Observateur or Le Monde. There's a real split!"[6]

When he said this, Boughedir could have been talking about *The Picnic*—the short film he made in 1972[7]—for he satirizes this "cultural bastardy" in the film, but does so in a way that functions precisely as an appeal to his countrymen to reclaim their cultural specificity, a style of cultural synthesis—their *tunisianité*—which he believes is Tunisia's best hope for becoming a "fully mature" society.[8] As we know, in *Halfaouine*, Boughedir developed the theme of tolerance as a key feature of the kind of *tunisianité* he believes his countrymen should promote, and in his second feature-length film, *A Summer in La Goulette* (1996), he pleads, almost to the point of television-movie didacticism, for the restoration of a live-and-let-live, multicultural/"Mediterranean" Tunisia that he fears has been lost or is fast disappearing.[9]

If Boughedir believes there is a problematic divide in Tunisian society along class or cultural lines—a tension between a Westernized class (that historically has looked to France as the model of modernity to which it aspires) and one that looks to Cairo (as the once-capital of the Arab world, when Arab nationalism and the prestige of Egyptian culture were at their height)—Moufida Tlatli, in an interview with Khélil in the same volume in which Boughedir's interview appears, suggests that the big divide in Tunisian society, which implicates her as a filmmaker, is a generational one:

> One is often disappointed by the response of [the Tunisian] public which, if I interpret it correctly, expects so much more from the cinema than the cinema can give. It almost expects the cinema to be a site of response to all the problems facing Tunisian society. During debates, young people say: "We want films about young people, about their lives, their difficulties. Why don't you see that? Why are you immersed in stories about Beys, about those who came before them, and those who came after? All that's the past. We are here, now. We are in this Tunisia, which never stops moving for a moment, and you don't pay attention!?"[10]

Tlatli then goes on to give the lie to a cherished myth: "In Tunisia, the people are not moviegoers [le public n'est pas cinéphile]. They have been warped by films of violence and sex. Getting people to see our films is already an enormous task" (203).[11]

Boughedir and Tlatli are both correct, as Bouzid confirmed in his 1994 "Sources of Inspiration" lecture. Describing his intellectual formation as a filmmaker in the 1960s and early 1970s, he referred to "the Golden Age of the Cinema":

> That was the era of the best Fellinis, Bergmans, Godards, Resnais, the best Japanese, Czech, Polish, Hungarian, Swedish, Canadian, and Indian films. It was also an auspicious era for the American cinema in New York, Free Cinema in England, Cinema Novo in Brazil, and the Latin American cinema. In Paris, the cultural center of cinema in the sixties, we saw the focal point move from the Champs Elysées to the Latin Quarter, with its flourishing art and experimental cinemas.[12]

This is a film culture that very few, if any, young Tunisians have today; and the Tunisians of Mohamed Bouazizi's generation (and of his social class, most especially) have not been nourished by the worldview that made this "Golden Age of the Cinema" possible.[13] When Bouzid added that "television viewers don't know what a film is anymore. They can't distinguish between a film, a television film, a drama and a series, all chopped up by commercial breaks," he implied that he was possibly already falling out of step with the viewing public that he would need for his films, if he wished to remain relevant as a public intellectual in his own country.

As we have noted, Bouzid believes that "cinema is the mode of expression associated with the best period of liberalism." He thinks of cinema as "the art of an era, of democratic and liberal ideas" and believes in the cinema as an institution that can, or should, play a unique and important role in fighting against what he calls "feudal ideas." Just as the Russian Revolution, in the words of Lenin, declared film to be "the most important art," so too does Bouzid's cohort of filmmakers see the cinema as post-Independence Tunisia's most important art—not as a propaganda tool, but as a means of education and enlightenment in the struggle to help their society become "modern." They understand this modernity above all in terms of freedom of expression and believe that if the cinema (and by implication the society) is not free, it dies (47).[14]

But by the time Bouzid comes to make what he calls his "last film," *Making Of* (2006), he recognizes that the problem in Tunisia is not that the cinema is unduly constricted by censorship, but that Ben Ali's regime is no longer responsive to criticism by the country's artists. Despite having a reflexive tendency toward censorship (especially at the level of script approval, when a filmmaker is seeking the small government subsidy that will allow a film to be officially called "Tunisian"), Ben Ali's regime is beyond caring—or perhaps even recognizing—what its critics have to say through allegory or satire. Nor do those who "hold the levers of the world system" (Jameson) care what the Tunisian cinema says or does: the forces of global capitalism are indifferent to the social, cinematic, and political project of the filmmakers of the New Tunisian Cinema.

Just at the point where Bouzid in effect asks whether he has lost the bet to win over "a badly educated public" (which is how he described the challenge facing his cohort of filmmakers when they first started to make movies), this public rose up in revolt against Ben Ali's regime and seemed to prove that they had learned something from their national cinema after all.

Taking "a subjective look back" in 2012 at the Tunisian films represented in the 2010 Carthage Film Festival, *Africultures* editor Olivier Barlet observes: "[It is] a Tunisian cinema that is going in circles; but this is not surprising, in a country where everything was ossified, and where the cultural policy was nepotistic and discriminated against the best [artists], like Nouri Bouzid, that eternal nonconformist [*empêcheur de tourner en rond*], whose *Making Of* was in perfect sync with the preoccupations of Tunisian society, especially its youth."[15] The fear that Tunisia's leading filmmakers had lost their gamble with destiny—that the liberal values they sought to promote in their films would, in a democratic moment, be overwhelmed by "feudal ideas"—was given voice during a roundtable discussion among filmmakers, scholars, and critics held in November 2011 at the *Festival des cinémas d'Afrique* in Apt, France, and is perhaps summed up by Amine Chiboub when he says:

> In Tunisia as well, different groups didn't talk to each other, [but] during the revolution, everybody was fighting for the same thing. Struggling against a common enemy brought people together. But when [the enemy] fell, everything changed, and everyone went back to his own group and its definition of things. We forget that we are all Tunisians. The reality has changed. Freedom of expression is fundamental, but it is an enormous responsibility, and we have to know how to use it. Today, we can freely talk about politics, but as soon as it touches on religion, there is a problem.[16]

Chiboub goes on to make the crucial point that it is not always, or only, the Salafists who are the "problem," but rather a widespread and deeply rooted conservatism that more accurately describes what the liberal secularists are up against. When, for example, on 7 October 2011 the animated film *Persepolis* (Marjane Satrapi and Vincent Paronnaud, 2007) was aired by the Tunisian private television company Nessma, it provoked a demonstration in front of the station the following day, and Nessma TV's owner subsequently faced trial in Tunis on charges of "violating sacred values" and "disturbing the public order."[17] "We assumed they were Salafists," Chiboub says, "but they were clean-shaven people [*des gens sans barbe*], like you and me, who were protesting and claiming that as Muslims they were offended. We don't know our own society. There were police in every mosque. The average Tunisian is profoundly conservative and attached to his Muslim values. It's the reality. We should not express ourselves to the point where we will be prevented from expressing ourselves at all! If we are moderates, we need to find a way to get our message across without provoking people" (338).

With *Making Of, le dernier film*, as its French title suggests, Bouzid more or less brings an end to what we have been calling the New Tunisian Cinema. In one of the film's "documentary" inserts, Bouzid (playing himself) actually says it is the last film he will make. He implies that the Tunisian dramatic narrative film—the feature-length fiction film (that in Europe and America never quite makes it out of the art house circuit and that we recognize as the story of a private individual destiny that is an allegory of the embattled situation of the public third-world culture and society)—is finished. It is finished as the chosen vehicle his cohort believed would be the most effective weapon in their fight for a democratic and liberal society. Bouzid all but abandons allegory, and his critique of the Ben Ali regime is up-front[18]—or rather, he pushes allegory into the blatant self-reflexivity of the film-within-the-film, which becomes its own kind of allegory (of the movie-as-pedagogy)—and he makes an unambiguous and emphatic plea for the preservation of the moderate, secular Tunisia of its founding intellectuals.

Nadia El Fani, too—forty years after Boughedir's *The Picnic* (that early attempt to make "the first specifically Tunisian film")—makes this same plea in the documentary she was making when the uprising occurred in early 2011: *Neither Allah, nor Master!* (*Ni Allah, ni maître!*, screened at the Cannes Film Festival 18 May 2011—the title, shortly after its release, changed to: *Laïcité, inch'Allah!*).[19] Near the beginning of the film, she records a crowded scene on the Place du Gouvernement in Tunis that includes a group of demonstrators holding up their signs ("NO WAR AGAINST RELIGIOUS SIGNS") and chanting, as they march: "Our constitution is the Qur'an, our motto is Islam!" We hear El Fani's murmured observation in voice-over: "Islamists. There are only men . . . " Her camera cuts to a bearded young man wearing an Afghani *pakul* (rebel hat) and sporting a *keffiyeh* around his neck, who explains (in halting French) what is happening:

YOUNG MAN. Here, then, are Islamists who want to come and take over Tunisia. There is no place for them—first, because the people are opposed to this. They are opposed to an Islamist government. But not to a Muslim government. Because we are Muslims.[20]

EL FANI. The problem with our current constitution is that Article 1 states that the religion of the Republic is Islam.[21] But what about the atheists? What about the Christians?

YOUNG MAN. There's room for everyone.

EL FANI. And the Jews? What about the Buddhists . . . who are Tunisian?

YOUNG MAN. (*Clearly at a loss.*) We never had problems.

DESTINY ANSWERS THE PEOPLE'S CALL FOR LIFE

EL FANI. We mustn't say we're only Muslims. We are a lot of other things as well. Everyone has the right to live in peace, to express himself.
YOUNG MAN. (*Looking very uncertain now.*) As it has been for centuries.
EL FANI. But it must be written down. It's important.
YOUNG MAN. (*Almost inaudible.*) Yes.

There is no such ambivalence or uncertainty, as we see it here in El Fani's bearded interviewee, in the point of view expressed by the Islamists in *Making Of*, which Bouzid contextualizes within a story about a Tunisian youth who is recruited to their cause during the United States–led invasion of Iraq in 2003 that toppled the regime of Saddam Hussein.

"The story takes place in Tunisia! Do you think people will believe you?" the young actor asks the director, in one of *Making Of*'s "documentary" sequences. Whether or not the viewer believes the Islamist threat is real in Tunisia, the film is a reminder that there is indeed, in Boughedir's phrase, a part of the Tunisian population that "has its eyes fixed on Cairo and reads everything that is written about the Middle East" (i.e., a part of the population that is preoccupied with Tunisia's Arab-Muslim identity). The leader of the Islamists in the film offers his new recruit a genealogy of humiliations suffered by Muslims, going back centuries, and the film's narrative offers some believable reasons rooted in the hero's quotidian reality that explain why he becomes drawn toward the Islamic fundamentalists and their ideology that prescribes a simple solution to the persistent crises of Tunisian society. These reasons amount to a harsh indictment not only of Ben Ali's regime, as one might expect, but of the free-market fundamentalist ideology of capitalist globalization as well, which has implications for an Islam that cannot cope with it; or for an Islam that has emerged as a vehicle to resist its devastating effects on societies like Tunisia.

The Islamists in the film call for a return to what they believe is the true spirit of Islam and to political programs based on Islamic principles, and they attack the rampant corruption in government (and, as they believe, the corruption in the society as well) with calls for piety.[22] Whether or not the Islamic component of Tunisian identity is the key issue confronting Tunisia today—and whether political Islam is a *symptom* of a complicated malaise, or whether "Islam" *tout court* is a *cause* of the malaise (as Bouzid implied in his "Sources of Inspiration" lecture over a decade earlier)—is a question the director leaves open. But using his film as a kind of mirror, Bouzid pushes the question of the authoritarianism of the state into a confrontation with its own image. He throws down the gauntlet and asks, quite simply: Why does the film's hero turn toward fundamentalism? Why is this attractive, reasonably intelligent, charismatic young man susceptible to the message of political Islam? Indeed, what is political Islam? How do we explain its increasingly virulent spread throughout the Arab world? And does Ben Ali's regime bear any responsibility for its rise in Tunisia?

The film's final scene, in which the hero blows himself up in a shipping container marked CAPITAL, suggests some of the complexity of the answers to these questions.

"Terrorists aren't born. They're made"[23]

Ben Ali, as the most obvious of the many contributing factors to Tunisia's malaise—that is, the factor that can most easily be *figured*, like a character in a melodrama—was a problem, certainly. But the problems confronting Tunisia—as an Arab and Muslim nation and as a third-world country—have clearly become larger than Ben Ali. At one point in *Making Of*, the hero Bahta (Lotfi Abdelli), who has been trying to arrange his escape from Tunisia on a boat that will take him to Italy, is told by the fisherman-smuggler (whom he has already paid): "Our project won't happen. It's over. No more crossings. Don't hang around here anymore." Bahta is incredulous: "What are you talking about? I gave you money, no?" The smuggler replies: "It's not my fault. The war in Iraq messed everything up. The Italians are supporting Bush. Their defense is solid as a rock. No Muslim can get past it." Bahta asks him: "What war?"

In other words, a "new world order" has emerged ("the war in Iraq messed everything up"); and Bahta will respond accordingly. He may very well ask why Iraq, George W. Bush, or the fact that he is a Muslim, should decide his destiny. The world used to be a simpler place: Tunisia had a dictator; Bahta decided to escape; he found the right person to bribe. But he has to rethink everything, now. Tunisia's filmmakers, too, Bouzid is saying, have to rethink their role as filmmakers and the kinds of films they will make. The "six constants" he identified in his cinema in 1994, which he believes "give our films an identity," now have to be understood in the context of globalization and its discontents.

Ben Ali's dictatorship and the Islamic fundamentalism that is in part a response to it are a far cry from the ideologically moderate and secular values of the New Tunisian Cinema's filmmakers. Indeed, the crude and systemic resort to violence in Ben Ali's police state, the regime's authoritarianism and its greed, are the mirror image of the Islamists' solution to society's ills. The secular modernists are in danger of being overtaken by the imperatives of an unscrupulous global free-market capitalism on one side and a ruthless ideology of religious fundamentalism on the other. The two sides are locked in an impossible embrace—there can be no reasonable dialogue between them—and Bouzid's film is an acknowledgment that the New Tunisian Cinema, with its attempts to blend popular and art house sensibilities, has come to the end of the road. It has become inadequate to the task of accounting for the evolving Tunisian reality. A new analysis of the Tunisian reality is needed, for the filmmakers' strategies of resistance to Ben Ali's regime have come to seem ineffectual, and Ben Ali's regime (as a symptom and synecdoche of the "six constants" Bouzid describes in his "Sources of Inspiration" lecture) is no longer the only, or necessarily the primary, enemy.

In one of his early conversations with Bahta, Abdallah (Lotfi Dziri), the Islamist leader of the cell in the port city of Radès where Bahta lives (Radès, the country's chief commercial port, is about nine kilometers southeast of Tunis), probes his young recruit with questions to discover the sources of his discontent:

ABDALLAH. What do you dream of?
BAHTA. I don't dream anymore. I want to go away. Get out of this country. I don't want to spend my time being chased by the cops. I don't want to die, be killed. My mother is living a nightmare. What's the good of a man without money, who has nothing? No education, no future. Not allowed to dream anymore. I'm out of here! I don't want to be here anymore.

Bahta is a break-dancer who aspires to a career in dancing, but the police, fearful of his high spirits, spot him for a troublemaker and harass him at every opportunity. Bouzid depicts the general climate of interdiction in Ben Ali's Tunisia as a sad symptom of the police state—no real reason, for example, is given for Bahta's arrest by the police when they find him dancing with his buddies in one of the city's street underpasses. Before we hear the police siren, and as the boys assemble for an impromptu competition to show off their break-dancing skills, we overhear one of the boys say, with bravado: "The street belongs to us!" (This, of course, is an ironic allusion by the director to the reality expressed by his oft-repeated remark: "The streets in Tunisia do not belong to us.") The street as a free and public space is an allegorical figure in the film representing the liberty that Tunisians lost under Ben Ali, which is why much of the film takes place on the streets, and why for most of it, Bahta is on the lam, not free to enjoy the liberty of walking down a street (much less express himself freely in dance, even when it is *under* the street) without being arrested by the police.

Tunisians' neurotic relationship with authority is expressed in the film primarily through the representatives of the law: Bahta's father (played by Mahmoud Larnaout), as the supreme authority within the family (there is a scene in the film in which Bahta's father gives him more than thirty lashes with his belt!);[24] his cousin Rezgui (Moez Kouki), who is a junior officer in the Radès police force; and Brigadier Gaddour (Taoufik El Bahri)—and it is articulated also through an obsessive discourse on manhood (Brigadier Gaddour, for example, is fond of taunting Bahta with the suggestion that he is "not a man"; and Abdallah, who insists on calling him "son," frequently exhorts Bahta to "be a man"). Bahta experiences the aspersions cast on his manhood as intolerable, which is precisely why those who seek to tease, hurt, or (in Abdallah's case) manipulate him invariably choose to play on his anxieties in this regard. As a popular ideology of social control, the discourse on neopatriarchal manhood remains a powerful one in Tunisia, revealing the limits of Tunisia's gains as a secular, modern society. Bahta's elders (the men of his father's generation)—whom Nouri Gana, in a tour-de-force article about manhood in modern Tunisia, would describe as "Bourguiba's sons," a "breed of men" who experience manhood as "melancholy"—in their turn make it difficult for Bahta to grow into a healthy sense of himself as a man:

> Sustaining a steadfast Westward gaze yet suffering from an enduring neopatriarchal hangover, Bourguiba's contradictions cannot be overstated, not least because they have never ceased to inform the psychodynamics of manhood in postcolonial Tunisia. Bourguiba's rule of Tunisia (1956–1987) produced a breed of men that might be aptly called Bourguiba's sons. Suspended in a state of mutability that is simultaneously cultivated

and frustrated, they have been able neither to come to terms with the challenges of modernity, of which gender equality is part and parcel, nor relinquish fully the protective shelter of traditional patriarchy, in which male supremacy is the grantor of psychosocial stability.[25]

In the film, the policeman is one of the prime representatives of this sought-after male supremacy, and a scene in which Bahta steals Rezgui's police uniform and masquerades as an officer for an afternoon offers a revealing glimpse of the troubling psychodynamics of manhood in Ben Ali's Tunisia. Bahta swaggers into a café, twirling his baton, as we hear snatches of friendly banter among the patrons. "What's this talk? No more dirty talk!" Bahta admonishes them. The camera pans across the café, and we see groups of men at tables, some playing cards, others smoking *chicha* pipes, most simply chatting or idly watching the television in the corner. We catch our first sight of Abdallah's henchmen, Ghazi (Foued Litaïem) and Bilel (Helmi Dridi), who are watching Bahta closely (a faint smile plays across Ghazi's lips, when he realizes that Bahta is not a real policeman). "Drop your head!" Bahta shouts at one man, who is looking at him in disbelief. "I'll sort you out!" He goes up to a table: "Take that *chicha* out of your mouth! Stop playing cards! A bit of order and discipline! It's a police officer talking to you! A bit of respect for the uniform!" A young man in a baseball cap slowly—too slowly for Bahta's liking—puts down his *chicha*. "What's that?" Bahta shouts at him. "Get up. Do you know, I could arrest you . . . and put you in prison?"

Bahta swings around and addresses the café at large: "Yessir! Prison. Prison can be for any citizen! You choose the best crime, and I'll send you to prison for it." He puts his hand across his chest: "You can count on me." At the table nearest to Bahta, a large, middle-aged man continues to play cards, pointedly ignoring this imposter-policeman. Bahta turns to him and asks: "Do you have something against dancers?" The man, looking him directly in the eye, replies: "I don't know anything about them." Turning again to a broad view of the patrons in the café, Bahta says solemnly: "The rule of law reigns in this country." The camera cuts to a man smoking his *chicha*. "The rule of law reigns in this country!" he repeats. "We give you a bit of democracy, and what have you done with it?" He turns to a young man: "*What have you done with it?*" The unnerved young man starts babbling: "It wasn't me! It wasn't me!" (Ghazi is looking at Bahta with admiration, coming to the conclusion that he would make an excellent recruit to the Islamist cause.)

"We're watching you!" Bahta tells the patrons in the café. "I'll give you all a passport! No more illegal emigration. Tomorrow you can pick up your visas. Go to the embassy... they'll welcome you with open arms. And pick up your visa. Go to Europe." He is now on a flight of fancy from which he cannot come down; Bahta's performance has become not so much disturbing (even to those who believe him to be a real—if somewhat deranged—policeman), as entertaining. "There, you'll find a rich blonde. Marry her. Marry, sort out your papers. But no naughty stuff!" The camera cuts to a close-up of an old man, who murmurs with gratitude: "Thank you, my son."

Then, assuming the crisp, military bearing of a policeman on parade, Bahta salutes his audience: "So, gentlemen. I have a mission." He does a pirouette and moonwalks, Michael Jackson–style, out of the café and into the sunny street. The men all stare after him, smiling—with, it would appear, a mixture of sadness, pity, and affection—in recognition of what has just happened. They seem to understand what sort of crisis Bahta is undergoing.

On the street, Bahta takes advantage of the uniform he is wearing to stop an attractive young woman and demand to see her identity card.[26] As far as the narrative is concerned, Bahta has now officially committed a crime—impersonating a policeman—and after Abdallah's men find him and bring him to their master (who offers him protection), his descent into paranoid desperation will gather momentum. Abdallah begins the process of Bahta's indoctrination by giving his young recruit a DVD to watch.

Alone in Abdallah's study, in a dire attempt to master his fears, Bahta silently enacts a despairing scene that seems to involve his arrest and torture by the police. Picking up an object on Abdallah's desk and theatrically "stamping" a piece of paper with it, he says aloud: "Refused!" Then he sits in Abdallah's chair, and enacts being manacled and then tortured with electric shocks, his body jerking spasmodically, until he loses consciousness.

When he "regains consciousness," he sees the DVD Abdallah has left for him, and puts it in the player next to the television monitor. The first image we see is of dead Palestinians, while the voice-over narration explains: "The massacre began in Sabra and Shatila...." Bouzid cuts to a close-up of Bahta's face, watching. Next, we see images of the jets flying into the World Trade Center towers on 9/11. Then an image of Osama Bin Laden giving a speech. He is saying: "It is spreading all over the land of Islam. The only way to rid ourselves of it is by *jihad* and suicide operations. Humiliation removed by bullet fire. A free man refuses to be dominated." The image of Bin Laden gives way to one of Iraqi prisoners being humiliated at Abu Ghraib.

Bahta suddenly feels ill and rushes to the corner of the room, where he throws up.

In the days that follow, during the course of several conversations between Abdallah and Bahta (whom Abdallah calls by his given name, Chokri, when he is not referring to him as "son"), we learn something of Abdallah's Islamist ideology—perhaps the most striking aspect of which is its profound misogyny.[27] One day, in the cemetery, during his apprenticeship as a restorer of tombstones (a metaphorically apt occupation, perhaps, for an Islamic fundamentalist), Bahta is told by Abdallah: "We have abandoned our religion. God has punished us. Women are in part responsible. They are everywhere . . . they stopped wearing the veil. They work. The cafés are full of them, the beaches, football stadiums."

When Bahta wants to know why, in the West, "they live better than us," Abdallah tells him: "The West looks out for its own interests against those of Islam. It imposes its point of view upon us. They sacked our lands, humiliated us. Took us back to a new prehistory."

Far from being one man's paranoid interpretation of history, Abdallah's explanation here is perfectly accurate. While Bouzid has no interest in theorizing Islamic alternatives to Western hegemony, he is fully aware that the rejection of secularism across large swathes of the Islamic world is part of Muslims' struggle for self-definition. Secularism, Anouar Majid reminds us, is originally a Western idea born out of specific historical circumstances:

> The secular worldview that emanated from the late eighteenth century and the first few decades of the nineteenth was the product of Enlightenment thought and a classical liberal philosophy whose goal was nothing less than the recalibration and redefinition of human morality to adjust it to a new social calculus that excluded traditional religious commitments (irrational as these might have been). Endowed with "natural rights" that extended into ownership of private property, individuals were sent into the world to maximize their self-interest and enter into all sorts of "contracts," whether with business partners, workers, or states.[28]

The ethos of trade that evolved out of Enlightenment philosophy became fetishized in the twentieth century (especially in the United States) as an ideology of modernization, which was understood to be inseparable from capitalist development. As an ideology, free-market capitalism "remains conveniently unexamined, almost unnamed in the United States," Majid observes. Meanwhile, "world cultures continue to be eroded by the escalating anarchy and oppression resulting from the abdication of authority still precariously monopolized by the nation-state" (14). Tony Judt makes a similar observation in *Ill Fares the Land* (2010), in which he historicizes the baleful ascendancy of global free-market capitalism thus:

> The materialistic and selfish quality of contemporary life is not inherent in the human condition. Much of what appears "natural" today dates from the 1980s: the obsession with wealth creation, the cult of privatization and the private sector, the growing disparities of rich and poor. And above all, the rhetoric that accompanies these: uncritical admiration for unfettered markets, disdain for the public sector, the delusion of endless growth.[29]

It is not surprising that when Abdallah explains to Bahta why "we must destroy the West," and Bahta protests: "But the West has democracy, fun, the good life!," the embittered Islamist replies: "Their democracy is a sin. It's based on false values, selfishness, and individualism."[30] The crisis of contemporary capitalism, in other words—to which political Islam is a response—"stems from its failure to produce a social imaginary that would give social existence a meaning that goes beyond the pursuit of productivity and consumption for their own sakes" (*Unveiling Traditions*, 41).

When "Lotfi" (as the actor Lotfi Abdelli, playing Bahta/Chokri) one day refuses to continue filming, because he believes he and his director are putting themselves in danger, Bouzid asks him: "What danger?" The actor replies: "I am a Muslim. If something touches Islam, it touches me. You're using me in this film to attack the Muslims. So, explain your relationship with religion to me. I'm not filming with you anymore if you don't explain your position to me. I'm not your puppet." Bouzid tells the other actors on the set to take a break, and then explains his position to Lotfi:

> Listen, Lotfi, before doing this film, I read the Qur'an. I read it in Arabic, and in French. The Qur'an contains everything. The Sufi can find what he

needs in it—peace and love. If someone wants war, he'll find the verses that suit him, especially during the last period of the great invasions. The Qur'an became a tool for the invasions.[31] Whoever talks about combat, *jihad*... I'm not one of those people who says one thing in front of foreigners, and talks of *jihad* with Muslims. No! In my opinion, Islam was useful in its time. Nowadays, we should be secular, leave the Qur'an as a belief, not a tool to resolve our daily problems, otherwise there will be hell to pay. We can't do *jihad* in the present day. I want to show how a young person can be brainwashed. That's why I'm doing this film.

Lotfi remains bewildered, suspicious. It is at this moment that the viewer begins to understand, if she or he has not done so already, that there is a cultural, intellectual, and generational divide separating Bouzid from his "actor" that is wider than might at first appear. (Has Lotfi read the Qur'an, for example? Either in Arabic or in French? One rather doubts it.) By way of apology, perhaps, for not having had more confidence in his director, Lotfi stutters: "I didn't say you were against me." To which Bouzid immediately adds: "Or against Islam!" Lotfi retreats into confusion: "Don't play with my words! I don't know how you feel about Islam... You can say what you like, I don't know what you are planning."

Bouzid decides to keep it simple: "My position is that I don't think Islam should mix with politics. My position is clear. Christianity and Judaism shouldn't mix with politics, either."

Lotfi looks at Bouzid as if for the first time or as if he were a complete stranger. "Who are you?" he asks simply. Bouzid replies: "I'm just an individual. I'm expressing my personal opinion. And you agreed to make this film with me, go forward, without knowing what will happen, just like in life."

But Bouzid is not "just an individual," like any other. He is a public intellectual with a powerful voice, and his "personal opinion" is being expressed in a bid to help shape Tunisian national identity. This exchange between the director and his actor reveals the extent and range of the differences that make up the divide—a "real split," to borrow Boughedir's phrase—between the filmmakers of Bouzid's generation and the Tunisians of Lotfi's generation.[32] The median age of the Tunisian population is twenty-nine—it is not a youth-bulge country—but the issues, clearly, are mostly elsewhere: they have to do with the world in which we now live (which contains individuals like Abdallah, who want to "destroy the West"); and a world that directors like Bouzid have been fighting to build or preserve (one that is liberal and secular); and the world on the threshold of which Lotfi is standing and into which he is ready to "go forward, without knowing what will happen" (one in which Bahta hopes there will be "democracy, fun, the good life").

New Realities

But "democracy, fun, [and] the good life" are, for the Bahtas of this world, unachievable in the present capitalist system.[33] As Majid points out, capitalism is inherently a system of uneven development: "In the Third World, introducing democracy simply means democratizing poverty and containing threatening alternatives" (42–43). The Third World, he writes, is still largely informed by the nineteenth-century modernist agenda of "catching up" with the West:

> [But] catching up with Western modernity is a nonprogressive, unrealistic option at this historical juncture. Not only is there no concrete geographical "West" to "catch up" with, but the continuing quest for integration in the global economy will certainly prolong the Muslims' dependency. Because the proposed culturalist solutions do not take the real destructive powers of capitalism into account, they block out the articulation of new paradigms whose main goal is the collective destiny of human societies, not the perpetuation of old, unsustainable cultural rivalries. (61)

There is no doubt that Tunisia has been in thrall to this modernist agenda since Independence, and it was perhaps inevitable that Bourguiba's Westernization project should result in a rearranged class system in which the petty bourgeoisie would focus on trying to attain what Bahta calls "the good life," while neglecting what has to be done to build a "democracy." The Tunisian narrator-hero of Albert Memmi's semi-autobiographical novel, *The Pillar of Salt* (originally published in Paris in 1953), comments on this kind of "catching up" and its consequences in his country when he observes the contempt that his benefactor, a pharmacist, appears to have for "those whose earnings were small." Hard work and thrift, and the pharmacist's "philosophy of profit and earnings" have allowed him to rise from poverty in the Jewish ghetto of Tunis to "Easy Street." Memmi/the narrator explains: "Our middle class is too recent to have much respect for professional scales of values or for a disinterested vocation. It still understands only commercial success and, of course, this opinion of our middle classes imposes itself on our other classes too" (87).

This middle class that "understands only commercial success," we note, became rampant in Ben Ali's Tunisia, creating another social divide complicating the task of the filmmakers. Who was to be their audience, now that the opinion of these middle classes—what Judt (referring primarily to American society) calls the rhetoric that accompanies the contemporary obsession with wealth creation—had successfully imposed itself on Tunisia's other classes too? Under Ben Ali, the worship of commercial success accelerated (along with consumerism and corruption), and its consequences became known as the "economic miracle," which Béatrice Hibou's analysis reveals would contribute to the regime's undoing. (Among the films discussed in this study, Mohamed Zran's *Essaïda*, we have said, illustrates the class divisions of this new Tunisia especially well.)

If Tunisian cinema began in the mid-1960s with attempts to forge a nationalist identity grounded in opposition to the colonial oppressor, and in the mid-1980s began to show, in Hélé Béji's phrase, that it understood "there are no longer two realities that confront each other, the colonial and the national, but two realities that intertwine,"[34] it began to alter its profile again around the start of the new millennium. Nadia El Fani's *Bedwin Hacker* is the first Tunisian film to signal an awareness that "the idea of the national," as Hobsbawm predicted, can no longer be contained within "nations" and "nation-states" as these used to be defined, either politically, economically, culturally, or even linguistically,[35] although the film does endorse and celebrate the notion that there are specifically local languages and cultures that are worth preserving as such. With *Making Of*, however, we see a reformulation of what Bouzid in 1994 described as the "social, cinematic and political project" of his generation of Tunisian filmmakers.

The day it dawns on Lotfi that the film they are shooting is about the making of a terrorist, he asks his director: "Where is this character taking me?... Do you know where we are now?... We are right now in terrorism!" Bouzid asks: "So what?" Lotfi has been disoriented by the film's narrative economy and by a recognition of the possible ramifications of the fact that the film will be seen all over the world; he seems to fear that the film will misrepresent Tunisia, give the wrong idea about who the Tunisians are—it is a question of national identity, in which, of course, his personal identity is implicated. "What do you mean, 'So what'?!" he cries: "You go from dancing to fundamentalism to terrorism!" Bouzid replies calmly: "It exists in our world, doesn't it?" When Lotfi protests that no one will believe that such a story could take place in Tunisia, Bouzid explains to him: "The phenomenon exists everywhere! It has been exported, don't you realize? [...] Come on, let's get this story over and done with. It could happen anywhere. Didn't you see on TV what happened in London? Didn't you hear that the day before yesterday, a boy blew himself up in Baghdad?" Lotfi dismisses these facts: "Nouri, nobody knows about it." But Lotfi is wrong. "I know about it," Bouzid says. "Didn't you hear about the trial of those people who went to Baghdad? It's in all the papers."

Lotfi falls silent. He does not know what to say.

Majid believes that those who believe "only a secular modernity can free Arabs from their long and deadly paralysis" are subscribing to a "familiar Orientalist thesis" (105). He has a number of (admirable) ideas—although some of them do seem rather vague and theoretical[36]—about how to resist the destructive tendencies of the global economic system, which he correctly sees as the real culprit responsible for the malaise of the Arab world. He believes that no emancipatory system can be complete without a thorough understanding of capitalism—a premise with which one cannot disagree—but, like all intellectuals willing to confront the question of how to challenge the reigning ideology of capitalism, Majid knows there is no quick and easy answer. What he does know is that "the nationalist secularist model of the postindependence period has utterly failed to emancipate the people and is now seen as a dismal failure" (118).

Majid gestures toward the necessity of "a thoroughly redefined Islam," one that exists "in dynamic relation to other cultures" (129). While he acknowledges that the term *Islam* itself "may evoke strong (mostly negative) reactions among Westernized Muslims"—especially as those Muslims (erroneously, he believes) perceive that "the religion of Islam acts as a barrier to women's fulfillment outside men's arbitrary control"—he insists that it is a male-manipulated interpretation of Islam, often encoded in an unexamined *shariʿa*, that has "allowed Orientalist prejudices to persist in the West and among Westernized Muslim elites" (128–129). Feminism, he argues, must be understood as a mode of intervention into *particular* hegemonic discourses and not as a universal response to an assumed universal patriarchy (129).

It is probably impossible, or too late, for the filmmakers of the New Tunisian Cinema—"Westernized Muslims," every one of them—to embark on a thorough redefinition of Islam along lines suggested by Majid—although directors like Bouzid do say, as he does in *Making Of*: "I am not anti-Islam, I am anti-terror. I accept the struggle against occupation—but as a political struggle, not in the name of Islam. Don't use religion. Why must I be ashamed of being a Muslim?" And acknowledging the identity crisis that (the character) Lotfi undergoes in *Making Of* when the young actor realizes that his character (Bahta) starts out as a dancer and ends up a terrorist, Bouzid points out to him: "The project they have for Bahta frightens you. Their idea for society frightens you."

It will be the next generation that decides which way to go and how to negotiate "a balance between reclaiming a national identity, reaffirming progressive elements of the indigenous culture, and the struggle to create a democratic, just, and coherently developed society."[37] Islamic identity in Tunisia remains insecure, and as a fraught element of the oppositional discourse in national politics during the Ben Ali era, Islam has become and is likely to remain for the foreseeable future too overheated to be useful as an ideological vehicle for the kind of societal change that the filmmakers would see as positive, for the unanswerable questions remain: "Whose Islam?," "Which Islam?"[38]

All that the filmmakers can do, as Bouzid has said, is clarify the fundamental issues. They cannot have the answer to everything—cinema should not be a replacement for politics or theory or science—but they should try to teach the public "a new way of seeing." This, the filmmakers of the New Tunisian Cinema have done.

Notes

Preface

1. The Constitution of Tunisia was adopted on 1 June 1959 and amended in 1988 and 2002, after the Tunisian constitutional referendum of 2002. Throughout this work, unless otherwise indicated, all references to Tunisia, its history, society, and so on, are to the status quo prior to the Tunisian revolution of 2010–2011.

2. In Morocco, "les années de plomb" (the years of lead—the 1960s through the 1980s) were marked by state violence against dissidents and democracy activists. After the death of King Hassan II, levels of state repression dropped perceptibly, but restrictions on freedom of expression remained draconian. In their 2007 report on the "10 countries where press freedom has most deteriorated," the New York City-based NGO Committee to Protect Journalists announced: "Morocco joins Tunisia as Arab world's leading jailer of journalists." (www.cpj.org/backsliders/index.html.)

3. Jameson, "Third-World Literature in the Era of Multinational Capitalism," 65. (It is the article's opening sentence.)

4. Cf. Friedman, "Newt, Mitt, Bibi and Vladimir," in which he remarked: "I sure hope that Israel's prime minister, Benjamin Netanyahu, understands that the standing ovation he got in Congress this year was not for his politics. That ovation was bought and paid for by the Israel lobby." Friedman's remark (and the theme of his article) is an early example of a growing trend in the United States of mainstream journalists and public intellectuals trying to make the argument that the activities of the Israel lobby do not reflect the majority opinion of American

Jews. As one of the anonymous, online responses to Friedman's article put it: "Israel is no more a democracy than we are. Neither government represents its people anymore."

5. A notable exception is my colleague, Warren Goldstein. See, for example, his response in the *Huffington Post* on 31 May 2010 to the Israeli blockade of Gaza, and Israel's attack on a flotilla of activists attempting to break the blockade and supply humanitarian aid to the beleaguered territory: "What Will Israel Not Do?" Goldstein concludes his posting with an address to the U.S. president: "It's high time for President Obama to hear this, not just from me, but from millions of American Jews. I do not want my tax dollars—any of them—supporting the military of a government that continues illegal settlements, continues the illegal blockade, and then blames the people being displaced and blockaded for not wanting peace."

In 2001, Steven Rosenthal, a professor of history at the University of Hartford, published *Irreconcilable Differences? The Waning of the American Jewish Love Affair with Israel*, a brisk and well-written compendium of factors informing the relationship between American Jews and the Jewish state, focusing on the first Palestinian Intifada, the case of the American Jewish spy Jonathan Pollard, the conflict between American Jews and Israelis over the "Who is a Jew?" question, and the Israeli invasion of Lebanon in 1982. (Despite its title, this admirable book is singularly weak on the American Jewish community's efforts to influence the U.S. government's involvement in Zionism- and Israel-related matters, i.e., the manifold activities of the Israel lobby.)

Starting in February 2011, Don Ellis, also a colleague, for a time maintained a blog at: http://www.middleeastmirror.com, which took "conflict resolution" as its theme and claimed to hold up an objective "mirror" to debates about politics and conflict in the Middle East, with particular attention to Israel and its neighbors.

6. Cf. Hacker and Pierson, *Winner-Take-All Politics: How Washington Made the Rich Richer—And Turned Its Back on the Middle Class*; Herman, *Taking Liberties: The War on Terror and the Erosion of American Democracy*.

7. The filmmakers whose works I discuss in this study were born between 1944 and 1960: Férid Boughedir (b. 1944); Nouri Bouzid (b. 1945); Moufida Tlatli (b. 1947); Moncef Dhouib (b. 1952); Mohamed Zran (b. 1959); and Nadia El Fani (b. 1960).

8. I thought I would be the first to name this group of films the "New Tunisian Cinema," but Sonia Chamkhi beat me to it, with her *Cinéma tunisien nouveau: Parcours autres*, published in 2002. Chamkhi looks at the Tunisian cinema of the period 1980–1995 through five representative films of the "second generation" of filmmakers (her filmmakers include: Néjia Ben Mabrouk, Nouri Bouzid, Moncef Dhouib, and Moufida Tlatli). In an article about Bouzid's *It's Scheherazade We're Killing* (1993) and *Making Of* (2006), published in spring 2011, Jeffrey Ruoff refers to "the Tunisian New Wave," which he describes as "a period, from approximately 1986–1996, when Tunisian cinema was simultaneously popular at home and abroad, attaining critical success at international film festivals. Many of the landmark works of this period—*Man of Ashes, Halfaouine, The Silences of the Palace*—were produced by Ahmed Attia of Cinétéléfilms. Not as consistent in its aesthetic and social vision as the French *nouvelle vague*, the Tunisian New Wave consists of a loosely affiliated group of filmmakers who all knew each other and often collaborated together." (Jeffrey Ruoff, "The Gulf War, the Iraq War, and Nouri Bouzid's Cinema of Defeat: *It's Scheherazade We're Killing* [1993] and *Making Of* [2006]," 33n8.)

Rather than rely on the notion of a "new wave"—which in effect ends when the public feels the novelty of the "new" cinema has worn off—I make the claim that the New Tunisian Cinema emerged as "new" because it was different from what came before it; and until another, recognizably new approach or style began to emerge in response to new or changed conditions, it remained the "new" cinema. The New Tunisian Cinema, thus, comes to an end around the time of Moncef Dhouib's *The TV Is Coming* (2006) and Bouzid's *Making Of* (2006), when the filmmakers of this cohort begin decisively to change their strategies of subversion and resistance vis-à-vis the Ben Ali regime.

9. Nouri Bouzid, *Sources of Inspiration*, 57.

10. Férid Boughedir, in publicity material for *Halfaouine* to accompany the screening of the film in the 1990 Cannes Film Festival.

11. Bouzid, "New Realism in Arab Cinema: The Defeat-Conscious Cinema," 249. Bouzid is talking about Arab cinema in general, not only Tunisian cinema; and he identifies the symbolic beginning of the contemporary sense of defeat experienced by all Arabs as the 1967 Arab–Israeli War, which "brought into question all belief systems and ideologies, thus upsetting any sense of confidence that had been engendered in the people and replacing it with suspicion and skepticism" (242). He singles out the Egyptian Youssef Chahine's 1972 film, *The Sparrow*, as "the ultimate in Arab cinema.... the only film to probe, as it were, into the hidden causes and roots of defeat; exploring and exposing not just its military aspect, but all its social ramifications, and rendering it, finally, as a sort of logical extension of the course of events" (245).

12. While some films like *Bedwin Hacker* are rooted firmly in the present or look toward the future, others seek to make a record of the past, before the past's vestiges in the present disappear from view or fade from memory. The documentary film genre, which until recently did not seem to lend itself as readily as the fiction film to the purposes of national allegory, belatedly found its place in the project of the New Tunisian Cinema, particularly in the films of Hichem Ben Ammar. (Owing to space limitations, and the dominance of the fiction film in the imaginary of what constitutes the New Tunisian Cinema, I have not included any documentary films in this study.) Perhaps contrary to expectations of what the documentary form can accomplish under a regime such as Ben Ali's—a regime that filmmakers understood could not bear the truth about its repressiveness, unless disguised as allegory (which the regime hoped, or assumed, the viewing public would not pick up on)—Ben Ammar's sympathetic, "character"-centered documentaries have found a way to tell a story that is both personal and national. El Fani acknowledged in an interview that with *Bedwin Hacker* she consciously chose the genre film (the cyber-spy thriller) to mount her indictment of the Tunisian police state; and we see that fiction films like *Halfaouine* (a comedy) or *The Silences of the Palace* (a melodrama) are distinguished by their authors' personal stamp, implying that their autobiographical qualities are inseparable from their pervasive nostalgia. But Ben Ammar's *And I Saw Stars* (2007), for example—an historical documentary about boxing in Tunisia—succeeds as an allegory of resistance, because Ben Ammar clearly understands what his political motives were in making it. "I made it my responsibility to listen to [the boxers'] voices without betraying them," he has said, for "the boxer is by definition the incarnation of a revolt against the injustice of society. How to restore the force of his protest? How to render it audible? There's the

challenge." (Hichem Ben Ammar interviewed by Leïla Elgaaïed: "Le documentaire comme combat.")

After the Arab Spring, there was a veritable explosion of documentary filmmaking in the Maghreb, prompting *Le Monde* to ask, in an article reporting on a roundtable discussion by filmmakers and critics held at La Clef theater in Paris on 1 December 2012: "Do we have a new 'golden age' of the documentary film in the Maghreb?" The discussion topic was the Tunisian revolution according to its films ("Quelle révolution tunisienne à travers les films?"). The discussants agreed that this proliferation of documentary films should not be described as a "new wave," because the films have been made by filmmakers of all ages: "It is not a question of one generation overtaking another; what unites the filmmakers is their fierce insistence on independence, to the point where some of them even refused aid from their countries!" (Fabre, "Vers un nouvel 'âge d'or' du documentaire au Maghreb?")

13. Nora, ed., *Realms of Memory: Rethinking the French Past*, 3.

1. The Nation, the State, and the Cinema

1. Rosen, *Change Mummified*, 265–266.

2. Hopwood, *Habib Bourguiba of Tunisia*, 104–105. Subsequent page numbers will be cited in the text. Cf. Willis, *Politics and Power in the Maghreb*: "To outside observers, Ben Ali's decision to move against Bourguiba in November 1987 and remove him in a swift and bloodless *coup d'état* might have appeared like a de facto takeover of the country's military. However, the reality was more complex. Firstly, Ben Ali's action enjoyed support well beyond the military. [. . .] Finally, there is evidence that Ben Ali did not act on behalf of the military in removing Bourguiba. Ben Ali only met the country's senior generals to secure their support in the hours *after* he had acted, although the fact that the commander of the presidential guard and the chief of the General Staff were contemporaries of Ben Ali's at the Saint Cyr military academy in France clearly facilitated this" (96–97).

3. Simon Hawkins points out that the nickname Bourguiba acquired during his anticolonial struggle, *al-Mujahid al-Akbar* (Supreme Struggler)—rendered in French as *Le Combattant Suprême*—carries an explicit connection to *jihad*, a religious term that refers not only to armed conflict but also to the daily struggles for justice, discipline, morality, and religion. (Hawkins, "Who Wears *Hijab* with the President," paraphrase from 40.)

4. Cf. Naccache, "Bourguiba et nous," 223–226. For a psychoanalysis of this malaise, especially as it affected Tunisian manhood, see Krichen, *Le syndrome Bourguiba*, and Gana, "Bourguiba's Sons."

5. Perkins, *A History of Modern Tunisia*, 175. (Subsequent page numbers will be cited in the text.) Mark Tessler, Gregory White, and John Entelis have described Bourguiba's regime toward the end as having declined into "atrophy, centralization, increasing authoritarianism and corruption. The exclusion of progressive, leftist, and democratic tendencies left it weakened in an increasingly heterogeneous and conflict-ridden political environment" (Tessler et al., "The Republic of Tunisia," 429).

1. THE NATION, THE STATE, AND THE CINEMA

6. Hopwood, *Habib Bourguiba*, 3. The Bey of Tunis was the Ottoman-appointed governor of Tunisia, which was a province of the Ottoman Empire. The French liked to view the Bey as an independent "prince," as this made him easier to manipulate than if they recognized his allegiance to the Sublime Porte.

7. Hurst and Barlet, "Interview with Nouri Bouzid (about *Poupées d'argile*)." Bouzid repeated this remark to me a few months later, in Tunis: "The streets [here, in Tunisia] do not belong to us."

8. Beaugé, "En Tunisie, un 'cycle d'injustice' se perpétue," 29–30.

9. For a succinct and excellent analysis of Tunisia's economy under Ben Ali, see Stephen J. King, *The New Authoritarianism in the Middle East and North Africa*. King explains that the "economic miracle" benefited rampantly rent-seeking urban and rural economic elites and enriched the president's family, while impoverishing workers and peasants. Béatrice Hibou offers a fascinating and detailed analysis of Tunisia's "political economy of repression" in *La force de l'obéissance*, where she explains why the so-called "economic miracle" was essentially a fraud. As the title of her book suggests, Tunisians paid a heavy price for their prosperity (which, in any event, as we have said, was enjoyed only by some). In the preface to the English-language edition of her book, Hibou remarks that for at least a decade prior to the 2011 uprising, official speeches constantly vaunted the Tunisian "economic miracle," which "had an effect that was not paradoxical (it was perfectly logical), but was certainly quite odd and unforeseen by the rulers: they aroused expectations, created hopes, and fueled frustrations" (*The Force of Obedience*, xv). The title of Nicolas Beau and Jean-Pierre Tuquoi's earlier book, *Notre ami Ben Ali: L'envers du "miracle tunisien*," signals plainly the theme of their critique, which can be summarized by a remark they quote of a Tunisian intellectual living in the capital: "This country is badly governed but well managed" (146). They also make the point that without Bourguiba's commitment to national education, family planning, women's emancipation, and other progressive initiatives, the "*miracle tunisien*" attributed to Ben Ali (and for which, of course, Ben Ali took full and sole credit), would not have been possible. They discuss at length "French complicity" in propping up Ben Ali's regime, and in their chapter, "Une diplomatie complaisante," even have a section entitled: "Le 'miracle tunisien' de Jacques Chirac."

10. Naccache, "Bourguiba et nous," 224. Subsequent page numbers will be cited in the text.

11. Perkins, *A History of Modern Tunisia*, 194. King refers to the "minority, transnational, violent, terrorist brand of political Islam that frightens people at home and abroad and can be reasonably described as neo-Islamic totalitarianism. Its presence gives authoritarian incumbents wide scope in their use of repressive measures. Often that repression is utilized against both religious and secular oppositions, and against Islamists who renounce violence" (*The New Authoritarianism*, 12).

12. Bellin, "Civil Society in Formation: Tunisia," 124.

13. Perkins, *A History of Modern Tunisia*, 129. For a detailed overview of "the democratic imperative vs. the authoritarian impulse" in the three states of the Maghreb, where (at the time of writing) "a robust authoritarianism" was flourishing and seemed "unlikely to be overturned anytime soon," see Entelis, "The Democratic Imperative vs. the Authoritarian Impulse."

14. Throughout this book, I perform my own kind of allegory when I refer to Tunisia as a police state, when the more accurate and meaningful description is *policing* state. In *The Force*

1. THE NATION, THE STATE, AND THE CINEMA

of Obedience (which is entirely about Tunisia as a "policing state"), Hibou writes: "The policing state is not a police state in the accepted sense of the term, but a system and modes of regulation that make it possible for people's behavior to be controlled. It is the 'set of mechanisms through which order, the channeled growth of wealth, and the conditions of maintenance [of the well-being of the population] can be ensured' [Foucault]" (279). Hibou explains: "I decided that the concept of the policing state was useful if we were to gain a better understanding of the way the Tunisian state operated, since it enables us to get beyond the myth of the Leader as well as the image of the exteriority of state to society" (279).

15. Naccache insists that it was Bourguiba who first turned Tunisia into a prison: "When we talk about Bourguiba, with the hindsight of the few years that separate us from the height of his power, we remember how we could not pursue our friendships, our loves, our passions—whether for others, or for a culture, or an idea—without always having to keep it hidden. We were already in prison, before we'd even been judged, and before the doors of '9 avril' had even closed behind us" (225–226). Naccache's reference to "9 avril" is to the Civil Prison situated on the Boulevard du 9 avril 1938 in Tunis, which was demolished in March 2007. References to "9 avril" are now more often to the University of Tunis (today's Faculté des Sciences Humaines et Sociales) on the same Boulevard du 9 avril. Built in 1960, the campus overlooks a cluster of government offices on the edge of the medina, including that of the prime minister, in the Kasbah section of the city. In 1981, a new flagship campus of the university was built 20 kilometers west of the city, in La Manouba, where, should the occasion arise, student unrest could be more effectively controlled by government security forces than was (or is) the case at the "9 avril" campus.

16. Cf. the first chapter of Beau and Tuquoi's *Notre ami Ben Ali*, which is entitled: "Un général devenu président" ["A General Turned President"].

17. Other works by Béji in the same vein include: *L'imposture culturelle* and *Nous, décolonisés*.

18. "J'imagine mes compatriotes, à cet instant immense où la liberté se met à traverser la rue et histoire à descendre l'escalier de notre petit monde familier" (Béji, *Désenchantement national*, 9). Subsequent page numbers will be cited in the text.

19. Bourguiba, quoted by Béji, *Désenchantement national*, 48.

20. Sharabi, *Neopatriarchy*, 65. Subsequent page numbers will be cited in the text.

21. Béji, *Nous, décolonisés*, 61.

22. Perkins notes that upon becoming Tunisia's new president, Ben Ali automatically also became head of the ruling PSD (Parti Socialiste Destourien), "suggesting that whatever transformations might flow from the 'Historic Change,' they would not include a disentangling of the thoroughly interwoven lines between the state and the party. To symbolize the advent of a new leadership, however, the PSD was renamed the Rassemblement Constitutionnel Démocratique (RCD—Democratic Constitutional Rally)" (185).

23. Béji, *Nous, décolonisés*, 68 (emphasis in original). Subsequent page numbers will be cited in the text.

24. The Democracy Index is an index compiled by *The Economist* examining the state of democracy in 167 countries. It focuses on five general categories: electoral process and pluralism, civil liberties, functioning of government, political participation, and political culture. The countries are categorized as "full democracies," "flawed democracies," "hybrid regimes,"

(all considered democracies), and "authoritarian regimes" (considered dictatorial). In 2008, Tunisia was classified as an authoritarian regime, ranking 141 out of the 167 countries studied.

25. "Je tente vainement, je l'avoue, d'imaginer ce que pourrait être aujourd'hui un *portrait du décolonisé*, version révisée du modèle mis au point par Albert Memmi" (Béji, *Désenchantement national*, 20).

26. An English translation has been published as *Decolonization and the Decolonized*.

27. In my analyses of individual films in subsequent chapters, I take up many of the themes and issues that Memmi considers in *Decolonization and the Decolonized*. Like Béji's books (*Désenchantement national* and *Nous, décolonisés*), Memmi's *Portrait du décolonisé* tries to identify the sources of malaise in the postcolonial world. His disappointment is deep and his judgment unequivocal: "The country of the decolonized is a country without law, where there is rampant institutional violence that can only be countered by even greater violence" (61). But his book should not be dismissed as an exercise in Orientalism—although some readers might wish to treat is as such—even when he writes: "The Arab world has still not found, or has not wanted to consider, the transformations that would enable it to adapt to the modern world, which it cannot help but absorb" (65). Memmi is a perceptive and sympathetic observer of the world in which he lives: "Even though it is painful to admit," he writes, "the progress acquired by the West is often more appropriate than traditional solutions. The situation is not one in which, as has been repeated so complacently, several civilizations clash. There is now a single, global, civilization that affects everyone" (44).

28. It need hardly be said that the roots of the postcolonial malaise identified by Béji and Memmi are myriad and too numerous to be examined with equal attention in this study. Where Sharabi identifies the root causes as having to do with what he calls neopatriarchy, there are other scholars who put their focus elsewhere. See, e.g., Kuran, *The Long Divergence*, in which the author suggests that democracy has been hindered in the Arab societies, Iran, Turkey, and the Balkan Peninsula by the historical dearth of autonomous nongovernmental associations serving as intermediaries between the individual and the state. The chronic weakness of civil society in the region can be traced to a number of factors, he writes, such as the rule of *shari'a* law (which prevailed until the establishment of colonial regimes in the late nineteenth century), which essentially precludes autonomous and self-governing private organizations, thus preventing democratic institutions from forming and facilitating the rise of modern Arab dictatorships.

29. Memmi observes that "the absence of a large working class, preventing the formation of a sufficiently robust labor movement, leads to old-fashioned paternalism rather than relative social justice, and to bondage beneath a façade of generosity" (*Decolonization and the Decolonized*, 11). He was proven correct, as suggested by a front-page headline in the *New York Times* the day before Ben Ali and his family fled into exile: "Behind Tunisia Unrest, Rage over Wealth of Ruling Family" (Kirkpatrick).

30. I want to agree with Memmi, but recognize that many of my views about religion have hardened into prejudice. For an interesting problematization of the kind of dismissal of religion and insistence on one version of secularism that we see in Memmi's remarks, see Asad, "Ethnography, Literature, and Politics."

31. Béji, *Nous, décolonisés*, 119.

1. THE NATION, THE STATE, AND THE CINEMA

32. Lamloum and Ravenel, eds., *La Tunisie de Ben Ali*, quotation from jacket copy.

33. Nacer Khemir, quoted in Armes, "The Poetic Vision of Nacer Khemir," 81. Subsequent page numbers will be cited in the text.

34. Armes quotes Khemir from: *Nacer Khemir: Das verlorene Halsband der Taube*, eds. Bruno Jaeggi and Walter Ruggle (Baden: Lars Müller/Trigon Film, 1992), 108.

35. Fredric Jameson, "Third-World Literature in the Era of Multinational Capitalism," 73. Subsequent page numbers will be cited in the text.

36. Khemir quoted in *Nacer Khemir: Das verlorene Halsband der Taube*, 108.

37. Jameson, in "A Brief Response" (26–27), was responding to Ahmad, "Jameson's Rhetoric of Otherness and the 'National Allegory.'" A version of Ahmad's article appeared later as a chapter of his book *In Theory: Classes, Nations, Literatures*.

38. Jameson, "A Brief Response," 27. The original text reads: [the first world is based] "far more even than military power, on the fact that American bankers hold the levels [sic] of the world system."

39. I am paraphrasing Imre Szeman in "Who's Afraid of National Allegory? Jameson, Literary Criticism, Globalization." He writes that Jameson's essay is "a sophisticated attempt to make sense of the relationship of literature to politics in the decolonizing world. . . . Indeed, the concept of *national allegory* introduces a model for a properly materialist approach to postcolonial texts and contexts" (804). Szeman later incorporated "Who's Afraid of National Allegory?" into his remarkable book, *Zones of Instability: Literature, Postcolonialism, and the Nation*.

40. Shohat and Stam, *Unthinking Eurocentrism*, 25. Subsequent page numbers will be cited in the text.

41. Three-worlds theory, which originally started in the 1950s, posited three worlds: the capitalist First World of Europe, the United States, Australia, and Japan; the "Second World" of the socialist bloc (with China's place in the schema, Shohat and Stam note, being the object of much debate); and the Third World proper. (Ibid., 25)

42. The word "authentic" should perhaps always be rendered in quotation marks. See below my discussion of *tunisianité* (which I leave in French, so as to avoid the inelegant and cumbersome "Tunisianness"), and how the notion is related to that of an "authentic" national identity.

43. I must reiterate that I have chosen films, not filmmakers, for this study; *The Silences of the Palace*, for example, is perhaps the most obviously and self-consciously allegorical of the films I have selected for analysis in these pages; and yet, in 2004 Tlatli made *Nadia and Sarra*, a melodrama about the relationship between a mother and daughter during the mother's difficult experience of menopause—a film that would appear to have no (national) allegorical content whatsoever.

44. Comaroff and Comaroff, "Millennial Capitalism," 325. Quoted by Szeman, "Who's Afraid of National Allegory?" 818.

45. Rosen, *Change Mummified*, 266.

46. Jameson, "Third-World Literature," 74. Emphasis added.

47. Bensmaïa, *Experimental Nations*, 68–69.

48. Palakeel, "Third World Short Story as National Allegory?" 98.

49. I must take Palakeel's word for it (noting that he is writing in 1996), when he states that "the short story is the most energetic literary activity in the Third World which is still alive in the wake of the multinational television culture" (98).

50. During the month of Ramadan, dozens of old films are broadcast on Tunisian national television, directors are interviewed, roundtable discussions are hosted, and so on. For an interesting article that focuses on the role television plays during Ramadan in "modern" families living in Tunis, see Chouikha, "La modernité au miroir du ramadan télévisuel," 187–204.

51. Said, "Figures, Configurations, Transfigurations," 1–2.

52. Szeman, "Who's Afraid of National Allegory?" 803. Subsequent page numbers will be cited in the text.

53. Szeman is referring to Jameson's 1971 essay, "Metacommentary," in which Jameson wrote: "Every individual interpretation must include an interpretation of its own existence, must show its own credentials and justify itself: every commentary must be at the same time a metacommentary" (10).

54. Xavier, "Historical Allegory," 351. Subsequent page numbers will be cited in the text.

55. Cf. Jameson, *Postmodernism, or the Cultural Logic of Late Capitalism*. Jameson argues that realism—a form taken to new heights of development in the nineteenth century to account for the social reality of the time—is now inadequate to the task of accounting for what we call totality. The new configuration of space and time and the more abstract nature of the social process in postmodernity requires new art forms to help us understand society and our position within it—not through representation in the classic sense of what realism does, but rather by offering what he calls "cognitive mapping" (51–52). Allegory (as it has been retheorized in recent times), we can say, is a form of cognitive mapping. I will argue that when Bouzid comes to make his "last film," *Making Of* (which, in Jameson's phrase, includes an "interpretation of its own existence"—a metacommentary), he is seeking a new form that can account for the contemporary Tunisian social reality, because he understands that Ben Ali's regime and Tunisian audiences have in some sense become immune to the mode of critique contained in the typical New Tunisian Cinema film.

56. Jameson, "Third-World Literature," 77–78.

57. Owens, "The Allegorical Impulse," 64.

58. As we have indicated, it is not only "third-world" cultures and societies that produce national allegories expressing their embattled situation. Consider the case of Israel, which is not a third-world culture or society, but which is certainly an embattled one, nearly all of whose films are national allegories. When I proposed a course on Israeli cinema in the Department of Cinema at the University of Hartford in 2008, the director of the university's Center for Judaic Studies objected strenuously to my teaching it, insisting that a professor in his own department would be better equipped to teach the course. He expressed his fears that if the course were taught by me—a non-Jew, as far as he knows—it risked being "propaganda." What this scandal revealed is that allegory is very much a matter of reception, a reader-response problem. The Center for Judaic Studies' director was afraid of how I would interpret the Israeli films, which, because they are allegories, cannot be trusted, as it were, to "speak for themselves."

59. It goes without saying that a prison film made in Hollywood for an American audience is not necessarily going to mean the same thing to contemporary viewers as a prison film made

1. THE NATION, THE STATE, AND THE CINEMA

in Tunisia for a Tunisian audience during the Ben Ali era; nor is a film like John Frankenheimer's *The Manchurian Candidate,* made in 1962 (to choose a random example of a boldly allegorical film made in Hollywood), going to signify in the same way as Jonathan Demme's remake of the film in 2004. Frankenheimer's film is about the "strange aftermath of a Korean War veteran's decoration and his mother's machinations to promote her Joseph McCarthy-like husband's career" (Maltin, *Leonard Maltin's 2007 Movie and Video Guide,* 830), while Demme's film encourages the viewer to see it as an allegory about big-business string-pulling and the sinister links between the U.S. Government (more specifically, the Bush–Cheney administration) and a multinational defense conglomerate that resembles the Halliburton Corporation (cf. A. O. Scott, "Remembrance of Things Planted Deep in the Mind").

60. Gollin, *A Viewer's Guide to Film,* 175–176.

61. Sonia Chamkhi also identifies this theme of incarceration (*l'enfermement*) in the films she examines in her landmark study, *Cinéma tunisien nouveau*: "Anyone who is interested in Tunisia's cinematic output during the years 1980–1995 will observe that the films unfailingly deal with imprisonment. Whether they are about the ignorance that limits the imagination, the persistence of ossified traditions, the habits and customs that ensure closed-mindedness, or even the inferior status of women, who frankly remain cloistered and excluded, the films—and sometimes in the narratives themselves—speak the unhappy disjunction between the lived experience of subjects caught between a dysphoric present and a desired and inaccessible elsewhere" (11).

62. Every time I talked to my students at the University of Tunis about the Tunisian cinema (both in 1993–1994 and in 2001–2003)—Had they seen the latest Tunisian film in the theaters? Did they look forward to seeing every new Tunisian film?—they exhibited a relative indifference to their national cinema. "The films don't speak to our concerns—to our hopes, desires, dreams, problems, frustrations . . . ," is what they would usually say. There are many ways to interpret this kind of response, but I think chief among the reasons these young people were so often unenthusiastic about Tunisian films is the fact that the films demand an essentially *political* response from the (Tunisian) viewer. If, as Ismail Xavier argues, allegory is the "language of crisis," it becomes understandable that, for those living in a police state—where any involvement in politics whatsoever, let alone the mildest expression of protest against the regime in power, is believed will bring disaster down upon their heads—the preferred genres will be popular (usually American) entertainments. A majority of Tunisians can watch Al Jazeera television anytime, and the Palestinian tragedy, with which they identify on many levels—a worst-case scenario/reality which is also a kind of allegory of their own "embattled situation"—is ever-present. If they have a choice between seeing *Spider-Man* (Sam Raimi, 2002) or *Fatma* (Khaled Ghorbal, 2002), my students told me, they will choose to see *Spider-Man* (another kind of allegory).

63. Morgan Corriou's detailed and fascinating article, "La consommation cinématographique: les plaisirs du cinéma en Tunisie au tournant de 1956," offers an account of the distribution and exhibition practices in Tunisia around the time of Independence, and the role of the ciné-club in the evolution of this "cinephilia" about which Boughedir writes.

64. For a sense of how Tunisian cinema has differed historically from the cinemas of its neighbors in the Maghreb (even before the emergence of the New Tunisian Cinema in the

1. THE NATION, THE STATE, AND THE CINEMA

mid-1980s), see Guy Hennebelle's "Introduction" in the 1981 "Cinémas du Maghreb" special issue of *CinémAction* co-edited by Mouny Berrah, Victor Bachy, Mohand Ben Salama, and Férid Boughedir. Boughedir contributed extensively to this issue, and also edited the section on Moroccan cinema and co-edited the section on Tunisian cinema with Victor Bachy. Twenty-three years later, *CinémAction* published another "Cinémas du Maghreb" issue, to which Boughedir contributed an article in which he traces how women have been represented in the Tunisian cinema from its beginnings to the present.

The 1981 "Cinémas du Maghreb" issue of *CinémAction* also contains Victor Bachy's very useful summary of "Les structures politico-économiques" that have underpinned the Tunisian film industry, including an account of the founding and fortunes of SATPEC (Société anonyme tunisienne de production et d'expansion cinématographique) and its movie studio complex, built in Gammarth in 1967. Because I offer no history or analysis of my own of the economic/industrial contexts in which Tunisian films are or have been made—or why the Tunisian cinema is in perpetual financial crisis—the interested reader is directed to Bachy's account as a good place to start. Florence Martin provides a brief, updated account in "Cinema and State in Tunisia." Mahmoud Jemni's very short "Essai d'une typologie du cinéma tunisien" (published online 5 August 2011) is also of interest for the way in which he combines a few remarks about the political economy of the Tunisian cinema (successive governments, recognizing the value of having a national cinema, but afraid of its potentially seditious power, have never properly funded its development), with an outline of what he sees as the main thematic periods and the dominant genres of the Tunisian cinema since Independence.

For a brief history of Algerian film production, see Armes, "From State Production to *Cinéma d'Auteur* in Algeria"; and also Hafez, "Shifting Identities in Maghribi Cinema." For a summary account of contemporary film production in Morocco, see Dwyer, "Morocco: A National Cinema with Large Ambitions"; see also Moulay Driss Jaïdi, "Une étude de cas: Le Maroc."

65. Boughedir, "Le cinéma tunisien."

66. Higbee, "Le cinéma maghrébin vu de l'autre côté de la Méditerranée," 103. Subsequent page numbers will be cited in the text.

67. Higbee derives his statistics from Patricia Caillé, "Interroger l'exploitation et la réception des cinémas contemporains du Maghreb en France dans un contexte postcoloniale (1997–2007)," SFSIC, Colloque international—"Mondialisation, culture et communication," 10–11 May 2008, Université de Jijel, Algeria.

68. Boughedir, "Les principales tendances du cinéma tunisien," 153.

69. Kchir-Bendana, "Ideologies of the Nation," 40. Subsequent page numbers will be cited in the text.

70. Bouzid's sketch in *Harb El Khalij . . . wa ba'd/La Guerre du Golfe . . . et après?/The Gulf War . . . What Next?* is entitled: *C'est Schéhérazade qu'on assassine/Murdering Shahrazad*. The other four films are: *Black Night Eclipse*, by Borhane Alaoui; *The Silence*, by Mustapha Darkaoui; *Research of Shaima*, by Néjia Ben Mabrouk; and *Homage by Assassination*, by Elia Suleiman.

71. Writing in the preface to the English edition of *The Force of Obedience* (8 February 2011), Hibou suggests that it is too soon to say whether the upheaval that resulted in the

departure of Ben Ali and the "clans" can be described in terms of revolution or will lead to democratic transition: "The palace revolution which sounded the death knell for the reign of Ben Ali was orchestrated by the general staff of the army and a section of the elite in power for over twenty years; it aimed at pre-empting this social upheaval so as to prevent it from being transformed into a revolution" (xiii). For our purposes, too, the question of whether the secular and liberal values of the social class to which the filmmakers belong will prevail in the new Tunisia remains to be seen. If we refer to the Tunisian Revolution of 2011, we must specify whether we are talking about the "palace revolution" or a (subsequent) revolution in the practice of governance or the governing national ideology. Ben Ali's regime was officially secular and democratic—which is how the filmmakers, not without difficulty, were able to make their films—but of course in reality it was not in the least democratic; and so the question will be whether a new version of the contradictory status quo will return, i.e., will liberal filmmakers, against the odds, continue to succeed in making films under the watchful gaze of a regime that is fundamentally hostile to their values? (For a lively discussion of these issues, see Barlet, "Apt 2011: Les débats du printemps arabe," and the roundtable discussion led by Tahar Chikaoui and Olivier Barlet at the same *Festival des cinémas d'Afrique* in Apt, France, in November 2011: Barlet et al., "Cinéma et Révolution.")

72. Boughedir, "Le cinéma tunisien."

73. Hibou, *The Force of Obedience*, 229. (Subsequent page numbers will be cited in the text.) Khayr ed-Din al-Tunsi is revered in contemporary Tunisia as the country's greatest precolonial reformer. As Mohamed Bey's prime minister from 1873 to 1877, he tackled administrative, financial, and tax reform. He his best known for writing *The Surest Path to Knowledge Concerning the Condition of Countries* (1868) and for founding Sadiqi College in Tunis in 1875.

74. Historians until recently linked the reformist project to the nineteenth-century construction and development of the nation-state as a response to European development. Tunisia, in this view, is still trying to "catch up" with the West, and reform is understood to be the best defense against neocolonialism. Hibou insists that "the myth of Tunisia 'at the crossroads of East and West' rests on facts whose importance is doubtless exaggerated but no less real" (228). She also writes: "It now seems that the thesis of reformism as a response to decline, internationalization, and the crisis of the nation-state in the Muslim world is a gross simplification: internationalization significantly predates the nineteenth century and has always contributed to the formation of the nation-state; reformism, furthermore, was a response to internal dynamics proper to Tunisian society" (228).

75. Tunisia is a "heterogeneous" society only in the sense that nearly every society is heterogeneous (with divisions between rich and poor, between urban and rural populations, and so on); otherwise, it is usually cited as a remarkably *homogeneous* society (with an ancient history as a state, which now, at least, has a nonsectarian population—98% Sunni Muslim—which is ethnically 98% Arab-Berber, and so on), its claims to a "Mediterranean" national identity notwithstanding.

76. In a note to me, Amy Kallander correctly points out that most Tunisians have a limited understanding of what the Ottoman Empire was all about or what it meant to be a part of it. Downplaying the Ottoman past is common in the former Arab provinces, where nationalist versions of grade-school history dominate. (Cf. Abbassi, *Quand la Tunisie s'invente*.)

1. THE NATION, THE STATE, AND THE CINEMA

77. In "The Nation Form: History and Ideology," Etienne Balibar writes: "Beginning from the core, national units form out of the overall structure of the world-economy, as a function of the role they play in that structure in a given period. . . . In a sense, every modern nation is a product of colonization: it has always been to some degree colonized or colonizing, and sometimes both at the same time" (Balibar and Wallerstein, *Race, Nation, Class*, 89).

78. Historically, as Hibou points out, the concept of *tunisianité* was in effect invented by the French colonizers when they formulated the "Tunisian Question" as a legal issue that sought to assert French power in the country by making distinctions and differences between the French and local juridical systems.

79. Tessler, "The Origins of Popular Support for Islamist Movements," 106. Subsequent page numbers will be cited in the text.

80. The BBC reported that "ten percent of the camp, which in total houses approximately 13,000 refugees, was virtually rubbed out by a dozen armored Israeli bulldozers" (Lee, "Jenin rises from the dirt"). Many residents of the Hawashin neighborhood, which was leveled, had no advance warning, and some were buried alive.

81. In "How Israel Gets Away with Murder," Geoffrey Wheatcroft writes: "Although Israel is sometimes described as an American client state, which receives huge financial subsidy from Washington, she is unique as a client state: she can do exactly as she likes in the knowledge that she will never be seriously restrained by her sponsor. Even when the White House is privately irritated by Israeli actions, Congress is absolutely reliable, never knowingly outbid in its unswerving loyalty. During the bombardment of Lebanon in the summer of 2006, the House of Representatives passed a resolution of total solidarity with Israel by 410 votes to eight, and the Senate has just passed another on a hand vote, not even bothering to take a formal tally."

82. Ajami, "Rebellion in the Land of the Pharaohs." (My quoting of Ajami in no way implies that I endorse his worldview. After selling his soul to the neoconservative wing of the Republican Party, Ajami urged the Bush–Cheney regime to topple Saddam Hussein, which he argued would send a message of strength and enhance America's credibility throughout the Muslim world. It is hard to forgive Ajami for his role in whipping up the paranoid anxieties of the Israel lobby and for encouraging the Bush–Cheney regime in its delusions. But he is an eloquent writer, and his remarks here about the Egyptians being both shamed and emboldened by the Tunisian example seem valid.)

83. Friedman, "Nostalgia, Nationhood, and the New Immigrant Narrative." Friedman quotes from Boym, *The Future of Nostalgia*, 15.

84. Bouzid, *Sources of Inspiration*. A decade later, in an interview with Heike Hurst published in *Le Monde libertaire*, Bouzid would describe his cinema as a "*cinéma d'intervention.*" Over the years, Bouzid has given a number of very interesting interviews about his filmmaking practice, and on 5 April 2006, he gave a lecture at the University of Rome 3 in the Panafricana Festival, in which he reviewed and refined some of the statements and general propositions he made in his Villepreux lecture twelve years earlier. (See Barlet, "La leçon de cinéma de Nouri Bouzid.")

85. Bouzid, *Sources of Inspiration*, 45. (Subsequent page numbers will be cited in the text.) The published lecture appears in both French and English in the same volume. All quotations here are taken from the English translation. An edited version of the lecture was also published in English as "On Inspiration" (Bakari and Cham, *African Experiences of Cinema*).

1. THE NATION, THE STATE, AND THE CINEMA

86. Bouzid judges his cohort to be "seven to ten directors" who have made "some twenty or thirty" films, all of which are stamped by a sense of "urgency" (48).

87. Sarris, "Notes on the Auteur Theory in 1962." Sarris seemed most interested in identifying auteurs working within the Hollywood studio system, where one perhaps least expected to find them. He and the critics publishing in the *Cahiers du cinéma* (which, throughout the 1960s, took up the *politique des auteurs* as their credo) tended to identify mise-en-scène as the vehicle of the auteur's distinctive style, expressed in decisions about staging, physical setting and décor, framing, cinematography, and sound.

88. While it is perfectly true that the filmmakers of the New Tunisian Cinema can be described as auteurs, this study does not take an auteurist approach to an analysis of their films, but is more concerned to discover what their films can tell us about Tunisians and their society between approximately 1986 and 2006.

89. Khayati, *Cinémas arabes*, 139. The chapter referred to is entitled: "Égypte/Tunisie: Le dépit amoureux" (which, the confusion between slashes and hyphens notwithstanding, could perhaps be translated as: "Egypt/Tunisia: A Love–Hate Relationship" or, if read from the Tunisian point of view, "Egypt/Tunisia: A Loving Scorn").

90. Khayati appears to be echoing Bouzid, who said this two years earlier in his "Sources of Inspiration" lecture.

91. The variety and range of the melodramatic form, however, is such that Moufida Tlatli can make a melodrama (*The Silences of the Palace*) and still be opposed to the type of film characterizing the Egyptian commercial cinema. Her approach will not be like that of, say, Douglas Sirk in the 1950s (in films like *All That Heaven Allows*), which display a self-conscious use of cliché and irony, but rather one that draws its power from a restrained and realistic performance style, an unemphatic but nevertheless subtly signifying mise-en-scène, and a bold use of allegory.

92. Bouzid elaborates his ideas about melodrama in an article about the sociopolitical context of what he calls the "New Realism" in Arab cinema, which appeared in Arabic in *Al-Tariq* (XLVII, no. 4 [September 1988]). The article was translated into English by Shereen el Ezabi and published as: "New Realism in Arab Cinema: The Defeat-Conscious Cinema."

93. For a theory and analysis of melodrama, both as a genre and a mode, see Lang, *American Film Melodrama*; or the French edition: *Le mélodrame américain*. For an analysis of this question of "fate" and its related term "destiny," as they apply to personal desire in conflict with tribal imperatives or national identity (from which we can infer just how exceptional Tunisia has been in its modern, nonmelodramatic, inclusive conception of national identity), see Lang, "Deconstructing Melodramatic 'Destiny.'"

94. Bouzid adds that the ideological preoccupations of the director should never dominate. "If ideology comes first, it's not cinema" (47).

95. The press in Tunisia has never been free, and so Bouzid's allusion to the (initially) negative reaction of the mainstream press to the films of the New Tunisian filmmakers—a subject too big and complex to treat here—is an oblique acknowledgment that the regime in power sensed the challenge to its authority and legitimacy that the films posed.

96. As always in French (the language in which Bouzid gave his Villepreux lecture), the gender of the "character" under discussion is determined by the gender of the word *personnage* (which is masculine) and does not reflect any sexism on Bouzid's part.

97. The notion of a "national cinematic language" is a broad and imprecise one, but is meant to indicate the kind of distinctions we make when we refer, say, to the production values of a Hollywood genre film or the narrative rhythms of an art house film made by a French auteur. While it is not possible to separate form and content, it is helpful in any discussion about "cinematic language" to try to identify characteristic forms (a certain use of the close-up, the frequency or semantic function of the long take, a dialectic between the stasis and movement of the camera, a particular attitude toward narrative economy, and so on) and characteristic content to be found in this or that cinema—as Siegfried Kracauer believed could be done for the German cinema "from Caligari to Hitler," or as the authors of *The Classical Hollywood Cinema: Film Style & Mode of Production to 1960* attempt to do when they analyze the American commercial cinema of the studio era.

98. For an analogous situation in the United States, we observe that the South intermittently reveals how it has been marked by this same sense of defeat since it lost the Civil War in 1865, a sense that was acutely exacerbated by the defeat of the Republicans (whose party had become increasingly a regional one, based in the South) when Barack Obama won the presidency in November 2008. Following Obama's victory at the polls, the Republican Party collapsed into know-nothing fundamentalism, right-wing extremism, incoherently expressed views, and frequently bizarre, anarchic manifestations of discontent.

99. I disagree with Bouzid that the body is "something fundamental" in drama, if by "drama" we mean a stage play like Sophocles' *Oedipus Rex*, which conforms to the principles of construction described by Aristotle in his *Poetics*; but in the cinema as we generally know it, the body, I would agree with Bouzid, is the mainstay.

100. *Making Of, le dernier film* is the French title of the film Bouzid made in 2006. Unfortunately, some of the resonances of this title are lost in the English translation, which is simply *Making Of*. As the film is about the "making of" an Islamic fundamentalist, and is itself structurally self-reflexive, in that it contains the making of a documentary film (which the French would call *"le 'making of'"*) of the fiction film we are watching, it expresses Bouzid's deeply held, secular view that we are all "made" by ideology/culture. ("I'm not a believer," he says in *Sources of Inspiration*, 61.)

2. "The freedom to be different, to choose your own life"

1. This retrospective took place during a (briefly) disastrous period in Franco-Tunisian relations. See "Une 'saison tunisienne'" in Beau and Tuquoi's *Notre ami Ben Ali* for an account of how a projected program of cultural events organized to take place in Paris and several other French cities celebrating Tunisian culture was nearly derailed by Ben Ali, who believed the motives behind the program were defamatory to both Tunisia and his own government. The cause of Ben Ali's discontent was an article in *Le Monde*, 6 March 1995, which (rather too truthfully) characterized the program as a homage to "artists caught between Islamism and political power. Children of Independence, they were twenty years old in 1968. The cream of the crop of a country that has no national cultural project, they await relief, which is slow in coming" (206–207).

2. THE FREEDOM TO BE DIFFERENT

2. Khayati, "Un cinéma sans tabou." What Khayati writes is: "Tous ces films vont, dans un cinéma moderne et une direction d'acteur impeccable, dans des scénarios cousus main et des thématiques résolument actuelles, s'attaquer aux tabous majeurs: la sexualité, la femme, la question juive, le pouvoir, l'idéologie intégriste, l'identité culturelle du pays, etc." (2). (The term "essay" is really too grand to describe Khayati's brief remarks, which were provided merely to orient the film viewer with little or no knowledge of the Tunisian cinema's specificity within the context of Arab film production.)

3. If Hachemi and Farfat represent two sides of the same character, as Bouzid himself insists, there is the implication that sexual abuse of youngsters is more widespread than is reported or perhaps thought. For every child whose abuse becomes known, as in Farfat's case, there are many more, like Hachemi, whose trauma remains a secret; moreover, different individuals will respond to the same (traumatic) event in different ways. Trauma, as Bouzid's film makes clear, always leaves its mark, whether or not we recognize it.

4. I assume that "Jacko" is a rendering of Jacquot, a pet form of the French personal name, Jacques.

5. Bouzid describes one of the six "constants" of his cinema as: "a feeling ... of helplessness faced with something we're being dragged into, something we haven't chosen" (cf. Bouzid's "Sources of Inspiration" lecture, discussed in the previous chapter).

6. Khélil, *Abécédaire du cinéma tunisien*, 49. Subsequent page numbers will be cited in the text.

7. What Khélil writes is: "Mais, s'il y a, dans cette onde de choc, un film absolument incontournable, c'est *L'homme de cendres* de Nouri Bouzid" (49).

8. Bouzid, "Note d'intention" (unpaginated document).

9. Hisham Sharabi, *Neopatriarchy*, 29.

10. Bouzid, *Sources of Inspiration*, 56. Subsequent page numbers will be cited in the text.

11. Barbencey, "Nouri Bouzid: Une société fondée sur le viol." Not surprisingly, Bouzid's comment ("Je crois que notre société est construite sur le viol") reappeared in a 2004 review of his new film, *Poupées d'argile*, whose protagonist, it becomes clear during the course of the narrative, was raped in his youth. See Claude-Marie Trémois, "Filles de l'air et du vent."

12. Like Sejra (Wassila Chaouki), the brothel-keeper in the film, Lévy represents a happier and more tolerant, multicultural past. When Hachemi visits "Monsieur Lévy" to invite him to the wedding, the old and lonely widower, accompanying himself on a lute, sings Hachemi a song and then gives him the lute as a present ("The song is for your wedding, and the lute is for you," he says). The song (in Arabic and written by Bouzid) is overwhelmingly nostalgic for a lost Tunisian society, about which Lévy asks Hachemi rhetorically: "Whatever happened to those happy evenings? The balconies full to overflowing ... Arabs, Jews, French, Italians ... Now, I never go out. There's no place to go":

I came to see you / But the doors were all closed / I remember the time / When the streets were so gay / The neighborhoods have lost their charm / No one sings in the courtyards or celebrates on the balconies / The doors no longer dance / The locks have fallen silent / The roofs break out in tears / As the swallows fly away / I remember the time / When the streets were so gay / On the strings of my lute / I've played you this song / To bring back to your face / Your smile of long ago / Let happiness reign and know no bounds.

2. THE FREEDOM TO BE DIFFERENT

13. hooks, "Reflections on Race and Sex," 57.

14. Cf. note 7 in the previous chapter explaining the context in which Bouzid, with this remark, acknowledges that Tunisia is a police state.

15. As it turns out, it was Farfat himself who wrote the graffito on the city wall announcing that he is "not a man" (*Farfat mush rājil*). The scene in which he tearfully tells his friends Touil and Hachemi this, late in the evening, sitting on a jetty at the boatyard, is a powerful indictment of their society's homophobia:

> TOUIL. I want to know who wrote on the walls. You don't deserve that. If I catch the one who did it ... I'll tear him to pieces!
> FARFAT. It was me. Tear me to pieces. Who has put his friends to shame? It's Farfat. The source of evil? It's Farfat. Of degeneration? It's Farfat. Of perversion? Depravity? The devil is Farfat. Always Farfat! Poor Farfat, they've got your number. Alas! Friendship is cruel. (*He starts to run down the jetty toward the sea.*)
> TOUIL. Farfat ... (*Running after him.*) Farfat!
> FARFAT. It's over, Farfat. You've been buried alive. (*He jumps into the sea.*)
> TOUIL. Come back, you'll drown!
> FARFAT. So what? I've no father.

16. In a boldly allegorical scene, Bouzid makes an unambiguous reference to Islam as a repressively patriarchal ideology internalized by Muslims when he shows a frustrated and miserable Hachemi on his bed masturbating, but unable to come. Both at the beginning of the scene, and at the end, the camera lingers on the framed religious inscription in gorgeous Arabic calligraphy above the bed: "In the name of Allah, the Most Gracious, the Most Merciful." (The scene is intercut with the first half of the scene in which Farfat attempts to drown himself.)

17. When Bouzid refers to "our society," it is not always clear whether he is referring to Muslim society, Arab-Muslim society, or even more specifically, Tunisian society, although he very probably means all three. In "Bourguiba's Sons: Melancholy Manhood in Modern Tunisia," Nouri Gana writes: "Without diminishing the importance of the political allegory of French colonial and neocolonial rape or Israel's rape of Arab lands following the 1967 war (both of which are at the origin of the persisting malaise of postcolonial nationhood and the agony of Arab nationalism), Bouzid's film [*Man of Ashes*] is concerned with the immediate material and psychoaffective effects of these wider historical and societal crises as they become manifest—in a rather condensed and indirect form—at the inscriptional level of individual history" (122n19).

18. Hoveyda, *Que veulent les arabes?*, 132–133.

19. Some of Bouzid's general statements about sexuality in his society (like those of several other Tunisian filmmakers, especially Férid Boughedir) seem also to have been borrowed from Bouhdiba's *La sexualité en Islam*, which, not surprisingly, appears to have been enormously influential among francophone Tunisian intellectuals. Like Bouhdiba, Bouzid sometimes takes a broad (and some would say Orientalist) and ahistorical view of sexuality in his society. For a critique of Bouhdiba's nevertheless fascinating and intelligent book, see Massad, *Desiring Arabs*, 144–151.

2. THE FREEDOM TO BE DIFFERENT

20. The astonishment is mine, not Bouhdiba's, although I suppose it scarcely makes any difference whether genital mutilation is dressed up as a "covenant with God" (as in Judaism) or is merely a sort of superstition, to which its adherents are attached in the name of tradition (as in Islam). Bouhdiba explains that circumcision "is a *sunna* act, that is to say, one that is strongly recommended." (A *sunna* is an "imitation of the Prophet." The *fiqh* refers to both the interpretations of Muslim scholars of the *shari'a* and the *Sunna*, which are the teachings and practices of Mohamed.)

21. Marcel Mauss, quoted by Bouhdiba, *Sexuality in Islam*, 179.

22. Bouhdiba explains that in the Muslim tradition, "just at the moment of the operation, a large red or black cockerel must be killed and the *tahhār* [the barber who has performed the circumcision] takes it away as payment" (177).

23. Mohamed Kerrou, however, in an ambitious article written at the time of the film's release, "Portraits d'individus," sees the film as a complex allegory of contemporary Tunisian society, with the opening shots representing a traditional society in a struggle with modernity, suffering a slow death (11).

24. As I suggest below, Ameur's dying words—"You will always be my apprentices. I nevertheless initiated you"—reveal the logic of circumcision in Muslim (and Jewish) societies as an expression of patriarchal control. Just as the circumcised boy is physically marked for life, so Farfat and Hachemi are psychologically marked for life. Ameur is saying that Farfat and Hachemi will always "belong" to him—they are bound to him in the same way that the trauma of circumcision binds all Muslims (and Jews).

25. Bouzid, *Sources of Inspiration*, 49. What Bouzid says in French (which I have translated as: "Go to hell, I'll do what I like,") is: "Je vous emmerde, je fais ce que je veux."

26. Bouzid, "Note d'intention." There are no figures available to give an indication of the prevalence of the phenomenon in Tunisia of men being forced to marry against their will. An interesting item appeared in *The Guardian Weekly* in July 2010, however, revealing that the problem exists in the United Kingdom (although it must be said that the report raises more questions than it answers—to what social/economic/ethnic groups or categories do these men belong, for example?): "An increasing number of men say they are being forced into marriage against their will, by relatives who suspect them of being gay, or bisexual. The Forced Marriage Unit—a joint Home and Foreign Office agency—dealt with 1,682 cases last year, of which 14% involved men" (Brown, "Doomed Grooms," 14).

27. In *Desiring Arabs*, Massad points out that Bouhdiba's logic, according to which the "separation of the sexes" was part of the corruption of an originary Islam, is naïve. Bouhdiba seems to think, writes Massad, that "if Arab society had adhered to originary Islam, heterosexuality would have reigned supreme in Muslim Arab history through the present.... The oppression of the women and the youth would not have pervaded Arab society as it does today were it not for this lack of adherence to the Islamic ideal and the continual degradation away from it. Bouhdiba summarized the result for 'us': 'as a religion, Islam makes possible a lyrical vision of life, but the Arabo-Muslim societies have almost succeeded in denying this lyricism by refusing it all foundation and by refusing it even to the point of denying self-determination'" (146).

28. Bouzid, "Note d'intention."

2. THE FREEDOM TO BE DIFFERENT

29. When Touil organizes the visit to Sejra's brothel, and Farfat becomes hysterical, fighting with Azaïez and swinging one of Sejra's poor cats around like a weapon, Touil apologizes to the old brothel-keeper, saying sadly: "I thought it was a good idea . . . to bring old friends together." Sejra replies with the wisdom and authority of her legendary status as the city's most beloved doyenne of a disappearing culture of elegantly housed and organized prostitution: "You have to separate them."

30. Haskell, *From Reverence to Rape*, 24. Subsequent page numbers will be cited in the text.

31. Homosociality, as I am using the term here, describes the transactions between men concerning the possession of women. (And I would say that, if Hachemi's mother "suffers" on his account, she brings this suffering upon herself, in accordance with the society's values to which she subscribes, and Hachemi can in no way be blamed for it.)

32. Bouzid, "Note d'intention."

33. It is in the nature of cinematic signification that Lévy as a Jew should be perceived to represent more than himself (i.e., as merely the grandfather of Hachemi's childhood friend). It is my guess that the negative reaction from some viewers toward Bouzid's indulgent portrayal of Lévy was not (necessarily) due to anti-Semitism on the part of those viewers, but to the lack of any sign in the film that Bouzid is opposed to the Israeli occupation of Palestinian territory. As in most societies, the educated classes in Tunisia are usually able to make the distinction between "Jews" and Israeli policy toward the Palestinians, although, with the stranglehold of the Israel lobby on American foreign policy in the Middle East and the unwavering support of the Jewish Diaspora in the United States for Israel, even during periods of pathological Israeli aggression against Palestinians and other Arabs in the region, it is becoming increasingly difficult, even for educated people, to maintain that distinction.

34. Bouzid, *Sources of Inspiration*, 57.

35. As quoted in the previous chapter, Bouzid said in his "Sources of Inspiration" lecture: "In our society the individual is nothing; it's the family that counts, the group. Our cinema is trying to destroy the edifice of the family and liberate the individual" (57).

36. Bouhdiba does not so much contradict himself as suggest that the Muslim male learns to live with trauma, as though it were a natural condition. He writes, for example, that "one can speak of a castration complex inherent in all Muslim child-rearing," and even draws attention "to the relation, often observed in Arab culture, between violence and love, which is merely another variant of the castration dialectic. The mutilated man rapes. The raped woman is mutilating" (184)—which appears to be at odds with his conclusion that "in the end, everything seems to settle down without too much difficulty and heartache" (183).

37. Bouzid, *Sources of Inspiration*, 52–53.

38. Bouhdiba's reference to "the early age of marriage, which follows soon after circumcision," is problematic, since the marriage age of men and women "in Islam" varies according to region, historical period, social class, and other factors. In contemporary Tunisia, marriage is neither "early" nor followed "soon after circumcision." Most men marry when they are in their mid-twenties, and boys are usually circumcised before the age of five. (In Boughedir's *Halfaouine*, the circumcision of Noura's brother takes place when the child is about two years old. Increasingly, among the secular, middle classes, the circumcision is performed in a medical

2. THE FREEDOM TO BE DIFFERENT

setting, without ceremony, shortly after the infant's birth.) For the marriage age of women in the Arab world, see Rashad et al., *Marriage in the Arab World*.

39. Bouhdiba's remark about the "exceptional place in our Arabo-Muslim societies" of sexual mutilation notwithstanding, excision (female genital mutilation) is not practiced in Tunisia, nor is it common practice in Arab societies.

40. I am referring to sexuality as it is understood by psychoanalysis, not sociology. From a sociological perspective, Bouhdiba has much to say about how different the Islamic conception of sexuality is from the Christian conception. For example, he writes: In the Islamic understanding of sexuality, unlike the Christian view, "there can be no question of drowning the sexual in the miracle of creation as if it were merely an epiphenomenon" (94). He explains that: "The whole of life, according to Islamic teaching, bathes in an atmosphere of sexuality. Sometimes this is carried to the point of obsession. One should marry. One should have sexual intercourse. Parents must marry off their children and among the duties of filial piety is that of getting a widowed parent to remarry. To make love is an overriding duty, from which there is no excuse, even devotion to God. Devotion itself is expressed in terms of the lawful satisfaction of desire. So, in its very practice, sexuality transcends earthly existence: the afterlife is again a sexual existence. Paradise implies orgasm and perpetual erection" (95).

41. If we accept that the Oedipus complex described by Freud is universal, then the meaning of masculine subjectivity and identity, as founded in a moment of patriarchal violence, will be the same for those societies comprehended by the Oedipus myth as for those in which, as Bouhdiba, Bouzid, Hoveyda, and others have suggested, the myth of Abraham dominates. Freud writes:

> Castration has its place, too, in the Oedipus legend, for the blinding with which Oedipus punished himself after the discovery of his crime is, by the evidence of dreams, a symbolic substitute for castration. The possibility cannot be excluded that a phylogenetic memory-trace may contribute to the extraordinarily terrifying effect of the threat—a memory-trace from the prehistory of the human family, when the jealous father would actually rob his son of his genitals if the latter interfered with him in the rivalry for a woman. The primeval custom of circumcision, another symbolic substitute for castration, is only intelligible if it is an expression of subjection to the father's will. (Compare the puberty rites of primitive peoples.) (Sigmund Freud, *An Outline of Psychoanalysis*, 92–93n11)

42. This comment, from which the French (and English) title of the film derives, is an allusion to the carnal, or erotic, component of the male–male friendship that is central to the film's themes and meanings. If I understand the dialogue correctly, Farfat was somehow implicated in the theft of the motorcycle Azaïez refers to. (Farfat probably borrowed the motorcycle, which was then stolen while it was in his care.)

43. Malkmus and Armes, *Arab and African Film Making*, 118.

44. Vergès, "Dialogue," 139.

45. And yet... Bouzid shows Hachemi weeping at the memory of his rape by Ameur years before. The scene immediately follows one in which we see Hachemi's mother covertly placing

a talisman under her son's pillow (to make him want to marry and produce children). Hachemi has just returned from visiting Mr. Lévy, to whom he was about to reveal that he was raped as a boy (but Mr. Lévy fell asleep, and Hachemi realizes that he will never be able to unburden himself of this awful secret from his past). We are given to understand, thus, that Hachemi (and Bouzid?) really does believe that his disinclination to marry is caused by the rape. If the viewer thinks Hachemi is/would be "gay" (but lives in a time and place where a gay identity is socially not yet an option or is inconceivable for otherwise "normal" men), this scene rather suggests that the director himself believes his protagonists' homosexuality is caused by their homosexual rape *or* that viewers who believe Hachemi and Farfat are homosexual will understand that the director has to frame his topic in this way for his Tunisian audience, who can only see homosexual identity as a catastrophe.

46. Stollery, "Masculinities, Generations, and Cultural Transformation in Contemporary Tunisian Cinema," 55.

47. *L'homme blessé* (Patrice Chéreau, 1983).

48. Bouzid, *Sources of Inspiration*, 46.

49. As we have said, Bouhdiba's view of what he calls "sexuality in Islam" is essentially a depressed one, his occasional attempts to put a positive spin on it notwithstanding. He concludes that "the sexual ethic experienced by Muslims and the vision of the world that underlies it have less and less to do with the generous declarations of the Qur'an and of Muhammad himself. One can even speak of a degradation, which began at a very early date, of an ideal model. The open sexuality, practised in joy with a view to the fulfillment of being, gradually gave way to a closed, morose, repressed sexuality" (231). As in much of the New Tunisian Cinema, the element of nostalgia is strong in Bouhdiba's view, which is indicated by the title of his concluding chapter: "The Crisis of Sexuality and the Crisis of Faith in the Arabo-Muslim World Today." Regardless of whether we agree with Bouhdiba's analysis of a contemporary "crisis of sexuality," we have to acknowledge that his view of "sexuality . . . in the Arabo-Muslim world" matches Bouzid's view, as we see it in *Man of Ashes*.

50. Murray and Roscoe, eds., *Islamic Homosexualities*, 306. We might do well to be suspicious of some of Murray and Roscoe's claims, for, as Massad points out in *Desiring Arabs*, the very title of their book is "indicative of their limited knowledge of Muslim societies (since 'Islamic' is an adjective referring to the religion Islam while 'Muslim' refers to people who adhere to it, [making it] unclear how 'Islam,' the religion, can have a 'homosexuality' let alone 'homosexualities'" (170). Massad remarks that the language-based errors and mistakes in their book are "too many to list here"—a statement I cannot refute. (For an update on the social status of homosexuality in Pakistan, see Meghan Davidson Ladly, "Gay Pakistanis, Still in Shadows, Seek Acceptance," *New York Times*, 3 November 2012. www.nytimes.com/2012/11/04/world/asia/gays-in-pakistan-move-cautiously-to-gain-acceptance.html?hpw.

51. I see no problem with repeating this observation by Murray and Roscoe. But the reader should be alert to the complexities of what is at stake when men are perceived to be "adopting the new terminology and self-conceptions of a gay identity under the influence of Western examples." See Massad's chapter in *Desiring Arabs*, "Re-Orienting Desire: The Gay International and the Arab World," in which he looks at "the serious ongoing attempts by the Gay International and their adherents to impose their own sexual taxonomy and transform the

medically and sociologically marginal figure of the 'deviant' (itself a European invention) into the 'homosexual' (*mithli*), a juridical subject endowed with legal rights (another more recent European invention), and then posit the existence of homosexuality as a communitarian societal group or category" (416).

52. Bouzid, *Sources of Inspiration*, 58. Subsequent page numbers, all of which refer to this published lecture, will be cited in the text.

3. Laughter in the Dark

1. *Halfaouine* sold 500,000 tickets in the first six months of its release in Tunisia in 1990—a remarkable record, considering there were only twenty-eight movie theaters in the country. "It beat *Titanic* and *Rambo*! People saw the film four or five times, they learned the dialogue by heart," remembers its author. (Boughedir [interview], "'Le multiplexe est le remède' au piratage des films en Afrique.")

2. Férid Boughedir, quoted in Armes, *Postcolonial Images*, 143. Subsequent page numbers will be cited in the text.

3. By "Mediterranean," Boughedir at the very least is referring to what Iain Chambers describes as "a contemporary Mediterranean where the Occident and the Orient, the North and the South, are evidently entangled in a cultural and historical net cast over centuries, even millennia." (Chambers, *Mediterranean Crossings*, 3.) Elsewhere, Boughedir has enthusiastically described himself as an advocate for a Tunisian culture of "*métissage*" or "*synthèse*."

4. Boughedir, in publicity material for *Halfaouine* intended to accompany the screening of the film at the 1990 Cannes Film Festival. His citation comes from the first sentence of Bataille's landmark work, *L'érotisme*: "De l'érotisme, il est possible de dire qu'il est l'approbation de la vie jusque dans la mort" (Bataille, *L'érotisme*, 1). The reference is a potentially risky proposition for Boughedir, considering the links Bataille develops in his book between eroticism, death, and murder.

5. Brahimi, *Cinémas d'Afrique francophone et du Maghreb*, 103: "Ce qui était au centre du film de l'Algérien Merzak Allouache, *Omar Gatlato*, c'est-à-dire le sentiment d'une incurable absence au cœur du trop plein, se retrouve dans *Halfaouine* de Férid Boughedir." Her phrase "absence au cœur du trop plein" is difficult to translate satisfactorily, as it suggests a heart that feels empty and yet also fit to burst (with ill-defined and confusing feelings that include love and frustration). (Subsequent page numbers will be cited in the text.)

6. One cannot help but think of how, from the early 1990s onward, President Ben Ali enthusiastically promoted the broad availability of the Internet in Tunisia, but at the same time sought to control it—as if the freedom of information exchange were something for which the Tunisians were not ready, not mature enough.

7. *Halfaouine* was made less than three years after Bourguiba was ousted by Ben Ali on 7 November 1987. As we have said, after more than thirty years in office, Bourguiba had become senile and increasingly (and arbitrarily) authoritarian—and although it is difficult to pinpoint when Tunisia can be said to have become a police state, it is a baleful irony that Ben

3. LAUGHTER IN THE DARK

Ali's dictatorship made the situation worse. Cf. Belhassen, "Les legs bourguibiens de la répression," 391–404: "To identify the main features of the practice of repression under Bourguiba's regime is to note that, in this area, there was no break between the two regimes, but rather two stages in the Bourguiba-Ben Ali practice of repression that differ, not in their nature, but in their forms and degree. One observes that there is a continuity, a progression from one phase to another, that has allowed repression, which was a constitutive element of Bourguiba's regime, to become a comprehensive and institutionalized *system* of repression with Zine El Abidine Ben Ali's accession to power" (391–392). Cf. also Florence Beaugé's "La Tunisie des illusions perdues," which was published in *Le Monde* on 7 November 2008, the twentieth anniversary of Ben Ali's accession to power on 7 November 1987.

8. Bataille, *L'érotisme*, 15: "En effet, bien que l'activité érotique soit d'abord une exubérance de la vie, l'objet de cette recherche psychologique, indépendante, comme je l'ai dit, du souci de reproduction de la vie, n'est pas étranger à la mort." (Subsequent page numbers will be cited in the text.)

9. As I discuss below, it is significant, however, that the shots of Noura in the women's *hammam* at the end of the film are almost, but not exactly, the same as those we see at the beginning of the film.

10. Friedman, "Nostalgia, Nationhood, and the New Immigrant Narrative."

11. Cf. Charrad, "Cultural Diversity Within Islam," 66. As Simon Hawkins observes in "Hijab: Feminine Allure and Charm to Men in Tunis": "While hijab is commonly seen as a marker of modesty, in practice it is read in different ways depending on the form of the hijab, the age and social identity of the wearer, her behavior, the context in which it is worn, and the social identity of the viewer" (2). In this charming scene on Halfaouine Street, the veil is shown to be an important prop in the erotic game of revelation and concealment—a key element of Boughedir's theater of flirtation.

12. Friedman makes a remark about the "new immigrant," that we can say equally applies to Noura and what he represents: "As long as he remains marginalized, as long as he remains an outsider, as long as he resists assimilation, he remains nostalgic."

13. Dames, *Amnesiac Selves*, 12; quoted in Maureen McKnight, "'Scarcely in the Twilight of Liberty.'"

14. Stone McNeece, "La lettre envolée," 74–75.

15. The actual period of the film's setting is never stated, but as a vaguely autobiographical work, *Halfaouine* is engaged in a complex allegorical dialogue between the late 1960s/early 1970s (when Boughedir would already have been in his twenties) and the period of the film's making, the late 1980s.

16. Abderrezak, "*Halfaouine, l'enfant des terrasses*: L'individu-oiseau face à la communauté," 83 (emphasis in original). Subsequent page numbers will be cited in the text.

17. There is a (single, brief) gratuitous scene of female nudity in Michel Khleifi's first film, the Palestinian *Wedding in Galilee* (1987), in which the bride is stripped naked and ritually washed by her attendants prior to the wedding.

18. I think it is useful to include a comparison here with the nude, sexual frolic in Désiré Écaré's *Visages de femmes* (Ivory Coast, 1985), for the controversy surrounding the scene in Écaré's film is similar to the one triggered five years later by *Halfaouine*: Is the nudity gratuitous?

3. LAUGHTER IN THE DARK

Frank Ukadike, in *Black African Cinema*, carefully and sensitively considers the status of the ten-minute "love scene" in Écaré's film and wonders if its inclusion renders the film, in some sense, less "African." His analysis of the issues raised by the scene is one that can, in nearly all its particulars, be applied to the *hammam* scenes in *Halfaouine*, including his remark that: "Écaré may argue (but perhaps not publicly) that this love scene is only a ten-minute nude sequence tagged for export and thrown in for the titillation of his Western audiences" (221). Critics of Boughedir's film tend to focus more on Noura's age than on the female nudity, however. This perhaps represents a displacement (in the Freudian sense) of the trouble these scenes may cause, and also some sort of tacit acknowledgment of the Tunisian filmmaker's "right" to fight censorship and to make a claim for Tunisia's self-representation as a "modern" society. One of Ukadike's concluding remarks about Écaré's *Visages de femmes* might equally be applied to Boughedir's *Halfaouine*: "In a sense, Écaré can be seen irreducibly [*sic*] moving with the times by willingly applying [an] antitraditional posture to the analysis of modern Africa" (222).

19. As Hawkins notes in "Hijab: Feminine Allure and Charm to Men in Tunis," a group that catcalls at women (as we see Moncef and Mounir do at the beginning of the film), "while seeming to display desire, must also be seen as building homosociality" (2). Noura's entrée into the world of heterosexual men begins here, with his desire to be accepted by these older boys/young men as one of them.

20. Apter, "Harem: Scopic Regimes of Power/Phallic Law," in *Continental Drift*, 103. Subsequent page numbers will be cited in the text.

21. Spurr, "Eroticization: The Harems of the West," in *The Rhetoric of Empire*, 170.

22. In the film, the tale is not told in its entirety. I discuss below its function as a warning to Noura about the potential dangers to a child of adult sexuality.

23. Jarrod Hayes, "The Joy of Castration: Childhood Narratives and the Demise of Masculinity," in *Queer Nations*, 260. Subsequent page numbers will be cited in the text.

24. The conversation is reminiscent of a similar conversation in Boughedir's earliest surviving short film, the forty-three-minute *The Picnic* (1972). Boughedir's sketch seeks to reveal the relationship of Tunisians to their government by having each character assert his politics through a remark that must be interpreted allegorically. The national debate about Tunisian identity, particularly the question of how to respond to government abuses (of civil rights, etc.), is revealed in remarks inscribed in the following discourses: (1) violence; (2) nepotism/cronyism; (3) passive grumbling about the government; (4) football (i.e., acceptance of the ruling party); (5) *khubzism*; and (6) *mektoub*. For an analysis of this rhetorical strategy employed by Boughedir, see Lang, "*Le pique-nique*, Férid Boughedir et la 'tunisianité,'" 231–242.

25. It is a common mistake of Westerners to refer to an Arab medina as "the casbah." The casbah (more correctly: *kasbah*, from Arabic القصبة for "citadel") is the quarter of the city in which the citadel is located—the fortress and military barracks encircled by walls with gates. (The exception perhaps is Algiers, where the natives themselves generally refer to the pre-1830 city of Algiers as "the Kasbah.")

26. Rosello, *Postcolonial Hospitality*, 164. Subsequent page numbers will be cited in the text.

27. Fukuyama, *Trust: The Social Virtues and the Creation of Prosperity*, 26. Subsequent page numbers will be cited in the text.

28. In Tunisian Arabic, "Sidi" means "Master" or "Saint," depending on the context (but more often is just a term of respect for an elder): "For example, older conservative Tunisian women call their husbands 'Sidi,' not by first name; older conservative Tunisians (both men and women) call their older brothers 'Sidi,' especially when there is a large age difference between them. There are two female equivalents of 'Sidi': 'Lella,' when used in a social context, and 'Sayyeda,' when speaking about female saints, for example '(Es)-Sayyeda El-Manoubiyya.'" (www.absoluteastronomy.com/topics/Sidi.)

29. Khemaïs' reaction to Abdelwahab and Sadok's attempt to restrain him is possibly another hint of the sexual abuse it seems likely he suffered as a boy.

30. Karim/Karama refers to generosity, nobility of character.

31. We recall that when Ali is first introduced in the film, we see a ram belonging to Ali tethered to a post in front of his wine shop. The boys greet the ram warily, before handing their empty wine bottles to the shopkeeper. This surely is a subtle allusion by Boughedir—although the viewer will not make the connection until later—to the role Ali takes in his sexual relationships with boys.

32. Naccache, "Bourguiba et nous." Subsequent page numbers will be cited in the text.

33. A literal translation of this last sentence I think would not convey Naccache's meaning. The original reads: "Et pour rester, il te fallait aussi faire des choses, t'inscrire dans le processus dans lequel les Tunisiens se sont faits" (224).

34. Although Salih, for example, appears to be an alcoholic—a fact of which most of Halfaouine seems to be aware, and of which nearly everybody, except Sheikh Mokhtar and Khemaïs, would seem to be fondly forgiving—Salih sternly forbids Noura to drink alcohol. He may have a libertine philosophy of life, but he takes his moral responsibility as a role model for the boys very seriously; he understands the connection between (what we could call) good fathering in the private sphere and good governance in the public sphere.

35. Bouhdiba, "Aïcha, que faisait donc ton père l'ogre?" 152.

36. Norton, "Associational Life," 32.

37. Salih is no doubt named for the subversive, comic singer Salah Khemissi, who died in 1958 at the age of forty-six.

38. *Laughter in the Dark* was the first of Vladimir Nabokov's novels to appear in English. It begins thus: "Once upon a time there lived in Berlin, Germany, a man called Albinus. He was rich, respectable, happy; one day he abandoned his wife for the sake of a youthful mistress; he loved; was not loved; and his life ended in disaster. This is the whole of the story and we might have left it at that had there not been profit and pleasure in the telling; and although there is plenty of space on a gravestone to contain, bound in moss, the abridged version of a man's life, detail is always welcome." Whether or not we think Boughedir is making an allusion to Nabokov's novel, the title of Salih's new play is an inspired touch on several levels; and just as Nabokov's witty judgment is correct—that there is "profit and pleasure" to be derived from the detailed telling of the story of a man's life—so too can it be said that there is "profit and pleasure" (most especially if it offers a national allegory) to be derived from the telling of the story of a boy's coming-of-age in a working-class neighborhood in the old city of Tunis.

39. See note 7, where I quote Souhayr Belhassen on the "Bourguiba-Ben Ali practice of repression." Whether or not the director of *Halfaouine* in 1990 could already see where things

were going, or (accurately, as it turns out) predict that the new president would be as dictatorial as the old, Bourguiba's legacy of repression would quickly metastasize into a comprehensive system of social control under Ben Ali.

40. *BBC News Online*, 27 May 2002, 15:11 GMT 16:11 UK, "Win Confirms Tunisia Leader in Power," http://news.bbc.co.uk/2/hi/middle_east/2009011.stm.

41. CPJ, "Attacks on the Press in 2002."

42. In "Masculinities, Generations, and Cultural Transformation in Contemporary Tunisian Cinema," Martin Stollery notes that "*Halfaouine* is primarily concerned with the renegotiation of relationships between father figures and sons" (59) and rather optimistically believes the film affirms "the possibility for gradual cultural change through the blurring of distinctions between gendered spaces and between hegemonic and subordinate masculinities" (58). He correctly observes that, to a certain extent, "Salih inhabits a subordinate masculinity due to his unmarried status, his drinking, his musical and theatrical performances, his political views, and his air of playful immaturity which makes him a natural ally of Noura's" (58).

43. Cf. Sciolino, *La Seduction: How the French Play the Game of Life*. Sciolino acknowledges that there is much that is unlovable about France, but she also observes that "the French still imbue everything they do with a deep affection for sensuality, subtlety, mystery, and play.... In every arena of life they are determined to stave off the onslaught of decline and despair. They are devoted to the pursuit of pleasure and the need to be artful, exquisite, witty, and sensuous, all skills in the centuries-old game called seduction. But it is more than a game; it is an essential strategy for France's survival as a country of influence" (7).

4. Sexual Allegories of National Identity

1. Throughout this conversation, the male tourists who have sex with hustlers like Roufa are referred to as "horses." And later in the movie, when Roufa asks his kid brother if he knows where Fred lives, Roufa will refer to the Frenchman as "your horse." Auteurists may find this interesting, as horses that are freighted with symbolic meaning figure in other of Bouzid's films, most notably *The Golden Horseshoes* (1989) and *Clay Dolls* (2002). In *Sexuality in Islam*, Bouhdiba observes that "the sexual significance of circumcision cannot be in doubt" (182), and he sheds some light on the metaphorical meaning of the horse in the traditional song sung in Tunisia on the occasion of a boy's circumcision:

> You begin with circumcision and you end in marriage, and still your horse neighs in the forest.
> You begin with circumcision and you end in youth, and still your horse neighs among the bachelors.
> Let us call quickly for his mother, let us call quickly for his aunt, let them come quickly and throw money on the procreative rod. (183)

Bouhdiba asks: "What is this horse if not the 'procreative rod' (*'ammāra*) on which one asks the female relations to come and throw propitiatory money. The money must match this 'ammāra, which must be strengthened, prepared, maintained, glorified and protected from the evil eye" (183).

2. Mulvey, "Visual Pleasure and Narrative Cinema" [1975], in *Visual and Other Pleasures*, 16–17.

3. Roland Barthes, *Camera Lucida: Reflections on Photography*, 12 (capitalization of the word "Photograph" in original). Subsequent page numbers will be cited in the text.

4. As Bouzid's narrative unfolds, his attention shifts almost exclusively to the point of view of his Tunisian characters, Khomsa and Roufa—which is not necessarily to say that the film abandons the Frenchman's point of view or that the viewer is expected to see him entirely as the "other." Such are the mysteries and vagaries of identification in the film-viewing process that a filmmaker's control over whom or what the viewer identifies with (and when and how) must always remain partial, provisional, contested, and contradictory. Or, to put it another way: while the (skillful) filmmaker exercises considerable control over what the viewer will identify with *formally*, the filmmaker has less control over who and what the viewer will identify with *emotionally*. A film such as Clint Eastwood's *Letters from Iwo Jima* (2006), for example, about the Second World War Battle of Iwo Jima, from the perspective of the Japanese who fought it, rather proves—on several levels—that while there are values and emotional structures that might be universal (suggesting that it *is* possible to "know" the other), each man's other, finally, will always be his own. If the epistemological question of knowing the other is an impossible one, it is nevertheless a question that must be asked, for not only is it universal, but one that happens to be at the heart of the Orientalist debate.

5. Of course, the plaque is not really intended to serve as protection for the entire medina against the "evil eye," but rather for the inhabitants of the house only, and perhaps the neighborhood as well (i.e., any area that falls within its sightlines). Cf. Dundes, "Wet and Dry, the Evil Eye." It is interesting that in Turkey—which was the former heart of the Ottoman Empire, of which Tunisia was a province—talismans against the evil eye take the form of blue eyes, possibly for the reason that northern Europeans, unaware of local customs, are likely to break the taboo on staring at or praising the beauty of children. (See especially 119–120 of Dundes' essay for this interpretation of the meaning of the blue evil eye and of the "like against like" use of blue-eye amulets used in Turkey and surrounding areas.)

6. Since 1990, Germans have comprised the highest number of visitors to Tunisia (an estimated 1 million German tourists visited Tunisia in 1999), although the figures changed after the attacks on the World Trade Center in 2001 and the attack on a synagogue in Djerba in southern Tunisia in April 2003, in which 19 people, including 14 German tourists, were killed. A summary of trends following these attacks was available on ArabDataNet.com (June 2003): "Travel to Tunisia is dominated by Europeans: of the 5.39 million tourists who visited Tunisia in 2001, more than 3.6 million were from Europe (mainly Germany, Italy, France, and Spain). Of all Tunisia's visitors, Germans are the biggest spenders; German tourists alone provided 38 percent of total tourism revenues in 2001."

7. Hédi Khélil, *Sens/Jouissance: Tourisme, érotisme, argent dans deux fictions coloniales d'André Gide*, 11–12 (emphases in original). (Subsequent page numbers will be cited in the text.) Khélil's poetic syntax is decidedly "French" and appears to have been influenced by the writings of Roland Barthes.

4. SEXUAL ALLEGORIES OF NATIONAL IDENTITY

8. "Carnets d'Égypte" is a travel diary of no more than thirty pages that Gide began on 31 January 1939 and ended during the third week of March of the same year. The diary can be found in the Pléiade edition of Gide's *Œuvres Complètes*. It has never been published in English.

9. Khélil notes: "To avoid all ambiguity, 'Pederasty' in this study will always refer to its first meaning ('carnal relations with boys') and never to its broader meaning ('male homosexuality')" (28n10).

10. Khélil lists among the pioneering works of postcolonial studies: Albert Memmi's *Portrait du colonisé, précédé de: Portrait du colonisateur*; Frantz Fanon's *Les damnés de la terre* and *Peau noire, masques blancs*; Aimé Césaire's *Discours sur le colonialisme*; and Guy de Boschère's *Autopsie de la colonisation*.

11. Khélil writes: "[I am] a 'colonized' reader whose own desire is inevitably motivated by the desire of the tourist, in a country where tourism has become a big business, and where every day the hotel infrastructure becomes more entrenched and sophisticated, and where a whole repertoire of exotic imagery is sold by travel agencies, brochures, guides, postcards. Any fiction that I might produce—I, who have been 'colonized' in my own country—cannot avoid the tourist's gaze, of which one finds several examples in Gide's text" (126).

12. In the second-to-last sentence of this quotation—"La mener ainsi, n'est-ce pas l'engager dans une traversée toujours insatisfaite?"—the use of the word *traversée* perhaps intentionally echoes the title of the well known 1982 Tunisian film, *Traversées* (*Ubûr/Crossing Over*) by Mahmoud Ben Mahmoud, in which two travelers, a cultivated Arab and an Eastern European refugee, find themselves caught in an endless back-and-forth journey on a ferry that runs between Ostend and Dover, because neither the Belgian nor the British authorities will allow them to enter their respective territories. As Kamel Ben Ouanès observed in his 1991 review of the film in *Le Temps* (Tunis): "It would seem that Mahmoud Ben Mahmoud is saying that our world sees its ideals and its attempts at rapprochement between cultures and between nations come to grief on the rocks of an aborted humanity. The film takes for its premise that there are universal values, and then, from an anthropological perspective, interrogates this premise, examining the nature of human connexion, beyond ethnic and cultural differences, for it is at the frontier, in this no-man's-land *par excellence*, where man finds himself at once outside and in search of a partial-space [*espace-partie*], of an exile-space, or again, of a refuge-space where destiny not only toys with a couple of anonymous figures who have gone astray, but also with the logic of the history of our time, producing antagonisms and collisions between well-provisioned and prosperous nations and others that are underdeveloped and needy." (Quoted in Moumen Touti, *Films tunisiens: Longs métrages, 1967–1998*, 97.)

13. Emphases in original. These allusions, of course (Africa as *counterfeit*, etc.), are to Gide's novel, *The Counterfeiters*.

14. The familial identity of this male member of the household is never revealed. He is more or less Roufa's age, but unlike Roufa, who shows anger and frustration at his situation, this young man seems to be suffering from a paralyzing psychological depression. Not only is he associated with the caged bird he keeps in the courtyard, he is clearly shown to be an excessive drinker, perhaps even an alcoholic.

15. Rivet, *Le Maghreb à l'épreuve de la colonisation*, 303. Subsequent page numbers will be cited in the text.

16. It is interesting to note that Khomsa never speaks French to the Frenchman (except on one occasion, when she asks him where his wife is), although it is obvious that she understands his language. This is one of the ways in which Bouzid's allegory seeks to present her as an ostensibly "authentic" representative of a Tunisian culture that has remained untouched and untainted by colonialism. She is the repository of the values of the "conquered nationality."

17. Jacques Lacan, *The Seminar of Jacques Lacan, Book II*, 49.

18. The word he uses is *"triglia,"* an Italian word that has entered the Tunisian language, referring to a red mullet (*rouget*, in French), which in this context, is vaguely pejorative, as it is meant to describe the fair-skinned European whose complexion reddens in Tunisia's sunny climate.

19. The boy's Arabic nickname is "Nizq," which does not translate as Navette. Only once in the movie is he referred to as Navette, and it is the Frenchman who calls him this.

20. According to Islamic tradition, as mentioned earlier, it was not Isaac, but his brother Ishmael whom Abraham prepared for the sacrifice. (The stele represented on the cover of Krichen's book dates from the sixth century, which is why I refer to Abraham's son here as Isaac.) In any event, the lesson is as much about the necessity of man's submission to the God of his faith, as it is about his submission to the authority of the father.

21. The stele includes the "hand of God" that stops Abraham from going through with the sacrifice; and in the top, right-hand corner can be seen the ram caught in a thicket, which God, at the very last moment, provides as a substitute object for sacrifice. As recounted by Marshal Mirkin in "Reinterpreting the Binding of Isaac," according to the Bible, an angel interceded, saying: "Lay not thy hand upon the lad, neither do anything to him." The angel continues, saying: "For now I know that thou fearest God, seeing thou hast not withheld thy son, thy only son from me." After the angel speaks, Abraham looks up and sees a ram caught in a thicket.

22. Krichen, *Le syndrome Bourguiba*, 52.

23. Bouzid, *Sources of Inspiration*, 57.

24. Cf. Lang, *"Midnight Cowboy's* Backstory," in *Masculine Interests* (140–179), in which I examine the question of why Joe Buck, the hero of *Midnight Cowboy* (John Schlesinger, 1969), chooses to become a hustler. The real (as opposed to stated) reasons a person becomes a hustler are invariably complex and are often opaque to the hustler himself.

5. The Colonizer and the Colonized

1. Béji, *Désenchantement national*, 16.

2. As indicated earlier, the beys were not princes, although, following the French after 1881, the Tunisians liked to think of their ruling bey and his family as royal. Until the Ottoman Empire was dismantled in 1923, the Bey of Tunis was nominally the Ottoman-appointed governor of Tunisia, which was a province of the Ottoman Empire. On 20 March 1956, Lamine Bey proclaimed the independence of Tunisia and became King of Tunisia with the style of His Majesty. Prime Minister Bourguiba put the king under house arrest 15 July 1957, and on 25 July, the Tunisian Constituent Assembly deposed the king and abolished the monarchy.

5. THE COLONIZER AND THE COLONIZED

3. The title of the film in Arabic, صمت القصور (*Samt al-Qusur*), translates as: *The Silence of the Palaces* (not, as the French and English titles would have it: *Les silences du palais/The Silences of the Palace*), which far better suggests Tlatli's intention that the film reveal something about the status of women in Tunisia, or of Tunisians in general, and not just of the women in the palace of her story.

4. As any reader of French can see in the distinction between the masculine and feminine endings of the two nouns (a nuance lost in the English translation), Tlatli wishes to draw attention to the colonial character of the condition of women under (neo)patriarchy; moreover, the phrase—*la colonisée du colonisé*—is a reminder that in her society the men, too, were (are) colonized, i.e., they suffer the indignities and oppression of nonsovereignty and subalternity.

5. Moufida Tlatli in an interview with Bernard Génin for *Télérama* (32–33).

6. Memmi, *The Colonizer and the Colonized*, 155–156.

7. Hélène Cixous ("The Laugh of the Medusa"), quoted by Apter, *Continental Drift*, 98.

8. Adult Alia is played by Ghalia Lacroix and young Alia is played by Hend Sabri.

9. Moufida Tlatli, "Moving Bodies" (interview with Laura Mulvey), 18. Subsequent page numbers will be cited in the text. (See note 40 for my comment regarding Tlatli's reference to "Islamic society.")

10. Béji, *Désenchantement national*, 16. If the dreams and hopes that Tunisians had invested in the revolution had not been fulfilled, it was because, as Béji herself recognized, getting rid of the French was one thing and building a state after the French had left was another: "National consciousness as movement, and the nationalism of the State as fixity, have functions that are radically opposed to one another in terms of freedom" (18).

11. Hochberg, "National Allegories and the Emergence of Female Voice in Moufida Tlatli's *The Silences of the Palace*," 43.

12. Gauch, *Liberating Shahrazad*, 29. Subsequent page numbers will be cited in the text.

13. In its primordial form, Hisham Sharabi explains in *Neopatriarchy*, the structure of the (Arab) family is indistinguishable from that of the tribe; but "the emergence of the extended and nuclear family as distinct from the clan family, represents a fairly recent development which is linked to urbanization and class stratification" (25).

14. Sharabi, *Neopatriarchy*, 41. Subsequent page numbers will be cited in the text.

15. In the tradition of melodrama, Tlatli seeks a "happy ending" for her film (signaled by Alia's decision to give birth to her child). But as we know, Alia will have to wait until 14 January 2011 to see the fall of the neopatriarchal dictator in control of her country at the time of the film's making, when, once again, she will find herself standing poised on a threshold of hope for a better future for her sex and for her countrymen. (In a curious example of life imitating art, Tlatli would become Minister of Culture in the interim government that was formed after Ben Ali fled to Saudi Arabia—but she was replaced a few weeks later.)

16. Sharabi, *Neopatriarchy*, 18–19; Sharabi is quoting Marshall Berman, *All That Is Solid Melts into Air*, 109.

17. Sharabi writes: "Patronage, and the satisfaction of needs that goes with it, makes it easier for the individual to accept his or her condition. Although alienation is not wholly overcome, one has the sense of belonging in a system which affords one protection and bestows upon one an occasional favor" (46). We are reminded of a moment in the film when Sidi

5. THE COLONIZER AND THE COLONIZED

Bechir's lover, the servant Fella, enters the prince's room one evening and finds him sitting cross-legged on his bed, smoking, and playing Solitaire. She climbs onto the bed with him, sweeps the cards to one side, and asks him coquettishly: "Do you prefer your cards, or me?" She moves toward him on her knees, as he removes her apron and starts to unbutton her frock. "And my earrings?" she asks softly. "I haven't forgotten," he answers. "It's not the right time." (One wonders if Sidi Bechir enjoys stringing Fella along, endlessly delaying the granting of his favors, which more properly should be called "payments for services rendered.")

18. Perkins, *A History of Modern Tunisia*, 135. (Subsequent page numbers will be cited in the text.) For a comprehensive comparative history and analysis of women's rights in Tunisia, Algeria, and Morocco showing how the logic of Islamic legal codes and kin-based political power affect the position of women, see Mounira M. Charrad's landmark study: *States and Women's Rights: The Making of Postcolonial Tunisia, Algeria, and Morocco*. See also Marzouki, *Le mouvement des femmes en Tunisie au XXème siècle*; Brand, *Women, the State, and Political Liberalization*.

19. Bourguiba, quoted by Ben Youssef Zayzafoon, *The Production of the Muslim Woman*, 106. Subsequent page numbers will be cited in the text.

20. Incidentally, five years after *The Silences of the Palace* was filmed, some changes were made in the law concerning single mothers: "Unlike the PSC of 1956, which recognized the 'Tunisian woman's' rights only as mother and wife," Ben Youssef Zayzafoon notes, "Article 74 in the reforms of 1998 allowed the single mother to use a paternity test to sue the biological father for child alimony. However, the natural children are given the right to claim only the father's name. The single mother cannot use her own name to get welfare from the state" (127). While there has been some evolution in women's rights in Tunisia since the PSC of 1956, in certain areas that evolution still lags behind international law. Ben Youssef Zayzafoon notes that the (Tunisian) law of 5 April 1996, for example, allows spouses to have joint ownership of properties acquired after marriage; but "even today international laws regarding gender equality in inheritance and sexual orientation are not recognized in Tunisia because they are deemed incompatible with the 'country's religious and cultural heritage'" (ibid.).

21. I am not suggesting that Alia (or the emerging, independent Tunisia she represents in the allegory) would be "saved" if she simply jettisoned Arabic as her language of bureaucratic communication and formal discourse, and switched to French; for, as Sharabi writes:

> Since the end of World War II, tens of thousands of Arab students have studied abroad and managed to obtain advanced degrees in the sciences and the humanities. Yet it can be argued that these "educated" have remained unchanged in their basic intellectual and "linguistic" orientations, and have maintained, except for the acquisition of certain professional expertise, the outlook and mode of thought characteristic of their neopatriarchal upbringing and background—whether in conservative, reformist, or secular form. (118)

22. Sharabi, *Neopatriarchy*, 86. Sharabi is quoting from Barakat, *Al-Mujtama' al-'Arabi al-Mu'asir*, 246.

23. Mulvey, "Visual Pleasure and Narrative Cinema" [1975], in *Visual and Other Pleasures*, 14. Subsequent page numbers will be cited in the text.

5. THE COLONIZER AND THE COLONIZED

24. Mohamed Arkoun, quoted by Sharabi, *Neopatriarchy*, 108–109 (emphasis added).

25. Slawy-Sutton, "*Outremer* and *The Silences of the Palace*: Feminist Allegories of Two Countries in Transition," 86. Subsequent page numbers will be cited in the text.

26. The Ottomans were, of course, not colonizers in the same sense that the British or the French were in the nineteenth century—for one thing, the claims of racial superiority and the "*mission civilisatrice*" of the European powers were absent from Ottoman goals and practices—but for our purposes in this essay, the Bey of Tunis can be seen as a colonizer.

27. See Charles-André Julien, *Et la Tunisie devint indépendante . . . (1951–1957)*, especially 154–155, for a description of the contradiction, or gap, between Lamine Bey's power "en droit" and his actual power.

28. Moncef Bey did sympathize with the nationalists and attempted to challenge the French; and for this he was replaced in 1943. He died in exile in 1948.

29. Mulvey, in Tlatli, "Moving Bodies," 18.

30. Memmi, *The Colonizer and the Colonized*, xii. Subsequent page numbers will be cited in the text.

31. Mark Sinker, "*Les silences du palais (Saimt el qusur*/The Silences of the Palace)," 53.

32. Memmi, *Decolonization and the Decolonized*, 4.

33. Gauch is quoting from Tlatli, in her interview with Mulvey, in which the director says: "[Poetry] frequently had to make use of symbols and metaphors to express something that could not otherwise have been spoken. Poetry allows this: it gives a fantastic freedom. You only have to have a small amount of imagination to extract another meaning from the words" (Tlatli, "Moving Bodies," 18).

34. Hassan, "Alternatives to Secular Modernity." (This is the first sentence of Hassan's review, published in the e-journal *Jouvert: A Journal of Postcolonial Studies*.)

35. Despite being surprised by the sudden collapse of Ben Ali's regime, Middle East and North Africa scholars were in no doubt about the causes of its collapse and were ready with analyses the day after the ousted dictator's flight out of the country. Cf. Michele Penner Angrist, "Morning in Tunisia: The Frustrations of the Arab World Boil Over."

36. Berman, *All That Is Solid*, 109; quoted in Sharabi, *Neopatriarchy*, 18.

37. We perhaps already have the answer to this question in the lyrics of a song Alia sings early in the film. Sitting by herself in a storage room of the palace, accompanying herself on Sarra's lute, she sings: "*Do you think my heart could ever trust you again? / That a word could make me relive the past? / That a gaze could make me believe in passion and tenderness again? / Those were the good old days.*" (She turns to notice that Sidi Ali is outside the room, listening, and watching her through the glass door. He smiles at her and applauds her performance. She smiles radiantly back at him.) The song suggests that, although far from having been "washed in the icy water of egotistical calculation," Alia will at least start putting her devotion to Sidi Ali in perspective, i.e., she will—indeed, she must—try to understand the nature of his betrayal or else fall a victim to neurosis. The lyrics of the song are in effect an authorial intrusion by Tlatli, for they provide an extradiegetic commentary on the evolution and meaning of Alia's relationship to Sidi Ali of which Alia herself is not yet aware.

38. To be precise: Alia only learns of Sidi Ali's death after she has taken her bath; but the symbolic effect is the same: she and Lotfi are experiencing a crisis in their relationship—as

signaled by her declaration that, over Lotfi's objections, she will not abort her unborn baby, as she has done to terminate previous pregnancies; and by the shot in which we see a worried Lotfi (while she is taking her bath) go to the refrigerator in the kitchen, grab an opened bottle of wine, and drink compulsively from it, as he shoots a nervous glance in the direction of the bathroom.

39. Brahimi, *Cinémas d'Afrique francophone et du Maghreb*, 13–14.

40. Olivier Roy, in *Globalized Islam: The Search for a New Ummah*, argues that "the culturalist approach, which states: Islam is the issue," is irrelevant to the contemporary debate on Islam. He notes that "there is a constant confusion between Islam as a religion and 'Muslim culture' (if the expression makes sense, which I doubt). Islam as a religion comprises the Koran, the Sunnah and the commentaries of the *ulama*; Muslim or Islamic culture includes literature, traditions, sciences, social relationships, cuisine, historical and political paradigms, urban life, and so on. Such a culture is difficult to spot outside cultures based in certain historical eras or geographical regions. We tend to explain all the problems of the contemporary Muslim world in terms of Islam. The status of women, terrorism and the absence of democracy are analyzed in terms of 'Islamic culture or religion'" (10). (To be fair to Tlatli: despite her reference to "Islamic society" in her interview with Mulvey, she is referring to her own, particular Muslim culture and society—the Tunisia she has known and lived in, which she locates historically and geographically in her film—and it is her film that stands as her statement about women's status and subjective experience in the neopatriarchal society that is Tunisia. It is precisely because Tlatli is aware that a phrase like "Islamic society" hardly begins to describe, explain, or express what she is trying to say, that she is a filmmaker, and uses "symbols and metaphors to express something that could not otherwise have been spoken.")

41. I was present on the first day of shooting for *The Silences of the Palace* (28 November 1993, at Khaznadar Palace, in a suburb of Tunis), when this scene was shot. Watching Tlatli direct her first scene, I remember thinking that, to film a photographer taking a photograph—like photographing a character looking into a mirror—is already to step into a realm of representation that self-consciously contains its own allegory.

42. The ambiguity of the song is in no way diminished when we see elsewhere in the film an old woman (possibly a former servant) named Beya paying the servants a visit in the palace kitchen.

43. The blatant symbolism of the caged bird occurs throughout the New Tunisian Cinema, where too often it appears as a cliché. In this film, however—a melodrama—it seems, for once, appropriate.

44. Martin, "Silence and Scream: Moufida Tlatli's Cinematic Suite," 181.

45. Apter, *Continental Drift*, 99.

46. Interview with Moufida Tlatli by Hédi Khélil, in Khélil, ed., *Le parcours et la trace*, 202–203.

47. Mernissi, *Le harem et l'Occident*, 8.

48. Sherzer, "Remembrance of Things Past: *Les silences du palais* by Moufida Tlatli," 56.

49. Ella Shohat, "Framing Post-Third-Worldist Culture: Gender and Nation in Middle Eastern/North African Film and Video," *Jouvert: A Journal of Postcolonial Studies* 1, no. 1 (1997). A broader version of this essay, dealing with post–Third-Worldist feminist films from

5. THE COLONIZER AND THE COLONIZED

the Americas and Australia as well as from the Middle East and North Africa, appears as: "Post-Third-Worldist Culture: Gender, Nation, and the Cinema," in Alexander and Mohanty, *Feminist Genealogies, Colonial Legacies, Democratic Futures*, 183–209.

50. Gauch writes that "Alia now seems to discover that no father or husband can authorize her life narrative for her. Sidi Ali may have praised her singing, and Lotfi may have taught her to read and write, but neither man 'authored' Alia as her life with her mother did. Nor does either man really want to hear the story that Alia has to tell." Alia recognizes that she must redeem her mother's life, tell this story that "she has too long permitted society to ignore" (*Liberating Shahrazad*, 32–33).

51. Lobbying for her husband's reelection to the presidency in 2009 for a final term, for example, Leïla Ben Ali addressed a national conference on 9 August 2007 on "Le régime républicain et le rôle de la femme dans l'enracinement des valeurs de citoyenneté et le renforcement du processus de développement" ["The republican system and the role of the woman in anchoring the values of citizenship and reinforcing the process of development"]. According to an article by El Hadji Gorgui Wade Ndoye in the 28 August 2007 issue of *ContinentPremier.com* ("Magazine africain en ligne"), Mme. Ben Ali "seized this opportunity to galvanize the Tunisian woman, who, according to her, is the very symbol of contemporary Tunisian modernity." In her speech, Leïla Ben Ali said: "On the one hand, we are devoted to maintaining the close connection between the emancipation of the [Tunisian] woman and the improvement of the condition of the Tunisian family, and on the other hand, we are committed to the building of the modern state, consolidating the attributes of the Republic, and stimulating the process of modernization." Ndoye writes: "This correlation, according to Leïla Ben Ali, has been strengthened by the reformist zeal [of the state], the accumulated gains of the Tunisian woman, and the accomplishments achieved [by the state] to benefit [the Tunisian woman] since 'The Change' of 7 November 1987, the twentieth anniversary of which our people are about to celebrate with pride and joy. For her, 'The Tunisian woman today represents a luminous symbol of the modernity of our society, a well-anchored pillar of its authentic identity, a powerful bulwark for our civilization's secular values and principles, and an unassailable shield against extremism, fanaticism, and self-withdrawal in all its forms.'" (Ndoye, "Mme. Leïla Ben Ali Première Dame de Tunisie.")

6. "It takes two of us to discover truth"

1. Zran quotes only the first two sentences of the following: "Should you really open your eyes and see, you would behold your image in all images. And should you open your ears and listen, you would hear your own voice in all voices. It takes two of us to discover truth: one to utter it and one to understand it." I have taken part of the last phrase of Gibran's maxim for the title of this essay, because I think it is more revealing of how the film functions as an allegory of resistance. The portion of the maxim Zran uses as an epigraph for his film ("Should you really open your eyes and see . . . ") merely describes the experience of his character Amine, whose relationship with the "Other," in the final analysis, is solipsistic.

6. "IT TAKES TWO OF US TO DISCOVER TRUTH"

2. Kevin Anderson makes this observation in a short but pithy article ("Philosophic Dialogue: Marx's *Eighteenth Brumaire* Today") that he wrote in the December 2002 edition of the online magazine/newsletter, *News & Letters*: there are remarkable parallels between Anderson's analysis of how, "in France [Bonaparte's coup] ushered in nearly two decades of authoritarian rule, as the Bonapartist state became a precursor of twentieth century fascism, setting up the first modern police state," and how in Tunisia Ben Ali's 1987 coup ushered in more than two decades of authoritarian rule that transformed Tunisia into a modern police state. The basic similarity between Napoleon III and Ben Ali was their focus on the economy (what in Tunisia was called the "economic miracle"), which allowed the rich to get richer, and made the poor poorer. Both leaders blackmailed their citizens into accepting a state that policed them, by claiming that they were providing the "security" needed for the economy to flourish.

3. Memmi, *Decolonization and the Decolonized*, 10. Subsequent page numbers will be cited in the text.

4. Khélil, *Abécédaire du cinéma tunisien*, 133. Subsequent page numbers will be cited in the text.

5. Khélil writes: "Mais ces effets de reconnaissance d'un réquisitoire social au premier degré ne sont que des appeaux."

6. The epigraph that appears at the beginning of the film is given in French: "*Regardons-nous tels que nous sommes pour être mieux que nous sommes.*"

7. Person, *On Freud's "A Child Is Being Beaten"*, ix. Subsequent page numbers will be cited in the text.

8. Stora, "The Maghrib at the Dawn of the Twenty-first Century," 1.

9. In an interesting touch, Zran has Amine immediately surrounded by a group of small boys when he gets off the train at Essaïda. They are fighting each other with wooden swords, in a game of battle, and Amine becomes caught up in it. If, as Marx has it, history is fueled by class struggle, who or what is the enemy in this mini-allegory of Essaïda's embattled situation?

10. Hibou offers some astonishing statistics: There were between 80,000 and 133,000 police in Ben Ali's Tunisia, a country with approximately 10 million inhabitants. The ratio of police to citizens, thus, is somewhere between 1:67 and 1:112, while in France, the most policed country in Europe, the ratio is 1:265, and in the United Kingdom, it is 1:380.

11. It is worth noting, however, that unlike, say, Libya, Tunisia has no tribal system. But with Ben Ali's largely successful attempts to weaken civil society in Tunisia, it is perhaps not surprising that denizens of Tunis who are originally from elsewhere in the country—sometimes even when they are second- or third-generation inhabitants of the capital—will often claim a sentimental, or even decisive, allegiance to the town or region of their forebears. When I was involved in a car accident in Tunis and in need of a body shop, for example, my landlord—whose father had come to the capital from Djerba some fifty years earlier and retained no formal or even familial ties to the island—insisted I take my car to a Djerban to be fixed, even if we did not know the Djerban personally or by reputation. Speaking as though the Djerbans were a tribe, my landlord explained that, as a [Tunis-born] "Djerban" himself, he felt he could "trust" a Djerban more than he could someone with roots elsewhere. (See Christopher Alexander, "Authoritarianism and Civil Society in Tunisia" [1997], in which Alexander notes: "Ben Ali . . . worked diligently to break the tie between elite and popular politics that

6. "IT TAKES TWO OF US TO DISCOVER TRUTH"

was so vital in the 1970s and 1980s. Ill-equipped to play position politics, he has tried to ensure that 'civil society' remains unavailable as a political weapon.")

12. Kerrou, "Le *zaîm* comme individu unique," 235–248. Quoted in Hibou, *The Force of Obedience*, 306n2.

13. Sharabi, *Neopatriarchy*, 21. Subsequent page numbers will be cited in the text.

14. The portrait is very messy and frenzied in its execution. But the viewer, no doubt, is meant to see it as "art." On one occasion, we see Amine grunting and thrusting his pelvis toward a drawing mounted on his easel, as he scratches savagely at the paper with a stick of charcoal. The scene ends on a shot of Nidhal's puzzled, embarrassed face. The notion of artistic creativity as fueled by a form of sexual energy or libido is an ancient one; but it raises the question again of the nature of the relationship between the artist and his subject. Here it is figured as sexually predatory; a Marxian analysis might identify Nidhal, who belongs to the lumpenproletariat, as being exploited by a representative member of the bourgeoisie.

15. Janmohamed, "The Economy of Manichean Allegory," 20. Subsequent page numbers will be cited in the text.

16. The question of when, how, and why Tunisia's educated classes mix Arabic and French in their speech is a complex subject that is too large to explore here, although it is obvious in *Essaïda* that Amine and Sonia's unselfconscious use of French in their speech is an indicator of their Westernized education and social class. The reader is referred to the Tunisian scholar Mahmoud Dhaouadi's very interesting study of the phenomenon, in which he pays particular attention to the gender of the speakers and the role this factor plays in their reasons for "code-switching": *Globalization of the Other Underdevelopment: Third World Cultural Identities*.

17. Said, *Orientalism*, 1. Subsequent page numbers will be cited in the text.

18. Cf. Hannah Arendt on why "neither oppression nor exploitation as such is ever the main cause for resentment; wealth without visible function is much more intolerable because nobody can understand why it should be tolerated." She writes: "According to Tocqueville, the French people hated aristocrats about to lose their power more than it had ever hated them before, precisely because their rapid loss of real power was not accompanied by any considerable decline in their fortunes. As long as the aristocracy held vast powers of jurisdiction, they were not only tolerated but respected. When noblemen lost their privileges, among others their privilege to exploit and oppress, the people felt them to be parasites, without any real function in the rule of the country." (Hannah Arendt, *Antisemitism*, 4.)

19. The situation is even a little more complicated than this, because Sonia belongs to the nouveau-riche social class of Ben Ali's so-called economic revolution. She hopes to marry Amine (who has the same name as the last Bey of Tunis), a member of Tunisia's old aristocracy, and thereby secure her membership in the bourgeoisie. The relative ease with which Amine moves between Carthage and Essaïda is an indication of the class confidence he possesses, which Sonia lacks. (And it is probably not an accident of casting that Rostom's character is twice Sonia's age; it is perhaps a way of referring to the sociocultural gap that exists between the traditional elite and the new ruling class.)

20. Hibou, "Domination and Control in Tunisia," 198. Subsequent page numbers will be cited in the text.

21. Bentley, *The Life of the Drama*, 261.

22. This image of the abandoned factory is loaded with symbolic meanings; indeed, it will be incorporated into the film's final shots. In a healthy industrial-capitalist economy, we infer, such a factory would provide employment for the working class to which Nidhal belongs.

23. Memmi, "Going Abroad," in *Decolonization and the Decolonized*, 67. Subsequent page numbers will be cited in the text.

24. Hatem is played by Khaled Ksouri, who plays Farfat in Bouzid's *Man of Ashes* (1986). In *Man of Ashes*, he is kicked out of the house by his father, whereupon he resolves to leave Sfax and move to Tunis. There is a sense in which Hatem is the same (now deracinated, psychologically and ethically damaged) character, several years later.

25. I do not mean to suggest that the RCD was a criminal organization, although in many ways it did function like a mafia, even in its less malignant aspects. Hibou describes how the RCD cells, "scattered across the whole territory, within businesses and administrative offices, in urban districts and villages, are there to gather and reply to the population's requests. No ideological backdrop distorts this desire to include all segments of society. The RCD is a network of interests and clienteles that provides employment, grants, administrative facilities, aid of every kind, lodging, banking facilities, free cards for medical treatment and transport. Nothing is officially demanded in return, but people are drawn along by example and by a desire for effectiveness" (*The Force of Obedience*, 90). Needless to say, "belonging to the party is a very effective instrument, since it determines citizenship, or at least social and economic citizenship. It is difficult to carry out economic activities and to succeed—obtain grants, add an extra room to your offices, gain access to seeds for sowing, profit from a subsidized credit, benefit from postponed repayment deadlines—without going through the RCD" (ibid.). Hibou also describes the advantages of party membership as a means of social advancement: "The active members of the RCD are not members out of either conviction or ideology, but in the hope of advancing their own interests, obtaining something, giving voice to desires, expressing a grievance or an aspiration, resolving internal conflicts or, on the contrary, exacerbating confrontations between groups" (92).

26. Hibou, *The Force of Obedience*, 90. Subsequent page numbers will be cited in the text.

27. After Ben Ali's ouster in January 2011, it was estimated by Abdelrazek Kilani, president of the Tunisian Bar Association, that "about 100 judges are totally corrupt" and needed to be removed. "They took bribes and followed orders from the Ministry of Justice," Mr. Kilani said in an interview. "They convicted people because the ministry told them to." (Thomas Fuller, "Reform Lawyer Says Tunisia Risks Anarchy.")

28. The state party includes the state bureaucracy, which regulates "the whole of daily life and [imposes] its logic down to the smallest detail" (110).

29. Hibou gives the example of the manufacturer who was asked by the government to make a product locally that was needed by farmers and was being imported. The industrialist, despite a state-backed guarantee from a public bank (and believing himself protected by the law) said he could not manufacture the product, for financial and other reasons. The state responded by punishing him and driving him into bankruptcy. "There was nothing political in this affair," Hibou remarks. "Rather, what we have here is a totalitarian view of social life. In order to face an economic and social demand, and to avoid any aggravation in the deficit of the trade balance, all means are permitted, including abuses of power and the flagrant violation of

the law by the executive. And this conception does not concern merely major economic activities and social elites. The little greengrocer, the craftsman or shopkeeper can be the victims of injustice in the same way, quite simply because it is not the law which is imposed, but the law of whoever is the strongest in society" (119).

30. Foucault, quoted in Hibou, "Domination and Control in Tunisia," 202.

31. Hibou, *The Force of Obedience*, 119.

32. Bouzid first made this remark in 1995, in an interview with *L'Humanité* (Pierre Barbencey, "Nouri Bouzid: Une société fondée sur le viol").

33. Bouzid, *Sources of Inspiration*, 57. Subsequent page numbers will be cited in the text.

34. Khélil, *Abécédaire du cinéma tunisien*, 134. Subsequent page numbers will be cited in the text.

35. The allegory contained in Nidhal's funeral procession is uncertain, however (which perhaps goes to the heart of Khélil's complaint about the frequent inability of the film to transcend the level of "anecdote"). But when (it seems) all of Essaïda joins in the noisy funeral procession, we understand that Nidhal is being depicted as a *victim*—the victim of an unjust society in which the gap between rich and poor is wide. The scene need not be allegorical of anything, however. We can see it as simply what it is: the funeral procession of a boy who has died tragically. But the location of the boy's story in a particular place—which, moreover, gives its name to the title of the film—suggests, as Jameson would put it, that this story of a private individual destiny has been an allegory of the embattled situation of the public third-world culture and society. (There is a sense in which we can say that Nidhal's death, and the outpouring of anger and grief we see from the residents of Essaïda, are prescient of Mohamed Bouazizi's death in January 2011, which led to the ouster of Tunisia's president, by then the symbol of everything that is unjust and hurtful to the Nidhals and Mohamed Bouazizis of their society.)

36. As I have noted, Nidhal *intends* to commit suicide—or at least he says he intends to—but appears to change his mind after his father begs him to come down from the pylon.

37. The film is dedicated "*à la jeunesse de mon pays, à la jeunesse . . .*"

7. "It takes a lot of unruly individuals to make a free people"

1. Online New Zealand Arts Calendar: www.artscalendar.co.nz/event/17965 (retrieved 15 October 2005).

2. "Avec ce film d'espionnage informatique je m'adresse soi-disant à l'Occident alors qu'en fait je touche directement la société tunisienne." (Interview with Olivia Marsaud, "La Tunisie sans tabous: *Bedwin Hacker* de Nadia El Fani.")

3. John Tomlinson, *Globalization and Culture*, 2. (Subsequent page numbers will be cited in the text.) For the reader interested in a statistical analysis of the globalization phenomenon and where Tunisia stands in relation to 208 other countries of the world, the KOF Index of Globalization is as good a place as any to start (KOF Swiss Economic Institute, Zurich, Switzerland; http://globalization.kof.ethz.ch; accessed 2 October 2009). The 2009 KOF Index of Globalization ranks France 1 and Tunisia 34 in the Political Globalization category. For the

degree of Social Globalization, France ranks 28 and Tunisia ranks 103. For the degree of Economic Globalization, France ranks 35 and Tunisia 66. For the overall degree of globalization in 2009, France ranks 16 and Tunisia ranks 64. Space limitations do not permit a description here of the KOF Index's methods of calculation, interesting and informative though these methods are. Briefly, however: the KOF index defines *economic globalization* as characterized by long-distance flows of goods, capital, and services, as well as information and perceptions that accompany market exchanges. *Political globalization* is characterized by a diffusion of government policies. And *social globalization* is expressed as the spread of ideas, information, images, and people. (See http://globalization.kof.ethz.ch/static/pdf/method_2009.pdf.)

4. Bauman, *Globalization*, 70. (Subsequent page numbers will be cited in the text.) The symbols of who or what represents these globalizing processes vary, but all tend to derive from the same image, which is summarized by Ella Shohat and Robert Stam in their description of "world systems theory" as: "a hierarchical global system controlled by metropolitan capitalist countries and their multinational corporations [that] simultaneously generates both the wealth of the First World and the poverty of the Third World as the opposite faces of the same coin" (Shohat and Stam, *Unthinking Eurocentrism*, 17). Protestors have long understood the character of this coin and know that their adversaries have vastly superior resources at their disposal—that the warfare between them is "asymmetrical"—and so they increasingly resort to guerrilla tactics, as did Selçuk Özbek, a student at Anadolu University in Turkey, when, on 1 October 2009, he threw a white sneaker at Dominique Strauss-Kahn, the managing director of the International Monetary Fund, shouting: "Get out of the university, I.M.F. thief!" (Strauss-Kahn filed no official complaint, and the student was freed by the police later in the evening.) According to the *New York Times* report of the incident, Mr. Özbek told NTV in a live broadcast: "I think this is how global capital should be welcomed wherever it goes. The anti-imperialist youth of any country responsible for their future should act this way." (Mr. Özbek said his shoe was returned to him after his protest.) (Arsu, "Another Shoe Flies, This Time in Istanbul at I.M.F. Chief.")

5. Pun intended (Julia seeks to *arrest* her adversary): Kalt's "freedom" is represented by her mobility; and Julia wants her imprisoned. (If Kalt is caught, Julia tells her lover Chams, "she's looking at twenty years.")

6. Kalt is not actually Kmar's aunt, although the girl reflexively calls her "auntie" (until Kalt is able to cure her of the habit). The unconventional familial arrangements depicted in the film are part of the film's critique of the neopatriarchy and its reflection/inscription in Tunisia's political structure (i.e., the president as an oppressively paternalistic/neopatriarchal figure committed to safeguarding and perpetuating his repressive regime).

7. Ghannouchi, "Interview with Rached Ghannouchi, Nahdha Chairman." Ghannouchi, who lived in exile in London until the uprising in 2011 and Ben Ali's sudden departure allowed him to return to Tunis, was the leader of the unauthorized Islamist opposition political party Ennahdha in Ben Ali's Tunisia.

8. I am well aware that the reader may be wondering why I would draw this parallel between El Fani's project and that of Rached Ghannouchi, given that Ghannouchi is the leader of Ennahdha, whose vision of a post–Ben Ali Tunisia has been revealed to be profoundly at odds with the one for which El Fani and the filmmakers of the New Tunisian Cinema are

7. IT TAKES A LOT OF UNRULY INDIVIDUALS

fighting. What is striking is that *before* he came to power, Ghannouchi's rhetoric was not unlike that of the secularists. For El Fani's view of Ghannouchi's record as an active leader in Tunisia's politics after Ben Ali's downfall, see Nadia El Fani, "'En politique, ce n'est pas grave de perdre'" (interview by Olivier Barlet about *Laïcité inch'Allah*), and El Fani's contribution to a roundtable discussion held at the *Festival des cinémas d'Afrique* in Apt, France, in November 2011): Olivier Barlet et al., "Cinéma et révolution."

9. "Interview with Rached Ghannouchi, Nahdha Chairman." I infer that the Bedwin Hacker's political agenda is similar to that of Ennahdha (at least, as it is described here by Ghannouchi), although the film offers no actual evidence that it is specifically concerned, for example, with the "issue" of the "lower social classes," and it steers clear of anything even remotely Islamist. In the character of Mourad, moreover, who is writing a Ph.D. dissertation about non-Islamic religious beliefs and practices in Tunisia, the film unambiguously endorses religious freedom (and by implication, the separation of powers, i.e., that religion should stay out of the public sphere). Ghannouchi, who is said to represent a progressive strain in Islamic reformism and has written several books on the subject, is (perhaps only) like the Bedwin Hacker in his belief in the need for "innovation against social injustice" and in "the importance of local culture." (Cf. http://en.wikipedia.org/wiki/Rashid_Al-Ghannushi. Accessed 16 March 2010.)

10. "Interview with Rached Ghannouchi, Nahdha Chairman."

11. It needs to be reiterated here that Julia represents the state: on the higher-allegorical level, she represents the Tunisian state; and on the conventional narrative-allegorical level, she represents the French state.

12. Bernanos, *Les enfants humiliés: Journal 1939–1940*, 77. What Uncle Salah actually says to Chams—in a slight alteration of Bernanos' text by El Fani—is: "Il faut beaucoup de jeunes fous pour faire un peuple libre" ("It takes a lot of crazy youth to make a free people").

13. Mehdi and his wife are still friends, but we infer that he and Frida no longer live under the same roof (or never for very long). Frida is bored by village life and admits to Kalt that she no longer loves her husband.

14. The great Tunisian filmmaker, Abdellatif Ben Ammar, once used almost exactly this phrase to explain why he made his film, *Une si simple histoire* (1970): "[In that film] I was preoccupied with the Other's perspective on us. My concern was to say to the foreigner: 'We are not what you think. We have our own civilization and our own identity'" (Ben Ammar, "Putting Forward a Clear View on Life," 113). The interview originally appeared in: Berrah et al., eds., *CinémAction* 14, "Cinémas du Maghreb."

15. Shohat and Stam, *Unthinking Eurocentrism*, 2. Subsequent page numbers will be cited in the text.

16. This question of *point of view* is always complex in the cinema. One can look at the film from a "Western" perspective (in which case, it is legitimate to say: "Kalt represents one of Europe's internal and external 'others'"); but when we share Kalt's point of view, we can say—with caveats of all kinds—that "Julia represents Europe's historically oppressive relation to this 'other.'" But even this representation of how identification and point of view work in *Bedwin Hacker* is inadequate, not to say simplistic. Most mainstream films use a certain number of the conventions of melodrama (e.g., El Fani, describes *Bedwin Hacker* as a "cyber-spy movie"), but viewers understand that melodrama's binary vision—like the "self" versus "other" structure

we see deployed in *Bedwin Hacker*—is nearly always inflected by dialectical operations of narration and reading, which give the films their interest.

17. Jameson, "Third-World Literature in the Era of Multinational Capitalism," 69. I of course agree with Shohat and Stam that Jameson's "totalization" of all third-world texts in his argument (i.e., that in third-world texts, the story of the private individual's destiny is *always* an allegory) is a gross generalization. ("It is impossible to posit any single artistic strategy as uniquely appropriate to the cultural productions of an entity as heterogeneous as the 'Third World,'" Shohat and Stam write. "And allegory is in any case relevant to cultural productions elsewhere, including those of the First World" [271].) Nevertheless, *Bedwin Hacker* is clearly an allegory in which Kalt represents not only Tunisia but also a transnational "nation" of the First World/Europe's internal and external "others."

18. Mohamed Bensalah, *Cinéma en Méditerranée*, 17. Bensalah goes on to ask rhetorically: "With these conditions, how can we be surprised by the sterility of the North/South dialogue, which would appear to be taking place in a hall of distorting mirrors? It is a dialogue between stereotypes deeply etched in the cultures by history" (18).

19. Jonathan Friedman, quoted by Bauman, *Globalization*, 100. Nearly everyone in Kalt's immediate circle occupies this "global, culturally hybrid, elite sphere." For example, Uncle Salah is a poet, Frida is an international singing star, Mourad is an academic, Chams is a journalist, and so on. But her message, through the Bedwin Hacker, is to all victims of state repression and the injustices of globalization.

20. In making Frida an Algerian national—and beginning the film with her arrest by the Paris police for not having a valid French visa—*Bedwin Hacker* is no doubt alluding to the uniquely conflicted relationship between France and Algeria, which dates at least from the time of Algerian War and the colony's independence from France in 1962, which brought to a head the confusion surrounding the question of who qualified as "French" when it came to (re)patriation in metropolitan France. (Frida's character, incidentally, might be very slightly confusing to some Maghrebi viewers, because the Tunisian actress who plays her was never able to master an Algerian accent for the role.)

21. Hakim Bey, quoted by Taggart, "The Digital Revolt."

22. Martin, "Transvergence and Cultural Detours: Nadia El Fani's *Bedwin Hacker* (2002)," 123. Subsequent page numbers will be cited in the text.

23. Bivona, "'Si vous n'aimez pas le bruit des bottes, portez des babouches!': Subversion, liberté et modernité dans le film *Bedwin hacker* de Nadia El Fani," 33–34.

24. The most famous of these, following the new, 2003 anti-terrorist legislation, were the young men arrested in the towns of Zarzis and Ariana. They were known respectively as the Youth of Zarzis (or the Internautes de Zarzis) and the Youth of Ariana. Cf. http://campaigns.ifex.org/tmg/prisoners.html; and the "Reporters sans frontières" report on the Internet in Tunisia: www.rsf.org/article.php3?id_article=10768 (retrieved 15 October 2005).

25. My statistics for this section on the Internet in Tunisia come from the International Fact-Finding Mission's *Report*, published in May 2005, on "Tunisia and the World Summit on the Information Society" (WSIS). The first phase of WSIS, which took place in Geneva from 10 to 12 December 2003 and was hosted by the government of Switzerland, involved 175 countries adopting a "Declaration of Principles and Plan of Action." The second phase took

place, quite absurdly, in Tunis, hosted by the government of Tunisia, from 12 to 18 November 2005. Following the first phase of preliminary meetings, three international NGOs, the International Centre for Human Rights and Democratic Development, the International Federation for Human Rights (La Fédération Internationale des ligues des droits de l'Homme), and the World Organization Against Torture (L'Organisation mondiale contre la torture), with the support of the Human Rights Caucus (composed of more than sixty NGOs participating in the WSIS), appointed a team of three experts in the new information technologies, the media, and human rights to undertake an investigation and dialogue mission in preparation for the second phase of the summit.

In "Repossessing the Dispossessed," Laryssa Chomiak and Robert P. Parks observe: "Even though Internet usage in Tunisia increased from six percent in 2003 to thirty-six percent in 2010, the International Telecommunications Union reports that fewer than forty percent of Tunisians accessed the internet in 2011."

26. According to the 2005 International Fact-Finding Mission's *Report*, there was a "total lack of trust" on the part of users of the Internet in Tunisia. For example, six out of seven Internet users "[had] no faith in the Tunisian ISPs" (12).

27. "What Do Barbara Streisand and the Tunisian president, Zine el-Abidine Ben Ali, Have in Common?" So, intriguingly, begins a short article in the 28 June–4 July 2008 issue of *The Economist*, "Blog Standard: Authoritarian governments can lock up bloggers. It is harder to outwit them." (The answer to this question is that Streisand and Ben Ali both tried to block material they disliked from appearing on the Internet.) The article goes on to explain: "In November 2007 Tunisia blocked access to the popular video-sharing sites YouTube and Dailymotion, which both carried material about Tunisian political prisoners. It was not for the first time, and many other countries have blocked access to such sites, either to protect public morals, or to spare politicians' blushes. What was unusual this time was the response. Tunisian activists and their allies organized a 'digital sit-in,' linking dozens of videos about civil liberties to the image of the presidential palace in Google Earth. That turned a low-key human-rights story into a fashionable global campaign" (67).

28. Rosello, *Postcolonial Hospitality*, 182n7. Subsequent page numbers will be cited in the text.

29. Charles Pasqua, Minister of the Interior from 1986 to 1988 and again from 1993 to 1995, gave his name to the 1986 law that restricts residency conditions in France and facilitates expulsions, and to the controversial 1993 reform that defines nationality law. (On 11 May 1987, Pasqua announced: "Some have reproached me for having used a plane, but if necessary I will use trains.") With the first Pasqua law in 1986, a child born in France of foreign parents can only acquire French nationality if, between the ages of sixteen and twenty-one, he or she demonstrates his or her will to do so by proving that he or she has been schooled in France and has a sufficient command of the French language. The regularization of the status of undocumented aliens was made more difficult (as were residency conditions for foreigners in general, as a consequence) by the second Pasqua law on "immigration control." And on 2 June 1993, Pasqua told *Le Monde*: "France has been a country of immigration; it doesn't want to be one anymore. Our aim, taking into account the difficulties of the economic situation, is to tend toward 'zero immigration'" ("L'objectif que nous nous assignons, compte tenu de la gravité de la situation économique, c'est de tendre vers une immigration zéro").

7. IT TAKES A LOT OF UNRULY INDIVIDUALS

30. As Leon S. Roudiez, the American translator of Kristeva's *Strangers to Ourselves*, points out, "the French title, *Étrangers à nous-mêmes* is more allusive as there is only one word in French to convey the meanings of four in English: foreigner, stranger, outsider, alien" (99n9).

31. Julia Kristeva, *Lettre ouverte à Harlem Désir* (Paris: Rivages, 1990). Harlem Désir (born 25 November 1959, in Paris), a French politician and Member of the European Parliament for the Île-de-France, was the first president (1984–1992) of the French antiracist organization, SOS Racisme.

32. To be faithful to the nuances of her argument, I must note that Kristeva writes as a foreigner and a cosmopolitan, i.e., from a position that—as she herself acknowledges—is "atopic (foreignness) and utopic (a concord of people without foreigners, hence without nations)." She does so "as a means to stimulate and update the discussion on the meaning of the 'national' today. For [she is] convinced that contemporary French and European history, and even more so that of the rest of the world, imposes, for a *long while*, the necessity to think of the *nation* in terms of new, flexible concepts because it is within and through the nation that the economic, political, and cultural future of the coming century will be played out" (Kristeva, *Nations Without Nationalism*, 50; emphasis in original).

The necessity of thinking of the nation in terms of new, flexible concepts was highlighted by the reaction in France to the discovery that the perpetrator of the "Toulouse and Montauban shootings" in March 2012—a series of three gun attacks targeting French soldiers and Jewish civilians, in which a total of seven people were killed, and five others injured—was 23-year-old Mohammed Merah, a native son of Algerian descent. In a *New York Times* editorial, "Who Gets to Be French?," Karl E. Meyer reported that four members of Parliament belonging to President Nicholas Sarkozy's center-right party issued a joint statement in which they insisted that Mr. Merah "had nothing French about him but his identity papers." The left-wing newspaper *Libération* retorted: "Merah is certainly a monster, but he was a French monster." A childhood friend of Mr. Merah elaborated: "Our passports may say that we are French, but we don't feel French because we were never accepted here. No one can excuse what he did, but he is a product of French society, of the feeling that he had no hope and nothing to lose. It was not Al Qaeda that created Mohammed Merah. It was France." Meyer writes that these opposing approaches to what it means to be French—one rooted in an uncompromising ideal of assimilation, the other grounded in the messy realities of multiculturalism—struck a chord with him. President Sarkozy articulated the exclusionists' position in 2011, when he said: "If you come to France, you accept to melt into a single community, which is the national community, and if you do not want to accept that, you are not welcome in France. We have been too concerned with the identity of the person who was arriving, and not enough about the identity of the country that was receiving him." And yet France today has Europe's largest Islamic minority, making up nearly 10 percent of its population, and Muslims remain a people apart. As a researcher for the Open Society Institute put it: "In France, you can be of any descent, but if you are a French citizen you cannot be an Arab." Composite identities such as Arab–French are, he added, "ideologically impossible." (Meyer, "Who Gets to Be French?")

33. Kristeva, *Nations Without Nationalism*, 54. Subsequent page numbers will cited in the text; emphases in original throughout.

34. For a short article clarifying some of these issues, especially as they apply to Chams's character (who seeks individual freedom but still feels the tug represented by Kalt, who militates for the freedom of the group), see Fukuyama, "Identity and Migration." Echoing Olivier Roy in his 2004 book, *Globalized Islam*, Fukuyama notes that the question of identity does not come up at all in traditional Muslim societies, but it becomes problematic precisely when Muslims leave traditional Muslim societies by, for instance, emigrating to Western Europe: "One's identity as a Muslim is no longer supported by the outside society; indeed, there is strong pressure to conform to the West's prevailing cultural norms. The question of authenticity arises in a way that it never did in the traditional society, since there is now a gap between one's inner identity as a Muslim and one's behavior vis-à-vis the surrounding society." Modern liberal societies, especially in Europe, have weak collective identities, Fukuyama observes. Their elites feel that they have evolved beyond identities defined by religion and nation. Chams, who is resident in France and has been largely shaped by his upbringing there, feels caught between conflicting paradigms of identity politics. Modern identity politics, Fukuyama tells us, springs from a hole in the political theory underlying liberal democracy: "That hole is liberalism's silence about the place and significance of groups." Modern political theory "understands the issue of political freedom as one that pits the state against individuals rather than groups."

35. Hayes, *Queer Nations*, 2. Subsequent page numbers will be cited in the text.

36. When Abdellatif Ben Ammar was asked by his *CinémAction* interviewer, "Why are your heroes always orphans?," he replied: "Perhaps to get them out of the dominance of the family. So they can be free to develop in the direction they wish, on their own, and not under pressure" (Ben Ammar, "Putting Forward a Clear View on Life," 113).

37. Georg Henrik von Wright (1997), quoted in Bauman, *Globalization*, 57.

38. Cf. McClintock, *Imperial Leather*; Stoler, *Carnal Knowledge and Imperial Power*.

39. The Tunisian motto, inscribed in the national Constitution, is: "Liberty, Order, Justice."

40. In the late eighteenth century, the English philosopher and social theorist Jeremy Bentham designed a type of building he called a Panopticon, a circular structure with an "inspection house" at its center that would allow the managers or staff of an institution (such as a hospital, school, poorhouse, asylum for the mentally ill, or prison) to observe inmates, without the inmates being able to tell whether or not they are being watched.

41. It is interesting to note that, as long ago as 1981, Abdellatif Ben Ammar, who directed the revolutionary, nationalist film *Sejnane* (1973), was already fearful of the consumerist trend he saw in his society, which he feels inhibits and undermines the ability to analyze the roots of repression and the will to resist: "The new generation, the ones with hope for the future, have taken a path which worries me. Their sole preoccupation is with consuming. The Tunisian middle class is accumulating domestic electrical appliances. Daily life is not enough for [them], [they] add gadgets: mixers, TV" (Ben Ammar, "Putting Forward a Clear View on Life," 114).

42. But see Bryan Turner's apparent refutation of this assertion in his remarks about modernization, which I shall quote again in chapter 8: Modernization is about "the conditions which give rise to the abstract citizen." It is "the triumph of global over local culture" (Turner, *Orientalism, Postmodernism and Globalism*, 136).

43. Anthony Smith (*National Identity*, 157), quoted by Tomlinson, *Globalization and Culture*, 100.

44. Smith, quoted by Tomlinson, *Globalization and Culture*, 101.

45. Tomlinson (quoting Iris Marion Young), *Globalization and Culture*, 157.

46. The (barely audible) French original—"*C'est toujours la même chose!*"—contains an ambiguity that an English translation does not allow. Is Kalt observing that, to open his computer, Chams uses the same password he uses to connect to the press agency? ("It's still the same [password]!") Or is she saying: "[With men like Chams] it's always the same thing!"? Julia will later inform Chams: "Did [Kalt] tell you she went on the Chaos Computer Club site, and since then you're on file? She used your code to connect to the Press Agency." Perhaps, merely, the viewer is meant to accept the film's cyber-logic as he or she would the "science" of science fiction movies, and Kalt's remark is meant to be taken as the explanation of how she figures out Chams's password.

47. The Chaos Computer Club (CCC), an organization of hackers, is the second-largest human-rights technology group in the world (after the San Francisco–based Electronic Frontier Foundation, a nonprofit digital rights advocacy and legal organization). The CCC was founded in Berlin in 1981, has about 4,000 members, and remains based in Germany. It should not be confused with the Chaos Computer Club France (CCCF), a fake hacker organization created in Lyon in 1989 by Jean-Bernard Condat, at the behest of the DST, to watch and to gather information about the French hacker community. (It is logical to assume, however, that Julia is referring to the CCCF.)

48. Bivona, "'Si vous n'aimez pas le bruit des bottes portez des babouches!': Subversion, liberté et modernité dans le film *Bedwin hacker* de Nadia El Fani," 36. My translation does not do justice to the French original (with its several, and finally untranslatable, meanings of "*fragile*"), which reads as follows: "Chams, ce garçon fragile dans ses sentiments, sa nationalité, son travail, ses capacités de discernement. Il est incapable de comprendre la vraie raison de son séjour en Tunisie, et de le dire à Julia et à Kalt, car le but de son voyage n'est autre que Bedwin Hacker, encore et toujours, ce visionnaire d'une époque, qui est en train de naître dans le glouglou des images télévisées."

49. www.footagefarm.com/truman.html (retrieved 25 October 2005).

50. "À ma grand-mère, 'Bibi,' qui m'inspire toujours le courage de résister. . . . " (Written also in Arabic.)

51. The film may discourage a literal-minded interpretation of its allegorical strategies, but at first I nevertheless had my own, preferred (and literal-minded) interpretation of Kalt's warning at the beginning of the film about the presence of "enemies": I understood her to be referring to enemies on Tunisia's cartographical left and right. On the one side, there was the political and cultural near-chaos of Algeria; and on the other, was the eccentric and authoritarian regime of Libya's charismatic leader, Muammar Qadhafi. The enemy "behind" was a reference perhaps either to the assorted ills of Africa (to the south) or to the predatory, capitalist-hegemonic tendencies of Europe (to the north).

But in her more careful reading of the scene, in her chapter devoted to the film in *Screens and Veils: Maghrebi Women's Cinema*, Florence Martin points out that in the same moment in which we hear the French-speaking female voice announcing "enemy on the right" (and then, "enemy on the left," and a moment later, "Careful—there is one in the back"), we see a cartoon camel leap from the right and superimpose itself on the television image (and then the same camel appears suddenly from the left, and a moment later, it emerges in the center of the screen, seemingly from the back). Clearly—as Martin suggests—the Bedwin Hacker's warning (albeit playfully and ironically conveyed) is to those still stuck in the mind-set of the Cold War era: "Here, the new colorful cartoon literally shakes up the old black-and-white vision of the Cold War era and suggests a radical change" (136).

52. Website of the Tennessee Valley Authority. "The Father of Public Power." www.tva.gov/heritage/lilienthal (accessed 25 October 2005).

8. Inventing the Postcolonial Nation/Constructing a Usable Past

1. For the sake of convenience, throughout this chapter I shall refer to the group of research scientists—who properly speaking constitute neither a company nor a television crew—as the "German television company."

2. The radio reporter will become the narrator of the short film the residents of El Malga decide to make (we infer that it will be what the French call a *"making of"*—a documentary about the preparations for the pageant—for we do not see the completed film, nor any of the footage shot by Ingrid, the German wife of the artist Kafza). Shooting begins with the reporter looking into the camera and saying: "Free men of the world, peoples of the civilized West: We know that you are living in the era of speed, and that you don't have the time to explore all our accomplishments. This is why we have taken the initiative of preparing a little film, as a sign of fraternity between our peoples: to give you an idea of what we have accomplished in the very short time since independence."

3. Van Wyck Brooks, "On Creating a Usable Past"; Eric Hobsbawm, "Introduction: Inventing Traditions."

4. Hazbun, "Images of Openness, Spaces of Control," 27. Subsequent page numbers will be cited in the text.

5. Pierre Nora, ed., *Les lieux de mémoire*. In this work of historiography about France (translated by Arthur Goldhammer for the 1996 Columbia University Press edition, *Realms of Memory: The Construction of the French Past*, edited by Lawrence D. Kritzman), Nora explains that he and his team of contributors sought to "institute a symbolic history better suited than traditional history to the civic as well as intellectual needs of our time" (xviii). "The point of departure, the original idea," he writes, "was to study national feeling . . . by analyzing the places in which the collective heritage of France was crystallized, the principal *lieux*, in all the senses of the word, in which collective memory was rooted, in order to create a vast topology of French symbolism" (xv). Subsequent page numbers from the English-language edition will be cited in the text.

6. Ayed is their handyman. He is a municipal employee and does odd jobs for the committee—everything from being the driver of the municipal minivan, to making tea for the committee during meetings.

7. Throughout the Maghreb, *"fantasia"* (or لعب البارود/*laâb el baroud*: "game of gunpowder") involves the celebratory galloping of horses and shooting of guns in the air, with the riders

decked out in traditional Bedouin garb. This equestrian performance, which nowadays is considered a cultural art and a form of martial art, is sometimes still organized to conclude the festivities of a traditional Berber wedding. *Fantasia* is essentially the theatricalized repetition of two cavalry movements during wartime: the rapid charge and the sudden retreat. In Morocco especially, and frequently as a tourist attraction, *fantasia* is practiced during local seasonal, cultural, or religious festivals.

8. Driss Abbassi, citing Stephen Benedict ("Tunisie, le mirage de l'État fort"), notes in *Quand la Tunisie s'invente* that Tunisia's youth do not first identify themselves as "Mediterranean," as Ben Ali's regime might have wished; nor, for the most part (as perhaps did previous generations), do they think of colonization and the struggle for independence as the starting point in the enterprise of constructing a national identity. Contemporary Tunisian youth think of themselves first as Muslims and Arabs and are "preoccupied with the Palestinian cause and the Gulf War and its prolongations" (130).

9. Of course, it makes no sense in a one-party state to talk about legal opposition to the ruling party. Like most dictatorships, Tunisia under Ben Ali was not officially a one-party state, but for all intents and purposes it was, and opposition parties had a phantom reality; they existed in a twilight zone between irrelevance and the preservation of the *idea* of democracy. The paradox, or irony—not to make too fine a point—is that the "law" of an authoritarian government is, in the final analysis, whatever the authoritarian government says it is on any given day or in any given circumstance. If the law (inscribed in the Constitution, for example, and embodied in the Supreme Court) is routinely subverted to serve the interests of the dictator, his family, cronies or class, then Salem would be right—there would be "no point" in trying to exercise one's right of opposition.

10. "Destiny answers the people's call for life, darkness will be dispelled, and chains will break," is my own preferred translation (by David Bond, of the Institut des belles-lettres arabes in Tunis) of the last two lines of the Tunisian national anthem, "Humat Al-Hima"/ "Defenders of the Homeland" (revised in 1987), written by Mustafa Sadiq Al-Rafi'i, incorporating lyrics by Aboulkacem Chebbi. A widely repeated version in unidiomatic English of these lines from the chorus is: "If one day, a people desires to live, then fate will answer their call, and their night will then begin to fade, and their chains break and fall." (Cf. Shadid, "Yearning for Respect, Arabs Find a Voice.") For an analysis of Chebbi's classic poem "The Will to Live" as a notable contribution to cultural resistance literature, and for the way in which it strengthened and galvanized the Tunisian revolution, see: Elbousty, "Abu al-Qasim al-Shabbi's 'The Will to Live.'"

11. The scene also alludes to the widespread perception that Egypt is no longer the leader of the Arab world (a theme of the film which I discuss briefly in this chapter) and to the growing conviction among Tunisians that a country like theirs, small as it might be, has no reason to feel culturally inferior to historically more influential players on the global stage, such as Egypt.

12. Cf. Larry Rohter's remark in his *New York Times* review of Che Guevara's memoir, *The Motorcycle Diaries*: "Che Guevara is widely remembered today as a revolutionary figure; to some a heroic, Christ-like martyr, to others the embodiment of a failed ideology. To still others, he is just a commercialized emblem on a T-shirt" ("Che Today? More Easy Rider Than

Revolutionary"). (I mention these remarks by Rohter because Sghaïer wears a Che Guevara T-shirt throughout the film.) And before the 2011 uprising in Tunisia, when the last two lines of the Tunisian national anthem would be repeated throughout the world as a mantra for what became known as the "Arab Spring," Aboulkacem Chebbi's name might have resonated with an added intertext for Tunisian viewers recalling that policemen during the Ben Ali era, when asking for a bribe, would sometimes ask for an "Aboulkacem Chebbi" (a thirty-dinar banknote, on one face of which was printed a portrait of the poet).

13. In their book, *Le syndrome autoritaire: Politique en Tunisie de Bourguiba à Ben Ali*, Michel Camau and Vincent Geisser describe how, during the struggle for Independence, Bourguiba succeeded in raising the morale of the colonized Tunisians and restoring their dignity, but made them understand that they would only succeed in overthrowing their colonizers if they submitted to the authority of an elite (*el nukhba*) under his firm leadership. This elite took it as an article of faith that the people needed not democracy, but a strong leader: "Left to themselves, the people would display their divisions and weaknesses; under the guardianship of an elite, they would [be able to] show themselves united and powerful" (120). Ben Ali's authoritarianism, so much more comprehensive than Bourguiba's, had its roots in Bourguiba's example, which did not take long to degenerate into a familiar pattern of repression, according to which criticism of the president's leadership became synonymous with "plotting against the security of the state" (149).

14. Lamine will also play the role of an informer when, in secret, he dictates a letter to Mabrouka that begins: "Monsieur le Ministre: It is my duty to inform you of what is going on here...."

15. Hibou's explanation in *The Force of Obedience* of why the majority of businesses in Ben Ali's Tunisia remained small makes for depressing reading: "Entrepreneurs are hampered by their fear of direct interference on the part of 'family,' 'clans' and 'friends,' by the generally predatory and corrupt atmosphere, by anxiety over arbitrary and unforeseeable tax levies, by the absence of the rule of law and by juridical insecurity, by the business climate and the degradation of the environment, by the worry that they might appear too powerful and thus arouse the possessive desire of power, becoming caught up in the *stratégie du pourtour*. As a result, it is claimed that they prefer to remain 'small'" (148). Bouzid's character, harassed enough already by the difficulties of running a small business (which include the petty thievery of his waiters), is now being asked, in the dubious guise of a "request" that he prove his patriotism, to give up a day's income.

16. Actually, throughout the film, Fitouri refers simply to "a foreign television," as if it were a state-controlled apparatus in the exclusive service of the regime in power (as Channel 7 was in Ben Ali's Tunisia). It does not seem to occur to him that it might be a private company providing programming for a particular market segment, based on viewer demand. (Fitouri even assumes that, because she is German, Ingrid will know the telephone number of "the TV" in Germany.) The title of the film suggests, too, that the citizens of El Malga (which, incidentally, in Tunisian dialect means "gathering place" or "meeting place") seem to think "the TV" that is coming to their village has a Europe-wide viewership.

17. Moments after this scene in which Bouzid's café proprietor agrees to let Fitouri turn his café into a movie set, Ingrid walks in, seats herself at a table, and asks the waiter for "a clean

ashtray, please." The puzzled waiter says: "An ashtray? The whole café is an ashtray!" Overhearing this, Fitouri commands the waiter to "go and fetch an ashtray, immediately!" (As in the scene in which Fitouri instructs Hadhria to wait until "the TV" comes to the village, before she supervises her drum majorettes in the picking up of any garbage littering the streets, Dhouib is acknowledging here the relative lack of civic spirit one sometimes finds in societies making the transition from allegiance to family, clan, and tribe to the more abstract kind of allegiance to the nation-state.)

18. Later, during the sudden storm that wrecks the pageant and the citizens' hope of being filmed by the German television company, the giant statue representing the "authentic" and "modern" Tunisian woman topples forward. With her one arm held high in a salute, and because of the way in which Dhouib films her fall, she reminds the viewer at this moment of the historic toppling of the statue of Saddam Hussein in Baghdad's Firdos Square on 9 April 2003. The radio reporter's warning to the West "not to export your so-called democracy to this noble land" is therefore very likely an allusion to the American invasion of Iraq in 2003 and a general warning to all foreigners with neocolonial designs on Tunisia.

19. Béji, *Nous, décolonisés*, 45.

20. Hartog, *Régimes d'historicité*, 163–164. Cited in Abbassi, *Quand la Tunisie s'invente*, 9.

21. After Egypt signed a peace treaty with Israel on 26 March 1979, Egypt's membership in the league was suspended, and the league moved its headquarters from Cairo to Tunis. Egypt was reinstated as a member in 1989, and the league's headquarters returned to Cairo in 1990.

22. Inevitably, this sense of belonging to the Arab world is always being qualified by historical events and global trends that reconfigure the national imaginary. Anouar Majid, in *Unveiling Traditions*, argues that the "Middle East," as an epistemological/regional designation, for instance, is a "fictitious stage" (as in a theater), and that the whole ideology of Arab nationalism is being displaced by transnational capitalism. As Islamic countries adopt more pragmatic outlooks "in a frenzy to cope with the massive and turbulent shifts engineered by global capitalism" (59), the old alliances of Arab nationalism are giving way—especially, he notes, since the Gulf War: "Even Maghreb unity, to the disappointment of older Arab nationalists, has turned out to be largely a myth" (182n41). "Tunisia, Algeria, and Morocco emphasized Arabism in the 1960s and 1970s, 'but in the early 1990s people are recognizing that they belong to several places. They are part of the Arab world, but also part of Africa, of the Mediterranean basin and, say, of Europe. The Tunisians and Algerians in particular are not happy with this complicated, ill-defined identity—the Moroccans are more satisfied with being simply Moroccan—but the change in emphasis away from Arabism may have the long-term practical benefit of discouraging dreaming and encouraging regional co-operation'" (183n41; quotation from: Michael Field, *Inside the Arab World*, 394–395).

23. With Barack Obama's election to the American presidency in 2008, the mainstream of the American media—the right-wing Fox Broadcasting Company notably excepted—became generally eager to denounce as patently false the "reasons" given by the Bush administration for the U.S. invasion of Iraq (i.e., the weapons of mass destruction threat); but the surreality of any discourse touching on the role of the Israel lobby in American politics persisted, as the media remained strangely silent about the real reasons the United States invaded and occupied Iraq. (Cf. Mearsheimer and Walt, *The Israel Lobby and U.S. Foreign Policy*, where they make it

8. INVENTING THE POSTCOLONIAL NATION/CONSTRUCTING

clear that American interests were inseparable from Israeli interests in the American decision to invade Iraq. See especially pp. 230–231.)

24. Perkins, *A History of Modern Tunisia*, 7. Subsequent page numbers will be cited in the text.

25. In *Halfaouine*, Boughedir acknowledges Tunisia's debt to Mustafa Kemal Atatürk's example when he shows Salih, the most sympathetic adult male character in the film, sleeping with a portrait of the founder of modern Turkey on the wall beside his bed. (Salih, of course, would endorse the secularization of Turkey that Atatürk sought to accomplish, not the dictatorship that accompanied it.)

26. For a detailed and harrowing description of Ben Ali's repression of "Islamism" in Tunisia, see Hibou's "Introduction" to *The Force of Obedience*. For an article tracing the shifting relationship of the Tunisian government with the Islamic Movement, first under Bourguiba, then under Ben Ali, see Allani, "The Islamists in Tunisia between confrontation and participation: 1980–2008."

27. Again, it was Bourguiba, the architect of modern Tunisia, who set the secular tone. The official attitude toward Islam in Tunisia is conventionally respectful; but in making Brahim's character blind, Dhouib suggests not only that Islam has its limitations as a guide in the business of navigating modern life, but also that it is in the state's interests to handicap the would-be Islamists (i.e., keep them in the dark and in a dependent position). While there are vestiges of belief in the proverbial dialectic between blindness and insight—as there are in many societies—there is no denying that blind people are at a disadvantage in this world. They may be consulted (in a political process that may or may not be a sham), but they cannot be allowed to lead. With Ben Ali's ouster in January 2011, the question of whether Islamic parties should be allowed to participate in the government would be revisited.

28. The reader will recall that *Rih Essed* is the Arabic title of Bouzid's *Man of Ashes* and refers to a strong wind that sweeps away everything in its path.

29. For a critique of the premises of Western secularism as the ideological embodiment of capitalism, see Majid, *Unveiling Traditions*. One of Majid's arguments, which I briefly discuss in chapter 9, is that Western-style "modernization" is but a code word for capitalist development, and as such, defines the only alternative to secular modernity as religious faith, which post-Enlightenment European thought inevitably reduces to fundamentalism and fanaticism.

30. Like Ben Ali's strategy of proclaiming Tunisia the most modern country in the Arab world (and holding up Tunisia's advanced Personal Status Code as "proof" of this), while ruthlessly suppressing all oppositional voices, Israel's long-deployed ideological strategy has been to tout itself as "the only democracy in the Middle East," while denying millions of Palestinians both within Israel and in the occupied territories their basic human rights. In a grotesque example of the power and influence of the "Israel lobby" in American politics, the Israeli government, with help from American marketing executives, began a marketing campaign in 2005, aimed primarily at Americans in the United States, to "brand Israel" as "relevant and modern," which culminated in Prime Minister Benjamin Netanyahu's address to the U.S. Congress in May 2011, in which he declared that Israel was the exception in the Middle East, "a region where women are stoned, gays are hanged, Christians are persecuted."

8. INVENTING THE POSTCOLONIAL NATION/CONSTRUCTING

31. "Benalism" (or *Benalisme/bénalisme*) is a pejorative term used by many of Ben Ali's detractors not only to describe his systemically baleful style of governance but also to allude to its oppressive longevity. (For some, the word also contains an allusion to Hannah Arendt's phrase, the "banality of evil," which she incorporated in the title of her 1963 work, *Eichmann in Jerusalem: A Report on the Banality of Evil* [New York: Viking].) Cf. "Réflexions sur les 21 ans de Benalisme," *La Tunisie profonde: Réflexions sur la Tunisie libre de toutes les idéologies obscurantistes* (*Le Nouvel Observateur* blog site, *nouvelobs.com*).

32. Abbassi, *Quand la Tunisie s'invente*, 35. Abassi acknowledges that he draws his remarks about Kahina's symbolic significance from: Jacques Alexandropoulos, "Mosaïques tunisiennes," in Alexandropoulos and Cabanel, eds., *La Tunisie mosaïque*, 10. For a chapter on Berber and Jewish resistance to the Arabs in which Kahina, "the warrior-priestess . . . famous for her supernatural powers," is discussed, see also Chouraqui, *Between East and West: A History of the Jews of North Africa*, 33–41.

33. Hannoum, *Colonial Histories, Post-Colonial Memories*, xv. Subsequent page numbers will be cited in the text.

34. When Elissa, sister of King Pygmalion of Tyre, fled Tyre (a city in ancient Phoenicia that today is about fifty miles south of Beirut, Lebanon) after the murder of her husband Acerbas, she eventually found refuge for herself and her followers on a small piece of land on the North African coast that would become the city of Carthage. The local Berber King Iarbas wished to marry the beautiful Elissa and threatened to make war on Carthage if she did not concede to his wish. Insisting on remaining faithful to her dead husband, Elissa chose to immolate herself on a commemorative funeral pyre rather than risk the destruction of Carthage and her people. (Accounts vary as to whether Elissa fell on a sword or threw herself onto the pyre, or killed herself with a sword and was afterwards burned on the pyre. Virgil's version of the story in his *Aeneid* introduces the Trojan hero Aeneas as Elissa/Dido's lover, which adds pathos to her suicide, so that she dies tortured by guilt over having betrayed the memory of Acerbas [or Sychaeus, as Virgil calls him].) (Hadhria seems to be referencing Virgil's Queen of Carthage when she tells Hichem that "[Elissa] was in love, and she kept her love secret.")

35. In "Who Wears *Hijab* with the President: Constructing a Modern Islam in Tunisia," Simon Hawkins observes: "The Tunisian state invokes the past and holds up historical figures for reverence, but they are not models to be emulated. Alyssa, the semimythical founding queen of Carthage, is given great visibility and held up as an inspiration for the contemporary strong role of women, but only in a general and abstract manner. . . . Her existence hints at the future that was to come, but the current age does not look to her for guidance. She remains a figure in tradition who can never become modern and whose value for modern individuals is limited" (48–49). (This is precisely why, gently poking fun at his character, Dhouib has Hadhria so admire the founding queen of Carthage: Hadhria is not as modern a woman as she thinks she is.)

36. Not to be confused with Khayr ed-Din al-Tunsi (1822–1890), Tunisia's reformist prime minister (1873–1877) and grand vizier of the Ottoman Empire (1878–1879), among whose most enduring achievements, as noted earlier, was the founding of the Collège Sadiqi in 1875, which made a secular Western education available to Tunisian students for the first time.

37. The so-called "Hilalian invasion" (which was probably more of an infiltration than an invasion, a process that took decades, perhaps longer) was mounted by the Fatimid dynasty of Egypt in an effort to bring their former vassals, the Zirids, a Berber dynasty based in Kairouan, back under their suzerainty and to punish them for having abandoned Shiism. The Banu Hilal were a confederation of Bedouin tribes from Upper Egypt, whose story is recounted in fictionalized form in the Arabic epic *Taghribat Bani Hilal* (also known as *Sirat Abu Zeid Al Hilali*), which was declared one of mankind's "Masterpieces of the Oral and Intangible Heritage of Humanity" by UNESCO in 2003.

38. Galley, "Arabic Folk Epics," 433, 434. Subsequent page numbers will be cited in the text.

39. Is Dhouib alluding to the acting style of Egyptian commercial cinema? Tunisian directors are proud of the more realistic performance style they strive for in their films, which serves their quite different kind of cinema.

40. Regardless of Dhouib's intentions here, the viewer who has seen *The Silences of the Palace* cannot fail to recall Hichem Rostom's performance in that film as an altogether less charming seducer.

41. *Distinctive Women: Blog des femmes qui veulent voyager autrement*. www.distinctivewomen.com/archive/2007/07/13/le-monde-feminin.html.

42. Harun al-Rashid (763–809), son of Caliph al-Mahdi, was the fifth and most famous Abbasid caliph. In 782, before becoming Caliph in 786, he was appointed governor of Tunisia, Egypt, Syria, Armenia, and Azerbaijan. Due to the way in which he and his magnificent court are fictitiously depicted in the tales of *The Thousand and One Nights*, Harun al-Rashid turned into a legendary figure that quite obscured his true historic personality. This is perhaps why Dhouib alludes to him here—to make a satirical point about how fact and fiction too often become intertwined when national histories (like the El Malgans' parade) are being written.

43. Dhouib is alluding to the fact that throughout the Ben Ali era, Tunisian men understood that if they wore a beard, their chances of successfully navigating the bureaucracy (to obtain an identity card, passport, or other document from the state) would be considerably diminished, as the wearing of a beard could be taken by the RCD as a political provocation—a sign of resistance to the regime or even outright support for the Islamists' cause.

44. In Arabic, as I hope I have conveyed in my English translation, Hadhria's comment contains the hint of a sexual pun, suggesting that the Tunisians had sex with (or were raped by) all of them.

45. Moore, *Tunisia since Independence*, 10.

46. In *Unveiling Traditions*, Majid describes a three-day, religious-nationalist meeting (25–27 September 1989) sponsored by the Lebanon-based Research Center for Arab Unity—historically the guardian of the Arab nationalist doctrine—of some fifty intellectuals in Cairo, in which Sheikh Mohamed al-Ghazali, a well-known *'alim*, defined himself as an "Egyptian man Arabized through Islam." Another participant reminded the audience that some of the major heroes of Islamic history, such as Salahuddin al-Ayubi (Saladin), were not ethnically Arab. And still another participant simply stated that there has been no Arabness without Islam (183n42).

47. It is impossible to do more here than mention very briefly how some of these names signify in contemporary Tunisia. According to Allen Fromherz, the very name Ibn Khaldun, for example, has become "thick" with more national and modern meaning than with historical meaning. He notes that although Ibn Khaldun's writings remain important among Tunisia's intellectual elite, the name and image of Ibn Khaldun has become a national, popular evocation of modernization or innovation within "legitimate" traditional bounds, both an evocation and a legitimization of new, national identities and of collective innovations. (Fromherz, *Ibn Khaldun*, 149–164.)

As for Hannibal, he is meant to evoke what Abbassi (in *Entre Bourguiba et Hannibal*) calls "the Mediterranean idea," which, even though it is "a piece that has been added to Tunisian identity" (239), offers Tunisians not only a heroic "ancestor" possessed of many impressive personal qualities, but also a historical pedigree rooted in the ancient past and in a specific location (the great Mediterranean empire of which Carthage was the capital). Abbassi describes how a published guide to the Bardo Museum in suburban Tunis notes that in the thirteenth century the Hafsid dynasty chose Tunis—which is fewer than 20 kilometers from Carthage—as their capital. (The earlier Zirid dynasty had established Kairouan, deep in the heartland, as their capital.) According to the author of the guide, this showed the renewed commitment of the "Ifriqiyans" to a Mediterranean sphere of influence. The author concludes his historical summary thus: "We have to wait until 1956 to see the Tunisians definitively claim their independence and form an entity that, by virtue of its history, will define itself as Arab, African, and Mediterranean" (227).

48. What Ingrid says, in Arabic, is "bel haq," which means: "That's true." The French subtitle reads: "Pur souche," which literally means "pure stock." Dhouib is not only making fun of Fitouri's prejudices and assumptions (he probably thinks that, like Ingrid, all Germans have blond hair and blue eyes), but is also critiquing every nationalism grounded in ethnic or religious exclusivity (Saudi Arabia or Hitler's Germany . . . or that most peculiar case of all, Israel), and with justifiable pride, he is endorsing Tunisia's commitment to a plural national identity.

49. In its blatant symbolism, this vehicle recalls the car in Boughedir's short film, *The Picnic* (1972/1975), which is a symbol of the East–West hybridity of Tunisia under the French protectorate. (The car [see figure 1.1] is of no recognizable make, because it has been assembled from the parts of cars of many different makes.) See Lang, "*Le pique-nique*, Férid Boughedir et la 'tunisianité,'" 231–242.

50. Anderson, *Imagined Communities*, 44. Subsequent page numbers will be cited in the text.

51. The construction of Tunisian national identity of course is an ongoing project, and I do not mean to imply—echoing Jameson's argument about all third-world texts being national allegories depicting "the embattled situation of the public third-world culture and society"—that Tunisians have in some sense (finally) won the "battle" in the wars of representation upon which their sense of sovereign worth in the world community of nations depends. Consider Bauman's remarks in *Globalization*—since I end this chapter with a few comments about Tunisians becoming "thoroughly familiar with, and lively participants in, global culture"—that:

> Contrary to what academics, themselves members of the new global elite, tend to believe, the Internet and Web are not for everyone and unlikely ever to become open

to universal use. Even those who get access are allowed to make their choices within the frame set by the suppliers, who invite them "to spend time and money choosing between and in the numerous packages they offer." As for the rest, left with the network of satellite or cable television with not as much as a pretention to symmetry between the two sides of the screen—pure and unalloyed watching is their lot. (53)

The project of modernization, in Bryan Turner's phrase, is nevertheless about "the conditions which give rise to the abstract citizen"—and whether or not Tunisians fully understand and welcome the inevitable trajectory of this project they have embraced, "modernization is the triumph of global over local culture" (Turner, *Orientalism, Postmodernism and Globalism*, 136).

9. "Destiny answers the people's call for life, darkness will be dispelled, and chains will break"

1. In Sidi Bouzid, for example, the unemployment rate was estimated by union leaders to be over 30 percent. For a brief journalistic summary of events surrounding Mohamed Bouazizi's self-immolation and how they led to the uprising that toppled Ben Ali's regime, see Wright, *Rock the Casbah: Rage and Rebellion Across the Islamic World*, 15–21. For a succinct chronology of the Tunisian revolution and the controversy over powers and prerogatives in the formation of the post-revolution Tunisian Constituent Assembly, see: Allani, "The post-revolution Tunisian Constituent Assembly." The best coverage of the revolution and its background, and also of "unrest in the Arab world," remains the *New York Times*' "Tunisia" entry in its "Topics" archive, which includes a "list of [hyperlinked] resources from around the Web about Tunisia [and about unrest in the Arab world] as selected by researchers and editors of *The New York Times*": http://topics.nytimes.com/top/news/international/countriesandterritories/tunisia/index.html?inline=nyt-geo.

2. The WikiLeaks cables were not the first published revelations of the corruption of Ben Ali's family. The publication in France in 1999 of Nicolas Beau and Jean-Pierre Tuquoi's *Notre ami Ben Ali: L'envers du "miracle tunisien"*, for example, was described by the popular French magazine *Télérama* as "the book all of Tunis is talking about." Focusing on Ben Ali's record of brutal repression, the book's authors accuse the president of having, little by little, transformed "tranquil Tunisia" into "an immense garrison house," but they also include a section on "the families that plunder Tunisia" and another on "Leïla and co." In October 2009, Nicolas Beau and Catherine Graciet's *La régente de Carthage: Main basse sur la Tunisie*, from the same publisher (La Découverte, which distributed the book for sale in the Relay chain of magazine stands and bookshops that can be found in train stations and airports throughout France), offered a portrait of Leïla Trabelsi Ben Ali and her ten brothers and sisters that is such a vivid indictment as to seem almost incredible. But for those protestors who had heard about the U.S. Embassy cables, their authorship and provenance gave the reports a uniquely authoritative sting that was encouraging to the uprising.

3. "US embassy cables: Tunisia—a US foreign policy conundrum," *The Guardian*, 7 December 2010, www.guardian.co.uk/world/us-embassy-cables-documents/217138 (accessed 24 January 2011).

4. In the *New York Times* on 27 January 2011, Robert F. Worth and David D. Kirkpatrick wrote:

> Al Jazeera has been widely admired for its aggressive coverage of the Tunisian uprising, which was largely ignored in most Western outlets. The channel succeeded despite serious obstacles: the Tunisian government had barred its reporters from the country, and a Tunisian-born anchor, Mohammed Krichen, arranged for an old friend, Lotfi Hajji, to work under cover as Al Jazeera's eyes and ears on the ground.
>
> Mr. Hajji, a freelance journalist who also calls himself a human rights activist, was followed and harassed by the secret police almost constantly. After the uprising started, local contacts began sending Mr. Hajji amateur videos of police violence over Facebook. Al Jazeera began showing the grainy cellphone videos on its broadcasts, as part of what the station sympathetically labeled "the Sidi Bouzid Uprising" after the town where a young man started it all by setting himself on fire on Dec. 17.
>
> Each time Al Jazeera broadcast the videos, more would flood into Mr. Hajji's Facebook account, in a cycle that blew the seeds of revolt across the country.

(Worth and Kirkpatrick, "Seizing a Moment, Al Jazeera Galvanizes Arab Frustration.")

For Al Jazeera's initial lack of coverage of protests in Egypt (which caused some Egyptian activists to complain bitterly that Mubarak must have cut a deal with the Qatari and Saudi governments), see Marc Lynch's blog on the *Foreign Policy* website, starting with his 25 January 2011 posting: "Watching Egypt (but Not Al Jazeera)," http://lynch.foreignpolicy.com/posts/2011/01/25/watching_egypt_and_lebanon_and_the_pa_and.

5. An excellent and informative article in the 22–28 January 2011 issue of *The Economist*, "Ali Baba Gone, but What About the 40 Thieves?" (31–33), begins with the statement: "Everyone knows what started it: the self-immolation on December 17th of a despairing, jobless youth named Muhammad [sic] Bouazizi in the main square of Sidi Bouzid, a town in Tunisia's hardscrabble interior" (31). The article then goes on to repeat a widespread factual error: Bouazizi, "a university graduate . . . had tried to scrape a living selling vegetables from a stall which was confiscated by the police" (32). The same week in which this issue of *The Economist* appeared on newsstands, a consultation of the *Wikipedia* entry for Mohamed Bouazizi would reveal that the online encyclopedia was in this instance better equipped to report the truth about Bouazizi's level of education than had been *The Economist*, *The Independent*, *The Guardian*, and the *International Business Times*: "Although multiple media outlets reported that Bouazizi had a university degree, his sister, Samia Bouazizi, stated that he had never graduated from high school, but that it was something he had wanted for both himself and his sisters" (http://en.wikipedia.org/wiki/Mohamed_Bouazizi [accessed 23 January 2011]).

Note: As late as 30 January 2011, CNN was still broadcasting false information about Mohamed Bouazizi's level of education, describing him as "a graduate student." (After this date, I lost track of what the reputable media outlets had to say on the subject.) For an analysis of Bouazizi's function, or role as a martyr, in the Tunisian revolution, see DeGeorges, "The social construction of the Tunisian revolutionary martyr in the media and popular perception."

6. Boughedir, interviewed by Khélil, *Le parcours et la trace*, 166. The key to Boughedir's conception of *tunisianité*, like that of Bourguiba, can be found in the bilingual/bicultural education they received at Sadiqi College. As Boughedir explains in his interview with Khélil: "My ideal of perfectly mastering both the East and the West is something I got from my education at Sadiqi College, which was committed to making us completely bilingual. It was my father who made me learn French, believing it would help me get ahead more quickly. He thought I would pick up Arabic later, and thanks to French, I could have a respectable career as a doctor, engineer, or lawyer. Afterwards, I should learn Arabic, because I live in an Arab country" (145). Boughedir goes on to say: "What you call 'hybridity' ['*métissage*'], I prefer to call 'synthesis' ['*synthèse*']. It's a kind of synthesis that says ours is basically a popular culture, one that is exceptionally rich, and which was, curiously enough, very coherent before Independence. Thanks to my education, I am able as a filmmaker to steal from the West the modernity of its cinema and offer Tunisian citizens a mirror in which they might see themselves and their culture—a Tunisia they can embrace, but not a simplistic, caricatured, naive, or folkloric Tunisia" (145).

7. *The Picnic*, made fifteen years after Tunisia celebrated its Independence, was made available to the public in 2003 for the first time as a "bonus" on the DVD release in France of *Halfaouine*. As noted earlier, it was originally one of three sketches in the omnibus film, *Fī Bilâd al-Tararanni/In Tararanni Country* (1975). At forty-three minutes, *Annouzha/Le pique-nique* is by far the longest of the three. Hamouda Ben Halima's *Al Fanous/Le réverbère* is twenty-five minutes long; and Hédi Ben Khélifa's *Azziara/La visite* is fifteen minutes long. The collective aim of its three directors was to make "the first specifically Tunisian film," which, according to Hédi Khélil in his *Abécédaire du cinéma tunisien*, derived from their conviction that "the essential task of the Tunisian filmmaker is to rediscover the authentic roots of the country, paying attention to daily life in all its forms, without being propagandistic or obviously subjective" (233). Boughedir has said that his own sketch is meant to evoke the universe of the French-language comic books he read as a child. In a sense, he succeeds in this aim, for *The Picnic* contains what Kchir-Bendana, in "Ideologies of the Nation in Tunisian Cinema," would describe as "a gallery of highly characteristic 'Tunisians' . . . a typology of more or less archetypal characters" (38).

8. For a nuanced attempt by a Tunisian sociologist to perform an arabo-specific analysis of the tensions between *tradition/authenticity* and *renewal/"modernization,"* see Abdelwahab Bouhdiba's chapter, "Des difficultés d'être soi-même: Açala-authenticité," in *Quêtes sociologiques*, 60–73. Boughedir's concept of *tunisianité* would appear to be similar to the Arab notion of *asala* discussed by Bouhdiba, who devotes a good part of his essay to the "rich," "polysemic," and "ambivalent" meanings of the word. Bouhdiba reluctantly acknowledges that one might begin by translating the word as *authenticity in/of tradition* but insists that "the formulation of the problematic as one between tradition and modernity needs to be reconsidered—not in terms of their opposition to one another, but rather in the ways that they are reciprocal. Tradition is a source of inspiration. Absolutely. It is not a matter of imitation and reflex. Only the refusal of reductionism, of all reductionism, will save us from ourselves" (67).

9. Anouar Majid, who believes that the late modern project of a global market, which can only be built on the ruins of the world's diverse cultures, implies that the focus of intellectuals like Boughedir is misplaced: "The proliferation of an academic terminology celebrating a hybridity caused by traumatic dislocations has effectively transformed symptoms of a global crisis with potentially apocalyptic proportions into virtues to be promoted as intellectual ideals in the postcolonial world" (*Unveiling Traditions*, 154–155).

10. Tlatli, interviewed by Khélil, *Le parcours et la trace*, 199. Subsequent page numbers will be cited in the text.

11. In "Essai d'une typologie du cinéma tunisien" (published 5 August 2011), Mahmoud Jemni observes: "The Tunisian people were once proud to call themselves cinephiles, but cinephilia is now moribund in Tunisia." In 1956, the year of Independence, there were 150 movie theaters in the country, "now there are 16 theaters for ten million inhabitants." Ciné-clubs had flourished throughout Tunisia under the umbrella of the Fédération Tunisienne des Cinéclubs (founded in 1950); and following Independence, the Fédération des Cinéastes Amateurs (1962) helped consolidate this already widespread film culture, the two associations complementing and working closely with each other. "[But] this enthusiasm for the cinema was curbed by the regime in power, which feared the raising of any consciousness that might challenge the political system. The successive governments representing Bourguiba's party even took various measures to erode the bases of a national film industry."

12. Bouzid, *Sources of Inspiration*, 46. Subsequent page numbers will be cited in the text.

13. The single best article about Tunisians' historical cinephilia (which Jemni refers to in his "Essai d'une typologie du cinéma tunisien," and which he is correct in observing is now more or less moribund) is Morgan Corriou's "La consommation cinématographique: les plaisirs du cinéma en Tunisie au tournant de 1956."

14. One only has to look at what happened to the revolutionary cinema of the Soviet avantgarde after Socialist Realism became the official style in 1932. The state prescription that films should have as their purpose the furtherance of the goals of socialism and communism effectively killed the cinema in the Soviet Union. By the time of Stalin's death in 1953, one of the great world cinemas had become moribund.

15. Barlet, "Le cinéma tunisien à la lumière du printemps arabe," 273.

16. Amine Chiboub, in Barlet et al., "Cinéma et révolution," 337–338. Subsequent page numbers will be cited in the text.

17. The film, a French production based on Satrapi's celebrated graphic memoir about her Iranian childhood, had been dubbed into Tunisian Arabic; and the scene that purportedly outraged the protesters most particularly is one in which God appears before a young girl (Satrapi) to teach her about forgiveness. The three hundred people who attacked Nessma's offices and tried to set fire to them claimed that the film denigrated Islam.

18. If *Making Of* seems to fall in line with official narratives about the threat to Ben Ali's secular regime of Islamic fundamentalism, it very clearly identifies Ben Ali's regime as the main *cause* of that threat.

19. A useful and interesting roundup of responses to the film in the French and Tunisian press, "TUNISIE: Ni Allah ni maître (Nadia El Fani)," can be found on the *brightsfrance.org*

9. DESTINY ANSWERS THE PEOPLE'S CALL FOR LIFE

("forum des brights de France et des environs") website at: www.brightsfrance.org/forum/viewtopic.php?f=10&t=2331(accessed 28 August 2011).

20. See Anthony Shadid, "Tunisia Faces a Balancing Act of Democracy and Religion," *New York Times*, 30 January 2012. This is the first article in the *New York Times* series: "The New Islamists: The Struggle Over Identity" (*"Articles in this series will explore the rise of political Islam in the Middle East, as Islamic movements struggle to remake the Arab world"*). Shadid quotes Abdelhalim Messaoudi, a journalist at Nessma TV (Tunis): "'Certain Islamist factions want to turn identity into their Trojan horse,' Mr. Messaoudi said. 'They use the pretext of protecting their identity as a way to crush what we have achieved as a Tunisian society. They want to crush the pillars of civil society.'" Shadid notes that the debates in Tunisia often "echo similar confrontations in Turkey, another country with a long history of secular authoritarian rule now governed by a party inspired by political Islam. In both, secular elites long considered themselves a majority and were treated as such by the state. In both, those elites now recognize themselves as minorities and are often mobilized more by the threat than the reality of religious intolerance." Shadid goes on to quote Hamadi Redissi, a columnist and professor, who predicted secular Tunisians might soon retreat to enclaves: "'We've become the *ahl al-dhimma*,' he said, offering a term in Islamic law to denote protected minorities in a Muslim state. 'It's like the Middle Ages.'"

21. "Article 1—Tunisia is a free, independent and sovereign state. Its religion is Islam, its language is Arabic and its type of government is the Republic."

22. I am paraphrasing Stephen J. King's description of political Islam as an ideology. Cf. *The New Authoritarianism in the Middle East and North Africa*, 12.

23. This is the tag line for *Making Of* in the promotional materials for the film.

24. Among the films in this study, scenes in which a father beats his son occur in: *Man of Ashes*, *Halfaouine*, and *Essaïda*. In *Making Of*, the scene in which Bahta's father beats him with his belt is treated allegorically, which is to say, not quite realistically. When Bahta is caught trying to steal his grandfather's savings, which the old man keeps stuffed under his mattress, Bahta submits to his punishment without a word, in a manner suggesting that this has happened many times before. The beating is conducted almost as a ritual, and apart from the strange, rhythmic sound of the belt across Bahta's back, it occurs in complete silence. We hear thirty lashes on the soundtrack, before the sound fades, like an ellipsis, suggesting that the beating is constant and continuous, psychological, metaphorical . . .

25. Gana, "Bourguiba's Sons: Melancholy Manhood in Modern Tunisia," 105.

26. In *The String* (Mehdi Ben Attia, 2009), there is a scene involving a man pretending to be a policeman that is decidedly less playful and more threatening to the victims. Two young men, Malik and Bilal, who have recently become lovers, go to the beach at Ghar el Melah (about fifty kilometers north of Tunis) for a swim. When they come out of the water, an unkempt and thuggish man approaches them.

MALIK. Can I help you?
MAN. ID.
MALIK. You're checking IDs on the beach?

9. DESTINY ANSWERS THE PEOPLE'S CALL FOR LIFE

MAN. On the beach, in the city, at the seaside. Always loyal to my country! There are laws, you know! ID!

MALIK, *getting up*. They're in the car. I'll go get them.

MAN. You stay here! If you move, I'll fuck you! Think you can leave me standing here, like an idiot?

(*Bilal gets up as well.*)

MAN. (*Addressing himself to Bilal.*) Do you want a calendar?

BILAL. A calendar?

MAN. A calendar, like in prison. I've got some great ones. How much have you got under you... on you? (*Muttering to himself.*) How do you talk to these guys? *Money, money* ...

BILAL, *bemused*. How much are your calendars?

MAN. (*Laughing mirthlessly.*) They're free. The money's so I don't throw you in jail. That's where the likes of you end up.

MALIK. Show me your badge.

MAN. My badge, motherfucker? I spit on your aunt's cunt! You dare to ask a state cop for his badge? This isn't Canada or Sweden. You can't go around stark naked, no laws, no ID, no license. Have you got any money?

BILAL. We have nothing.

(The man glances up to the bluff above them, his demeanor suddenly changes, and he quickly flees. The camera cuts to a shot of a policeman on horseback, looking down at the scene.)

27. The most shocking scene in the entire film is the one in which Bahta violently attacks his girlfriend, Souad (Afef Ben Mahmoud), smashing her head against a column in the underground parking garage where he has cornered her and knocking her to the floor as he screams: "Bitch! I'll teach you! [...] Dirty bitch! Damn you! God curse you!" Breathless and sobbing, she tells him: "You think you're a man? Go on, hit me again. ... God will punish you. You're not a man!" Bahta becomes more hysterical, spits on her, and hits her again: "You dare to talk about virility? Piece of shit! Adulterer! How dare you! Wear a veil! Otherwise ... I'll burn your face! God curse you!"

28. Majid, *Unveiling Traditions*, 2. Subsequent page numbers will be cited in the text.

29. Tony Judt, "Ill Fares the Land" (*New York Review of Books*, 29 April 2010). This essay is drawn from the opening chapter of Judt's book *Ill Fares the Land*.

30. This exchange between Abdallah and Bahta illustrates both the paradox and hypocrisy of America's claim that its invasion of Iraq in 2003—called "Operation Iraqi Freedom"—was motivated by a desire to bring democracy to Iraq. The "freedom" of the Iraqis was the least of the concerns of the Bush–Cheney administration.

31. Even Abdallah will admit to Bahta: "People will only act if religion is connected to politics." Seeing the invasion of Iraq as an opportunity to spread the Islamists' message, he explains the link between religion and terrorism thus: "That's the only way to make death commonplace. If the Iraqis sow terror amongst the occupiers—if the occupiers feel they are in danger—the relationship will be inversed. Terrorism is the solution."

9. DESTINY ANSWERS THE PEOPLE'S CALL FOR LIFE

32. Cf. Richard Cincotta, "Tunisia's Shot at Democracy: What Demographics and Recent History Tell Us."

33. For a roundup of statistics that put into sharp perspective what we mean by capitalism's "uneven development" and the contemporary global "consolidation of inequality and exclusion," especially as it affects the Arab world, see Suad Joseph's 2011 MESA Presidential Address, "History and Its Histories: Story-Making and the Present."

34. Béji, *Désenchantement national*, 16.

35. Hobsbawm, *Nations and Nationalism since 1870*, 150–152, 160–162; referenced by Majid, *Unveiling Traditions*, 59.

36. Majid calls for "a rebuilding of human-scale economies and a creative form of delinking from the expanding and intensified process of capitalist exploitation." He writes: "A postnationalist, Islamically progressive identity can contribute not only to Muslims' autonomy but also to the forging of new cultural solidarities in a polycentric world" (72).

37. Tohidi, "Modernity, Islamization, and Women in Iran," 142; quoted by Majid, *Unveiling Traditions*, 130.

38. When Ennahdha won 89 out of 217 seats in the 23 October 2011 elections for the constituent assembly tasked with writing a new constitution for the country, Jean Daniel remarked in a short essay in the *New York Review of Books* that "every aspect of this episode has been ambiguous, uncertain, and unlikely." While Ennahdha's leader, Rached Ghannouchi, had said repeatedly that he intended to create the most democratic model of government in the Arab world, he made a number of statements that belied the image he had been at pains to create of Ennahdha as a moderate Islamist party intent on reconciling Islamic identity with the defense of civil liberties. Two days before the elections, for example, Ghannouchi named the minimum threshold of votes he expected to receive and resorted to threats, saying that he would not hesitate to order troops into the streets if those votes failed to materialize. Daniel wrote: "It is a little late now for the proponents of a 'modern' Tunisia to express disappointment and tell themselves that they just didn't know their own people.... The modernists can certainly reproach themselves—as can we along with them—for having underestimated both the share of votes achieved by the revolutionary Islamist party and also its ability to inflame the feelings and imaginations of the Tunisian voters." The Tunisians have reminded us, he wrote, that "an uprising against a tyrant, even a successful one, may not amount to a revolution against a religion." Daniel concluded that: "The prospect of a Western-style democracy and complete freedom of religion now seems nothing but a fleeting memory. The mystique of loyalty to tradition has won out over the romanticism of the triumph of liberty." (Jean Daniel, "Islamism's New Clothes," *New York Review of Books*, 22 December 2011, 72.)

Filmography

RIH ESSED (ريح السد) (1986)
Man of Ashes (International English title)/*L'homme de cendres* (French title)

Production: Ahmed Baha Eddine Attia (Cinétéléfilms—Tunisia); SATPEC
Direction: Nouri Bouzid
Screenplay: Nouri Bouzid
Cinematography: Youssef Ben Youssef
Editing: Mika Ben Miled
Set design: Claude Bennys; Mohsen Raïs
Costume design: Lilia Lakhoua; Leïla Ben Mahmoud
Sound: Fawzi Thabet; Riadh Thabet
Music: Salah Mehdi
Running time: 109 minutes

Cast (in alphabetical order): Khadija Abaoub (the exorcist); Sarra Abdelhadi (Hachemi's sister, Amna); Mustapha Adouani (Ameur); Khaled Akrout (the grandfather); Yacoub Bchiri (Monsieur Lévy); Mourad Bejaoui (Anis); Habib Belhadi (Touil); Mahmoud Belhassen (Mustapha, Hachemi's father); Noureddine Ben Ayed; Souad Ben Sliman; Fathia Chaâbane (Aïcha, Hachemi's paternal aunt); Wassila Chaouki (Sejra); Hamadi Dekhil; Jamila Dhrif; Mohamed Dhrif (Azaïez); Habiba Gargouri; Khaled Ksouri (Farfat); Imad Maâlal (Hachemi); Sonia Mansour (Amina); Lamine Nahdi; Alham Nissar; Mouna Noureddine (Nafissa, Hachemi's mother); Mongi Ouni; Hedi Sanaâ; Chafia Trabelsi

FILMOGRAPHY

Release dates: France: May 1986 (Cannes Film Festival); Belgium: 15 September 1988 (Ghent); Netherlands: 11 May 1990; France: 16 February 1994

'USFÛR STAH (عصفور السطح) (1990)
Halfaouine: Child of the Terraces (International English title)/*Halfaouine: L'enfant des terrasses* (French title)

Production: Ahmed Baha Eddine Attia (Cinétéléfilms—Tunisia); Eliane Stutterheim (Scarabée Films—France); Hassen Daldoul (France Média—Paris); La SEPT (Paris); Westdeutscher Rundfunk (WDR—West German Broadcasting); Centre national du cinéma et de l'image animée (CNC—France); Ministère de la Culture et de l'Information (Tunisia); Tunis Air; Office National du Tourisme Tunisien (ONTT—Tunisia); Hubert Bals Fund—International Film Festival Rotterdam (Netherlands); NOS; NCO; Channel 4 (United Kingdom); FAS
Direction: Férid Boughedir
Screenplay: Férid Boughedir
Cinematography: Georges Barsky
Editing: Moufida Tlatli
Set design: Taïeb Jallouli; Claude Bennys
Costumes: Naâma Jazi
Sound: Hachemi Joulak
Music: Anouar Brahem
Running time: 98 minutes

Cast (in alphabetical order): Mustapha Adouani (Si Azzouz); Rabia Ben Abdallah (Lella Jamila); Zahira Ben Ammar (deaf-mute *hammam* attendant); Salem Ben Hassine (Jaâfar, the bum); Fatma Ben Saïdane (Salouha); Selim Boughedir (Noura); Aziza Boulabiar (Zakia); Hélène Catzaras (Latifa); Taoufik Chabchoub (Colombo); Carolyn Chelby (Leïla); Mohamed Driss (Salih); Abdelhamid Gayess (Sheikh Mokhtar); Tarak Harbi (Sadok, Mounir's father); Aïssa Harrath (Ali); Fethi Haddaoui (Khemaïs); Mustapha Koudhai (Hamadi Karama); Radhouane Meddeb (Mounir); Slah Msadek (butcher/ogre); Jamila Ourabi (matron in charge of the *hammam*); Jamel Sassi (Moncef); Kamel Touati (barber)
Release dates: United States: 1990 (IFC—International Film Circuit); Canada: 14 September 1990 (Toronto International Film Festival); France: 26 September 1990; Netherlands: 8 March 1991; Sweden: 10 April 1992; Finland: 17 July 1992; United States: 8 September 1995 (re-release); DVD release in France: 2003 (Gaumont Home Vidéo); DVD release in United States: 2004 (Kino Video)

FILMOGRAPHY

BEZNESS (بزناس) (1992)
Bezness (International English title)

Production: Ahmed Baha Eddine Attia (Cinétéléfilms—Tunisia); Jean-François Lepetit (Flach Film—France); Le Studio Canal Plus (France); Festival TransMéditerranée (FTM—France)
Direction: Nouri Bouzid
Screenplay: Nouri Bouzid
Cinematography: Alain Levent
Editing: Kahena Attia
Set design: Khaled Joulak
Costumes: Naâma Jazy; Pierre-Yves Gayraud
Sound: Hachemi Joulak
Music: Anouar Brahem
Running time: 92 minutes

Cast (in alphabetical order): Mustapha Adouani (police commissioner); Manfred Andrae (the German); Sondes Belhassen (Ghalia); Adel Boukadida (Aziz); Najoua Hafedh (Fatma); Claire Jolivet (girl by the pool); Abdellatif Kechiche (Roufa); Ghalia Lacroix (Khomsa); Jacques Penot (Fred); Ahmed Ragoubi ("Nizq"/"Navette"); Jamel Sassi ("Flash")
Release dates: France: 10 June 1992 (Cannes—Quinzaine des réalisateurs); Egypt: 1992 (Cairo); United Kingdom: 1992 (London); Burkina Faso: 1993 (Festival Panafricain du Cinéma de Ouagadougou—FESPACO); Netherlands: 11 February 1993 (Rotterdam); Zimbabwe: 1993 (Harare)

SAMT AL-QUSUR (صمت القصور) (1994)
The Silences of the Palace (International English title)/*Les silences du palais* (French title)

Production: Ahmed Baha Eddine Attia (Cinétéléfilms—Tunisia); Magfilm (Tunisia); Richard Magnien (Mat Films—France)
Production management: Tarak Harbi (Tunis); Dora Bouchoucha Fourati (Tunis); Joëlle Kondo (Paris)
Direction: Moufida Tlatli
Assistant direction: Mounir Baâziz; Marc Bodin Joyeux; Adel Koudhaei
Screenplay: Moufida Tlatli; Nouri Bouzid
Cinematography: Youssef Ben Youssef
Editing: Moufida Tlatli
Art direction: Claude Bennys; Mondher Dhrif
Sound: Faouzi Thabet; Gérard Rousseau; Frédéric Ullmann
Music: Anouar Brahem
Running time: 127 minutes

Cast (in alphabetical order): Zahira Ben Ammar (Habiba); Khedija Ben Othman (Sarra); Fatma Ben Saïdane (Mroubia); Hatem Berrabeh (Selim); Sami Bouajila (Lofti); Sabah Bouzouita (Shema); Hélène Catzaras (Fella); Christian Chartain (Hussein's friend); Kamel Fazaâ (Sidi Ali); Bechir Feni (the Bey); Amel Hedhili (Khedija); Michket Krifa (Lella Memia); Ghalia Lacroix (adult Alia); Sonia Meddeb (Lella J'neina); Najia Ouerghi (Khalti Hadda); Hichem Rostom (Si Bechir); Hend Sabri (young Alia); Kamel Touati (Hussein)

Release dates: Greece: 1994 (Thessaloniki International Film Festival); France: 7 September 1994; Canada: 13 September 1994 (Toronto International Film Festival); United States: 30 September 1994 (New York Film Festival); United States: October 1994 (Chicago International Film Festival); Netherlands: 9 February 1995; United Kingdom: 10 March 1995; United States: 1 September (San Francisco); Spain: 13 September 1995; Australia: 28 September 1995; Finland: 3 November 1995; Denmark: 1 December 1995; Norway: 8 August 1997; Sweden: 19 September 1997; Germany: 20 November 1997; Japan: 30 October 2000 (Tokyo International Kanebo Women's Film Festival); Indonesia: 12 November 2000 (Jakarta International Film Festival); Italy: 10 November 2003 (television premiere); Argentina: 15 April 2005 (Buenos Aires International Festival of Independent Cinema); United Kingdom: 24 February 2008 (Women's Cinema from Tangiers to Tehran)

ESSAÏDA (السيدة) (1996)
Essaïda (International English title)

Production: Sangho Films; Thouhami Kochbati
Direction: Mohamed Zran
Screenplay: Mohamed Zran; Pascal Arnold
Cinematography: Jean-Claude Couty
Editing: Francis de Délémont
Art direction: Tahar M'Guedmini
Costumes: Lilia Lakhoua
Make-up: Fatma Jaziri
Sound: Hachemi Joulak
Music: El Hamam El Abyadh; "Les Colombes"
Running time: 100 minutes

Cast (in alphabetical order): Aïcha Abdellaoui (grandmother); Mahmoud Abderrahman (crazy man); Abderrahman Abidi (Adel); Wafa Ajroudi (Nadia); Lotfi Akremi (Nawfel); Myriam Amarouchène (Sonia); Mohamed Arfa (bootblack); Fawzia Badr (Zeineb); Raoudhia Ben Salem (Selma); Abdelkader Boughanmi (Sami); Chedli Bouzaiane (Nidhal); Taoufik Chabchoub (Godfather); Khelifa Chtiri (Jabeur); Mabrouka Chtiri (Donia); Zakaria el Kobbi (Zea); Olfa Ghallab (Aïcha); Nejib Guibene ("Charlie Chaplin"); Larbi Khemiri (servant); Khaled Ksouri (Hatem);

Abdallah Mimoun (Omar); Tayeb Oueslati (Souleyman); Maïthé Pontanier (Sœur Hélène); Hichem Rostom (Amine); Mohamed Tebini (police superintendent)
Release dates: Tunisia: 28 October 1996; France: 1 October 1997; Italy: 14 November 2003 (television premiere)

BEDWIN HACKER (بدوين هاكر) (2002)
Bedwin Hacker (International English title)

Production: Z'Yeux Noirs Movies
Co-production: ERTT (Établissement de la radiodiffusion-télévision tunisienne—Tunisia) and ANPA (Agence Nationale de Promotion de l'Audiovisuel—Tunisia); 2M-SOREAD (Morocco); Sedat/Canal+ Horizons (Tunisia); ACC (France); Ministère de la Culture (Tunisia); Office National du Tourisme Tunisien (ONTT—Tunisia); Agence Intergouvernementale de la Francophonie (AIF); Hubert Bals Fund—International Film Festival Rotterdam (Netherlands)
Executive production: CTV Services (Tunisia); executive producers: Nadia and Bechir El Fani; Abdelaziz Ben Mlouka; associate producers: Ken and Romaine Legargeant
Direction: Nadia El Fani
Screenplay: Nadia El Fani
Cinematography: Tarek Ben Abdallah
Camera: Sofian El Fani
Editing: Claude Reznik
Set design: Mohsen Raïss; Hatem Miladi
Costumes: Nadia Anane
Sound: Hachemi Joulak; Mikaël Barre
Music: Milton Edouard
Running time: 103 minutes

Cast (in alphabetical order): Ikram Azzouz (customs officer at Tunis-Carthage Airport); Néjib Belkadhi (Mourad); Alberto Canova (DST boss); Rinda Dabbegh (Salma); Xavier Desplas (Zbor); Atilio Di Constanzo (Paris police inspector); Bechir El Fani (Uncle Salah); Lilia Falkat (Kmar); Sonia Hamza (Kalt); Ahmed Hafiane (Mehdi); Hamadi Maâroufi (Zarga); Mohamed Said (hairdresser/informer); Nadia Saïji (Frida); Tomer Sisley (Chams); Muriel Solvay (Julia/Agent Marianne); Habiba Trabelsi (Raja); Najoua Zouheir (Malika)
Release dates: Tunisia: October 2002 (Carthage Film Festival); Canada: May 2003 (Montréal Vues d'Afrique Festival); France: 16 July 2003; Tunisia: 19 January 2004; television broadcast on TV5 (France): April–December 2004; television broadcast annually in July on 2M (Morocco): 2005 to present; DVD release in United States: March 2006

FILMOGRAPHY

TALFAZA JAYA (التلفزة جاية) (2006)
The TV Is Coming (International English title)/*La télé arrive* (French title)

Production: Manara Productions (Tunis); Rougemarine (Paris)
Direction: Moncef Dhouib; *first assistant*: Hanane Ben Mahmoud
Screenplay: Moncef Dhouib
Cinematography: Ahmed Bennis; *camera*: Ali Ben Abdallah
Production management: Lamia Saïdane
Editing: Charlène Gravel
Production design: Taïeb Jallouli
Costume design: Nedra Gribaâ
Sound: Fawzi Thabet
Music: Rabie Zammouri
Running time: 95 minutes

Cast (in alphabetical order): Ali Abdelwahab (Salem); Raouf Ben Amor (visiting dignitary); Fatma Ben Saïdane (Hadhria); Chawki Bouglaïa (Sghaïer); Elaïd Bououni (Stoufa); Ammar Bouthelja (Fitouri); Nouri Bouzid (café owner); Leïla Chebbi (Selma); Abdelkhader Dkhil (Bahoussi); Tawfik El Bahri (Ayed); Abdelhamid Gayess (radio reporter); Aïssa Harrath (Brahim); Intidhar Kamarti (Madonna); H'mida Laâbidi (Kafza); Bernadette Machillot (Ingrid); Hichem Rostom (Hichem, "the Egyptian"); Jamel Sassi (Lamine)
Release dates: Tunisia: 18 July 2006 (Carthage Film Festival); United Arab Emirates: 13 December 2006 (Dubai International Film Festival); Egypt: December 2006 (Cairo International Film Festival)

AKHIR FILM (آخر فيلم) (2006)
Making Of (International English title) / *Making Of, le dernier film* (French title)

Production: Abdelaziz Ben Mlouka (CTV Production—Tunisia); Nouveau Regard Films; Centre Cinématographique Marocain (Morocco); Albarès Productions (France)
Direction: Nouri Bouzid
Screenplay: Nouri Bouzid
Cinematography: Michel Baudour
Editing: Karim Hamouda
Set design: Khaled Joulak
Costumes: Nabila Cherif; Rim Saïdane
Make-up: Fatma Jaziri
Sound: Michel Ben Saïd
Music: Nejib Charradi
Running time: 115 minutes

Cast (in alphabetical order): Lotfi Abdelli (Bahta/Chokri); Afef Ben Mahmoud (Souad); Fatma Ben Saïdane (Bahta's mother, Halima); Mohamed Ali Boum'Nijel (Bahta's younger brother); Sofiane Chaâri (Mongi Scala, the smuggler); Helmi Dridi (Bilel); Lotfi Dziri (Abdallah); Taoufik El Bahri (Brigadier Gaddour); Mostafa Hattab (Bahta's grandfather); Moez Kouki (Rezgui); Mahmoud Larnaout (Bahta's father); Foued Litaïem (Ghazi); Dorra Zarrouk (Abdallah's wife)

Release dates: Tunisia: 14 November 2006 (Carthage Film Festival); Italy: 20 June 2007 (Taormina Film Festival); United Kingdom: 31 October 2007 (Edinburgh Africa in Motion); Greece: 16 November 2007 (Thessaloniki International Film Festival); United Arab Emirates: December 2007 (Dubai International Film Festival); United States: 10 June 2008 (DVD premiere); Germany: 28 May 2009; France: 28 October 2009

Glossary

ALHAMDULILLAH "All praise is due to Allah" or "Praise be to God"
'ALIM see: 'ulama
ALLAHU AKBAR "Allah is greater"
AL-NAHDHA reformist ideas underpinning the "Arab Renaissance" in the nineteenth and twentieth centuries; the Islamic Renaissance Movement; see also: Ennahdha
ASALA authenticity in/of tradition
ATFD Association Tunisienne des Femmes Démocrates/Tunisian Association of Democratic Women, created in 1989
ATI Agence Tunisienne d'Internet/Tunisian Internet Agency
BABOUCHE a heelless slipper; also called *belgha*
BACLAWA phyllo pastry dessert filled with chopped nuts and soaked in honey
BELDI urban elite of the Tunis medina
BEY the governor of a district or province in the Ottoman Empire. Formerly used in Turkey and Egypt as a courtesy title; "the Bey": the former native ruler of Tunis or Tunisia
BEZNESS a generic expression in Tunisia for someone resourceful, or the activities of such a person, who tries to set up a "small business" with no capital at all; a hustler; the activity of hustling
BOUKHA fig brandy (its name means "alcohol vapor" in Judeo-Tunisian Arabic dialect), with an alcohol percentage ranging between 36 and 40 percent. It originated in Tunisia, where most of it is still produced
BURNOUS cloak

GLOSSARY

CHANGEMENT, LE/THE CHANGE the way in which Ben Ali's regime referred to itself and the "medical coup d'état" that ousted Bourguiba on 7 November 1987; see also: *Le Renouveau*

CHAOUCH French variation of the Turkish, *tchaouch*; porter, usher, doorkeeper, guide, camel driver

CHECHIA close-fitting traditional wool skullcap (usually red) worn in Tunisia

CHICHA Oriental tobacco pipe with a long flexible tube connected to a container where the smoke is cooled by passing through water

CLANDESTIN illegal immigrant (France)

CODE DE LA NATIONALITÉ FRANÇAISE French nationality law

CREDIF Centre de Recherche, d'Etudes, de Documentation et d'Information sur la Femme; initiated by the Tunisian government in 1990 with the aim of consolidating women's rights, the center permanently observes and evaluates the position of women in Tunisia, and thus plays an intermediary role between diverse governmental and nongovernmental institutions

DESTOUR Constitutional Liberal Party founded in 1920, which had as its goal the liberation of Tunisia from French colonial control; see also: Néo-Destour

DJEBBA traditional, medium-length caftan worn by men (Tunisia)

DST La Direction de la Surveillance du Territoire/Directorate of Territorial Surveillance (France), created in 1944

EID AL-ADHA "Festival of Sacrifice" or "Greater Eid" (in Tunisia more commonly referred to as *Eid al-Kabir*, the "Lesser Eid" being *Eid al-Fitr*); an important religious holiday celebrated by Muslims worldwide to commemorate the willingness of Abraham (Ibrahim) to sacrifice his son Ishmael (Isma'il) as an act of obedience to God, before God intervened to provide him with a sheep to sacrifice instead

EID AL-FITR the Muslim holiday that ends the Islamic holy month of Ramadan

ENNAHDHA RENAISSANCE PARTY (TUNISIA) founded under the name of *Movement of the Islamic Tendency* in 1981; in 1989, its name changed to *Hizb al-Nahdha*

FANTASIA celebratory equestrian performance involving galloping of horses and shooting of guns in the air, with the riders decked out in traditional Bedouin garb

FEZ a felt cap (usually red) for a man; shaped like a flat-topped cone with a tassel that hangs from the crown; also called a *tarboosh*

FIQH Islamic jurisprudence

FIS Front Islamique du Salut/Islamic Salvation Front (Algeria)

FITNA sedition or civil strife

FUSHA The Arabic name for what is known in English as literary or modern standard Arabic

HADITH a report of the sayings or actions of the Prophet Mohamed or his companions, together with the tradition of its chain of transmission

HALWA a dense, sweet confection, in Tunisia usually made from sesame paste and sugar, with other ingredients and flavorings often added, such as pistachio nuts, cocoa powder, orange juice, vanilla, or chocolate

HAMMAM Turkish variant of a sauna, distinguished by a focus on water, as opposed to steam

HAREM the part of a Muslim household reserved for wives, concubines, and female servants; the wives (or concubines) of a polygamous man

GLOSSARY

HUDNA truce or cease-fire
IJTIHAD the independent or original interpretation of problems not precisely covered by the Qur'an or *hadith*; the making of a decision in Islamic law by personal effort, independently of any school of jurisprudence (*fiqh*)
IMAM the person who leads prayers in a mosque; in Islam, a recognized leader or a religious teacher
JAHILIYYA pagan ignorance
JIHAD struggle or effort
KANOUN terra-cotta brazier
KASBAH the citadel of a city in northern Africa or the Middle East; the area surrounding such a citadel, typically the old part of a city
KEFFIYEH a traditional Arab headdress or scarf fashioned from a square of cotton and having a distinctive woven check pattern (in Tunisia, usually black and white)
KHAMSA Arabic word for the number five; the name for "The Hand of Fatma" (talisman to ward off the "Evil Eye")
KHUBZ (OR KHOBZ) Tunisian (Arabic) for *bread*
LABLABI hearty soup made from chickpeas and day-old bread, flavored with garlic and cumin
LELLA a feminine title of respect (Madam); the feminine equivalent of "Sidi" (Sir)
LTDH Ligue Tunisienne des droits de l'Homme/Tunisian League for Human Rights, founded in 1976
MARABOUT a Muslim hermit or saint, especially in northern Africa; the tomb of such a hermit or saint
MEDINA the old Arab or non-European quarter of a North African town or city
MEKTOUB destiny; "It is written"
MÉTISSAGE hybridity
NÉO-DESTOUR New Constitutional Liberal Party founded in 1934, following a rupture with the Destour; renamed the Parti Socialiste Destourien (PSD) in 1964
PSC Personal Status Code (Tunisia) Promulgated on August 13, 1956 by beylical decree; came into effect January 1, 1957
PSD Parti Socialiste Destourien/Socialist Destourian Party (formerly the Néo-Destour), the ruling political party from 1964 to 1988, headed by President Bourguiba
QUR'AN the sacred writings of Islam revealed by God to the Prophet Mohamed during his life in Mecca and Medina
RCD Rassemblement Constitutionnel Démocratique/Constitutional Democratic Rally (the former PSD), so renamed by President Ben Ali in 1988
RENOUVEAU, LE/"THE RENEWAL"/"THE NEW ERA" one of the names for the Ben Ali regime; see also: *Le Changement*
SAFSARI a length of white, lightweight cloth worn by Tunisian women as an outer garment, which covers the head and reaches to mid-calf
SALAFI the term used for the most conservative of Islamists
SANS-PAPIERS undocumented aliens (France)
SHARI'A Islamic law based on the teachings of the Qur'an and the traditions of the Prophet (*Hadith* and *Sunna*), prescribing both religious and secular duties and sometimes retributive penalties for lawbreaking

GLOSSARY

SHEIKH a religious official; leader of an Arab family or village

SIDI "Master" or "Saint" (depending on context); a masculine title of respect, meaning "my master"; "Si" means "Mister" or "Sir"

SUNNA the way of life prescribed as normative in Islam, based on the teachings and practices of Mohamed and on exegesis of the Qur'an

TAHHĀR the barber who performs a circumcision

TARBOOSH see: fez

TUNISIANITÉ Tunisianness

TVA Tennessee Valley Authority; a corporation owned by the U.S. government that provides electricity for 9 million people in parts of seven southeastern states at prices below the national average

UFT L'Union des Femmes de Tunisie, created in 1944 by the Tunisian Communist Party

UGTT Union Générale des Travailleurs Tunisiens/Tunisian General Workers' Union, founded in 1946

'ULAMA religious scholars; the body of *mullahs* (Muslim scholars trained in Islam and Islamic law); pl. of *'alim*, wise, learned; active participle of *'alima*, to know

UMFT L'Union Musulmane des Femmes de Tunisie, created in 1936

UMMA worldwide community of believers (Islam)

UNFT L'Union Nationale des Femmes Tunisiennes, created in 1956

WATAN homeland

ZAÎM chief, leader, or spokesman of a group of individuals such as a tribe

Bibliography

Abbassi, Driss. *Entre Bourguiba et Hannibal: Identité tunisienne et histoire depuis l'indépendance.* Aix-en-Provence/Paris: IREMAM/Karthala, 2005.

Abbassi, Driss. *Quand la Tunisie s'invente: Entre Orient et Occident, des imaginaires politiques.* Collection Mémoires/Histoire, no. 146. Paris: Éditions Autrement, 2009.

Abderrezak, Hakim. "*Halfaouine, l'enfant des terrasses*: L'individu-oiseau face à la communauté." *Expressions maghrébines* 5, no. 1 (Summer 2006): 83–96.

Ahmad, Aijaz. "Jameson's Rhetoric of Otherness and the 'National Allegory.'" *Social Text* 17 (Fall 1987): 3–25.

Ahmad, Aijaz. *In Theory: Classes, Nations, Literatures.* London: Verso, 1992.

Ajami, Fouad. "Rebellion in the Land of the Pharaohs." *Wall Street Journal*, 29 January 2011, http://online.wsj.com/article/SB10001424052748703956604576110131980631472.html. Accessed 6 February 2011.

Alexander, Christopher. "Authoritarianism and Civil Society in Tunisia: Back from the Democratic Brink." *Middle East Report* 205, 27 (Winter 1997), www.merip.org/mer/mer205/authoritarianism-civil-society-tunisia.

Alexander, M. Jacqui, and Chandra Talpade Mohanty, eds. *Feminist Genealogies, Colonial Legacies, Democratic Futures.* New York: Routledge, 1997.

Alexandropoulos, Jacques, and Patrick Cabanel, eds. *La Tunisie mosaïque.* Toulouse: Presses Universitaires du Mirail, 2000.

Allani, Alaya. "The post-revolution Tunisian Constituent Assembly: controversy over powers and prerogatives." *Journal of North African Studies* 18, no. 1 (January 2013): 131–140.

BIBLIOGRAPHY

Allani, Alaya. "The Islamists in Tunisia between confrontation and participation: 1980–2008." *Journal of North African Studies* 14, no. 2 (June 2009): 257–272.

Amnesty International Report 2003: Tunisia, 28 May 2003, www.unhcr.org/refworld/docid/3edb47e118.html.

Anderson, Benedict. *Imagined Communities: Reflections on the Origin and Spread of Nationalism* [1983]. Revised Edition. London: Verso, 1991.

Anderson, Kevin. "Philosophic Dialogue: Marx's *Eighteenth Brumaire* Today." *News & Letters*, December 2002, www.newsandletters.org/Issues/2002/December/PhilD_Dec02.htm.

Appadurai, Arjun. *Modernity at Large: Cultural Dimensions of Globalization*. Minneapolis: University of Minnesota Press, 1996.

Apter, Emily. *Continental Drift: From National Characters to Virtual Subjects*. Chicago: University of Chicago Press, 1999.

Arendt, Hannah. *Antisemitism*. New York: Harcourt, Brace & World, 1951.

Armes, Roy. "From State Production to *Cinéma d'Auteur* in Algeria." In Gugler, *Film in the Middle East and North Africa*, 294–305.

Armes, Roy. "The Poetic Vision of Nacer Khemir." *Third Text* 24, no. 1 (January 2010): 69–82.

Armes, Roy. *Postcolonial Images: Studies in North African Film*. Bloomington: Indiana University Press, 2005.

Arsu, Sebnem. "Another Shoe Flies, This Time in Istanbul at I.M.F. Chief." *New York Times*, 2 October 2009, www.nytimes.com/2009/10/02/world/europe/02shoe.html?_r=1&th&emc=th.

Asad, Talal. "Ethnography, Literature, and Politics: Some Readings and Uses of Salman Rushdie's *The Satanic Verses*." *Cultural Anthropology* 5, no. 3 (August 1990): 239–269.

Ashcroft, Bill, Gareth Griffiths, and Helen Tiffin, eds. *The Post-Colonial Studies Reader*. London: Routledge, 1995.

Bachy, Victor. "Les grands thèmes: Un miroir de la société tunisienne." *CinémAction* 14 (Spring 1981): 149–152.

Bakari, Imruh, and Mbye Cham, eds. *African Experiences of Cinema*. London: British Film Institute, 1996.

Balibar, Etienne. "The Nation Form: History and Ideology." In Etienne Balibar and Immanuel Wallerstein. *Race, Nation, Class: Ambiguous Identities*. Translation of Etienne Balibar by Chris Turner. London: Verso, 1988, 86–106.

Barakat, Halim. *Al-Mujtam'a al-Arabi al-Mu'asir* [*Contemporary Arab Society*]. Beirut: Center for Unity Studies, 1984.

Barbencey, Pierre. "Nouri Bouzid: Une société fondée sur le viol." *L'Humanité*, 17 October 1995, www.humanite.fr/1995-10-17_Articles_-Nouri-Bouzid-une-societe-fondee-sur-le-viol.

Barlet, Olivier. "Apt 2011: Les débats du printemps arabe." In Caillé and Martin, *Les cinémas du Maghreb et leurs publics*, 312–319.

Barlet, Olivier et al. "Cinéma et révolution" (roundtable discussion led by Tahar Chikaoui and Olivier Barlet at the *Festival des cinémas d'Afrique*, Apt, France, 6 November 2011). *Africultures: Le site et la revue de référence des cultures africaines*, 16 November 2011, www.

africultures.com/php/index.php?nav=article&no=10480. Reprinted in Caillé and Martin, eds., *Les cinémas du Maghreb et leurs publics*, 330–340.

Barlet, Olivier. "Le cinéma tunisien à la lumière du printemps arabe." In Caillé and Martin, *Les cinémas du Maghreb et leurs publics*, 270–280.

Barlet, Olivier. "La leçon de cinéma de Nouri Bouzid." *Africultures: Le site et la revue de référence des cultures africaines*, 18 April 2006, www.africultures.com/php/index.php?nav=article&no=4385.

Barthes, Roland. *Camera Lucida: Reflections on Photography*. Trans. Richard Howard. New York: Hill and Wang, 1981.

Barthes, Roland. *Writing Degree Zero*. Trans. Annette Lavers and Colin Smith. New York: Hill and Wang, 1968.

Bataille, Georges. *L'érotisme*. Paris: Minuit, 1957.

Bauman, Zygmunt. *Globalization: The Human Consequences*. New York: Columbia University Press, 1998.

Beau, Nicolas, and Catherine Graciet. *La régente de Carthage: Main basse sur la Tunisie*. Paris: La Découverte, 2009.

Beau, Nicolas, and Jean-Pierre Tuquoi. *Notre ami Ben Ali: L'envers du "miracle tunisien"*. Paris: La Découverte, 1999.

Beaugé, Florence. "L'économie tunisienne, miracle ou mirage?" *Le Monde*, 25 April 2008. In Beaugé, *La Tunisie de Ben Ali*, 78–81.

Beaugé, Florence. "En Tunisie, un 'cycle d'injustice' se perpétue." *Le Monde*, 11 June 2003. In Beaugé, *La Tunisie de Ben Ali*, 29–30.

Beaugé, Florence. *La Tunisie de Ben Ali: Miracle ou mirage?* Paris: Éditions du Cygne, 2010.

Beaugé, Florence. "La Tunisie des illusions perdues." *Le Monde*, 7 November 2008. In Beaugé, *La Tunisie de Ben Ali*, 68–72.

Béji, Hélé. *Désenchantement national: Essai sur la décolonisation*. Paris: François Maspero, 1982.

Béji, Hélé. *L'imposture culturelle*. Paris: Stock, 1997.

Béji, Hélé. *Nous, décolonisés: Essai*. Paris: Arléa, 2008.

Belhassen, Souhayr. "Les legs bourguibiens de la répression." In Camau and Geisser, *Habib Bourguiba: La trace et l'héritage*, 391–404.

Bellin, Eva. "Civil Society in Formation: Tunisia." In Norton, *Civil Society in the Middle East*, 120–147.

Ben Ammar, Abdellatif. "Putting Forward a Clear View on Life." In Downing, *Film and Politics in the Third World*, 109–117.

Ben Youssef Zayzafoon, Lamia. *The Production of the Muslim Woman: Negotiating Text, History, and Ideology*. Lanham, Md.: Lexington, 2005.

Benedict, Stephen. "Tunisie, le mirage de l'état fort." *Esprit*, March–April 1997: 27–42.

Bensalah, Mohamed. *Cinéma en Méditerranée: Une passerelle entre les cultures*. Aix-en-Provence: Édisud, 2005.

Bensmaïa, Réda. *Experimental Nations: Or, the Invention of the Maghreb*. Princeton, N.J.: Princeton University Press, 2003.

Bentley, Eric. *The Life of the Drama*. New York: Atheneum, 1967.

Berman, Marshall. *All That Is Solid Melts Into Air: The Experience of Modernity.* New York: Simon & Schuster, 1982.

Bernanos, Georges. *Les enfants humiliés: Journal 1939–1940.* Paris: Gallimard, 1949.

Berrah, Mouny, Victor Bachy, Mohand Ben Salama, and Férid Boughedir, eds. "Cinémas du Maghreb." Special issue, *CinémAction* 14 (Spring 1981).

Bertin-Maghit, Jean-Pierre, ed. *Lorsque Clio s'empare du documentaire,* vol. 2. Paris: L'Harmattan, 2011.

Bertin-Maghit, Jean-Pierre, and Geneviève Sellier, eds. *La fiction éclatée: Petits et grands écrans français et francophones, Volume 1: Études socioculturelles.* Paris: Ina-L'Harmattan, 2007.

Bivona, Rosalia. "'Si vous n'aimez pas le bruit des bottes, portez des babouches!': Subversion, liberté et modernité dans le film *Bedwin hacker* de Nadia El Fani." *Expressions maghrébines* 5, no. 1 (Summer 2006): 27–41.

Blanchard, Pascal, Nicolas Bancel, and Sandrine Lemaire, eds. *La fracture coloniale: La société française au prisme de l'héritage colonial.* Paris: La Découverte, 2005.

Bodman, Herbert L., and Nayereh Tohidi, eds. *Women in Muslim Societies: Diversity Within Unity.* Boulder, Colo.: Lynne Rienner, 1998.

Bordwell, David, Janet Staiger, and Kristin Thompson. *The Classical Hollywood Cinema: Film Style and Mode of Production to 1960.* New York: Columbia University Press, 1985.

Boughedir, Férid. "La communauté juive dans le cinéma tunisien." Harissa.com. 15 May 2012. www.harissa.com/news/article/la-communauté-juive-dans-le-cinéma-tunisien.

Boughedir, Férid. "Le cinéma tunisien: Du triomphe aux interrogations…" 27th Festival des 3 Continents, 22–29 November 2005, www.3continents.com/f3c2005/tunisie.html.

Boughedir, Férid. "La victime et la matrone: les deux images de la femme dans le cinéma tunisien." *CinémAction* 111 (Spring 2004): 103–112.

Boughedir, Férid. "'Le multiplexe est le remède' au piratage des films en Afrique" [interview]. Agence France Presse, 22 October 2007.

Boughedir, Férid. "Les principales tendances du cinéma tunisien." *CinémAction* 14 (Spring 1981): 153–159.

Bouhdiba, Abdelwahab. "Aïcha, que faisait donc ton père l'ogre?" *L'imaginaire maghrébin: étude de dix contes pour enfants.* Tunis: Cérès, 1994, 113–119.

Bouhdiba, Abdelwahab. *La sexualité en Islam.* Paris: Quadrige/Presses Universitaires de France, 1975.

Bouhdiba, Abdelwahab. *Quêtes sociologiques: Continuités et ruptures au Maghreb.* Tunis: Cérès, 1995.

Bouhdiba, Abdelwahab. *Sexuality in Islam.* Trans. Alan Sheridan. London: Saqi, 2004.

Bouzid, Nouri, trans. Shereen el Ezabi. "New Realism in Arab Cinema: The Defeat-Conscious Cinema." *Alif: Journal of Comparative Poetics* 15 (1995): 242–250.

Bouzid, Nouri. "Note d'intention: Extraits d'interview donnée par le réalisateur à des journaux tunisiens." In *Rih Essed* press kit, 1986. Unpaginated document. Clippings archive of the Museum of Modern Art Film Study Center, New York.

Bouzid, Nouri. "On Inspiration." In Bakari and Cham, *African Experiences of Cinema,* 48–59.

Bouzid, Nouri. *Sources of Inspiration*. Lecture 5. Amsterdam: SOURCES, an Initiative of the MEDIA program of the European Union/Dutch Ministry of Culture, 1994.

Boym, Svetlana. *The Future of Nostalgia*. New York: Basic, 2001.

Brahimi, Denise. *50 ans de cinéma maghrébin*. Paris: Minerve, 2009.

Brahimi, Denise. *Cinémas d'Afrique francophone et du Maghreb*. Paris: Nathan, 1997.

Brand, Laurie A. *Women, the State, and Political Liberalization: Middle Eastern and North African Experiences*. New York: Columbia University Press, 1998.

Braudy, Leo, and Marshall Cohen, eds. *Film Theory and Criticism*, 6th ed. New York: Oxford University Press, 2004.

brightsfrance.org. "TUNISIE: Ni Allah ni maître (Nadia El Fani)." brightsfrance.org. www.brightsfrance.org/forum/viewtopic.php?f=10&t=2331. Accessed 28 August 2011.

Brooks, Van Wyck. "On Creating a Usable Past." *The Dial*, 11 April 1918, 337–341.

Brown, Derek. "Doomed Grooms." *Guardian Weekly*, 9–15 July 2010, 14.

Burguière, André. "L'historiographie des origines de la France: Genèse d'un imaginaire national." *Annales: Histoire, Sciences Sociales* 58, no. 1 (January–February 2003): 41–62.

Caillé, Patricia, and Florence Martin, eds., with the collaboration of Kamel Ben Ouanès and Hamid Aïdouni. *Les cinémas du Maghreb et leurs publics*. Paris: L'Harmattan, 2012.

Camau, Michel, and Vincent Geisser, eds. *Habib Bourguiba: La trace et l'héritage*. Paris: Karthala, 2004.

Camau, Michel, and Vincent Geisser. *Le syndrome autoritaire: Politique en Tunisie de Bourguiba à Ben Ali*. Mayenne, France: Presses de Sciences Po, 2003.

Carpenter-Latiri, Dora. "'Née à Tunis virgule Tunisie': *Avenue de France* de Colette Fellous." *Expressions maghrébines: Revue de la coordination internationale des chercheurs sur les littératures maghrébines* 5, no. 1 (Summer 2006): 97–111.

Chambers, Iain. *Mediterranean Crossings: The Politics of an Interrupted Modernity*. Durham, N.C.: Duke University Press, 2008.

Chamkhi, Sonia. *Cinéma tunisien nouveau: Parcours autres*. Tunis: Sud Éditions, 2002.

Charrad, M. M. "Cultural Diversity Within Islam: Veils and Laws in Tunisia." In Bodman and Tohidi, *Women in Muslim Societies*, 63–79.

Charrad, Mounira M. *States and Women's Rights: The Making of Postcolonial Tunisia, Algeria, and Morocco*. Berkeley: University of California Press, 2001.

Chomiak, Laryssa, and Robert P. Parks. "Repossessing the Dispossessed." *Jadaliyya*, 9 January 2013. http://www.jadaliyya.com/pages/index/9485/repossessing-the-dispossessed. Accessed 30 January 2013.

Chouikha, Larbi. "La modernité au miroir du ramadan télévisuel. Le cas des familles et des citadins de Tunis." In Ossman, *Miroirs maghrébins*, 187–204.

Chouraqui, André N. *Between East and West: A History of the Jews of North Africa*. Trans. Michael M. Bernet. Philadelphia: Jewish Publication Society of America, 1968.

Cincotta, Richard. "Tunisia's Shot at Democracy: What Demographics and Recent History Tell Us." *New Security Beat*, 25 January 2011, www.newsecuritybeat.org/2011/01/tunisias-shot-at-democracy-what.html.

Comaroff, Jean, and John L. Comaroff. "Millennial Capitalism: First Thoughts on a Second Coming," *Public Culture* 12, no. 2 (2000): 291–343.

Corriou, Morgan. "La consommation cinématographique: Les plaisirs du cinéma en Tunisie au tournant de 1956." In Caillé and Martin, *Les cinémas du Maghreb et leurs publics*, 116–140.
CPJ: Committee to Protect Journalists: An Independent, Nonprofit Organization Dedicated to Defending Press Freedom Worldwide. "Attacks on the Press in 2002," www.cpj.org/attacks02/mideast02/tunisia.html.
Dames, Nicholas. *Amnesiac Selves: Nostalgia, Forgetting, and British Fiction, 1810–1870*. Oxford: Oxford University Press, 2001.
Davidson Ladly, Meghan. "Gay Pakistanis, Still in Shadows, Seek Acceptance." *New York Times*, 3 November 2012, www.nytimes.com/2012/11/04/world/asia/gays-in-pakistan-move-cautiously-to-gain-acceptance.html?hpw.
DeGeorges, Thomas P. "The social construction of the Tunisian revolutionary martyr in the media and popular perception." *Journal of North African Studies* 18, no. 3 (June 2013): 482–493.
Delay, Jean. *La jeunesse d'André Gide*. Paris: Gallimard [1956–57], 1992.
Dhaouadi Mahmoud. *Globalization of the Other Underdevelopment: Third World Cultural Identities*. Kuala Lumpur: A. S. Noordeen, 2002.
Distinctive Women: Blog des femmes qui veulent voyager autrement. www.distinctivewomen.com/archive/2007/07/13/le-monde-feminin.html. Accessed 1 July 2009.
Downing, John D. H., ed. *Film and Politics in the Third World*. Brooklyn, NY: Autonomedia, 1987.
Dundes, Alan. "Wet and Dry, the Evil Eye: An Essay in Indo-European and Semitic Worldview." In *Interpreting Folklore*, 93–133. Bloomington: Indiana University Press, 1980.
Dwyer, Kevin. "Morocco: A National Cinema with Large Ambitions." In Gugler, *Film in the Middle East and North Africa*, 324–338.
Economist, The. "Ali Baba Gone, but What about the 40 Thieves?" *The Economist*, 22–28 January 2011, 31–33.
Economist, The. "Blog Standard: Authoritarian Governments Can Lock Up Bloggers. It Is Harder to Outwit Them." *The Economist*, 28 June–4 July 2008, 67, www.economist.com/node/11622401?story_id=11622401.
Elbousty, Moulay Youness. "Abu al-Qasim al-Shabbi's 'The Will to Live': galvanising the Tunisian revolution." *Journal of North African Studies* 18, no. 1 (January 2013): 159-163.
El Fani, Nadia. "'En politique, ce n'est pas grave de perdre'" [interview with Olivier Barlet]. *Africultures: Le site et la revue de référence des cultures africaines*, 11 January 2012, www.africultures.com/php/index.php?nav=article&no=10571. Reprinted in Caillé and Martin, *Les cinémas du Maghreb et leurs publics*, 298–303.
Elgaaïed, Leïla. "Le documentaire comme combat" (interview with Hichem Ben Ammar). *Africultures, Le site et la revue de référence des cultures africaines*, 22 January 2007. http://www.africultures.com/popup_article.asp?no=4701.
Entelis, John P. "The Democratic Imperative vs. the Authoritarian Impulse: The Maghrib State Between Transition and Terrorism." *Middle East Journal* 59, no. 4 (Autumn 2005): 537–558.
Entelis, John P., ed. *Islam, Democracy, and the State in North Africa*. Bloomington: Indiana University Press, 1997.

Fabre, Clarisse. "Vers un nouvel 'âge d'or' du documentaire au Maghreb?" *Le Monde*, 29 November 2012, www.lemonde.fr/culture/article/2012/11/29/vers-un-nouvel-age-d-or-du-documentaire-au-maghreb_1797325_3246.html.

Fédération Panafricaine des Cinéastes/Panafrican Federation of Film Makers, ed. *L'Afrique et le centenaire du cinéma/Africa and the Centenary of Cinema*. Paris and Dakar: Présence Africaine, 1995.

Field, Michael. *Inside the Arab World*. Cambridge, Mass.: Harvard University Press, 1994.

Freud, Sigmund. "Mourning and Melancholia" (1917). In *The Standard Edition of the Complete Psychological Works*. Ed. James Strachey and trans. James Strachey et al., 14: 237–258, London: Hogarth Press and the Institute of Psycho-Analysis, 1953–1974.

Freud, Sigmund. *An Outline of Psychoanalysis*. Trans. James Strachey. New York: Norton, 1949.

Friedman, Natalie. "Nostalgia, Nationhood, and the New Immigrant Narrative: Gary Shteyngart's *The Russian Debutante's Handbook* and the Post-Soviet Experience." *Iowa Journal of Cultural Studies* 5 (Fall 2004), www.uiowa.edu/~ijcs/nostalgia/friedman.htm.

Friedman, Thomas L. "Newt, Mitt, Bibi and Vladimir." *New York Times*, 13 December 2011, www.nytimes.com/2011/12/14/opinion/friedman-newt-mitt-bibi-and-vladimir.html?_r=1&hp.

Fromherz, Allen James. *Ibn Khaldun: Life and Times*. Edinburgh: Edinburgh University Press, 2011.

Fukuyama, Francis. *The End of History and the Last Man*. New York: Free Press/Simon & Schuster, 1992.

Fukuyama, Francis. "Identity and Migration." *Prospect* 131 (25 February 2007), www.prospect-magazine.co.uk/article_details.php?id=8239.

Fukuyama, Francis. *Trust: The Social Virtues and the Creation of Prosperity*. New York: Simon & Schuster, 1995.

Fuller, Thomas. "Reform Lawyer Says Tunisia Risks Anarchy." *New York Times*, 21 February 2011, www.nytimes.com/2011/02/22/world/africa/22tunisia.html?hp.

Galley, Micheline. "Arabic Folk Epics." In Honko, *Religion, Myth, and Folklore in the World's Epics*, 425–438.

Gana, Nouri. "Bourguiba's Sons: Melancholy Manhood in Modern Tunisia." *Journal of North African Studies* 15, no. 1 (March 2010): 105–126.

Gauch, Suzanne. *Liberating Shahrazad: Feminism, Postcolonialism, and Islam*. Minneapolis: University of Minnesota Press, 2007.

Génin, Bernard. "Interview with Moufida Tlatli." *Télérama*, 7 September 1994, 32–33.

Ghannouchi, Rached. "Interview with Rached Ghannouchi, Nahdha Chairman." *BICNews*, 25 July 1997, www.iol.ie/~afifi/BICNews/Mag/mag6.htm.

Gide, André. "Carnets d'Égypte." *Journal 1939–1949—Souvenirs*. Paris: Gallimard/Bibliothèque de la Pléiade, 1954, 2, 1049–1077.

Gide, André. *Les faux-monnayeurs* (1925). Paris: Gallimard, 1978.

Goldstein, Warren. "What Will Israel Not Do?" *Huffington Post*, 31 May 2010, www.huffingtonpost.com/warren-goldstein/what-will-israel-not-do_b_595462.html.

Gollin, Richard M. *A Viewer's Guide to Film: Arts, Artifices, and Issues*. New York: McGraw-Hill, 1992.

Grell, Jacques, Rachid Toumi, and Hatteb Sedkaoui. *Les XVIe et XVIIe siècles pour la quatrième année de l'enseignement secondaire*. Tunis: Société tunisienne de diffusion, 1969.

Guardian, The. "US Embassy Cables: Tunisia—A US Foreign Policy Conundrum." *Guardian*, 7 December 2010. www.guardian.co.uk/world/us-embassy-cables-documents/217138.

Gugler, Josef, ed. *Film in the Middle East and North Africa: Creative Dissidence*. Austin, Tex.: University of Texas Press, 2011.

Hacker, Jacob S., and Paul Pierson. *Winner-Take-All Politics: How Washington Made the Rich Richer—And Turned Its Back on the Middle Class*. New York: Simon & Schuster, 2010.

Hafez, Sabry. "Shifting Identities in Maghribi Cinema: The Algerian Paradigm." *Alif: Journal of Comparative Poetics* 15 (1995): 39–80.

Hannoum, Abdelmajid. *Colonial Histories, Post-Colonial Memories: The Legend of the Kahina, A North African Heroine*. Portsmouth, N.H.: Heinemann, 2001.

Hartog, François. *Régimes d'historicité. Présentisme et expériences du temps*. Paris: Seuil, 2003.

Haskell, Molly. *From Reverence to Rape: The Treatment of Women in the Movies*. New York: Holt, Rinehart and Winston, 1974.

Hassan, Waïl S. "Alternatives to Secular Modernity" [review of Anouar Majid, *Unveiling Traditions: Postcolonial Islam in a Polycentric World*]. In "Growing Up Elsewhere," eds. Elaine Orr and Deborah Wyrick. Special double issue *Jouvert: A Journal of Postcolonial Studies* 6, nos. 1–2 (Fall 2001), http://english.chass.ncsu.edu/jouvert/v6i1-2/hassan.htm.

Hawkins, Simon. "Hijab: Feminine Allure and Charm to Men in Tunis," *Ethnology* 47, no. 1 (Winter 2008): 1–21.

Hawkins, Simon. "Who Wears *Hijab* with the President: Constructing a Modern Islam in Tunisia." *Journal of Religion in Africa* 41 (2001): 35–58.

Hayes, Jarrod. *Queer Nations: Marginal Sexualities in the Maghreb*. Chicago: University of Chicago Press, 2000.

Hazbun, Waleed. "Images of Openness, Spaces of Control: The Politics of Tourism Development in Tunisia." *Arab Studies Journal* 15, no. 2/16, no. 1 (Fall 2007/Spring 2008): 10–35.

Hennebelle, Guy. "Introduction: 3 pays, 120 films, 45 millions de Maghrébins." *CinémAction* 14 (Spring 1981): 5–7.

Herman, Susan N. *Taking Liberties: The War on Terror and the Erosion of American Democracy*. New York: Oxford University Press, 2011.

Hibou, Béatrice. "Domination and Control in Tunisia: Economic Levers for the Exercise of Political Power." *Review of African Political Economy* 108 (2006): 185–206.

Hibou, Béatrice. *La force de l'obéissance: Économie politique de la répression en Tunisie*. Paris: La Découverte, 2006.

Hibou, Béatrice. *The Force of Obedience: The Political Economy of Repression in Tunisia*. Trans. Andrew Brown. Cambridge: Polity, 2011.

Higbee, Will. "Le cinéma maghrébin vu de l'autre côté de la Méditerranée: cinéma national/transnational/diasporique." In Caillé and Martin, *Les cinémas du Maghreb et leurs publics*, 102–114.

Hjort, Mette, and Duncan Petrie, eds. *The Cinema of Small Nations*. Bloomington: Indiana University Press, 2007.

Hobsbawm, E. J. *Nations and Nationalism since 1870: Programme, Myth, Reality*. Cambridge: Cambridge University Press, 1990.

Hobsbawm, Eric. "Introduction: Inventing Traditions." In Hobsbawm and Ranger, *The Invention of Tradition*, 1–14.
Hobsbawm, Eric, and Terence Ranger, eds. *The Invention of Tradition*. Cambridge: Cambridge University Press, 1983.
Hochberg, Gil. "National Allegories and the Emergence of Female Voice in Moufida Tlatli's *The Silences of the Palace*." *Third Text* 50 (Spring 2000): 33–44.
Honko, Lauri, ed. *Religion, Myth, and Folklore in the World's Epics: The Kalevala and Its Predecessors*. Berlin: Mouton de Gruyter, 1990.
hooks, bell. "Reflections on Race and Sex." *Yearning: race, gender, and cultural politics*. Boston: South End, 1990, 57–64.
Hopwood, Derek. *Habib Bourguiba of Tunisia: The Tragedy of Longevity*. New York: St. Martin's, 1992.
Houimdi, Othman, and Aboulkacem Kerrou. *Cours d'histoire pour le cycle primaire conformes aux programmes officiels du secrétariat à l'éducation nationale*. Vol. 1, *Pour la cinquième année*, 1st ed., Tunis, 1959.
Hoveyda, Fereydoun. *Que veulent les arabes?* Paris: FIRST, 1991.
Huntington, Samuel P. "The Clash of Civilizations?" *Foreign Affairs* 72, no. 3 (Summer 1993): 22–49.
Hurst, Heike. "'Poupées d'argile,' entretien avec Nouzi Bouzid." *Le Monde libertaire: L'hebdomadaire de la Fédération anarchiste*, no. 1369 (30 September–6 October 2004). www.monde-libertaire.fr/n1369-30-sept-6-oct-2004/12120-poupees-dargile-entretien-avec-nouzi-bouzid.
Hurst, Heike, and Olivier Barlet. "Interview with Nouri Bouzid about *Poupées d'argile*, Namur [France], September 2002." *Africultures: Le site et la revue de référence des cultures africaines*, 9 January 2003, www.africultures.com/index.asp?menu=revue_affiche_article&no=2658.
Jaïdi, Moulay Driss. "Une étude de cas: Le Maroc. Situation paradoxale d'une cinématographie en devenir." In Caillé and Martin, *Les cinémas du Maghreb et leurs publics*, 208–218.
Jameson, Fredric. "A Brief Response." *Social Text* 17 (Fall 1987): 26–27.
Jameson, Fredric. "Metacommentary." *Proceedings of the Modern Language Association* 86 (1971): 9–17.
Jameson, Fredric. *Postmodernism, or the Cultural Logic of Late Capitalism*. Durham, N.C.: Duke University Press, 1991.
Jameson, Fredric. "Third-World Literature in the Era of Multinational Capitalism." *Social Text* 15 [vol. 5, no. 3] (Fall 1986): 65–88.
Janmohamed, Abdul R. "The Economy of Manichean Allegory: The Function of Racial Difference in Colonialist Literature." *Critical Inquiry* 12, no. 1 (1985). Reprinted in Ashcroft et al., *The Post-Colonial Studies Reader*, 18–23.
Jemni, Mahmoud. "Essai d'une typologie du cinéma tunisien." *Africiné: Le Site de la Fédération Africaine de la Critique Cinématographique*, 5 August 2011, www.africine.org/?menu=art&no=10356, accessed 17 February 2012.
Jemni, Mahmoud. *Quarante ans de cinéma tunisien: Regards croisés*. Gabès, Tunisia: SOGIM, 2006.
Joseph, Suad. "History and Its Histories: Story-Making and the Present." *Review of Middle East Studies* 46, no. 1 (Summer 2012): 6–23.

BIBLIOGRAPHY

Judt, Tony. *Ill Fares the Land*. New York: Penguin, 2010.

Julien, Charles-André. *Et la Tunisie devint indépendante . . . (1951–1957)*. Paris: Jeune Afrique, 1985.

Kchir-Bendana, Kmar. "Ideologies of the Nation in Tunisian Cinema." *Journal of North African Studies* 8, no. 1 (Spring 2003): 35–42.

Kerrou, Mohamed. "Portraits d'individus—Autopsie d'une société—étude sociologique d'un film tunisien: *L'homme de cendres* de Nouri Bouzid." Special supplement, *Utruhāt*, nos. 11–12, 1987: 13–19.

Kerrou, Mohamed. "Le *zaîm* comme individu unique." In *L'individu au Maghreb* (Actes du colloque internationale de Beit el-Hikma, Carthage, 31 October–2 November 1991), eds. Mohammed Arkoun and Héchmi Dhaoui, 235–248. Tunis: Éditions TS, 1993.

Khalil, Andrea, ed. *North African Cinema in a Global Context: Through the Lens of Diaspora*. London: Routledge, 2008.

Khayati, Khémaïs. *Cinémas arabes: Topographie d'une image éclatée*. Paris: L'Harmattan, 1996.

Khayati, Khémaïs. "Un cinéma sans tabou." *Journal Programme: Cinéma* 4—Institut du Monde Arabe, Paris (January–February–March, 1995): 1–2.

Khélil, Hédi. *Abécédaire du cinéma tunisien*. Tunis: SIMPACT, 2007.

Khélil, Hédi, ed. *Le parcours et la trace: Témoignages et documents sur le cinéma tunisien*. Salammbô, Tunisia: MediaCom, 2002.

Khélil, Hédi. *Sens/Jouissance: Tourisme, érotisme, argent dans deux fictions coloniales d'André Gide*. Tunis: La Nef-Démeter, 1988.

King, Stephen J. *The New Authoritarianism in the Middle East and North Africa*. Bloomington: Indiana University Press, 2009.

Kinzer, Stephen. "Third World's Answer to Group of 7." *New York Times*, 14 June 1997, www.nytimes.com/1997/06/14/business/third-world-s-answer-to-the-group-of-7.html.

Kirkpatrick, David D. "Behind Tunisia Unrest, Rage over Wealth of Ruling Family." *New York Times*, 13 January 2011, www.nytimes.com/2011/01/14/world/africa/14tunisia.html?ref=africa&pagewanted=all.

Kirkpatrick, David D. "Tunisia Leader Flees and Prime Minister Claims Power." *New York Times*, 14 January 2011, www.nytimes.com/2011/01/15/world/africa/15tunis.html?_r=3&ref=daviddkirkpatrick.

Korany, Bahgat. "The Maghrib." In *Politics and Government in the Middle East and North Africa*. Ed. Tareq Y. Ismael and Jacqueline S. Ismael. Miami: Florida International University Press, 1991, 513-537.

Kracauer, Siegfried. *From Caligari to Hitler: A Psychological History of the German Film*. Princeton, N.J.: Princeton University Press, 1947.

Krichen, Aziz. *Le syndrome Bourguiba*. Tunis: Cérès, 1992.

Kristeva, Julia. *Nations Without Nationalism*. Trans. Leon S. Roudiez. New York: Columbia University Press, 1993.

Kristeva, Julia. *Strangers to Ourselves*. Trans. Leon S. Roudiez. New York: Columbia University Press, 1991.

Kuran, Timur. *The Long Divergence: How Islamic Law Held Back the Middle East*. Princeton, N.J.: Princeton University Press, 2011.

Lacan, Jacques. *The Seminar of Jacques Lacan, Book 2, The Ego in Freud's Theory and in the Technique of Psychoanalysis, 1954–1955.* Ed. Jacques-Alain Miller and trans. Sylvana Tomaselli. New York: Norton, 1988.

Lamloum, Olfa, and Bernard Ravenel, eds. *La Tunisie de Ben Ali: La société contre le régime.* Paris: L'Harmattan, 2002.

Lang, Robert. *American Film Melodrama: Griffith, Vidor, Minnelli.* Princeton, N.J.: Princeton University Press, 1989.

Lang, Robert. "La décolonisation et le boxeur tunisien: *J'en ai vu des étoiles* (2007)." In Bertin-Maghit, *Lorsque Clio s'empare du documentaire,* 149–163.

Lang, Robert. "Deconstructing Melodramatic 'Destiny': *Late Marriage* (Dover Koshashvili, 2001) and *Two Lovers* (James Gray, 2008)." *Film Journal* 1 (September 2010), www.ucl.ac.uk/silva/filmjournal/deconstructing2011. Accessed 11 September 2011.

Lang, Robert. *Masculine Interests: Homoerotics in Hollywood Film.* New York: Columbia University Press, 2002.

Lang, Robert. *Le mélodrame américain: Griffith, Vidor, Minnelli.* Trans. Noël Burch. Paris: L'Harmattan, 2008.

Lang, Robert. "*Le pique-nique*, Férid Boughedir et la 'tunisianité.'" In Bertin-Maghit and Sellier, *La fiction éclatée,* 231–242.

Lee, Ken. "Jenin Rises from the Dirt," *BBC News*, 24 June 2003, http://news.bbc.co.uk/2/hi/middle_east/3015814.stm.

Levigne, Noëlle. *Manuel d'histoire (1500–1848) à l'usage des élèves de deuxième année de l'enseignement moyen.* Tunis: Publications de l'Office pédagogique, 1961.

Long, David E., and Bernard Reich, eds. *The Government and Politics of the Middle East and North Africa.* Boulder, Colo.: Westview, 1995.

Lynch, Marc. "Watching Egypt (but Not Al Jazeera)." *Foreign Policy* website, 25 January 2011, http://lynch.foreignpolicy.com/posts/2011/01/25/watching_egypt_and_lebanon_and_the_pa_and.

Maddy-Weitzman, Bruce, and Daniel Zisenwine, eds. *The Maghrib in the New Century: Identity, Religion, and Politics.* Gainesville: University Press of Florida, 2007.

Majid, Anouar. *Unveiling Traditions: Postcolonial Islam in a Polycentric World.* Durham, N.C.: Duke University Press, 2000.

Malkmus, Lizbeth, and Roy Armes. *Arab and African Film Making.* London: Zed, 1991.

Maltin, Leonard. *Leonard Maltin's 2007 Movie and Video Guide.* New York: Penguin, 2006.

Marsaud, Olivia. "La Tunisie sans tabous: *Bedwin Hacker* de Nadia El Fani." *Afrik.com*, 9 July 2003, www.afrik.com/article6344.html.

Martin, Florence. "Cinema and State in Tunisia." In Gugler, *Film in the Middle East and North Africa,* 324–338.

Martin, Florence. *Screens and Veils: Maghrebi Women's Cinema.* Bloomington and Indianapolis: Indiana University Press, 2011.

Martin, Florence. "Silence and Scream: Moufida Tlatli's Cinematic Suite." *Studies in French Cinema* 4, no. 3 (2004): 175–185.

Martin, Florence. "Tunisia." In Hjort and Petrie, *The Cinema of Small Nations,* 213–228.

Martin, Florence. "Transvergence and Cultural Detours: Nadia El Fani's *Bedwin Hacker* (2002)." *Studies in French Cinema* 7, no 2 (2007): 119–129.

Marx, Karl. *The Eighteenth Brumaire of Louis Bonaparte.* New York: International Publishers, 2003.

Marzouki, Ilhem. *Le mouvement des femmes en Tunisie au XXème siècle: Féminisme et politique.* Paris: Maisonneuve-Larose (Collection Enjeux), 1994.

Massad, Joseph A. *Desiring Arabs.* Chicago: University of Chicago Press, 2007.

McClintock, Anne. *Imperial Leather: Race, Gender and Sexuality in the Colonial Contest.* New York: Routledge, 1995.

McKnight, Maureen. "'Scarcely in the Twilight of Liberty': Empathic Unsettlement in Charles Chesnutt's *The Conjure Woman.*" *Iowa Journal of Cultural Studies* 5 (Fall 2004), www.uiowa.edu/~ijcs/nostalgia/mcknight.htm.

Mearsheimer, John J., and Stephen M. Walt. *The Israel Lobby and U.S. Foreign Policy.* New York: Farrar, Straus and Giroux, 2007.

Memmi, Albert. *The Colonizer and the Colonized* [1957], expanded ed. Trans. Howard Greenfeld. Boston: Beacon, 1991.

Memmi, Albert. *Decolonization and the Decolonized.* Trans. Robert Bononno. Minneapolis: University of Minnesota Press, 2006.

Memmi, Albert. *The Pillar of Salt.* Trans. Edouard Roditi. Boston: Beacon, 1992.

Mernissi, Fatima. *Le harem et l'Occident.* Paris: Albin Michel, 2001.

Meyer, Karl E. "Who Gets to Be French?" *New York Times,* 11 April 2012, http://www.nytimes.com/2012/04/12/opinion/who-gets-to-be-french.html?_r=0.

Miller, Toby, and Robert Stam, eds. *A Companion to Film Theory.* Oxford: Blackwell, 2004.

Mirkin, Marshal. "Reinterpreting the Binding of Isaac." *Tikkun* 18, no. 5 (September–October 2003), 61–65.

Moghadam, Valentine M., ed. *Gender and National Identity: Women and Politics in Muslim Societies.* London: Zed, 1994.

Moore, Clement Henry. *Tunisia since Independence: The Dynamics of One-Party Government.* Berkeley: University of California Press, 1965.

Mulvey, Laura. *Visual and Other Pleasures.* Bloomington: Indiana University Press, 1989.

Murray, Stephen O., and Will Roscoe, eds. *Islamic Homosexualities: Culture, History, and Literature.* New York: New York University Press, 1997.

Nabokov, Vladimir. *Laughter in the Dark* [1932; first English translation in 1936, by Winifred Roy]. Trans. Vladimir Nabokov. Indianapolis: Bobbs-Merrill, 1938.

Naccache, Gilbert. "Bourguiba et nous." *Expressions maghrébines* 5, no. 1 (Summer 2006): 223–226.

Ndoye, El Hadji Gorgui Wade. "Mme. Leïla Ben Ali Première Dame de Tunisie: 'La femme tunisienne représente un symbole lumineux de la modernité.'" *ContinentPremier.com— Magazine africain en ligne,* 28 August 2007, www.continentpremier.com/magazine21/modules.php?name=News&file=article&sid=1302.

Nora, Pierre, ed. *Les lieux de mémoire.* 3 tomes. Tome 1, *La République* (1 vol., 1984); Tome 2, *La Nation* (3 vols., 1987); Tome 3, *Les France* (3 vols., 1992). Paris: Gallimard.

Nora, Pierre, ed. *Realms of Memory: Rethinking the French Past.* Vol. 1, *Conflicts and Divisions.* Trans. Arthur Goldhammer. New York: Columbia University Press, 1996. English-language edition edited and with a foreword by Lawrence D. Kritzman.

Norton, Augustus Richard. "Associational Life: Civil Society in Authoritarian Political Systems." In Tessler et al., *Area Studies and Social Science*, 30–47.

Norton, Augustus Richard. *Civil Society in the Middle East*, vol. 1. Leiden: Brill, 1995.

Nouvel Observateur, Le. "Réflexions sur les 21 ans de Benalisme," *nouvelobs.com*, 3 November 2008, accessed 1 July 2009, http://latunisieprofonde.blogs.nouvelobs.com/archive/2008/11/03/reflexions-sur-les-21-ans-de-benalisme.html.

Ossman, Susan, ed. *Miroirs maghrébins: Itinéraires de soi et paysages de rencontre*. Paris: CNRS Éditions, 1998.

Owens, Craig. "The Allegorical Impulse: Toward a Theory of Postmodernism (Part 2)." *October* 13 (Summer 1980): 59–80.

Palakeel, Thomas. "Third World Short Story as National Allegory?" *Journal of Modern Literature* 20, no. 1 (Summer 1996): 97–102.

Penner Angrist, Michele. "Morning in Tunisia: The Frustrations of the Arab World Boil Over," *Foreign Affairs*, 16 January 2011, www.foreignaffairs.com/articles/67321/michele-penner-angrist/morning-in-tunisia.

Perkins, Kenneth J. *A History of Modern Tunisia*. Cambridge: Cambridge University Press, 2004.

Person, Ethel Spector, ed. *On Freud's "A Child Is Being Beaten"*. New Haven: Yale University Press, 1997.

Rashad, Hoda, Magued Osman, and Farzaneh Roudi-Fahimi. *Marriage in the Arab World*. Washington, D.C.: Population Reference Bureau, September 2005, http://www.prb.org/Publications/Reports/2005/MarriageintheArabWorld.aspx.

Read, Alan, ed. *The Fact of Blackness: Frantz Fanon and Visual Representation*. London: Institute of Contemporary Arts/Seattle: Bay Press, 1996.

Rivet, Daniel. *Le Maghreb à l'épreuve de la colonisation*. Paris: Hachette, 2002.

Rohter, Larry. "Che Today? More Easy Rider Than Revolutionary," *New York Times*, 6 May 2004, www.nytimes.com/2004/05/26/world/letter-from-the-americas-che-today-more-easy-rider-than-revolutionary.html?pagewanted=all&src=pm.

Rosello, Mireille. *Postcolonial Hospitality: The Immigrant as Guest*. Palo Alto, CA: Stanford University Press, 2001.

Rosen, Philip. *Change Mummified: Cinema, Historicity, Theory*. Minneapolis: University of Minnesota Press, 2001.

Rosenthal, Steven T. *Irreconcilable Differences? The Waning of the American Jewish Love Affair with Israel*. Hanover, NH: Brandeis University Press, 2001.

Roy, Olivier. *Globalized Islam: The Search for a New Ummah*. New York: Columbia University Press, 2004.

Ruoff, Jeffrey. "The Gulf War, the Iraq War, and Nouri Bouzid's Cinema of Defeat: *It's Scheherazade We're Killing* (1993) and *Making Of* (2006)." *South Central Review* 28, no. 1 (Spring 2011): 18–35.

Said, Edward. "Figures, Configurations, Transfigurations." *Race & Class* 32, no. 1 (1990): 1–16.

Said, Edward. *Orientalism*. New York: Random House, 1979.

Sarris, Andrew. "Notes on the Auteur Theory in 1962." *Film Culture* (Winter 1962–1963). Reprinted in Braudy and Cohen, *Film Theory and Criticism*, 561–564.

Schulman, Sarah. "Israel and 'Pinkwashing.'" *New York Times*, 22 November 2011, www.nytimes.com/2011/11/23/opinion/pinkwashing-and-israels-use-of-gays-as-a-messaging-tool.html?_r=1&hp. Accessed 23 November 2011.

Sciolino, Elaine. *La Seduction: How the French Play the Game of Life*. New York: Times Books/Henry Holt, 2011.

Scott, A. O. "Remembrance of Things Planted Deep in the Mind." *New York Times*, 30 July 2004, www. http://movies.nytimes.com/2004/07/30/movies/30MANC.html.

Serceau, Michel. "20 ans déjà!" Special "Cinémas du Maghreb" issue, *CinémAction* 111 (2004): 7–9.

Serceau, Michel, ed. "Cinémas du Maghreb." Special issue, *CinémAction* 111 (2004).

Shadid, Anthony. "Tunisia Faces a Balancing Act of Democracy and Religion," *New York Times*, 30 January 2012, www.nytimes.com/2012/01/31/world/africa/tunisia-navigates-a-democratic-path-tinged-with-religion.html?.

Shadid, Anthony. "Yearning for Respect, Arabs Find a Voice," *New York Times*, 29 January 2011, www.nytimes.com/2011/01/30/world/middleeast/30arab.html?_r=1&hpw.

Sharabi, Hisham. *Neopatriarchy: A Theory of Distorted Change in Arab Society*. New York: Oxford University Press, 1988.

Sherzer, Dina. "Remembrance of Things Past: *Les silences du palais* by Moufida Tlatli." *South Central Review* 17, no. 3 (Autumn 2000): 50–59.

Shohat, Ella. "Framing Post-Third-Worldist Culture: Gender and Nation in Middle Eastern/North African Film and Video." *Jouvert: A Journal of Postcolonial Studies* 1, no. 1 (1997), http://english.chass.ncsu.edu/jouvert/vli1/SHOHAT.HTM.

Shohat, Ella, and Robert Stam. *Unthinking Eurocentrism: Multiculturalism and the Media*. London: Routledge, 1994.

Sinker, Mark. "*Les silences du palais* (*Saimt el qusur/The Silences of the Palace*)." *Sight and Sound* 5, no. 3 (1995): 53.

Slawy-Sutton, Catherine. "*Outremer* and *The Silences of the Palace*: Feminist Allegories of Two Countries in Transition." *Pacific Coast Philology* 37 (2002): 85–104.

Smith, Anthony. *National Identity*. London: Penguin, 1991.

Smolin, Jonathan. "Political Malaise and the New Arabic Noir." *South Central Review* 27, nos. 1–2 (Spring-Summer 2012): 82–90.

Smyth, A.S.H. "Aiding and Abetting" [interview with Dambisa Moyo]. *Prospect Magazine* 160 (July 2009), www.prospect-magazine.co.uk/article_details.php?id=10911.

Spurr, David. *The Rhetoric of Empire: Colonial Discourse in Journalism, Travel Writing, and Imperial Administration*. Durham, N.C.: Duke University Press, 1993.

Stoler, Anne Laura. *Carnal Knowledge and Imperial Power: Race and the Intimate in Colonial Rule*. Berkeley: University of California Press, 2010.

Stollery, Martin. "Masculinities, Generations, and Cultural Transformation in Contemporary Tunisian Cinema." *Screen* 42, no. 1 (Spring 2001): 49–63.

Stone McNeece, Lucy. "La lettre envolée: l'image écrite dans le cinéma tunisien." *CinémAction* 111 (2004): 67–76.

Stora, Benjamin. "The Maghrib at the Dawn of the Twenty-first Century." In Maddy-Weitzman and Zisenwine, *The Maghrib in the New Century*, 1–9.

Szeman, Imre. "Who's Afraid of National Allegory? Jameson, Literary Criticism, Globalization." *South Atlantic Quarterly* 100, no. 3 (Summer 2001): 803–827.

Szeman, Imre. *Zones of Instability: Literature, Postcolonialism, and the Nation.* Baltimore: Johns Hopkins University Press, 2003.

Taggart, Will. "The Digital Revolt: Resistance and Agency on the Net." Working Papers on New Media and Information Technology in the Middle East http://nmit.wordpress.com/2008/09/06/the-digital-revolt-resistance-agency-on-the-net, posted 6 September 2008, accessed 25 October 2008.

Tessler, Mark. "The Origins of Popular Support for Islamist Movements." In Entelis, *Islam, Democracy, and the State in North Africa*, 93–126.

Tessler, Mark, Gregory White, and John Entelis. "The Republic of Tunisia." In Long and Reich, *The Government and Politics of the Middle East and North Africa*, 423-446.

Tessler, Mark, ed., with Jodi Nachtwey and Anne Banda. *Area Studies and Social Science: Strategies for Understanding Middle East Politics.* Bloomington: Indiana University Press, 1999.

Tlatli, Moufida. "Moving Bodies" [interview with Laura Mulvey]. *Sight and Sound* 5, no. 3 (1995): 18–20.

Tohidi, Nayereh. "Modernity, Islamization, and Women in Iran." In Moghadam, *Gender and National Identity*, 110–141.

Tomlinson, John. *Globalization and Culture.* Chicago: University of Chicago Press, 1999.

Touti, Moumen. *Films tunisiens: Longs métrages, 1967–1998.* Tunis: Répertoire, 1998.

Trémois, Claude-Marie. "Filles de l'air et du vent." *Réforme*, 30 September 2004, www.reforme.net/archive2/article.php?num=3096&ref=87.

Turner, Bryan S. *Orientalism, Postmodernism and Globalism.* London: Routledge, 1994.

Ukadike, Frank. *Black African Cinema.* Berkeley: University of California Press, 1994.

United Nations. *Human Development Report: Tunisia* (2008), http://hdrstats.undp.org/2008/countries/country_fact_sheets/cty_fs_TUN.html.

Vergès, Françoise. "Dialogue." In Read, *The Fact of Blackness*, 132–141.

Waterbury, John. "From Social Contracts to Extraction Contracts: The Political Economy of Authoritarianism and Democracy." In Entelis, *Islam, Democracy, and the State in North Africa*, 141–176.

Wheatcroft, Geoffrey. "How Israel Gets Away with Murder." *The Independent*, 11 January 2009, www.independent.co.uk/opinion/commentators/geoffrey-wheatcroft-how-israel-gets-away-with-murder-1299401.html.

Willis, Michael J. *Politics and Power in the Maghreb: Algeria, Tunisia and Morocco from Independence to the Arab Spring.* New York: Columbia University Press, 2012.

Worth, Robert F., and David D. Kirkpatrick. "Seizing a Moment, Al Jazeera Galvanizes Arab Frustration." *New York Times*, 27 January 2011, www.nytimes.com/2011/01/28/world/middleeast/28jazeera.html?_r=1&hp.

Wright, Robin. *Rock the Casbah: Rage and Rebellion Across the Islamic World.* New York: Simon & Schuster, 2011.

Xavier, Ismail. "Historical Allegory." In Miller and Stam, eds., *A Companion to Film Theory*, 333–362.

Index

Abbassi, Driss, 235, 245–246, 248–249, 292n76, 327n8, 331n32, 333n47
Abderrezak, Hakim, 75–76, 97
Abraham: as Founding Father of Islam, 44, 239. *See also* "Sacrifice of Abraham"
Abu Ghraib prisoner and torture abuse, 273
Ajami, Fouad, 29–30, 293n82
Al Fanous/Le Réverbère (Ben Halima), 336n7
Al Jazeera, 26, 261, 290n62, 335n4
Alexander, Christopher, 315–316n11
Algeria, 5, 25, 29, 231, 321n20, 325n51, 329n22
Algerian cinema, 22–23, 32, 291n64
Algerian War (1954–1962), 321n20
All That Heaven Allows (Sirk), 294n91
Allani, Alaya, 330n26
allegory, 13–22, 14, 25, 154, 224, 266, 285n14, 288n43, 289n58, 289–290n59, 290n62, 321n17
al-Qaeda, x, 323n32

Ambassadors, The (Ktari), 22
American Civil War (1861–1865), 295n98
Amnesty International, 4, 116
And I Saw Stars (Ben Ammar), 283n12
Anderson, Benedict, 199, 256–257
Anderson, Kevin, 315n2
anti-Semitism, 58, 245–246, 299n33
Appadurai, Arjun, 199
Apter, Emily, 77, 154–155
Arab League, 235, 329n21
Arab Spring, 194, 284n12, 328n12, 334n1. *See also* Tunisia: Revolution (2011)
Arab world, 24–25, 37, 46, 166, 174–175, 191, 199, 235, 241, 244, 258, 278, 281n2, 287n27, 293n82, 327n11, 329n22, 340n33, 340n38
Arab-Israeli War (1967), 26, 28, 283n11, 297n17
Arafat, Yasser, x
Arendt, Hannah, 316n18, 331n31
Arkoun, Mohamed, 138

INDEX

Armes, Roy, 13, 59, 68, 291n64
art, 168–169, 171–172, 177–178, 316n14
Asad, Talal, 287n30
asala, 336–337n8
Association Agreement (European Union), 29
Atatürk, Mustafa Kemal, 239, 330n25
Attia, Ahmed Baha Eddine, 22, 282n8
authoritarianism, 5, 10, 21, 166; in the private sphere, xiii, 44, 46, 55, 57–58, 68–69, 73, 82, 89, 92, 117, 148, 161, 163, 167, 187, 189, 247, 270, 300n41, 338n24; of the state, xiii, 39, 44, 46, 55, 69, 82, 89, 92, 95, 123, 128, 145, 148, 175, 187, 214, 224, 229, 231–232, 247, 268–269, 284n5, 285n11, 285n13, 286n14, 287n24, 303n7, 315n2, 319n6, 327n9, 338n20. *See also* Ben Ali, Zine El Abidine; Bourguiba, Habib; neopatriarchy
Aziza (Ben Ammar), 22
Azziara/La Visite (Ben Khélifa), 336n7

Bab' Aziz—The Prince That Contemplated His Soul (Khemir), 13
Baccar, Selma, 22
Bachy, Victor, 291n64
Balibar, Etienne, 26, 293n77
Baliseurs du désert, Les (Khemir), 14, 22
Barakat, Halim, 136
Barlet, Olivier, 264, 292n71
Barthes, Roland, 103, 104, 307n7
Bartky, Sandra Lee, 154
Bataille, Georges, 68, 71, 302n4, 303n8
Bauman, Zygmunt, 193, 198, 212–216, 333–334n51
Beau, Nicolas, 285n9, 286n16, 295n1, 334n2
Beaugé, Florence, 3, 4, 303n7
Bedwin Hacker (El Fani), xvi, 191–222, 277, 283n12, 320n9, 320–321n16, 321n17
Béji, Hélé, 7–8, 10–12, 14, 123, 126, 146, 234, 277, 286n17, 286n18, 287n25, 287n28, 310n10
Belhassen, Souhayr, 96, 303n7, 305n39

Belkadhi, Néjib, 22
Bellin, Eva, 5
Ben Ali, Leïla Trabelsi, 146, 156, 251, 260–261, 314n51, 334n2
Ben Ali, Zine El Abidine: as allegorical figure, 5, 12–13, 78, 268; authoritarianism of, ix, xvi, 5–6, 11–12, 89, 92, 95, 146, 328n13; coup d'état (1987), ix, xii, 1, 174, 284n2, 315n2; cult of personality, 146, 203; dictatorship, xii–xiii, xvi, 146, 201, 229, 259, 264, 269, 303n7, 327n9, 337n18; extended family, xv, 11, 21, 146, 260–261, 334n2; as host of "World Summit on the Information Society," 200–202, 321–322n25; legacy, 4, 146; ouster of, ix, xvi, 29, 146, 154, 259, 262, 292n71, 318n35, 319n7, 330n27, 334n1; personality of, 5; secularism of, 5
Ben Ammar, Abdellatif, 320n14, 324n36, 324n41
Ben Ammar, Hichem, xvi, 283–284n12
Ben Mabrouk, Néjia, 282n8
Ben Mahmoud, Mahmoud, 32
Ben Ouanès, Kamel, 308n12
Ben Saïdane, Fatma, 244
Ben Salama, Mohand, 291n64
Ben Youssef Zayzafoon, Lamia, 132, 134, 311n20
Benalism, 331n31
Bendana, Kmar. *See* Kchir-Bendana, Kmar
Benedict, Stephen, 327n8
Bensalah, Mohamed, 197–198, 321n18
Bensmaïa, Réda, 16–17
Bentham, Jeremy, 215, 324n40
Bentley, Eric, 182
Berman, Marshall, 129–130, 147
Bernanos, Georges, 196, 214–215, 220, 222
Berque, Jacques, 111
Berrah, Mouny, 291n64
Bey of Tunis, 3, 140–142, 144, 153, 252, 285n6, 309n2. *See also* Lamine Bey; Mohamed Bey; Moncef Bey

INDEX

Bey, Hakim, 198–199, 211
Bezness (Bouzid), xiv, 99–122, 165
Bin Laden, Osama, 272–273
Bivona, Rosalia, 199, 221, 325n48
Black Night Eclipse (Alaoui), 291n70
Bonaparte, Louis-Napoléon (Napoleon III), 157, 315n2
Bond, David, 327n10
Bouazizi, Mohamed, 154, 259–260, 263, 318n35, 334n1, 335n4
Bouazizi, Samia, 335n5
Bouchoucha, Dora, 22
Boughedir, Férid, 22–24, 32, 148, 262–263, 267, 282n7, 291n64, 297n19, 302n1, 336n6, 337n9
Bouguarche, Ahmed, 76
Bouhdiba, Abdelwahab, 46, 50, 54–58, 64, 91–92, 297n19, 298n20, 298n22, 298n27, 299n36, 299n38, 300n39, 300n40, 301n49, 306n1, 336–337n8
Bourguiba, Habib: as allegorical figure, 8, 12–13; authoritarianism of, xii, xvii, 5–6, 9–10, 89–90, 92, 95, 131, 270, 284n5, 302n7, 328n13; cult of personality, 146; death, 4, 89–90; as "Father" of the nation, 5, 8, 90; health of, 1–2; legacy, xvi–xvii, 4, 174, 270, 285n9, 286n15, 303n7, 306n39; modernist vision, ix, xi–xii, 24, 72, 147, 177, 239, 276, 285n9, 330n27; ouster of, xii, 1–2, 12, 116, 284n2, 302n7; personality, 1, 4–6, 8, 90, 286n15; "President for Life", 1; secularism of, 5–6, 24; as "Supreme Combatant", 1, 284n3; Westernized character, 5, 32, 239, 336n6
Bourguiba, Wasila, 2
Bouthelja, Ammar, 231
Bouzid, Nouri, xiii–xiv, 3, 42–43, 61, 65, 117, 187–188, 265–266, 268, 274–279, 282n7, 282n8, 283n11, 285n7, 294n92, 294n94, 295n99, 295n100, 297n19, 299n33; jail sentence, 3; as *"lieu de mémoire"*, 232–233; membership in socialist youth group, 3; "Sources of Inspiration" lecture, 31, 43, 62–63, 263–264, 267–269, 293n84, 293n85, 294n90, 296n5, 299n35
Boym, Svetlana, 31
Brahimi, Denise, 23, 69–70, 73, 81, 84, 148, 302n5
Brand, Laurie A., 311n18
Brooks, Van Wyck, 223
Brown, Derek, 298n26
Bush, George W., xi, 194, 220, 268, 339n30

Caillé, Patricia, 23, 291n67
Camau, Michel, 328n13
capitalism, 14, 16, 18, 21, 101–102, 146–147, 166–167, 174–175, 192, 212–216, 225, 256–259, 267–269, 274, 276–278, 319n4, 325n51, 329n22, 330n29, 340n33, 340n36
Césaire, Aimé, 197, 308n10
Chahine, Youssef, 33–34
Chambers, Iain, 302n3
Chamkhi, Sonia, 282n8, 290n61
Chaos Computer Club (CCC), 325n47
Chaos Computer Club France (CCCF), 325n46, 325n47
Charles I, King of Spain (Charles V, Holy Roman Emperor), 248
Charrad, Mounira M., 303n11, 311n18
Chebbi, Aboulkacem, xvii, 229–230, 259, 327n10, 328n12
Chiboub, Amine, 265
Chikaoui, Tahar, 292n71
Chouikha, Larbi, 289n50
Chouraqui, André N., 331n32
Cincotta, Richard, 340n32
ciné-clubs, 337n11, 337n13
circumcision, xiii, 42–43, 46–49, 51, 54–56, 59, 61, 86, 100, 298n20, 298n22, 298n24, 299–300n38, 306n1
Citizen Kane (Welles), 105, 168–169, 233
citizenship, 205–209, 218, 220–221, 322n29, 323n32, 324n34

INDEX

civil society, 1, 5, 194, 287n28, 315n11
Cixous, Hélène, 124, 154
"clash of civilizations" (Huntington), xi, 242, 287n27
class, xv, 123, 131, 136, 138–140, 142–144, 157–160, 164, 171, 174–175, 177–178, 180–181, 184–186, 188, 263, 277, 287n29, 299n38, 316n14, 316n16, 316n18, 316n19, 317n22, 324n41
Clay Dolls (Bouzid). *See Poupées d'argile* (Bouzid)
Cleopatra, 252
Club de la Jeune Fille Tunisienne, 134
Code du Statut Personnel (CSP). *See* Personal Status Code (PSC)
"cognitive mapping" (Jameson), 289n55
Collier perdu de la colombe, Le (Khemir), 14
colonialism, 7, 9, 75, 108, 142, 145, 147, 152, 166, 173, 193, 196–197, 208, 214, 246–247, 252, 293n77, 309n16, 310n4, 328n13. *See also* neocolonialism
Comaroff, Jean, 16
Comaroff, John, 16
Condat, Jean-Bernard, 325n47
Corriou, Morgan, 290n63, 337n13
coup d'état (1987), ix, xii, 1, 174, 284n2, 315n2
CPJ (Committee to Protect Journalists), 96, 97, 281n2
Crossing Over (Ben Mahmoud), 22, 308n12

Daldoul, Hassan, 22
Dames, Nicholas, 73–74
Daniel, Jean, 340n38
Davidson Ladly, Meghan, 301n50
De Beauvoir, Simone, 154
De Boschère, Guy, 308n10
De Tocqueville, Alexis, 316n18
Delay, Jean, 107
Democracy Index (*The Economist*), 11, 286–287n24
Democratic Constitutional Rally (RCD). *See* RCD (Democratic Constitutional Rally)

Désir, Harlem, 323n31
Destour Party, 111. *See also* Néo-Destour Party
Dhaouadi, Mahmoud, 316n16
Dhouib, Moncef, 282n7, 332n39
Dido. See Elissa (Queen of Carthage)
Douaji, Ali, 97
Dubai (United Arab Emirates), 216
Dundes, Alan, 307n5
Dwyer, Kevin, 291n64

Écaré, Désiré, 304n18
Egypt, 27, 29–30, 241, 243, 253, 258, 327n11, 329n21, 332n37, 332n39, 335n4
Egyptian cinema, 32–34, 62, 294n89, 294n91, 332n39
Eisenstein, Sergei, 35
El Fani, Nadia, 191, 266, 282n7, 283n12, 319–320n8
Ellis, Don, 282n5
Elissa (Queen of Carthage), 245, 247–248, 250, 252, 331n34, 331n35
Enlightenment: in Western secular tradition, 273–274, 330n29
Ennahdha (Tunisia), 194, 319n7, 319n8, 320n9, 340n38
Entelis, John P., 284n5, 285n13
Essaïda (Zran), xv, 82, 85, 157–190, 277, 338n24
"Eurocentrism" (Shohat and Stam), 196–197
"evil eye," 104–105, 120, 307n1, 307n5

Facebook, 259, 261, 335n4
Fanon, Frantz, 7, 60, 308n10
Farouk, King of Egypt and Sudan, 144
Fatma (Ghorbal), 290n62
Ferdinand and Isabella (the "Catholic Monarchs"), 248
Fî Bilâd al-Tararanni (Ben Halima et al), 2, 29, 336n7
Field, Michael, 329n22

INDEX

Foucault, Michel, 78–79, 182, 186, 286n14
French Revolution (1789), 25
Freud, Sigmund, 55, 78, 103, 161–162, 300n41
Friedman, Natalie, 31, 72, 303n12
Friedman, Thomas L., 281–282n4
friendship, 50–51, 57, 163, 172, 183, 300n42; and homosociality, 51
Fromentin, Eugène, 111
Fromherz, Allen James, 333n47
Fukuyama, Francis, 84–86, 324n34

Galley, Micheline, 249–250
Gana, Nouri, 270, 284n4, 297n17
Gauch, Suzanne, 127, 133, 145, 156, 314n50
Gaza War (2008–2009), 29
Geisser, Vincent, 328n13
Germany, 307n6
Ghannouchi, Rached, 194–195, 319n7, 319–320n8, 320n9, 340n38
Ghazali, Sheikh Mohamed al-, 332n46
Ghriba synagogue bombing (2002), 307n6
Gibran, Khalil, 157, 190, 314n1
Gide, André, 107–110, 308n8, 308n13
Giscard d'Estaing, Valéry, 206
globalization, ix, xiv, 23, 30, 103, 117, 147, 163, 193, 197–198, 212–217, 226, 258, 267–268, 274, 276, 278, 318–319n3, 319n4, 321n19, 326n2, 333–334n51, 340n33; defined, 193, 217
Godard, Jean-Luc, 35
Golden Horseshoes, The (Bouzid), xiv, 82–83, 117, 187, 306n1
Goldstein, Warren, 282n5
Graciet, Catherine, 334n2
Graiouid, Saïd, 76
Guevara, Che, 236, 327–328n12
Gulf War (1990–1991), 24, 26, 28, 327n8, 329n22
Gulf War . . . What Next?, The (Alaoui et al), 23–24, 37, 291n70

Hacker, Jacob S., 282n6
Hafez, Sabry, 291n64
Hajji, Lotfi, 335n4
Halfaouine: Child of the Terraces (Boughedir), xiii–xiv, 24, 67–98, 163, 248, 262, 282n8, 283n12, 299n38, 302n1, 302n7, 303n15, 304n18, 306n42, 338n24
Hannibal, 253, 333n47
Hannoum, Abdelmajid, 246–247
harem, 76–81 passim, 124, 155
Hartog, François, 235
Harun al-Rashid, 250, 332n42
Haskell, Molly, 51, 53
Hassan II, King of Morocco, ix, 281n2
Hassan, Waïl, 145–146
Hawkins, Simon, 284n3, 303n11, 304n19, 331n35
Hayes, Jarrod, 80, 209–210
Hazbun, Waleed, 224–225, 231
Hennebelle, Guy, 291n64
Herman, Susan N., 282n6
Hibou, Béatrice, 24–27, 30, 96, 164, 180–186, 231, 277, 285n9, 286n14, 291–292n71, 292n74, 293n78, 315n10, 317n25, 317n29, 328n15, 330n26
Higbee, Will, 22–23
Hilalian Invasion, 248–249, 332n37
Hiroshima mon amour (Resnais), 105
history, xvi–xvii, 7, 14, 90, 101, 139, 213, 217, 223, 225–226, 238, 240–242, 245–246, 248, 251–253, 255, 258, 261, 273, 292n76, 315n9, 326n5
Hobsbawm, Eric, 223, 277
Hochberg, Gil, 126–127
Homage by Assassination (Suleiman), 291n70
homme blessé, L' (Chéreau), 62, 301n47
homosexuality. *See* sexuality: and homosexuality
hooks, bell, 44
Hopwood, Derek, 2–3
Hoveyda, Fereydoun, 46, 59
Hurst, Heike, 293n84
Hussein, Saddam, 28

373

hybridity. *See métissage*
Hyenas' Sun (Behi), 22

Ibn Dhakwam, Al-Hassan, 58
Ibn Khaldun, 199, 250, 253, 333n47
identification, 20
Institut du Monde Arabe (Paris), 40
International Monetary Fund (IMF), 319n4
Invisible Man, The (Whale), 39
Iran, 287n28
Iraq War (2003–2011), 26, 28, 235–236, 267–268, 327n8, 329n22, 329–330n23, 339n30, 339n31
Islam, xi, 5, 8, 11–13, 21, 43, 62, 177, 189, 194, 229, 237–242, 247–248, 267, 274–275, 278–279, 313n40, 324n34, 331n35, 332n46, 340n36; as allegorical/culturalist term, 39, 148, 297n16, 313n40; in the Constitution, 338n21; and fundamentalism, 5, 65, 203, 211, 265–269, 272–274, 278–279, 285n11, 295n100, 320n9, 330n26, 330n27, 337n17, 337n18, 338n20, 338n22, 339n27, 340n38; and language, 136–138
Islamic Salvation Front (Algeria), 5
Israel, xi, 27–28, 236, 241, 281–282n4, 282n5, 289n58, 293n81, 297n17, 299n33, 329n21, 330n30, 333n48; "Israel lobby", xi, 281n4, 282n5, 293n82, 299n33, 329–330n23, 330n30
Israeli cinema, 289n58
It's Scheherazade We're Killing (Bouzid), 282n8

Jadoui, Sliman al-, 111
Jaïdi, Moulay Driss, 291n64
Jameson, Fredric, x, 13–21, 163, 197, 213, 264, 288n39, 289n53, 289n55, 318n35, 321n17, 333n51
Janmohamed, Abdul R., 173
Jebali, Taoufik, 83
Jemni, Mahmoud, 291n64, 337n11

Jenin Massacre (2002), 28–29, 293n80
jihad, 273, 275, 284n3
Joseph, Suad, 340n33
Jowitt, Kenneth, 214
Judaism, 43
Judt, Tony, 274, 277
Julien, Charles-André, 312n27

Kahina, the Berber, 245–247, 250, 331n32
Kallander, Amy, 292n76
Kchir-Bendana, Kmar, 23, 24, 336n7
Kerrou, Mohamed, 166, 298n23
Khair ad-Din ("Barbarossa"), 248
Khayati, Khémaïs, 32, 38, 294n89, 294n90, 296n2
Khayr ed-Din al-Tunsi, 24, 292n73, 331–332n36
Khélil, Hédi, 41–42, 44, 48, 106–110, 120, 122, 159–160, 188–189, 262, 296n7, 307n7, 308n9, 308n11, 318n35, 336n7
Khemir, Nacer, 13, 32
Khemissi, Salah, 305n38
Kilani, Abdelrazek, 317n27
Kilito, Abdelfattah, 76
King, Stephen J., 285n9, 285n11, 338n22
Kirkpatrick, David D., 287n29, 335n4
KOF Index of Globalization, 318–319n3
Kracauer, Siegfried, 295n97
Krichen, Aziz, 116–118, 284n4
Krichen, Mohamed, 335n4
Kristeva, Julia, 112, 122, 206–209, 323n32
Ksouri, Khaled, 317n24
Kuran, Timur, 287n28

Lacan, Jacques, 114–115
Laïcité, inch'Allah! (El Fani), 266–267, 338n19
Lamine Bey, 140, 252, 309n2, 312n27, 316n19
Lamloum, Olfa, 12, 26
Lang, Robert, 294n93, 304n24, 309n24, 333n49

INDEX

language, 137–138, 204–205, 212, 256–258; Arabic, xvii, 121, 135–138, 175, 212, 220, 257–258, 275, 311n21, 316n16, 333n48, 336n6, 338n21; cinematic, 295n97; French, 36, 118, 121, 135–136, 166–167, 175–176, 178, 257, 266–267, 275, 294n96, 295n100, 309n16, 310n4, 311n21, 316n16, 322n29, 323n30, 325n46, 325n48, 336n6; Italian, 309n18; Latin, 256–257; Ottoman Turkish, 257

Laughter in the Dark (Nabokov), 305n37

Lebanon War (1982), 28, 282n5

Lebanon War (2006), 29, 236, 293n81

Lee, Ken, 293n80

Lenin, Vladimir Ilyich, 264

Letaïef, Ibrahim, 22

Letters from Iwo Jima (Eastwood), 307n4

Libya, 315n11, 325n51

Ligue Tunisienne de défense des droits de l'Homme. *See* Tunisian League for Human Rights (LTDH)

Lilienthal, David, 222

Lynch, Marc, 335n4

Maghreb, the, ix, 25–26, 235, 290–291n64, 329n22

Maghrebi cinema, 22–23, 291n64

Majid, Anouar, 145, 273–274, 276, 278–279, 329n22, 330n29, 332n46, 337n9, 340n36

Making Of, le dernier film (Bouzid), xii, 264–268, 270–272, 277, 279, 282–283n8, 289n55, 295n100, 337n18, 338n23, 338n24

Malkmus, Lizbeth, 59

Maltese Falcon, The (Huston), xii

Maltin, Leonard, 290n59

Man of Ashes (Bouzid), xii–xiii, 11, 22–24, 40–66, 82, 88, 116–117, 187, 282n8, 297n17, 301n49, 317n24, 330n28, 338n24

Manchurian Candidate, The (Demme), 290n59

Manchurian Candidate, The (Frankenheimer), 290n59

Martin, Florence, 152, 199, 291n64, 325–326n51

Marx, Karl, 147, 157, 164, 166, 254, 315n9

Marzouki, Ilhem, 311n18

Massad, Joseph A., 297n19, 298n27, 301n50, 301–302n51

Mauss, Marcel, 47

McClintock, Anne, 324n38

McNeece, Lucy Stone. *See* Stone McNeece, Lucy

Mearsheimer, John, 329–330n23

melancholy, xiv, 71, 123, 126, 132, 139, 151–152, 270, 284n4, 297n17, 308n14

melodrama, 33, 146, 148, 156, 182, 186, 190, 268, 283n12, 288n43, 294n91, 294n92, 294n93, 310n15, 313n43, 320–321n16

Memmi, Albert, xi, 11–12, 124, 143–145, 158–159, 165, 184, 190, 276–277, 287n25, 287n27, 287n28, 287n29, 287n30, 308n10

Merah, Mohammed, 323n32

Mernissi, Fatima, 155

Messaoudi, Abdelhalim, 338n20

metacommentary (Jameson), 289n53, 289n55

métissage, 30–31, 262, 302n3, 336n6, 337n9

Meyer, Karl E., 323n32

Michaux-Bellaire, Édouard, 111

Midnight Cowboy (Schlesinger), 309n24

Mirkin, Marshal, 309n21

modernity, 276, 278. *See also* Tunisia: modernity of

Mohamed Bey, 292n73

Mohamed, Prophet, 43, 298n20, 301n49

Moncef Bey, 312n28

Montesquieu, Charles-Louis de Secondat, Baron de La Brède et de, 207, 209

Moore, Clement Henry, 251–252

375

Moroccan cinema, 22–23
Morocco, ix, 329n22; "years of lead", 281n2
Mubarak, Hosni, 30, 253, 335n4
Mulvey, Laura, 125–126, 137–138, 142
Murray, Stephen O., 64, 301n50, 301n51
Mzali, Mohammed, 2

Nabokov, Vladimir, 305n37
Naccache, Gilbert, 4, 6, 89–90, 95, 284n4, 286n15, 305n33
Nadia and Sarra (Tlatli), 288n43
Nasser, Gamal Abdel, 27
"national ideology" (Béji), 9
National Union of Tunisian Women (UNFT), 131, 133–134, 243
nationalism, 1, 118, 246, 329n22
"nationalitarianism" (Béji), 30
Ndoye, El Hadji Gorgui Wade, 314n51
Neither Allah, nor Master! (El Fani). *See Laïcité, inch'Allah!* (El Fani)
neocolonialism, xi, xiv, 7, 103, 118, 142, 192, 197–198, 215, 234, 292n74, 329n18
Néo-Destour Party, 131, 243
neopatriarchy, xiii, 8–9, 21, 37, 44, 66, 91, 102, 117, 127–128, 131–132, 137–140, 142, 148, 167, 174, 188, 247, 270, 287n28, 319n6; defined, 167
Netanyahu, Benjamin, 281n4, 330n30
New Tunisian Cinema: characteristics, xii–xiii, 40, 66, 116, 125, 154, 163, 269, 290n61, 293n84, 301n49, 313n43, 332n39; defined, xi–xii, 12, 15, 22, 24, 32, 282–283n8, 294n86, 294n88; and documentary film, 283–284n12, 295n100. *See also* Bouzid, Nouri: "Sources of Inspiration" lecture
"9/11" (11 September 2001), x, xvi, 5, 194, 247, 272
Nora, Pierre, xvi–xvii, 225–226, 235, 255, 326n5
Norton, Augustus Richard, 92
nostalgia, xiii, 31, 71–74, 79, 81, 90, 159, 168, 301n49, 303n12

Obama, Barack, 295n98
Oedipus complex (Freud), 37, 45–46, 55, 78, 151, 187, 300n41
Oedipus Rex (Sophocles), 295n99
Omar Gatlato (Allouache), 69, 302n5
Orientalism, 59, 76–77, 99, 102–103, 108, 110, 121, 155, 176, 178–179, 278, 287n27, 297n19, 307n4
Ottoman Empire, 25, 37, 123, 140–141, 145, 248, 251, 285n6, 292n76, 307n5, 309n2, 312n26, 331n36
Owens, Craig, 19
Özbek, Selçuk, 319n4

Palakeel, Thomas, 16–17, 289n49
Palestine Liberation Organization (PLO), 27–28
Pasqua, Charles, 206, 322n29
patriarchy, xiii, 8–9, 43, 62, 92, 127–128, 132, 136, 138–139, 142, 146, 156, 166–167, 174, 187, 279, 298n24. *See also* neopatriarchy
Penner Angrist, Michele, 312n35
Pépé le Moko (Duvivier), 83–84
Perkins, Kenneth, 5, 27–28, 130–131, 237–239, 286n22
Persepolis (Satrapi and Paronnaud), 265, 337n17
Personal Status Code (PSC), 29, 130–132, 244, 311n20, 330n30
photography, 99, 102–106, 114, 313n41
Picnic, The (Boughedir), 29, 262, 266, 304n24, 333n49, 336n7
Pierson, Paul, 282n6
Poetics (Aristotle), 295n99
Poupées d'argile (Bouzid), 3, 94, 296n11, 306n1
poverty, xv, 157–159, 165, 167, 170, 175, 177, 180, 184, 188, 190, 243, 259, 274, 276, 285n9, 318n35, 319n4. *See also* underdevelopment
"primal scene" (Freud), 150–151

INDEX

PSD (Parti Socialiste Destourien). *See* Néo-Destour Party; RCD (Democratic Constitutional Rally)

Qadhafi, Muammar, 325n51

Rabin, Yitzhak, x
Rafi'i, Mustafa Sadiq al-, 259, 327n10
Rambo (Stallone), 302n1
Ramses II (Egypt), 253
rape, 42–46, 49, 51, 61, 64, 88, 144, 150–152, 173, 186–187, 296n3, 296n11, 297n17, 299n36, 300–301n45; and allegory, xiii, 45–46, 60, 187
Ravenel, Bernard, 12, 26
RCD (Democratic Constitutional Rally), 10, 184–185, 202, 229, 231, 243–244, 286n22, 317n25, 332n43
realism, 35, 289n55, 294n92
Redissi, Hamadi, 338n20
reformism. *See* Tunisia: reformism discourse
religion, 238–239, 265–266, 275, 287n30, 332n46, 339n31. *See also* Islam
Research of Shaima (Ben Mabrouk), 291n70
Rhodesia, x–xi
Rivet, Daniel, 111
Rohter, Larry, 327n12
Roscoe, Will, 64, 301n50, 301n51
Rosello, Mireille, 83, 205–206
Rosen, Philip, 1
Rosenthal, Steven, 282n5
Roudiez, Leon S., 323n30
Roy, Olivier, 313n40, 324n34
Rubin, Gayle, 154
Ruoff, Jeffrey, 282n8
Russian Debutante's Handbook, The (Shteyngart), 72

Sabra and Shatila massacre (1982), 272
"Sacrifice of Abraham," 37, 43, 64, 116, 187, 189, 237, 309n20, 309n21
Sadiqi College (Tunis), 292n73, 332n36, 336n6
Said, Edward, 17–18, 176, 178

Saint Regaïa, 120
Salahuddin al-Ayubi (Saladin), 332n46
Sarkozy, Nicholas, 323n32
Sarris, Andrew, 32, 35, 38, 294n87
SATPEC (*Société anonyme tunisienne de production et d'expansion cinématographique*), 291n64
Saudi Arabia, 178, 333n48
Sciolino, Elaine, 306n43
Scott, A. O., 290n59
Section Féminine de L'Association des Jeunes Musulmanes, 134
secularism, 287n30, 295n100, 330n25; as Western idea, 273, 330n29
Sejnane (Ben Ammar), 324n41
sexuality: as allegorical discourse, 21, 44, 116, 163, 209; in Arab-Muslim society, xiii–xiv, 37–39, 46, 49, 298n27, 300n41, 300–301n45, 301n49, 301n50, 301–302n51; in *Bezness*, xiv, 99–122 passim; and compulsory heterosexuality, 53–54, 57, 62, 298n26, 300n40, 301n45; and fantasy, 60–61, 80, 118, 150–151, 162, 165; frank treatment of in New Tunisian Cinema, 38–40, 163; in *Halfaouine*, 67–98 passim; and homophobia, 50–53, 59, 114, 297n15, 301n45; and homosexuality, 50–51, 57, 59–60, 64, 84, 88–89, 102, 107, 114, 172, 200, 209–212, 214, 301n50, 301–302n51, 305n31, 306n1, 308n9, 309n24; and homosociality, 51, 299n31, 304n19; and Islam, 37, 49, 65, 273, 297n19, 298n27, 300n40, 301n49, 301n50; in *Man of Ashes*, xiii, 40–66 passim; and masculine identity, xiv, 40–66 passim, 77, 87, 89, 99–122 passim, 250, 270, 284n4, 297n15, 297n17; and pedophilia, 57–58, 88, 93, 107, 109–110, 172–173, 308n9; and prostitution, xiv, 99–122 passim, 155, 164–165, 299n29, 306n1, 309n24; and trauma, 42–44, 46, 48–49, 51, 54–56, 59–61, 80–81, 84, 147, 151–152, 297n17, 298n24, 299n36, 300n41, 301n45, 305n29

377

Shadid, Anthony, 327n10, 338n20
Sharabi, Hisham, 8–9, 43, 127–129, 136–138, 166–167, 174–175, 188, 287n28, 310n13, 310n17, 311n21
shari'a, 278, 287n28
Sherzer, Dina, 155
Shohat, Ella, 15, 155–156, 196–197, 288n41, 319n4, 321n17
Sidi Ben Issa, 238
Silence, The (Darkaoui), 291n70
Silences of the Palace, The (Tlatli), xiv–xv, 24, 123–156, 249–250, 282n8, 283n12, 288n43, 294n91, 310n3, 332n40
Sinker, Mark, 143
Slawy-Sutton, Catherine, 139
Smith, Anthony, 217
Socialist Realism (Soviet Union), 337n14
Sparrow, The (Chahine), 283n11
Spector Person, Ethel, 162–163
Spider-Man (Raimi), 290n62
Spurr, David, 78–79
Stam, Robert, 15, 196–197, 288n41, 319n4, 321n17
Stoler, Ann Laura, 324n38
Stollery, Martin, 60–61, 306n42
Stone McNeece, Lucy, 74–75
Stora, Benjamin, 163
Strauss-Kahn, Dominique, 319n4
String, The (Ben Attia), 338–339n26
subalternity, 19, 150
Suleiman I ("the Magnificent"), 248
Summer in La Goulette, A (Boughedir), 248, 262
surveillance, xvi, 80, 82, 164, 184, 192–193, 198, 202, 215, 315n10, 324n40. *See also* Tunisia: and the Internet; Tunisia: as a police state
Szeman, Imre, 18–19, 288n39

Taggart, Will, 199–200
television, xvi, 17, 191–193, 196, 198, 202, 221, 253–258, 261, 263, 265, 289n49, 289n50, 328n16, 334n51, 335n4. *See also* Al Jazeera
Tessler, Mark, 28, 284n5
Third World, x, 14–21, 24, 75, 101–103, 118, 122, 145, 153–156, 159, 166, 184, 191–193, 197, 200, 203, 213, 219, 234, 268, 276, 288n41, 289n58, 319n4, 321n17
Thousand and One Nights, The, 38, 332n42
Titanic (Cameron), 302n1
Tlatli, Moufida, 124–126, 145, 148, 155, 262–263, 282n7, 282n8, 310n15, 312n33, 313n40
Tomlinson, John, 193, 216–218
Touch of Evil (Welles), xii
Toulouse and Montauban shootings (2012), 323n32
Trace, The (Ben Mabrouk), 22
tribalism, 43, 47, 55, 166, 310n13, 315n11
Truman, Harry, 221–222
Tunisia: Constitution (1959), 281n1; constitutional amendment (2002), 96, 281n1; Constitution of 1861, 5, 25, 29; and corruption, xv, xvii, 11, 21, 102, 123, 127, 146, 156, 158–159, 165, 174, 180–181, 184–186, 251, 260–261, 267, 277, 284n5, 317n25, 317–318n29, 334n2; defensive nationalism of, 30; "economic miracle", xv, 4, 29–30, 96, 146, 156, 158, 174, 277, 285n9, 315n2, 316n19, 328n15, 334n2; as an *etatist* state, 8–9; exceptionalism, 24, 29; as French Protectorate, 3, 75, 123, 139–140, 143, 333n49; Fundamental Pact of 1857, 25; and globalization, 30, 112, 116–117, 163, 225; human rights record, ix–x, xvii, 3–4, 96, 146, 194, 201, 244, 286n15; Independence (1956), ix, 7, 74–75, 126, 333n47; and the Internet, xv–xvi, 29, 96–97, 146, 191–222 passim, 258, 261, 302n6, 321–322n25, 322n26, 322n27, 333–334n51; Jewish population, 27, 51, 241, 246,

266, 296n12, 299n33; justice system, 4, 185–186, 317n27; as a "Mediterranean" society, xiii–xiv, xvi, 67–98 passim, 262, 292n75, 302n3, 327n8, 329n22, 333n47; modernity of, ix, xii, xiv, 11, 24, 122, 134, 147, 161, 166–167, 174, 177, 191, 200–201, 224, 229, 242, 254, 262, 264, 276, 292n74, 298n23, 304n18, 314n51, 329n18, 330n30, 331n35, 336n6, 340n38; monarchy, 1, 127, 131, 140–141, 285n6, 309n2, 312n27; "national ideology" (Béji), 7–9; national motto, ix, 215, 324n39; and Palestine-Israel conflict, 27–29, 228, 235–237, 241, 254, 279, 290n62, 299n33, 327n8; as a police state, ix, xii–xiii, 6, 11, 31, 67–98 passim, 122, 146, 159, 164, 174, 191, 198, 202–203, 209, 215, 231, 269–271, 283n12, 285–286n14, 286n15, 290n62, 297n14, 302n7, 315n10, 338–339n26; postcolonial malaise, xiv, 1, 4, 7–8, 10–11, 14, 69, 73, 122–123, 125–126, 151, 287n27, 287n28, 297n17, 310n10; reformism discourse, 24–26, 146, 292n73, 292n74, 314n51, 331n36; Revolution (2011), 24, 258–260, 264–265, 281n1, 291–292n71, 334n1, 335n4, 340n38; as a "tolerant" society, ix, xiv, xvi, 31, 67–98 passim, 224, 231, 241–242, 262; and tourism, x, xvi, 27–28, 99–122 passim, 224–258 passim, 307n6, 308n11; and the United States, 27–28; Westernized character, 27, 122, 176–179, 211; and women's rights, xvi, 29, 40, 123, 125, 127–134, 140, 154–156, 159, 201, 211, 228, 242–245, 285n9, 290n61, 298n27, 303n11, 310n3, 310n4, 311n18, 311n20, 313n40, 314n51

Tunisian Association of Democratic Women (ATFD), 4

Tunisian League for Human Rights (LTDH), 4, 29, 96, 194

tunisianité, 15, 22, 24, 26, 29–30, 154, 262, 288n42, 293n78, 304n24, 333n49, 336n6, 336n8

Tuquoi, Jean-Pierre, 285n9, 286n16, 295n1, 334n2

Turkey, xii, 64, 239, 287n28, 307n5, 330n25, 338n20

Turner, Bryan S., 324n42, 334n51

TV Is Coming, The (Dhouib), xvi–xvii, 223–258, 261, 283n8

Ukadike, Frank, 304n18

Um Kalthum, 50, 200

umma, 24–25, 43, 132, 258

underdevelopment, 8, 10–11, 116–117, 165, 238, 308n12. *See also* Third World

Une Si Simple Histoire (Ben Ammar), 320n14

Union des Femmes de Tunisie (UFT), 134

Union des Jeunes Filles de Tunisie (UFJT), 134

Union Musulmane des Femmes de Tunisie (UMFT), 134

Union Nationale des Femmes Tunisiennes (UNFT). *See* National Union of Tunisian Women (UNFT)

University of Tunis, x, 176, 286n15, 290n62

Vergès, Françoise, 60

Visages de femmes (Écaré), 303–304n18

Von Wright, Georg Henrik, 213

Walt, Stephen, 329–330n23

Weber, Max, 166, 215

Wedding in Galilee (Khleifi), 303n17

Wheatcroft, Geoffrey, 293n81

White, Gregory, 284n5

WikiLeaks, 260–261, 334n2

Wikipedia, 261, 335n5

Williamson, Judith, 154

Willis, Michael J., 284n2

women's rights. See Tunisia: and women's rights. *See also* Personal Status Code (PSC)
World Summit on the Information Society (December 2003/November 2005), 201–202, 321–322n25

Wright, Robin, 334n1

Xavier, Ismail, 18–20, 290n62

Zezia, the Hilalian, 232, 245, 248–251
Zran, Mohamed, 162, 282n7

FILM AND CULTURE
A series of Columbia University Press
Edited by John Belton

What Made Pistachio Nuts? Early Sound Comedy and the Vaudeville Aesthetic
    Henry Jenkins
Showstoppers: Busby Berkeley and the Tradition of Spectacle
    Martin Rubin
Projections of War: Hollywood, American Culture, and World War II
    Thomas Doherty
Laughing Screaming: Modern Hollywood Horror and Comedy
    William Paul
Laughing Hysterically: American Screen Comedy of the 1950s
    Ed Sikov
Primitive Passions: Visuality, Sexuality, Ethnography, and Contemporary Chinese Cinema
    Rey Chow
The Cinema of Max Ophuls: Magisterial Vision and the Figure of Woman
    Susan M. White
Black Women as Cultural Readers
    Jacqueline Bobo
Picturing Japaneseness: Monumental Style, National Identity, Japanese Film
    Darrell William Davis
Attack of the Leading Ladies: Gender, Sexuality, and Spectatorship in Classic Horror Cinema
    Rhona J. Berenstein
This Mad Masquerade: Stardom and Masculinity in the Jazz Age
    Gaylyn Studlar
Sexual Politics and Narrative Film: Hollywood and Beyond
    Robin Wood
The Sounds of Commerce: Marketing Popular Film Music
    Jeff Smith
Orson Welles, Shakespeare, and Popular Culture
    Michael Anderegg
Pre-Code Hollywood: Sex, Immorality, and Insurrection in American Cinema, 1930–1934
    Thomas Doherty
Sound Technology and the American Cinema: Perception, Representation, Modernity
    James Lastra
Melodrama and Modernity: Early Sensational Cinema and Its Contexts
    Ben Singer
Wondrous Difference: Cinema, Anthropology, and Turn-of-the-Century Visual Culture
    Alison Griffiths
Hearst Over Hollywood: Power, Passion, and Propaganda in the Movies
    Louis Pizzitola

Masculine Interests: Homoerotics in Hollywood Film
    Robert Lang
Special Effects: Still in Search of Wonder
    Michele Pierson
Designing Women: Cinema, Art Deco, and the Female Form
    Lucy Fischer
Cold War, Cool Medium: Television, McCarthyism, and American Culture
    Thomas Doherty
Katharine Hepburn: Star as Feminist
    Andrew Britton
Silent Film Sound
    Rick Altman
Home in Hollywood: The Imaginary Geography of Hollywood
    Elisabeth Bronfen
Hollywood and the Culture Elite: How the Movies Became American
    Peter Decherney
Taiwan Film Directors: A Treasure Island
    Emilie Yueh-yu Yeh and Darrell William Davis
Shocking Representation: Historical Trauma, National Cinema, and the Modern Horror Film
    Adam Lowenstein
China on Screen: Cinema and Nation
    Chris Berry and Mary Farquhar
The New European Cinema: Redrawing the Map
    Rosalind Galt
George Gallup in Hollywood
    Susan Ohmer
Electric Sounds: Technological Change and the Rise of Corporate Mass Media
    Steve J. Wurtzler
The Impossible David Lynch
    Todd McGowan
Sentimental Fabulations, Contemporary Chinese Films: Attachment in the Age of Global Visibility
    Rey Chow
Hitchcock's Romantic Irony
    Richard Allen
Intelligence Work: The Politics of American Documentary
    Jonathan Kahana
Eye of the Century: Film, Experience, Modernity
    Francesco Casetti
Shivers Down Your Spine: Cinema, Museums, and the Immersive View
    Alison Griffiths
Weimar Cinema: An Essential Guide to Classic Films of the Era
    Edited by Noah Isenberg

African Film and Literature: Adapting Violence to the Screen
   Lindiwe Dovey
Film, A Sound Art
   Michel Chion
Film Studies: An Introduction
   Ed Sikov
Hollywood Lighting from the Silent Era to Film Noir
   Patrick Keating
Levinas and the Cinema of Redemption: Time, Ethics, and the Feminine
   Sam B. Girgus
Counter-Archive: Film, the Everyday, and Albert Kahn's Archives de la Planète
   Paula Amad
Indie: An American Film Culture
   Michael Z. Newman
Pretty: Film and the Decorative Image
   Rosalind Galt
Film and Stereotype: A Challenge for Cinema and Theory
   Jörg Schweinitz
Chinese Women's Cinema: Transnational Contexts
   Edited by Lingzhen Wang
Hideous Progeny: Disability, Eugenics, and Classic Horror Cinema
   Angela M. Smith
Hollywood's Copyright Wars: From Edison to the Internet
   Peter Decherney
Electric Dreamland: Amusement Parks, Movies, and American Modernity
   Lauren Rabinovitz
Where Film Meets Philosophy: Godard, Resnais, and Experiments in Cinematic Thinking
   Hunter Vaughan
The Utopia of Film: Cinema and Its Futures in Godard, Kluge, and Tahimik
   Christopher Pavsek
Hollywood and Hitler, 1933–1939
   Thomas Doherty
Cinematic Appeals: The Experience of New Movie Technologies
   Ariel Rogers

GPSR Authorized Representative: Easy Access System Europe, Mustamäe tee 50, 10621 Tallinn, Estonia, gpsr.requests@easproject.com